SPYCRAFT

SPYCRAFT

Tricks and Tools of the Dangerous Trade from Elizabeth I to the Restoration

NADINE AKKERMAN & PETE LANGMAN

YALE UNIVERSITY PRESS
NEW HAVEN AND LONDON

European Research Council
Established by the European Commission

Chapter 1 is part of a project that has received funding from the European Research Council (ERC) under the European Union's Horizon 2020 research and innovation program (Grant agreement No. 864635, FEATHERS).

For information about this and other Yale University Press publications, please contact:
U.S. Office: sales.press@yale.edu   yalebooks.com
Europe Office: sales@yaleup.co.uk   yalebooks.co.uk

Set in Adobe Garamond Pro by IDSUK (DataConnection) Ltd
Printed and bound in China

Library of Congress Control Number: 2024932814

ISBN 978-0-300-26754-9

A catalogue record for this book is available from the British Library.

10 9 8 7 6 5 4 3 2

MIX
Paper | Supporting
responsible forestry
FSC® C016973

CONTENTS

ILLUSTRATIONS

A NOTE ON DATES, SOURCES AND CURRENCIES

In 1582, the wildly inaccurate Julian calendar was replaced by a newly calculated version, the Gregorian calendar. As this had been ordered by Pope Gregory, the resolutely Protestant England stuck with the Julian version, ensuring that English dates remained ten days behind those of Europe until 1752. England and her enemies thus occupied different time zones, as 10 September in England was 20 September just across the channel in the Spanish Netherlands. These two systems were referred to at the time as *stilo veteri* (s.v., Old Style: the Julian calendar) and *stilo novo* (s.n., New Style: the Gregorian calendar), and still are. As we mostly deal in the Anglophone world, dates are given in Old Style (although exceptions are made for European dates such as the assassination of William the Silent, whose demise came about on 10 July on mainland Europe – 30 June in England). As with most historians, however, we take the new year to begin on 1 January rather than 25 March (Lady Day, the feast of the Annunciation).

The principles set out below have been applied to all primary sources, whether in manuscript or in print, including editions such as *The Correspondence of Elizabeth Stuart*.

Original punctuation, which is often non-existent where it does not appear to have been scattered randomly upon the page, has been lightly edited to aid reader comprehension. In similar fashion, we also eradicate unnecessary capitalisation. Seventeenth-century orthographical practice, spellings and contractions have been silently modernised in favour of readability. There are five exceptions to this rule:

1. When citing from a document that is also shown as an image on the same or following page. In this case, our transcription will be diplomatic, that is, we will write what is there, including contemporary abbreviations such as wch for which, y^t for that, y^e for the, and Y^{rs} for Yours, etc.

2. When discussing ciphers. Some of the works we discuss have idiosyncrasies that are a part of the cipher themselves, and to modernise these would cause no little confusion. (The English alphabet, for instance, had twenty-four letters, eliding i/j and u/v. Sometimes, the 'w' was also left out. Italians saw little use for the letter 'h', and in Scots, 'wh' was rendered 'quh'.)

3. When modernising a spelling might give the wrong impression: for instance, we write 'bisket bread' instead of 'biscuit bread' because, while it may be that the words are related, the actual formulation of 'bisket bread' is still a matter of dispute. To render 'bisket' in this instance as 'biscuit' would provide a false sense of familiarity.

4. When the original spelling is particularly evocative – we keep 'naughtie inke', for example.

5. Poetry (even bad poetry) we do not alter.

—◇—

As for currencies, while we have used the standard £.s.d or pounds, shillings and pence (where 12 pence make a shilling and 20 shillings make a pound), we have, on occasion, inserted a rough idea of how these sums might translate into modern terms – to do so we have used the calculator supplied by The National Archives, Kew (https://www.nationalarchives.gov.uk/currency-converter/). Do be aware that these sums are relatively arbitrary, as the things that we value today are very different from those that were valued back then. A horse, for example, is now a luxury; then it was a primary mode of transport.

ACKNOWLEDGEMENTS

The plethora of images in *Spycraft*, as well as a number of vital archival trips, have only been allowed by the grace of the Dr Hendrik Muller Prize which was awarded to Nadine in 2021, while a one-year Visiting Senior Research Fellowship at Jesus College, Oxford was invaluable in allowing us to revisit manuscripts and other sources last seen almost a decade ago. The intellectual discussions at All Souls College, Oxford that same year were also enlightening. Leiden University Centre for the Arts in Society (LUCAS) ought to be thanked for allowing Nadine more time away from the lecture theatre. Her ERC-Consolidator Grant FEATHERS enabled Chapter 1 to be published open access, as some secrets ought to be shared widely. We are indebted to our agent Michael Alcock at Johnson & Alcock, who persuaded Heather McCallum at Yale University Press that *Spycraft* was worth publishing, and for the whole team at Yale who have helped us to produce a book we are very proud of.

Such a work as *Spycraft* is always a collaborative endeavour in so many ways, as its wildly interdisciplinary nature has necessitated that we draw heavily on the expertise of others: it has only been made possible due to those giants on whose shoulders we have stood as we wrote.

Numerous individuals have helped us gain access to collections, told us where manuscripts were loitering with intent, or helped with translations. These include Jackie Eales for confirming that Lady Brilliana's letters as edited by Lewis were still in private hands; Edward and Victoria Harley and the Harley Estate for their generous hospitality; Alexia Grosjean for translations of Mary, Queen of Scots's letter regarding invisible ink; Angham Abdullah for decoding Arabic terms for lemons; Ioanna Iordanou for chasing down waterproof garments and Paolo Sarpi in Venetian archives and liaising with the Museo Correr; David van der Linden for assisting us with the Lyon Public Library; and Meagen Smith from Lambeth Palace Library for providing us with access to Morland's secret proposals.

Several people have helped by putting their modelling, re-creating and conceptual skills to the test for us, including Tony Curtis with his beautiful calligraphy and knowledge of quills; Jana Dambrogio and her astonishing facility for re-creating letter-foldings; Laura James who did absolutely stirling work on reproducing and testing methods of counterfeiting seals and various inks; Richard Lawrence who demystified printer's ink; Will Scott who provided mathematical and chemical advice; Daniel Starza Smith who lent us the sheaf of snakes seal and provided advice on papered-seals; and Simon Wilkinson for helping us to conceptualise the perspective box, and for facilitating our repeated counterfeitings of Robert Cecil's signature.

A book such as *Spycraft* needs well-chosen and -reproduced images. Amongst those we would like to thank for helping us in this particular endeavour are Catherine Angerson at the British Library for the imaging of several seals; Max Ferguson who brought post-production photographic expertise; Kersten Luts for his facility with a camera; Neil Johnston from The National Archives for providing multi-spectral light imaging of the Babington cipher; and Stuart Orme for giving us John Thurloe and in general for his stewardship of the Cromwell Museum.

On more than one occasion we have needed help and advice from those with more expertise in specific areas than we could muster. These include Thony Christie with his encyclopaedic knowledge of early modern scientific endeavours; Peter Davidson who provided information on Sir Christopher Wren, Nicholas Owen and Jesuits in general; Roger Farnham who helped us understand James Watts's print-copying device; Lotte Fikkers who provided contemporary legal advice; Catherine Fletcher who helped with our understanding of both the literal and symbolic impact of various powder weapons; John Guy who untangled Mary, Queen of Scots's early cryptographical education; Ineke Huysman whose knowledge of Constantijn Huygens was indispensible as always; Kathryn James who tweeted about mirror writing; Michael Netten and the Scots Brigade of the Sealed Knot who helped us understand some of the physical realities that accompanied matchlocks and wheellocks; Ivo Roessink for his surprising knowledge of toads and toxicity; Jane Stevenson for her invisible ink comments; Alan Stewart for his thoughts on waxy matters Baconian; and René van Stipriaan for his unpicking of William the Silent's sticky end.

A small but indefatigable team of readers have helped us by reading chapters in various states of undress, aiding us immeasurably in our attempts to render some of the more complex subjects comprehensible. These include Janet Dickenson who kept our Cecils in line; George Lasry, Satoshi Tomokiyo, Norbert Biermann, Alan Marshall and Alison Wiggins who read the cipher code chapter; Glynn Redworth who provided generous and helpful comments on various chapters; the FEATHERS team – Lotte Fikkers, Clodagh Murphy, Jonathan Powell, Holly Riach – who did great work with the proofs; and Hanna de Lange who checked the Bibliography.

Several generous scholars have provided us with references that we could not quite corner and capture ourselves, or brought to our attention items of which we were unaware but definitely needed to know. These include Henric Jansen who checked Tacticus; Clodagh Murphy who brought the stuffing of Mary Tudor's corpse with letters to our attention; Emily Montford who directed us to Cecil's cipher habits and a letter with its address written across its lock; Anthony Ossa-Richardson who provided us with the Lucian and Hippolytus references; and Filippo de Vivo who provided pointed remarks regarding Sarpi's unfortunate incident!

The list of those to whom we owe a debt is long, and if we have missed anyone, we can only apologise and blame it on those pesky spies who, in league with Titivillus, continually stole our manuscripts, altered our texts, introduced random misspellings and grammatical howlers into previously perfect sentences, and generally hung around invisibly causing mayhem. Finally, we would like to state that if your copy of *Spycraft* should glow in the dark, be assured that no glow-worms were harmed during its production, nor were any toads.

Nadine & Pete
Leiden and Adderbury / Adderbury and Leiden, 2023

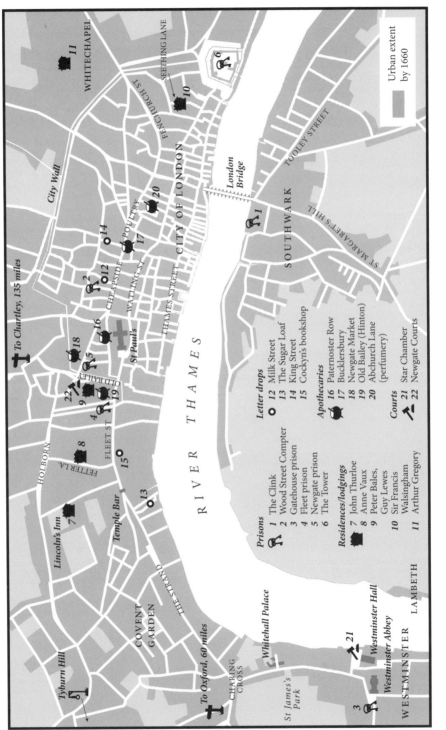

The London Netherworld, 1558–1660

Prisons
1 The Clink
2 Wood Street Compter
3 Gatehouse prison
4 Fleet prison
5 Newgate prison
6 The Tower

Residences/lodgings
7 John Thurloe
8 Anne Vaux
9 Peter Bales,
   Guy Lewes
10 Sir Francis
   Walsingham
11 Arthur Gregory

Letter drops
12 Milk Street
13 The Sugar Loaf
14 King Street
15 Cockyn's bookshop

Apothecaries
16 Paternoster Row
17 Bucklersbury
18 Newgate Market
19 Old Bailey (Hinton)
20 Abchurch Lane
   (perfumery)

Courts
21 Star Chamber
22 Newgate Courts

Urban extent
by 1660

PRELUDE: THE SKELETON KEY

A stranger entering Arthur Gregory's Whitechapel home in 1596, or perhaps his workshop in the Tower of London in 1606, would have been forgiven for believing it was occupied by an apothecary or alchemist. On its shelves, sticky with lumps of beeswax and the stumps of long-dead tallow candles, bottles of shellac, turpentine, quicksilver and linseed oil jostled for space with jars of oak galls, dried fish glue, alum and vitriol, while metal boxes sat uneasy atop one another, peeling paper labels marking their contents: verdigris, litharge, ceruse, sal ammoniac. Attached to the desk by a metal frame, a small wooden box containing a crystal lens hovered above a half-written letter. On the letter lay a small pair of spectacles. Quills cut from goose, swan and crow lay beside a penknife, a comb and some signets. A lattice of leather strips tacked onto the dark wood-panelled walls embraced unopened letter-packets and slips of paper covered in symbols; a tangle of horse's hair, ribbon and floss hung expectantly from an exposed nail, waiting their turn to strap, tie and bind. The fireplace was crowded with the kettles, stills and pots that brewed the room's thick atmosphere; in front of it sat a low bench of thick, blackened oak, like those used for the slaughter of pigs. Piles of paper crowded the floor while individual sheets hung like sleeping bats amongst the rafters. A viol, new wire strings draped over its tuning pegs, lay trapped in a thicket of rolled-up maps, plans for fortifications and complex automata. And there were books. His was a world busy with secrets.

You may not recognise many of the objects and substances described here, just as you may not recognise Arthur Gregory, who died 400 years ago in 1624. This is a book about both: a book about early modern spycraft, the tricks and tools employed by spies and counterspies as they plied their trade, whether that meant smuggling a letter through enemy lines, intercepting ciphered communications, or plotting to assassinate a head of state. These technologies were perfected through long, and often very messy, experience. While his room might suggest otherwise, Gregory was no alchemist, nor was he an apothecary. He was a counter-espionage agent who both used and developed those technologies, not merely a keeper but an inventor of secrets. He worked on and off for various members of the English establishment during the late sixteenth and early seventeenth centuries, seeking – but for a long time failing – to secure permanent employment. In many respects he epitomises those individuals who played vital parts in well-known plots and conspiracies, but who even then lurked in the shadows of a world already shadowy enough, the world of the spy. And there they have remained.

Many of the items in Gregory's room were used for manipulating letters. This was by far his most important skill: the primary job of a spy was (as it still is) to access information which they, or most likely their masters, might use against their enemies. In this period the *only* viable method of transmitting information over distance other than by word of mouth was with pen and paper, and once written down these paper secrets were folded into the packets we know as letters and sent on their way. It was at this point, when they were in transit, that the secrets were at their most vulnerable: like a messenger, a letter could be intercepted and interrogated. A spy's life might depend on their ability to protect the information contained in their letters from the prying eyes of the counterspy: a counterspy's career (and perhaps the life of their employer) might depend on their ability to capture that very same information and thus uncover and frustrate the spy's intentions. Perhaps the greatest asset either possessed was invisibility – it is no surprise that so few portraits exist of those who played this game. Neither side wished the other to be aware of their activities. The stakes were often high. Letters were not always tedious accounts of administrative meanderings; in times of conflict they were all too often a matter of life and death.

Arthur Gregory was not without fame in his lifetime, finding himself lauded in William Camden's famous history of the reign of Queen Elizabeth I, the *Annales* of 1616. In this book, published a decade after Gregory had retired from the world of espionage in favour of the comforts of suburbia and the

Fig. 1: Next to letters, writing implements such as a penknife, a quill, scissors, a piece of scorched sealing wax and even a comb, are given centre stage on this 'necessary board'.

office of mayor of Lyme Regis, Camden praised his work for Sir Francis Walsingham, privy councillor and secretary of state. Gregory, he wrote, could open and refold a letter-packet so neatly that 'it was not to be perceived that they had been unsealed'.[1] In 1662, Thomas Fuller would repeat Camden's praise, crediting Gregory with 'the admirable art of forcing the Seal of a Letter; yet so invisibly, that it still appeared a Virgin to the exactest beholder'.[2] This may still not sound all that significant to the modern historian, which goes some way to explaining why Gregory himself has remained relatively invisible ever since, despite his intimate involvement in foiling some of the more iconic plots of the era. Another reason why historians have allowed Gregory to become invisible again is that so much of the texture of his employment is flattened out by the printed page, just as his techniques, when they are discussed at all, are mentioned without consideration of their physical and temporal qualities.

The modern eye does not view objects in the same way as the early modern one. This is apparent in the period's trompe l'oeil paintings of so-called necessary boards. Depicting a collection of small objects such as quills, penknives, razors, spectacles, scissors and combs held onto a board by leather straps, these paintings were created in such a way as to give the impression of three dimensions – the phrase 'trompe l'oeil' means 'deceive the eye'. While this style of painting deceives the viewer into inferring a dimension that is not present, *Spycraft* aims to peel back the layers of deception and help the reader appreciate that there are dimensions to seemingly ordinary objects that are not at first apparent. Take Hoogstraten's painting, for example (Fig. 1). While the comb may look out of place amongst the writing implements on display, it was no mere symbol of earthly vanity as is often assumed – by drawing its tines across the paper, a scribe created a series of barely perceptible but straight and evenly spaced lines that were invaluable for keeping writing orderly.[3] *Spycraft* aims to show the reader how such everyday implements could have other, more shadowy uses than may at first appear. It will show how the ordinary world blended into the world of espionage, and how the boundaries between criminal and counterspy were often as blurred as those between secretary and spy.

The tricks and tools described in *Spycraft* were used by conspirator and criminal, impostor and intelligencer alike. Where successful spies were skilled at keeping their secrets, less committed actors were prone to collapsing under interrogation and all too readily betraying their craft. Where such instances shed light on otherwise invisible techniques, we have not been afraid to give the more peripheral and dubious characters centre stage. The various methods of counterfeiting a signature, for instance, remain the same whether one is forging a receipt to make some cash on the side or a passport needed to create a new identity for a life-or-death mission deep into enemy territory. The very tangibility of these techniques, however, can be the key to understanding some of the more occluded events of history.

SPIES AND THE DARK ARTIFICER

Arthur Gregory was, by any estimation, knee-deep in the surreptitious and secretive world of espionage, but was he a *spy* in the modern sense? The word 'spy' is as slippery as those it aims to describe. In the late medieval world the lines between messengers, diplomats and spies were somewhat blurred, and by the sixteenth century secretaries were considered primarily responsible for 'secret matters'.[4] As the first resident ambassadors were installed, men whose official mission it was to gather intelligence (that is, secret, confidential information) in the foreign state, diplomacy and intelligence became increasingly synonymous.[5] Many felt it necessary to state that ambassadors, though feeding on intelligence, were 'honourable spies', implicitly contrasting them to an ordinary, lowly and dirty version.[6]

Certainly, the word 'spy' came with a trunkful of negative connotations. This is perhaps understandable: the very qualities that made for an effective spy – the ability to skulk in the shadows unobserved, to lie undetected and to cheat unsuspected – made the job 'an office unbecoming a gentleman', its practitioners 'treacherous and morally corrupt' (though this did not mean that the higher echelons of society were not active in espionage).[7] In fact, many of the spy's everyday tasks were illegal: eavesdropping, counterfeiting, smuggling, bribery, perhaps even murder. Forging documents, for instance, was a dangerous game – since 1563, it had been punishable by means of a fine and by the guilty party being 'set upon the pillory in some open market town or other open place, and there to have both his ears cut off, and also his nostrils to be slit and cut and seared with a hot iron, so as they may remain for a perpetual note or mark of his falsehood'.[8] It is unsurprising, therefore, that the line in the sand that separated criminal from spy was often so trampled upon as to be invisible. Robert Cecil, secretary of state both for Elizabeth I and James I, recruited from the most insalubrious of venues: some of his spies came with the personal recommendation of Sir William Waad, lieutenant of the Tower.[9] Little wonder that Cecil remarked on 'how usual it is for buffoons to be used as spies'.[10] Such unfortunate beginnings ensured that intelligencers were criticised by virtually every part of society, and the stain of criminal immorality tainted everyone in the dangerous trade, from dark artificer and spy to secretary of state.[11] No one was exempt.

The poet and playwright Ben Jonson, who was known to have worked in the dangerous trade himself, equated spies with the period's most common source of artificial light, the tallow candle: 'Spies, you are lights in state, but of base stuff,/ Who, when you've burnt yourselves down to the snuff,/ Stink, and are thrown away. End fair enough.'[12] Made from the rendered fat of cattle or sheep, the tallow candle's light was accompanied by greasy and malodorous smoke, so the comparison was more than apt. Many of the individuals we examine in *Spycraft* were such as these, men and women who, no matter their skills, were all too often discarded once they had outlived their usefulness. In many cases, the secret techniques they had mastered accompanied them into obscurity – for spy handlers and spies alike, it was best to leave no trace of their presence behind.

A spy was fundamentally an individual who sought to discover and trade confidential information that they hoped would fuel action that either protected or undermined the state. Arthur Gregory slides into this definition somewhat obliquely: he spent most of his time sat behind a desk or in a workshop rather than eavesdropping behind tavern doors. But defining the spy is as difficult as unmasking them: as Bosola, the antihero of John Webster's 1612–13 play *The Duchess of Malfi*, put it, a spy or intelligencer was 'a very quaint invisible devil, in [the] flesh'; it has been suggested, however, that before the 1650s such activities were so amateur that there was no such thing as a spy, merely 'spying', and an awful lot of it.[13]

Definitions notwithstanding, Gregory was, in effect, the early modern equivalent of James Bond's gadget specialist Q. By the 1660s, a different kind of gadget specialist, but one who was also interested in invisible inks, the experimental scientist Robert Boyle, used the word 'artificer' to refer to some of the many assistants he employed. These men were essential: they built the devices Boyle used to demonstrate his ideas at the Royal Society and elsewhere, but they were rarely, if ever, mentioned by those who reported on these proceedings.[14] They were often anonymous, and have remained so. If remaining invisible was a talent to be nurtured amongst those who worked at the sharp end of espionage, those who developed and perfected the methods that allowed them to better carry out their tasks undetected were doubly invisible. Because of the nefarious nature of espionage, and the often dubious legality of the actions carried out by men such as Gregory as they plied their trade, we have adopted and adapted Boyle's terminology, and refer to these men (and the occasional woman) as the *dark* artificers.

THE MOTHER OF INVENTION

We concentrate our analysis on the development and use of spycraft techniques between 1558 (the year of the accession of Queen Elizabeth I and the publication of the period's most influential 'book of secrets', Giambattista della Porta's *Magiae Naturalis*) and 1660 (the year of the Restoration of King Charles II to the throne of England and the founding of the Royal Society, the famous academy devoted to the furthering of scientific knowledge), though we will draw on material from the entire early modern period (loosely, 1500–1720). Spying is rightfully characterised as the second-oldest profession, and technologies never develop out of a vacuum or in a linear fashion.[15] It is within this period, however, that we can best trace the evolution of espionage from amateur status to at least some measure of semi-professionalism, an evolution that was mirrored by contemporary technical advances. We cease our investigations around the dawn of the modern period because not only does the Industrial Revolution herald a radical change in available technology, but also because these times are already well-served by works of history.[16]

For the majority of Elizabeth I's reign, Protestant England faced an existential threat in the shape of the Catholic empire of Spain. This was exacerbated by Pope Pius V's 1570 declaration that the English queen was a heretic and Catholic subjects were not bound to obey her. Contrary to the propaganda surrounding the Elizabethan 'Golden Age', England was poor, weak and isolated. It was threatened on all sides (and from within), and unable to make much headway in the European rush to empire (though it would more than make up for this slow start). Catholic Spain, for instance, was still plundering unfeasible quantities of gold from the Americas, and was happy to use this wealth in an attempt to return this upstart island state to the one true faith – the Spanish king, Philip II, had, after all, been married to Elizabeth's half-sister and predecessor on the English throne, Mary I. The imprisonment of Elizabeth's cousin, the widow of a French king and rival for the English crown, Mary, Queen of Scots, ensured that the Catholic threat was felt both within and without. Elizabethan England was thus a hotbed of conspiracy, shot through with spies and traitors, and riddled with Jesuits. Elizabeth's response to Pius's declaration was to strengthen the laws against treason, extending it to include those attempting to convert her subjects to Catholicism, and allowing for the use of torture to extract evidence and confessions. Counter-espionage was the order of the day, and English agents were less responsible for protecting state secrets than they were for protecting the state itself (in the shape of its monarch), often by persecuting individuals considered threatening or even merely suspicious. Elizabethan England, however, lacked a dedicated 'secret service' in the mould of, to take one example, the Venetian 'Council of Ten', the quasi-autonomous body whose specific remit was counter-espionage and the protection of state secrets such as manufacturing techniques.[17] Even though England had long lagged behind other European states when it came to spycraft, the volatility of the sixteenth century ensured that it rapidly caught up and even overtook its rivals – there was no choice, it was adapt or die. While the use of spies in England diminished during the reign of King James, not least as one of his first acts after coming to the throne of England was to conclude a peace with Spain, they would prove as necessary during his son's reign in the 1640s and under the Commonwealth of Oliver Cromwell in the 1650s as they had in the 1580s.[18] This rapid development of espionage apparatus makes the techniques used by spies more visible than in those countries with more settled and organised secret services.[19] It is for this reason that, while *Spycraft* will consider techniques drawn from across Europe as a whole, and in some cases trace their development back to the Arab, Chinese and classical worlds, it will draw examples of their use primarily from the Anglophone world.

SENSORY INSTRUMENTS

The seventeenth-century edition of an Italian book of emblems, *Iconologia* by Cesare Ripa, included a line drawing of a spy with his tools: 'A man in a noble habit, hides most of his face with his hat; his cloak woven with eyes, ears and tongues; a lantern in one hand; his feet wing'd; a spaniel by him on the ground; his nose in full scent after his game.' His head and face are mostly covered with a hat and his 'noble habit', so that he might 'pass incognito, never discovering his designs' in all social circles. His lantern allows him to 'spy night and day'. His canine assistant symbolises 'their smelling out men's actions, and their inquisitiveness'. His cloak is covered in images of ears and eyes but also tongues, depicting the gathering and dissemination of intelligence. These sensory organs, so the accompanying text explains, 'are the instruments they use to please their patrons'.[20] Ripa knew that those in the dangerous trade could not exist without patrons, powerful individuals who helped them advance their careers and protected them in return for faithful service, such as acting as the patron's eyes and ears. To get ahead, the Arthur Gregorys of this world used their tongues to both flatter prospective patrons and convince them of their own invaluable skills in hope of gaining favour.

The patronage system defined Gregory's life and core essence in many ways; his cautious nature was a direct result of it. An inventor and innovator, Gregory was capable of rather more than Camden and Fuller had given him credit for. He certainly rated himself more highly, claiming expertise in 'secret employment [in] sundry ways, And also in matters of Architecture, Description, Fortification, Enginery [i.e., engineering], or whatsoever is mechanical, mathematical or martial'.[21] Notes found in the chamber of the imprisoned adventurer Thomas Arundell confirm this as no mere braggadocio:

> Arthur Gregory hath a device to make a ship go alone for a mile or two, which striking on any other ship shall take fire & burn both . . . & so to burn a whole fleet. He hath also a means to make a ship go much faster than she did & better, by mending her sails &c. He hath a way to make two men able to manage a cannon in a ship . . .[22]

Gregory would nevertheless have understood why Camden's portrait was not only brief but touched only upon his manipulation of letters. While he was more than happy to boast of his abilities and his innovative and imaginative inventions in oblique terms, he never committed his secrets to paper and thus never secured them for posterity. Quite the opposite: Gregory deliberately kept their details – the recipes of his potions and pastes, the mechanical workings of his instruments, and suchlike – close to his chest. Gregory had an ageing father and a growing family to support, so could not lose any opportunity for remunerative employment.[23] With so many seeking patronage from government officials, details of his techniques were better left unshared so as not to offer the competition a headstart.

Many of Gregory's letters in the 1580s were direct pleas for patronage, and by 1587 they were beginning to pay off: Walsingham now began to refer to Gregory as 'my servant'. The reciprocity of the client–patron relationship was not merely expressed in coin – other, often more valued rewards, such as preferment and enhanced social status, were available.[24] Gregory was primarily interested in a secure income, however; in 1599 he was handsomely rewarded for engineering defence works at Upnor Castle, and in 1603 was granted the office of 'scrutator' – or investigator – in the port town of Poole, before being called back to espionage work in 1606. He eventually became mayor of Lyme Regis, and was granted a life pension for services rendered.[25]

Finding the right patron was far from easy, especially when it was not apparent whom to single out as in charge. England's lack of a centralised secret service meant that there was no individual head of intelligence. Walsingham's involvement in intelligence gathering, for instance, was undertaken in adjunct to his secretarial duties. Walsingham, despite his reputation, only handled half a dozen spies at any given time.[26] Those few individuals he did directly control enjoyed no permanent employment but were attached to him as a function of the client–patron relationship, just as he was attached to his queen. The title so often given to Walsingham, 'Elizabeth I's Spymaster', is as inaccurate as it is anachronistic.[27] The queen's various advisors and courtiers – the Cecils, Walsingham, Leicester, Essex et al. – collected intelligence both to direct upwards but also, and often primarily, for their own private purposes. They would then effect any state policy passed down to them through their own spy networks when appropriate, but their efforts were rarely co-ordinated. These were the patrons the Gregorys of the dangerous trade appealed to, but they in turn needed to remain in the queen's good books. They were, in effect, rival spy chiefs.

Elizabeth had no shortage of eyes in her service; Walsingham did not control all of them. In 1586, for example, Elizabeth closed a letter to Robert Dudley, 1st earl of Leicester, with an early modern emoji acknowledging his status: 'Now will I end, that do imagine I talk still with you, and therefore loathly say farewell, ôô'.[28] Leicester used the same symbol to sign off his letters to the queen (see Fig. 2). He was not the only man who drew himself

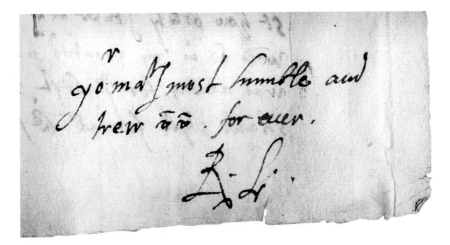

Fig. 2: Leicester's metonymic identification with his monarch's eyes went back at least sixteen years – in 1570 he had signed a letter to his queen with the words 'Yo.[r] Ma[ts] most humble and trew ôô . for euer. R.L.'

as a vital part of his queen's sensory equipment: the courtier and later lord chancellor Sir Christopher Hatton referred to himself as her eyelids, begging her in one letter 'forget not your liddes that are so often bathed with tears for [your] sake'.[29] While the intelligence she received came from multiple sources, the queen had the final word. Not surprisingly therefore, the top dogs not only competed against one another, but sometimes hated each other to boot. Just as favour was passed down the line, so the opposite was true – if a courtier fell out of favour with the queen, their network of clients followed suit, even to the point of losing their livelihoods. This made choosing one's patron a matter of grave importance, especially for those working in the dangerous trade. This was particularly problematic when it was the protection of the patron that prevented your technically illegal work from being publicly acknowledged as such. Hitching your wagon to the wrong horse could be disastrous, if not fatal, as some of those who relied on Robert Devereux, 2nd earl of Essex, would discover to their cost following his somewhat ill-advised rebellion against Elizabeth I in 1601.

In similar fashion, the perfectly natural death of a patron also meant the termination of employment – especially in a business as fickle as espionage. When Walsingham died in 1590, the lord treasurer William Cecil, Lord

Burghley, either 'paid off or abandoned' the majority of the late secretary's spies.[30] One of these spies appears to have been Gregory, as he later wrote to Edward Reynolds, secretary to the earl of Essex, 'I am worn as far out, of reparation in stuff and instruments . . . as I am out of knowledge and hope of preferment for my best services'. Nevertheless, he had a plan: 'I will show you many things the next week to conjure the devil withal.'[31] Luckily for Gregory, Essex was unmoved, so he turned his attentions to another potential patron, Burghley's son Robert Cecil, reminding him of his 'secreat services' and his work to advance spycraft.[32] This time, Gregory was successful, but many were not so fortunate. The other members of the Privy Council – a group of high-ranking and privileged advisors to the queen – had their own networks, so did not necessarily need extra pairs of eyes, and quite possibly did not trust Walsingham's old client-intelligencers in any case.

Employing intelligencers was not without risk for the patron. Spies were automatically considered of a low, base nature, and though the information they supplied was effectively laundered through their patron, the stains of immoral activities such as 'dissimulation, simulation, and out-right lying' were often impervious to erasure, and seeped slowly upwards. The distrust permeating the whole system sometimes narrowed the distance between patron and spy.[33] Libels circulating following the death of Robert Cecil characterised him as an 'archetypal malignant spider' and a 'dissembling smooth-faced dwarf'.[34] Thomas Scott, Parliament's intelligence chief before John Thurloe, was known to consider brothels and taverns as institutions ripe with intelligence, and thus suitable for close surveillance. This habit rather backfired, and he developed a reputation for having rather too intimate a relationship with the denizens of these tawdry establishments, not least those of a bawdy-house called the Sugar Loaf at Charing Cross.[35]

Their association with the dangerous trade influenced the pet names so often used by monarchs for these secretaries of state. King James referred to Robert Cecil as his 'little beagle': like the hunting dog that sniffed out foxes, Cecil worked to root out conspirators. (In this respect, the king might also have been slyly referring to an appellation for Robert's father William Cecil, 'the fox'.) This comparison of beagle to spy may have begun with Sir Walter Raleigh, who wrote that any sensible monarch had 'beagles or listeners in every corner, and all parts of the realm'.[36] Elizabeth had a crueller streak within her, endorsing one letter to Robert 'To the Ελφε [Elf]', having called him 'pigmy' before.[37] In doing so, she was perhaps referencing his physical deformities as well as linking him to a certain type of dark magic, a connection which also surfaces in another, more publicly ascribed nickname, 'the toad': a piece of paper with the words 'Here lieth the toad' was nailed to the doors of both his house in London and his rooms at court by a pastry cook in the service of the earl of Essex.[38]

SECRET SERVICES

Gregory would be employed again and again because he had kept his secrets to himself; no rival could imitate him. Circumspection could be costly, however: when Walsingham needed to counterfeit a postscript on an intercepted letter in 1586, Gregory was passed over in favour of a self-promoting London scrivener, Peter Bales. This unexpected usurpation by a rival taught Gregory the power of advertising, and the need for personal demonstration. By 1594, Gregory would be telling Robert Cecil how he would 'instruct your honour in the secret use' of one of his inventions.[39] He would later remind him (somewhat disingenuously) that 'your Lordship hath had a present trial of that which none but myself hath done before, to write in another man's hand'.[40] This propensity towards the 'show, don't tell' method of self-promotion also gives us evidence of the height of Gregory's ambition. When he wrote to Robert's father William, Lord Burghley, then lord treasurer, recounting his eighteen years of service and requesting a room in the Tower from which to work, he followed his flourishing signature by 'Commending his own services done to Her Majesty, and his ability to do her more'.[41] Rather than blazon his 'secret services' on paper, he wished to demonstrate his skills in person, preferably during an audience with the queen. This reluctance to record his methods led to many of his innovations disappearing into the mists of time, just as his successes with counterfeiting seals and discovering, revealing and ultimately counterfeiting letters written in invisible inks were soon forgotten. It is, perhaps, an enduring irony that some of the techniques he does mention are inferable from a printed book that was available to all.

UNNATURAL MAGIC

Many of Gregory's innovations were at the very least influenced by a pan-European bestselling 'book of secrets' called *Magiae Naturalis*, or *Natural Magick*. It was published in 1558 by the Neopolitan magus Giambattista della Porta, who both dedicated and personally presented it to the Catholic King Philip II of Spain. It included chapters on 'secret writing' and 'opening letters without suspicion', matters close to the heart of any dark artificer.[42] Della Porta also published an influential book on cryptography, *De Furtivis Literarum Notis* (*On the Secret Symbols of Letters*) in 1563. These works were intended not as dry compendia of theoretical knowledge, but as spurs to demonstration through which the natural magician could learn the secrets of nature.[43] The natural magic that della Porta promoted was in no way akin to witchcraft, which sought power through the manipulation of spirits. Natural magic was the art of exerting power through knowledge of the natural world.[44] Della Porta's publication was also no simple recipe book – purchasing it would not grant the casual reader the immediate power to mix invisible inks, or to open and reseal letters undetected. These 'secrets' may have been in plain sight, but they still required a considerable investment in both time and effort to interpret, and no little skill to put into practice. Gregory knew this from long, and sometimes literally painful, experience.

Whether or not the association of Elizabeth's 'elf' Robert Cecil with the warty amphibian was intended to communicate supernatural connotations, there is no doubt that some felt that some of the arts practised by intelligencers *were* akin to witchcraft. The Chinese first believed invisible ink to be witchery, and when the cipher keys of Philip II were broken he thought it was through black magic.[45] In 1574, della Porta was himself suspected of sorcery, and 'invited' by the Inquisition to visit Rome and explain his views on magic and witchcraft. He was eventually released, on condition that he devote more time to his literary works (della Porta was also a playwright) and dissolve his Accademia dei Segreti, an amorphous collection of natural philosophers (that is, proto-scientists), who met periodically to discuss their investigations into the nature of things and demonstrate their 'discoveries'. In reality, neither the Accademia nor della Porta's published work concerned

Fig. 3: Giambattista della Porta, the 'great sorceror of Naples'.

themselves with white or dark magic but with what we might call 'stage magic' – their purpose was to investigate nature through demonstration and experimentation.[46] But six years later the accusations resurfaced, as the German physician Johann Wier used della Porta's explanation that 'witch salve' was a hallucinogenic drug that convinced users that they were flying as an argument against the persecution of witches. The French jurist Jean Bodin, Wier's antagonist, was a firm believer in the reality of witches and promptly dubbed della Porta 'Naples's great sorcerer' (see Fig. 3).[47] Della Porta sought to protect himself against spurious accusations of impropriety by acknowledging the dangers of the technologies he described falling into the wrong hands. He wrote in *De Furtivis* that his ciphers were designed to protect the messages of the authorities should they be intercepted by 'bandits, spies or governors, who serve in far-off places'.[48]

BLACK BOOKS

That the generation of intelligencers that followed Gregory had to rediscover his skills for themselves is largely the result of the secrecy impelled by his need for patronage and to avoid accusations of impropriety and even witchcraft. When he died intestate in 1624, there was no manuscript *Workes* or *Spycrafte: A Manual* lurking amongst his effects, which is also one of the reasons that, bar a few scholarly speculations on his claims to have improved the 'sweetness and loudness' of the viol, if Gregory is remembered at all it is with the words of Camden or Fuller.[49] There is hardly any mention of his spectacular efforts in cleaning up the remnants of the Gunpowder Plot, and none of how, *exactly*, he achieved it.[50] *Spycraft* is the first study to reveal this (see Chapter 4, pp. 184–8). Gregory's need for patronage, and the precarity and rivalry the patronage system encouraged, meant he did not see the value of co-operative ventures. Gregory may have been granted his room in the Tower, and he may have eventually received the preferment and the pension he believed his talents deserved, but his was a lone victory. It would be another half-century or so before dark artificers like Gregory would work co-operatively, on a daily basis, with regular remuneration, and in the same room. These counter-intelligence units became known as *cabinets noirs* or 'black chambers', and those intelligencers who comprised them used many of the very same techniques Gregory had perfected. *Spycraft* follows the movement from lone genius to collaborative, standard intelligence units, the birth of an espionage service that is more recognisable to modern sentiments.

Generations of English spy chiefs complained about there being no tangible structure to the way in which intelligence was done. Such a structure is usually found in institutional archives, but there was no such archive that could tell them how the game was played. They knew full well what was needed.[51] It was not a simple process, however. When Queen Mary I died in 1558, for example, many of her ministers and secretaries also lost their jobs. William Cecil, already chief advisor to the new monarch, Mary's half-sister Elizabeth Tudor, tried to take possession of those documents and letters the Catholic queen had left behind her. While happy to co-operate, her ex-secretary John Boxall was perhaps a little embarrassed when forced to admit to the fate of the late queen's documents: 'The letters are in 2 packets, the one of the last year the other of this part. The two kinds whereof I spoke unto you of cannot be found. They were left in the bed chamber of the late Queen's highness to be signed with her hand, and at the ceringe of the corpse (as [Susan] Clarencius sayeth) counted to that use.'[52] ('Ceringe' here refers to the embalming of a corpse and/or shutting or sealing a corpse in a coffin.)[53] The papers that Cecil had hoped would form the basis of an official archive for the new queen had been used to stuff the body of the old one. Perhaps Clarencius, Mary I's favourite lady-in-waiting, had wanted to get rid of sensitive or incriminating evidence.

Later secretary-intelligencers would not fare much better in their attempts to hold onto their employer's documents. Robert Beale recalled the death of Walsingham in 1590 as a dark day, on which the secretary of state's 'papers and books both public and private were seized on and carried away, perhaps by those who would be loath to be used so themselves'. The once-circling vultures could now feed on the state papers with impunity, as no notary protected them: 'those things which were public have been culled out and gathered into private books, whereby no means are left to see what was done before or to give any light of service to young beginners'.[54] Burghley watched and learned. He drew up a will specifying that all of his papers regarding Her Majesty should be 'advisedly perused' by his son Robert.[55] He was to have first pickings. It was Robert who appointed a keeper of records at Whitehall, Thomas Wilson, transferring some of his father's archive to London. After Robert Cecil's own death, a warrant was issued that allowed Wilson, along with another of Cecil's former secretaries Levinus Munck, to take possession of his papers in Whitehall and Salisbury House. The papers now at Hatfield House are those that Wilson and Munck failed to remove from Salisbury House, and their sheer volume pays testament to the difficulty of sifting private papers from public ones.

During his tenure as keeper of records, Wilson complained bitterly to King James about the impossibility of his assignment. Men were reluctant to release papers (and thus their secrets), and 'embezzled & reserved to their own use' documents Wilson was meant to gather for the newly created State Paper Office.[56] He did not abandon the idea of an archive of state papers, confiscating libraries of ambassadors and private collectors, such as Sir Robert Cotton, who ran state papers to ground with the passion of the huntsman.[57] Despite Wilson's best efforts, the successors of the Cecils would be left largely in the dark when it came to papers concerning 'secret services'. This failure to replicate the almost compulsive archivisation that typified the Venetian intelligence service would frustrate the next generation of English spy chiefs.[58]

We, however, are in the privileged position of being able not only to access the various archives of individual spy chiefs and private collectors, no matter where they are physically located, but also turn them into a meta-archive which we can then search and cross-reference at our leisure. And we can do so largely from the comfort of our own homes on our laptops: the most important collections have been digitised. Where digital access is insufficient for our purposes – and the nature of spycraft is assuredly tangible – we can interrogate the documents themselves for those physical clues to their form and purpose; access to the scattered papers of sixteenth- and seventeenth-century intelligencers is readily obtainable in the south-east of England. The ease of access does not, however, make reading these documents as simple as reading the Sunday papers. Traditional archival skills such as palaeography as well as newer competencies demanded by, for example, the relatively new field of letterlocking (see below, pp. 56–66) are still vital. These letters and documents must still be transcribed, translated and sometimes decoded before they can be put to use. The researcher still has to act as a spy to catch a spy, painstakingly piecing together evidence while paying attention to the whispers in the wind.[59]

Spycraft is ultimately scholarship with the gloves off, not least as it often demands that techniques be reproduced so that we can better understand their working and thus their influence. By considering the physical nature of spycraft, we can read beyond the words on the page, and in doing so reach new conclusions regarding often iconic stories from history. It reveals, for example, how it was the three cipher secretaries of Mary, Queen of Scots, men who are often sidelined if mentioned at all in biographies, who were the most important actors in the Babington Plot and the fate of the queen (see below, pp. 91–5, 98, 101–3). It also shows her to have been a more savvy political operator than she is often given credit for. By showing the actual work involved in undertaking to counterfeit a seal or write a letter in cipher, we can better understand events in history. What is more, by tending to the techniques we render visible those who have largely remained invisible, and thus give voice to these dark artificers (no matter how much they strove to keep themselves hidden from view).

SECRETIVE PUZZLES

The documents and letters on which we have based our study are by nature elusive, cryptic and fragmentary. We cannot hope to be comprehensive, nor do we aim to be. We operate within physical and temporal constraints as much as we do linguistic ones – there are physical as well as semantic differences between how different languages manifest on the page, so we cannot hope to investigate examples from every country. This is why we have chosen to present these techniques as they were employed in specific case studies. There are many excellent overviews of the many and various acts of espionage that took place during this period, but we are interested in the technical details of early modern spycraft that remain unexplained and unexplored in such overviews and even in more detailed studies.[60]

Spycraft aims to situate itself in reality rather than in theory. We will only describe a technique if we have evidence of its use in the field, an intention to use it, a claim of having used it, or if it is important to understanding the development of spycraft in general. Cryptological manuals of this era, for example, were often more concerned with the mathematical exploration of ciphers and codes than with their practical application – the gap between theory and practice was often considerable.[61] There are many delightful 'techniques' which exist only in theory but were of no practical use, such as Jesuit polymath Athanasius Kircher's eavesdropping system made of gigantic imitation conch shells embedded in the walls of a courtyard. As this appears only as a two-dimensional image in a book, and there is no indication that anyone even considered building it, it has no place here.[62]

Within these parameters, we must take care not to overread our source materials – sometimes, a comb is just a comb. To take one example, in 1588 a new system of secret writing was brought to light, particularly useful when 'a man may have occasion to write that which he would not have every one acquainted with, which being set down in these characters, he may have them for his own private use only'.[63] This writing system, now known as shorthand, found its first iteration in Timothy Bright's book *Characterie, An Arte of shorte, swift and secrete writing by Character*.[64] It seems quite plausible that he conceived of it as a result of his work compiling a manuscript presentation copy of the highlights of della Porta's *De Furtivis*, which he had crafted at the behest of William Davison (a member of Walsingham's secretariat) the year before (see Chapter 2, pp. 80–2). Its primary purpose was to allow the user to 'write as fast as a man speaketh', or so Peter Bales would soon promise with his alternative system, 'Brachigraphie', which involved 'writing but one letter for a word'.[65] Shorthand could easily be confused with cipher, the secret language of diplomats and spies, however.

In 1589, Jane Seagar, for instance, presented a book of poetry to Elizabeth I in which each verse was accompanied by a string of mysterious symbols on its facing page (Fig. 4). Recently, it was alleged that in doing so she purposely presented herself as an intelligencer to Elizabeth I, as 'a code-breaker'.[66] Shorthand is not code however, and by extension, Seagar sadly cannot be seen as a 'code-breaker'. This does not detract from her exquisite mastery of the quill, but she simply used Bright's system.[67]

Likewise, for over a hundred years, Samuel Pepys's diary was thought to have been written in cipher. It is still talked about as if this were the case, even though we now know it is written in an adapted version of the short-hand espoused by Thomas Shelton in his books *Tachygraphy* (1641) and its companion *Tutor to Tachygraphy* (1642). It is often said, for instance, that John Smith, a student of Magdalene College, Cambridge, was the first to 'break' Pepys's code. He managed to read it by comparing it with a text that used the same shorthand system for which an English version still existed. He later discovered, doubtless much to his embarrassment, that Shelton's texts were to be found on the college's heaving library shelves.

If shorthand had any value within espionage, however, it was probably in allowing the rapid transcription of both documents and speech: during an interrogation, for instance, a scribe could set down the exact words of a suspect. To our knowledge, however, there are no spy-related shorthand documents loitering in the archives. Shorthand, therefore, seems to have had its secret usage in the realms of the private, for women like Seagar who wanted to convey the mysticism of biblical poetry, or diary writers such as Pepys, who wanted to save time: the opportunity it afforded him to record his many affairs and dalliances in a way that hid them from his wife was presumably an added bonus.

A SMORGASBORD OF TECHNIQUES

Each of *Spycraft*'s chapters takes a separate trick or tool as its focus, providing a general overview of its development, the intentions behind it and its use in the field. The chapters progress more or less logically in that each largely covers the ways in which spies, intelligencers and other secret operatives tried to overcome the weakness of the techniques discussed in the preceding chapter – though this did not, of course, preclude them from using multiple techniques simultaneously, mixing ciphers and invisible ink, for instance.[68] Wherever possible (and where such instructions are not liable to cause bodily harm – though heed our warnings), we provide either instructions on how to reproduce the technique, or refer to experiments that we have conducted or have had conducted to assess their feasibility.

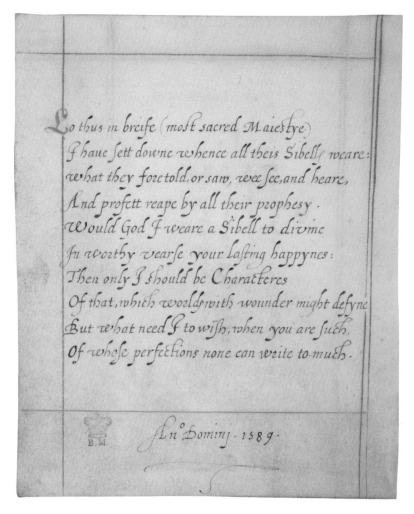

Lo thus in breife (most sacred Maiestye)
I haue sett downe whence all theis Sibells weare:
what they foretold, or saw, wee see, and heare,
And profitt reape by all their prophesy .
Would God I weare a Sibell to divine
In worthy vearse your lasting happynes:
Then only I should be Charactres
Of that, which woeldswith wounder might defyne
But what need I to wish, when you are such,
Of whose perfections none can write to much .

An° Domini . 1589 .

Fig. 4: Facing pages of one of Jane Seagar's poems as presented to Elizabeth I.
What looks like cipher is, in fact, the poem rendered into shorthand.

In Chapter 1, 'Fraud & Forgery', we detail the ways in which letters were opened, their contents extracted, and then either resealed or remade by spy and counterspy alike. Aware that their letters were liable to interception, spies sought other ways to protect their contents: through cryptography. Chapter 2, 'Ciphers & Codes', examines this burgeoning art and the culture that surrounded it. Using the Babington Plot, perhaps the period's most celebrated instance of a conspiracy fought by desk-bound cryptanalysts, as an indicative example, we explain how ciphers were actually used in the field. Ciphers, however, suffered from the manner in which they advertised their nature: as soon as an interceptor opened a ciphered letter, the symbols that stared back revealed that a secret was hidden within it. In Chapter 3, 'Disguise & Distraction', we consider the ways in which spies tried to overcome this problem and sought to hide the fact that their letters were bursting with sensitive information using linguistic and other tricks, how they sought to

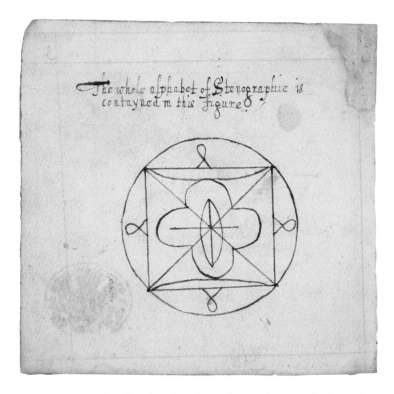

The whole alphabet of Stenographie is contayned in this figure

Fig. 5: A reminder that shorthand was designed primarily for utility rather than secrecy is writ large in John Willis's diminutive *The Art of Stenographie*. This image purports to contain every penstroke necessary for writing shorthand.

conceal letters and even the messenger using dead drops, priest-holes and other methods such as cross-dressing. Far better than hiding secret writing was to make it entirely invisible, however, and in Chapter 4, 'Inks & Invisibility', we investigate the challenge that the many different invisible inks posed to spy and counterspy alike, showing how Arthur Gregory used his ability as a counterfeiter and his knowledge of della Porta to develop a way to accurately copy a letter using invisible ink. We do so by considering the aftermath of the Gunpowder Plot, the conspiracy that 'would become the texual paradigm for all the versions and variants of plot and conspiracy that would follow later in the century'.[69] Fittingly, after a chapter discussing perhaps the most oft-told story of a botched assassination, Chapter 5, 'Stilettos & Storytelling', looks at the last resort of the spy, murder. The spy's primary weapon was stealth, and we look at three ways in which this stealth could kill: the stiletto; the pocket pistol or 'dag'; and, stealthiest of all, poison. Counter-intelligence used the inventiveness of spies against them: even more effective and deadly than these weapons were the feelings of fear and distrust they promoted. The public foiling by prominent spy chiefs of fictitious assassination plots was a feature of this age of suspicion. We have provided a set of appendices, 'Lessons: the School of Spycraft', to explain particularly complicated or technical details, such as the specific differences between a keyword cipher and an autokey cipher, or the various ingredients used to make invisible ink. These are referred to as either 'Lesson' or 'Lessons' in the endnotes.

Finally, in our 'Coda: The Black Chamber', we look at how the virtual witchcraft of the lone dark artificer developed into the deskcraft of an intelligence institution, how techniques allowing the rapid counterfeiting of seals sat alongside the use of ingenious devices such as a proposed copying machine, fuelling the most effective technique of all: the black chamber. In the end, we hope that our readers will understand that a spy had to bring more than just petticoats and lemon juice to the table if they were to make their mark.

1

FRAUD & FORGERY

In December 1560, King François II of France died from an ear infection, leaving his seventeen-year-old queen consort, Mary Stuart, a widow. While Mary had lived most of her life in France, her husband's death left her with but one title, the sovereign Queen of Scots. In August 1561, Mary returned to the land she had left as a five-year-old in order to assume her throne and take over the reins of power. Within five years, her rule imploded amidst a rash of murders, conspiracies, duplicity, two ill-considered marriages and open rebellion. Mary was imprisoned at Lochleven Castle by a group of rebellious Scottish lords. It was there, in 1567, that she abdicated her throne in favour of the fruit of her second marriage, the infant James. Escaping from her Scottish prison in May 1568, she fled to England, only to find herself placed under house arrest; William Cecil, Queen Elizabeth I's Protestant secretary of state, would neither allow her to return to her Catholic relatives in France, nor to Scotland and possible (though unlikely) restoration. An opportunity to make her house arrest more permanent arose in the shape of the so-called Casket Letters, which had been brought to his attention by Mary's illegitimate half-brother, the Protestant earl of Moray. A bundle of paperwork comprising eight letters, twelve sonnets and two draft marriage contracts, the Casket Letters were – according to Moray, at least – proof both of Mary's infidelity and of her collusion in the murder of Lord Darnley, her second husband.[1]

Moray was anxious to hold onto his position as regent during the minority of James VI, while Cecil was keen to neutralise the threat posed by this Catholic queen who had asserted her claim, albeit unsuccessfully, to the throne of England in 1558. Elizabeth's secretary of state proposed a tribunal to assess the letters and the case they presented against Mary. In effect, the tribunal was to rule on the authenticity of the letters: if they were deemed authentic, Mary would be guilty as charged. If they were forged, as Elizabeth believed, then her 'sister and cousin' could be exonerated. The case rested largely on whether the letters were in Mary's own hand or not: if they were, she would be convicted not on the evidence of others, but 'by the testimony of her own handwriting'.[2]

The tribunal soon turned into a virtual trial; Cecil had only ever been interested in one result. He concentrated on the hand itself, reporting that the 'manner of writing and fashion of orthography' of the Casket Letters compared favourably with other letters sent by Mary to Elizabeth that were known to be authentic. He had, in effect, declared the letters genuine and Mary guilty in absentia (she had been barred from taking part). It was at this point that Elizabeth, unhappy about the direction being taken, curtailed the proceedings. The tribunal ended with Mary, Queen of Scots left in a legal limbo, declared neither guilty nor innocent.[3]

The tribunal had changed nothing, merely muddied the waters, and Mary remained under house arrest. The original Casket Letters disappeared in 1584, leaving us only with contemporary copies and translations – some bearing Cecil's annotations – from which to draw our conclusions.[4] Nevertheless, modern scholars consider that the letters were forgeries, a mere collage or copy-paste work concocted from some of Mary's actual letters and other sources. It seems highly likely that Cecil knew full well that this was the case.

Though the tribunal proved ultimately inconclusive, the Casket Letters cast a slur on Mary's reputation, while her supporters continued to assert that they were forged. No one denied that they *appeared* to be in Mary's hand – it was merely suggested that her hand was not particularly idiosyncratic. For instance, the Scottish author Adam Blackwood, vice-chancellor of the University of Paris and Mary's apologist, argued that the identity of the writer could not be reliably deduced from the hand alone. 'It is well known', he wrote, 'that the letters of Mary Beaton, one of Her Majesty's ladies of honour, resembled so nearly those of her mistress, that it is not possible to discern the one handwriting from the other'. The letters may indeed have been written by a Scottish woman called Mary, but not necessarily the Mary her accusers alleged. This differentiation was important, as one's hand was effectively one's voice: a treason written was as damning as a treason uttered.[5] If the letters were in the hand of Mary, Queen of Scots, then they were powerful evidence of her misdemeanours. This made it all the more suspicious that the letters themselves had not been presented as evidence to the public. Mary herself was clear in her assertions that the letters, or, at least, those parts of the letters that were purported to prove her complicity in Darnley's murder, were forgeries.

Blackwood suggested that Cecil's disingenuous use of a set of confected correspondence had led to an increase in speculative forgery: 'you have also at this day by your juggling . . . now brought in the realm a most devilish and lewd practice, that many have learned of you to counterfeit men's hands'. Blackwood had a yet more powerful argument up his sleeve, however. 'We know not', he asserted, 'what time they [the Casket Letters] were written, nor by whom, nor where, neither superscribed nor endorsed with the name or person or any person, nor signed, nor sealed, nor the writing known or challenged of any'.[6] That is to say, the letters lacked any identifying or authenticating devices. Quite apart from the discussions over the hand, they bore no superscription (such as an indication of a place of origin), or signature, and lacked the final, authoritative kiss of a wax or wafer seal. It was not as if the recipient had even identified the writer in an endorsement, as was common practice. Blackwood may have been as biased a source as those he railed against, but he did name those material features which were considered necessary to authenticate a letter, and, by extension, what features must be reproduced to create an entirely convincing forgery. This was a lesson taken to heart by those who occupied the less salubrious corridors of power: if you wanted to ensnare a queen with a series of forged letters, they had better be convincing.

That Elizabeth's government employed individuals who could produce counterfeit letters accurate enough to convince the supposed writers themselves, and could do so with all the authenticating features necessary, is the clear message of William Camden's comments on the talents of Arthur Gregory. Opening and resealing a letter without anyone noticing necessitated a facility with seals, for example, that went beyond their careful removal and reattachment: it required an ability to counterfeit them. In an era when the primary method of transmitting information over distance was the humble letter, the mastery of every facet of their construction was the key ability required to operate as a dark artificer. Much of a spy's work boiled down to this, and so, therefore, did the work of the counterspy. The war between spy and counterspy was often an epistolary one, fought out on battlefields of paper, ink and wax. Whether or not the reported upsurge in counterfeiting was, as Blackwood suggested, merely the result of people taking their cue from governmental activities, there were a certain number of skills that needed to be mastered if one wished to counterfeit a letter convincingly. It is certainly the case that over the next decades many individuals worked hard to master the techniques necessary to fake each and every one of these authenticating devices.

THE MAN WITH THE GOLDEN PEN

If the forging of handwriting was a widespread phenomenon, it was not always done well. In 1596, for example, the hand of Robert Cecil was reported as having been 'grossly counterfeited' a mere month after he had finally succeeded his father as secretary of state.[7] Some years later, in 1602, legal authorities in Essex acquainted Cecil with another such 'fowle practice': 'your Honour hath been abused by a counterfeit letter produced under your name'. The counterfeiter, 'one John Gliberye, a known lewd person', was quickly brought to justice.[8] A true expert in the counterfeiting of hands, however, was one who could make you 'mistake your own handwriting, and approve and allow that for yours which hath been falsified by them, and you never did see with your eyes before'.[9] That is to say, their work was so good it could convince even the individual they imitated. Such men were known to exist, and that same year Cecil was warned of a Frenchman called Arnott, 'a very dangerous person and one that can counterfeit any man's hand. It is dangerous for you to give him a passport under your hand, lest he abuse it to counterfeit your hand'.[10] A skilled counterfeiter was a valuable weapon in the armoury of any spy or spy chief; and while there are no handwriting spy manuals from which we might learn their techniques, the life and work of one self-proclaimed 'master of writing' – and would-be spy – casts invaluable light onto the process by which a hand might be copied. This master of writing was Peter Bales. Bales ran a writing-school-cum-copy-shop, 'in the

Old Bailey, next to the sign of the Dolphin'. There he taught his students and promised to make copies of 'anything fair written in any kind of hand usual; and Books of Copies; such as you shall bespeak'.[11] The Old Bailey, home of criminal courts and adjacent to Newgate prison, was frequented by individuals from every echelon of society, from lawyers to labourers, prosecutors to poets. This provided Bales with an endless stream of clients.

Bales was not lacking in self-belief. He was willing to take on any scribe or scrivener to prove he had the best hand in the land (or at least in London). The 'Challenge of the Golden Pen' of 1596 was the result of a trading dispute between Bales and the owner of another writing school in the vicinity who also claimed pre-eminence at his craft. Bales could not stomach the possibility that people might think that anyone but he was the master scrivener. The challenge took the form of three separate competitions: 'The first, for best & fairest writing of all kind of hands usual: The second for Secretary & Clerklike writing: The third, for best teaching.' The prize was a real pen, fashioned by a London goldsmith from £20's worth of gold, the two belligerents having each put down half that amount as a winner-takes-all wager. Bales's victory appears to have been something of a foregone conclusion. The second task, for instance, was further defined by him as 'to write truest, best, and speediest, most Secretary, and Clerklike, from a man's mouth, reading, or pronouncing either English, or Latin'. As Bales's challenger knew no Latin, the outcome of this part of the challenge was hardly a surprise, and sure enough, the sign of the Dolphin was soon swimming above the Old Bailey alongside a hand holding a golden pen.[12] Bales would later go to great lengths to justify the competition, its supposed fairness and its importance, possibly because he was accused of having filled the judging panel and audience with his own friends.

Twenty years prior to this somewhat cynical and rather hollow triumph, Bales had been seeking employment in the counter-espionage trade. His letter of application came in the form of a jaw-dropping display of penmanship presented as a gift to Queen Elizabeth I at Hampton Court in 1575. This was a tour de force of micrographia, or small writing, in which Bales crammed the Lord's Prayer, the Credo, the Decalogue (i.e., the Ten Commandments), two short Latin prayers, his name, motto and the date of presentation 'within the circle of a single penny, encased in a ring and border of gold, and covered with a crystal so accurately wrought, as to be very plainly legible'.[13] It was a master-stroke to include the magnifying lens, or 'crystal', necessary to read his text in the setting of the ring, as it allowed everyone to admire his expertise, preferably when displayed upon the finger of his queen.

Bales's gift attracted Elizabeth's 'great admiration', and she reportedly wore this bejewelled feat of miniaturisation often.[14] Impressive as it was, this demonstration does not appear to have resulted in immediate employment, and it is unclear whether Walsingham saw the potential of micrographia as a spycraft technique. Bales was nothing but tenacious, and while by 1591 he was in the service of the lord chancellor, Sir Christopher Hatton, he craved more esteemed employment. Petitioning William Cecil, now Lord Burghley, for a position in the College of Arms – preferably as York Herald, but, failing that, as Rouge Croix Pursuivant – he not only reminded the queen's chief minister and closest confidant that he had 'been always willing and ready to do Her Majesty service with my pen or otherwise to my power', but could not resist commenting on the unsuitability of his competitors. He had no compunction in asserting that the incumbent Pursuivant, Ralph Brooke, not only 'preposterously seeketh to be preferred' but was 'notoriously detested, and for language or Latin insufficient to be advanced'.[15] Burghley begged to differ: not only was Brooke promoted to Herald, but Bales was passed over for the position of Pursuivant that Brooke's promotion had opened up.[16] Nevertheless, Bales still craved his hard-won expertise being put to legitimate use in the secret services of his queen, and, signing himself as 'Your Honour's most humble Peter Bales, *Cypherary*', he even offered his skills as a New Year's Gift to Burghley.[17] He would later boast that the 'best of this Land' held him in high regard because 'of some special service by him done, both abroad, and at home'.[18]

The opaque nature of his apparent service to his country and his outrageous talent for self-promotion did not detract from the fact that Bales was the possessor of extraordinary technical skills, and this was reflected in the clientele that frequented his scribal emporium: his quill was hard at work producing documents for men such as John Puckering, keeper of the Great Seal, and the translator John Osborne. The fact that one of the playwright Thomas Middleton's characters was required to 'draw any mark with a pen, which should signify as much as the best hand that ever old Peter Bales hung out in the Old Bailey [the sample scripts outside his shop]' shows that Bales's name was well known in London and that Middleton expected his audience to connect Bales with handwriting.[19] Bales was renowned for the clarity and consistency of his hands, with one source even stating that he could imitate printed typefaces convincingly.[20]

Bales's assertion that he was master of every act of the pen attracted characters even less savoury than playwrights to his shop. In 1599 he found himself drawn into the unholy mess that was the late career of Robert Devereux, 2nd earl of Essex. In a statement given on 31 July 1600, Bales recounted how he was approached at the beginning of Lent in 1599 by John Daniel, a ne'er-do-well who had once been described as 'either employed for the queen, or . . . a notable knave in no mean matters'.[21]

Daniel was a rather creative freelance intelligencer who worked on a 'spy now, pay later' basis, although the information he peddled seems to have been mostly concocted. In 1581 he wrote to Burghley, volunteering 'to go to Spain to mix with Irish traitors who had sailed there seeking help from Philip II', but his 'want of ability' (that is, lack of cash) prevented him from doing so.[22] Burghley's answer to this shameless request for money is not recorded, but by November 1590 Daniel seems to have gained the earl of Essex as a patron: Essex now lobbied the earl of Derby on Daniel's behalf, referring to Daniel as 'my servant'.[23] Some years later Daniel had successfully infiltrated various Catholic groups of interest in the Spanish Netherlands. He saw assassination plots everywhere. In March 1594, doubtless angling for some reward, Daniel sent Burghley 'a list of names of persons of sundry nations, with every man's mark, age and stature, who should come from parts abroad to kill the queen'. It is an indication of the bogus – or at least highly imaginative – nature of Daniel's information that the Jesuit and spy-handler Hugh Owen remarked that the list included individuals with 'no more to do with these doings of killing the queen than the man in the moon', and that one of its alleged assassins was 'a sorry fellow' who 'would not kill a cat if she looked him in the face'.[24] What Burghley thought of this latest offering is unclear, but in August 1594, Daniel was still in Essex's good books – not only did Essex lobby the dean of Christ Church, Oxford on his behalf, but Daniel soon married Jeanne van Kethulle, one of the countess of Essex's Flemish ladies-in-waiting.[25]

When the earl was arrested in 1599 following his unapproved return from campaign in Ireland, the countess, 'amid fears of the search or seizure of his papers', gave Daniel and his wife a locked casket containing some of her correspondence with the earl.[26] The trust the countess placed in the pair was entirely misplaced, however, as the moment that Essex was censured in Star Chamber – the court which dealt with the upper echelons of society – Daniel reverted to type and opened the box. After all, there was no reason to hide these letters unless they contained sensitive information, and an intelligencer's first loyalty was always to himself. Essex's 'ragged Roman hand' (i.e., a non-cursive script with upright letters) was, in the words of Anthony Bacon, elder brother to Francis and a secretary-intelligencer in Essex's pay, 'as hard as any cipher to those that are not thoroughly acquainted therewith'.[27] Daniel thus needed an expert to read it. (It is typical of this era that 'deciphering' could mean both the reading of apparently illegible handwriting, as it does here, and also a rather more spy-like activity related to cipher codes.)[28] And who better than Peter Bales at the sign of the Golden Pen? His reputation as 'a most notable and experienced decipherer of old and imperfect writing' had been enhanced by reading those parts of George Ripley's alchemical writings which their editor, Ralph Rabbards, could not.[29]

Bales had a straightforward, if time-consuming, method of deciphering difficult hands. In order to understand the words, the scrivener would endeavour 'first to conceive them himself'. In other words, Bales imitated hands in order to read them. Over the next three weeks, Bales copied the letters repeatedly, with Daniel watching his every move. Daniel paid the scrivener what seems like a very reasonable 1 shilling for each epistle (a mere £8 in modern terms, which perhaps explains Bales's desire to find alternative employment).[30] For Bales, deciphering a hand was a process that involved understanding the letterforms of a hand and how they functioned in context, and, of course, a deep appreciation of the mechanics of both pen and ink.

THE MECHANICS OF PEN AND INK

The type and condition of writing implement and the ink used all contributed to the way in which writing appeared on the page. Peter Bales had not only mastered the physicality of transferring ink onto paper, but he was also keen to share his knowledge. He had even written a textbook, *The Writing Schoolemaster* (1590), which included 'The Key of Calygraphie: that is, of fair [i.e., aesthetically pleasing] writing'. The first item of business was learning how to choose the correct knife with which to cut your quill, so he helpfully provided his students with a 'plain English verse' as an aide-memoire:

> Provide a good knife; right Sheffield is best.
> A razor is next, excelling the rest.
> A whetstone likewise of hoane that is white,
> Will make your knife cut your penne well to write.[31]

Different feathers suited different tasks: goose feathers were best for everyday writing, swan feathers suited large lettering, and crow feathers enabled fine lines. The unfortunate bird would generally have its left wing plucked, as those feathers 'curve outward and away from a right-handed writer'.[32] Cutting one's quill was a serious business.

It was not merely the quill that influenced the writing. If the paper was too rough it would damage the pen, if too smooth 'it will be too slipperie, that you cannot write heavily thereon'. Overly smooth paper could be helped by rubbing it with 'stanchgrain'.[33] While it may seem irrelevant to the spy or counterspy wishing to forge a letter, only by understanding the physical properties of quill and paper and how they affected the finished product could a perfect forgery be made. Indeed, Bales's technique of deciphering hands was, in essence, a method of counterfeiting. More practical advice followed: 'But when any letter seemeth more hard to be made, then it is very good to take a dry pen, and to trace over the same letter so often, until with your wet pen, you can well make the same.' Bales also provided the counterfeiter with a particularly useful piece of information:

> A, B, and M, if rightly you them make,
> Three quarters of the Alphabet doo take:
> Then of the rest, but six in all remaines,
> This have I shewen, to ease you of some paines.[34]

'For the choice of your quills, and the making of your pen'

'Choose the second or third quill of every wing, being round and hard; you may know them by the narrowness of the feather towards the end thereof, and cleanse them well with the back of your knife.'

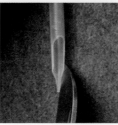

'Turn upright the back of the quill, and giue thereon a little cut, and with the end of the quill make the slit thereof very clean without raggedness or teeth.'

'In the nicking or last cut of your pen, (which is the making or marring thereof) you must be very wary, that you cut not the right side too short: for then your pen will bear too much on the left hand, and so scratch the paper and scatter the ink.'

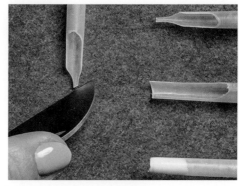

'You may harden your soft quills, by putting them into hot ashes, till they be for your purpose.'

Fig. 6: Peter Bales's recommended method for the making of a suitable quill, as found in *The Writing Schoolemaster* (1590), Q3v.

If so much of the alphabet can be written from just the strokes that make up these three letters, the vigilant counterfeiter could boil down an individual's hand to its most common features, not only simplifying the task, but also rendering it more regular, and less liable to error. Bales's final words, perhaps unsurprisingly for a 'schoolemaster', concerned diligence and continuous practice. He drummed his technique of repetition and imitation into his client as he worked, eventually presenting him with the blueprint to mimicry. Bales made his art personally available to any aspiring writer: *The Writing Schoolemaster's* title page notes that it was 'to be sold at the author's house in the upper end of the Old Bailey, where he teacheth the said arts'. In doing so, though perhaps unwittingly, he also produced a how-to guide for the budding counterfeiter.

What is missing in all of this is the ink. Fortunately, a large number of contemporary recipes have survived. For normal, black ink, few used anything other than iron gall ink, a recipe as old as it was ubiquitous. To make this ink you needed galls – the woody growths that form on the buds, leaves and other fleshy parts of trees and other plants in response to a gall wasp's laying its eggs in them – and some source of iron, usually copperas, the chemical we now call ferrous sulphate but was then commonly known as green vitriol or simply vitriol.[35] First you ground up dried galls and soaked them in rainwater (some recipes recommended using wine), with the length of time they steeped correlating to the strength, and thus darkness, of the resulting ink. Galls are rich in gallotannic acid (galls sourced from different plants created solutions of varying acidity – oak galls were a very common ingredient), which forms gallic acid during the steeping process. The gall-water was then strained and added to the copperas, forming ferrous gallate, which combines with oxygen to form ferrous pyrogallate, the dark pigment seen in the finished ink. Iron gall ink is not water-soluble, but over time its acidic nature can damage the paper on which it is used.[36]

In most recipes, the basic ingredients – gall-water, copperas and gum arabic – were the same; only the quantities and the length of time you were to soak your galls varied:

> *To make a perfect black ink to write or limme withall*
> Take one pound of galls, one pound of gum arabic, or vitriol an
> ounce, bruise your galls and vitriol, and put them into a vessel fit for your

purpose, fill it with white wine, that all your stuff may be covered above a hand breadth: then set it in the sun and stir it daily.[37]

Gum arabic was added to adjust the viscosity of the resulting liquid to make it more appropriate to the situation: a fast hand suited a runnier formula; more formal documents might suit a thicker, darker ink. If your ink was already too viscous, vinegar was often preferred over water as a thinning agent: too much water led to a dimming of the colour.[38] One correspondent suggested adding sugar to give the ink a glossy finish.[39]

Ink was usually home-made, and could be produced in great quantities, as we can see from a recipe used by Sir Thomas Roe, a diplomat and copious correspondent, which made 3 gallons of ink at once, enough to serve an entire embassy.[40] If you were travelling, it might have been sensible to use ink powder, which could be reconstituted by the simple addition of a suitable and available liquid (often, this liquid appears to have been urine).[41] This powdered ink, which came recommended by the sixteenth-century mathematician, cartographer and alchemist Girolamo Ruscelli (who, like della Porta, had an 'Academy of Secrets' in Naples), was made by adding charcoal derived from peach and/or apricot kernels with gum arabic to dried galls and vitriol. This recipe, he suggested, was also particularly good for reviving a bad ink: 'If you have naughtie inke, put to it a little of said powder, and it will become immediately very black, and have a good gloss.'[42]

While the majority of letters from this period were written in black ink, even if it now has generally faded to various degrees of brown, other colours were available. They were somewhat more exotic than the usual recipes, too:

An Emerald Green
Take verdigris [copper carbonate], litharge, quicksilver [mercury] brayed [crushed] to powder, and ground with the pisse of a young child.

For to make colour like Gold
Take saffron dried, beaten into powder, and put to it as much glistering orpiment [arsenic trisulphide] that is scaly and not earthy, then

with the gall of an hare or a pike, bray them together, put them in some phial under a dunghill five days, then take it out and have it, for it is the colour of gold.[43]

When confronted with the task of reproducing a convincing facsimile of a particular document, it was essential for spy and counterspy alike to colour-match their ink as they mixed it, while adjusting its viscosity and the cut of their quill to suit the style of hand to be copied. We regularly find letters which have postscripts or signatures that appear in a different shade of brown to the letter's body text. The volatile nature of contemporary ink makes it impossible to tell whether these variations relate to the time at which these additions were made or to their ink – the original writer might, for example, add a postscript to a letter previously composed, and thus end up using a different ink. This fact made it easier for a forger, of course, to add a postscript to a genuine letter, as the colour of the ink at least would not matter so much.

IMITATING THE EARL'S Ps AND Qs

It would not be long before John Daniel began the second part of his plan, doctoring the correspondence between the earl and countess of Essex, the very letters entrusted to him by the latter. One of the earl's letters contained a sentence even Bales thought dangerous: 'The Queen's commandment may break my neck; but my enemies at home shall never break my heart'. Bales later swore he only continued with his work to ascertain whether the letters contained anything more that he ought bring to the attention of a magistrate. Now Daniel wanted Bales to insert that one particular sentence in several of the other letters – in effect, following the method of those who created the more famous Casket Letters by using genuine passages to create a convincing collage. When Bales asked what purpose these letters served, Daniel answered it was at the behest of the countess that 'in the end he might the better gull somebody'. Though now in a state of 'perplexity', Bales did as he was asked. He would later swear that he 'did not imitate so near as I could': he purposely underperformed in his role as counterfeiter in order to prevent the copies from being put to nefarious use (Bales being Bales, this was presumably true, as having his work thought of as substandard would have stuck in his craw).[44]

Daniel left the scrivener at his travails, but possibly having noticed Bales's unease, he did not return to the shop. There was no need. By following Bales's example and taking up the pen himself, he had also learned to reproduce the earl's hand. He employed his new-found counterfeiting skills, adding postscripts to the letters at his own leisure. Daniel's motives were less than savoury: he was intent on blackmailing the countess with these letters written 'in her husband's hand', the contents of which were at best toxic, at worst treason – letters which were at the very least partially fabricated.[45] Since he now could make any number of copies, he purposed to sell these explosive documents again: having blackmailed the countess, why not sell the letters on to the authorities as 'intelligence'? He would later claim to be working as a government spy, explaining that 'the earl's letters were hardly written & not counterfeited but imitated for the Queen's Service': that is to say, the individual characters were copied in order that he might read the text to determine whether the earl spoke badly of the queen, not to counterfeit them for his own purposes.[46]

Bales, meanwhile, had confided in a London friend, a scurrilous individual called Peter Ferryman, who persuaded him to check the accuracy of Daniel's tale with the countess. Bales thought that some good might come of it: the countess might be thankful for his honesty, and he was still hoping that Essex would 'recover his credit, and then obtain an office' for him. The countess persuaded him to set down a declaration, which was countersigned by her secretary and Ferryman in April 1600.[47]

In the end, the countess still paid Daniel £1,750 for the return of the letters, the equivalent of a quarter of a million pounds in today's money. To finance the deal, she had to sell her jewellery, though it is unknown whether her actions were based on Daniel's newly discovered skill as a counterfeiter, or whether the stolen letters were, in themselves, potentially damaging enough. Her revenge was swift and merciless, however, as she promptly had him convicted in Star Chamber, with Bales appearing as a witness for the prosecution. Daniel was eventually fined to the tune of £3,000, imprisoned in the Fleet and punished as a counterfeiter: his ears were nailed to the pillory and he was forced to remain standing there accompanied by a notice reading 'A Wicked Forger and Imposter'.[48] He would remain in prison until the accession of King James to the throne of England.

Bales had nonetheless backed the wrong horse in his alleged loyalty to the earl. Once a royal favourite, Essex had topped off a few years of bad choices by leading a rebellion against his former patron, Elizabeth I, in 1601. A miserable failure, it resulted in the earl's execution and that of several of his circle. Robert Cecil appears to have protected Bales from the worst of the chaos that followed the abortive rebellion, which included the discussion of the letters in Star Chamber. Either Cecil saw the value of having a specialist scrivener beholden to him, or he was careful to keep individuals who had already been engaged in under-the-radar operations onside.[49] The 'small writer' even gained some measure of favour under James I: he was later appointed to the position of writing master to Prince Henry for the grand fee of a crown a day. Luck did not appear to follow Bales, however, and after nine months of tutoring the prince, he wrote to Cecil complaining that he was yet to receive a single penny by way of recompense. Furthermore, he had received no reward for 'writing and presenting to His Majesty his *Basilicon Doron* [James's treatise on government] for the Prince in a small volume to be worn as a tablet book'. He reminded Cecil of the value of his secret services: 'And I shall not only be ready to deliver to His Majesty a most secret Cipher impossible to be deciphered by where the observations are shown; But will also disclose . . . the manner of close conveyance of His Majesty's letters of greatest importance, that they shall pass without finding them about the messenger by any search whatsoever.' This time he signed himself as 'Peter Bales, the Small Writer, Writing-School Master to the Prince'.[50]

Of Bales's cipher or his method for secretly conveying letters (which may have involved his gift for micrographia) there remains no trace. Nor, after this date, is there any trace of the master scrivener himself. Perhaps he was altogether too ostentatious and well known a figure to fully trust with state secrets, or perhaps he simply did not know when to shut up. If indeed it was he who wrote in the crown prince's copy book that 'Prince Henry has such a childish hand that he is hardly worthy of even mediocre praise as a writer', then the latter seems likely.[51]

PRINTER'S INK AND CANDLE SMOKE

While John Daniel presented counterfeited letters as written entirely in Essex's own hand, it was common practice amongst those in positions of influence – exactly the kind of person a spy might wish to imitate – to have a secretary or amanuensis write a letter's body text and merely add their signature as authorisation. Other documents that were produced in this way were the kind of receipts and claims for petty cash that governmental departments churned out in their hundreds. In such cases, all that was necessary for those members of society who walked on the darker side of the street was to find someone with good enough secretary hand for the script to look convincingly anonymous and have them re-create the document in question. All the document would lack would be the appropriate signature. Luckily, or unluckily, depending on your position, it was possible to re-create a signature without any calligraphic skill whatsoever. All it took was a signature-stamp, a device not unknown in government circles – in 1569 a warrant was drawn up to allow for a series of Queen Elizabeth's letters to be authorised in this manner.[52]

The way in which these stamps were fashioned and then used is to be found in the examinations of two men, Christopher Porter and Guy Lewes, who were brought in front of two Middlesex justices of the peace in July 1600. Porter was a pursuivant, that is, a messenger ordinary of Her Majesty's Bedchamber. A pursuivant's responsibilities included apprehending recusants and other transgressors, acting as couriers for documents and suchlike, making their activities something akin to modern police work.[53] On 6 June 1600, for example, Porter was issued with a warrant to 'apprehend William Holliday, merchant, of London, and to bring him before their Lordships [i.e., the Privy Council]'.[54] Porter had spied an opportunity, and was intent on using signature-stamps to authorise fake expenses claims which he could then exchange for cold, hard cash. Lewes was the Old Bailey resident he employed to engrave his stamps in brass. He was also the man who reported Porter to the authorities. The three names Porter wished to counterfeit with his brass stamps were not insignificant. The lowliest was Thomas Smythe, customer (collector of customs duties), alderman and soon-to-be sheriff of London.[55] Next came William Waad, clerk of the Privy Council and latterly lieutenant of the Tower of London.[56] The most grand of the trio was without doubt Sir Robert Cecil. The combined signatures of Waad and Cecil were the authorising marks on expenses forms that messengers such as Porter redeemed at the royal household's chests following a job (Fig. 7).

In his own statement to the justices, the engraver Lewes claimed that Porter had approached him a fortnight before, bearing a piece of paper with a name written upon it in 'Roman letters'. Porter wished Lewes to 'engrave that name in a piece of brass . . . So that the same might imprint upon any paper either with printer's ink, or the smoake of a candle'.[57] Lewes was to make a small, portable printing press that could only reproduce one thing: a signature.

The stamp would be engraved much as if it were a piece of moveable type, to enable 'relief' printing – that is, where the signature itself stands above

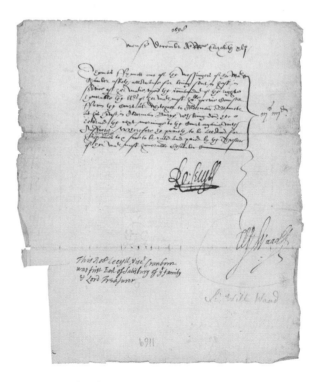

Fig. 7: An invoice for the payment of 3s 4d claimed by the pursuivant Thomas Fynnett 'for being sent in hast in service of her Majestie'.

the rest of the printing implement, which is then inked and applied to the paper as necessary. (The intaglio method, as used in copperplate engraving, would be totally unsuitable for such a surreptitious device.) The stamp would not work with the sort of ink described earlier in the chapter, the kind that a letter-writer would routinely use to scratch out words with their quill. Indeed, it would only work with printer's ink, as Porter had insisted. Following a demonstration in a printer's shop, the pursuivant knew enough about the process of printing to understand that paper was always moistened before it received the kiss of the printer's press, as this helped flatten out the inconsistencies in the paper's surface, thus preventing misprints. Printing on dry paper would cause drop-outs, small areas where no ink had reached the paper, a tell-tale sign that this signature was not written with a quill. Following this part of the process was vital, as the printer had explained to Porter: 'the wetting of the paper doth make it take their ink without suspect, so that the print will not be seen of the back side'.[58]

Printer's ink was thick and oleaginous, designed to stick to the metal type used in the printing process rather than drain through the cut nib of a quill.[59] It might have proved a little awkward to use, as on a printing press it was usually applied to typeface with large, leather balls which had a thin layer of ink upon them. These would have been impractical when it came to inking something as small as Porter's stamp, which would have been roughly the same size as a seal impress, but once applied (perhaps by a small piece of leather), this ink would have worked handsomely. Porter's stamp, however, was to be usable with both printer's ink and 'the smoake of a candle'.

While using a candle may seem strange, even given that a piece of metal held above a candle will rapidly acquire a thin layer of carbon, it makes far more sense when you consider that the majority of candles at this time were made not of wax but of tallow – beef or mutton fat – and thus produced a far more noxious, greasy smoke than modern paraffin wax candles, and that a good source of black pigment used in most printer's ink was found in 'lamp black', the carbon deposits accreted in lamps. This method of 'inking' would have been as useful to the spy as to the thief, as tallow candles were the most common producers of artificial light, and so these stamps would not require the counterfeiter to be in constant possession of small quantities of printer's ink.

Porter's understanding of how to use a signature-stamp undetected, and perhaps to charge it not with ink but with candle smoke, reminds us that he was up to no good, even if he at first denied it, claiming that he was merely doing his job as a pursuivant. When caught with his counterfeit stamps, therefore, Porter claimed that he was not intent on defrauding the crown, anything but – he was trying to uncover those who, he said, were already using such stamps to counterfeit 'bills in the pay house'.[60] As part of his plan, he meant first to discover if what he had been told by 'some of the ancient pursuivants', namely that such counterfeit stamps had been successfully used in the 1570s, was actually true.[61] In this case Porter was certainly onto something, as records tell us that in 1578 no fewer than eleven pursuivants had been accused of submitting a total of 110 fraudulent claims to the sum of over £400 using the counterfeited signature of secretary of state Walsingham.[62] Porter told his inquisitors that the best way to catch those he suspected of repeating this fraud was to get some stamps made, use

Fig. 8: A reproduction of Porter's signature-stamp with the resulting signature rendered in printer's ink.

them, and from this learn how to distinguish the real signatures from the stamped.

Unfortunately for Porter, he was not an accomplished liar, and while the position of pursuivant came with a wage (in 1612 it was set at £4 5s per annum plus another 2s 6d for 'daily board-wages'), it was plainly not so great that it removed the temptation to slip in the odd extra expenses claim for 3 shillings or so. This temptation was presumably rendered all the more enticing every time he returned home to be greeted by his wife and their clamouring brood of eight children.[63] Porter was not going the extra mile in honest service to the crown but had instead overstepped the bounds of legality in the interests of lining his own pockets. Having been left to stew for a few days by the authorities, Porter abandoned his defence of seeking out fraudsters, and admitted that he had been searching 'both to see if he could find any bill so stamped with any stamp like them, whereby he intended to make the like, and to pass into the payhouse for his own private gain'.[64] Porter was committed to prison, where he remained for quite some time.

Porter's scheme did not fail because his stamps failed to work. It failed because the engraver, Lewes, having pocketed the 2 shillings and sixpence Porter paid him for each signature carved out of brass, decided to 'reveal the matter unto Thomas Hicocke the Clerk of Newgate', upon which Porter was arrested. Lewes claimed that he had not recognised the signatures of Smythe, Waad and Cecil when Porter had first brought them to him. Certainly, by his account Porter pretended that the signature which read 'Tho: Smythe' referred not to Thomas Smythe the collector of customs but to a woman 'much given to play at cards [who] was loath to forgo her game to write her name'. He clearly hoped that a charitable soul would conclude that 'Tho:' was a diminutive of Thomasina rather than Thomas. The second signature belonged to Waad, by Porter's account 'the said woman's brother', while Cecil's was needed for the signing of a will.[65] It does not take a great leap of imagination to conclude that Lewes was lying about falling for this story, and that he had turned Porter over to the authorities in the expectation of some small reward on top of the cash he had already earnt. Working on the wrong side of the law was a dangerous game.

Cecil might have kept Porter incarcerated as an act of personal retribution: this messenger had, after all, been passing himself off as the secretary of state himself, and such behaviour must have had some effect on Cecil's authority. The disgraced pursuivant would later describe himself as 'distressed' and 'cast into prison against Her Majesty's injunction' as he petitioned for his freedom.[66] Porter was certainly released at some point (most probably at the accession of James to the English throne), but his propensity for getting into trouble continued – he was listed as a serving messenger of the Chamber in 1611–12, but in 1615 a warrant was issued to the keeper of the Gatehouse, 'to enlarge and set at liberty Christopher Porter, messenger'.[67] No mention is made of Porter's ears, but whatever indiscretion it was that led to this second residence at His Majesty's pleasure did not appear to have had an impact on his employability, as no sooner had he been set free than Porter was once more plying his former trade of pursuivant.[68] It is not beyond the bounds of possibility that he had been sent to prison this second time not as punishment but in order to act as a stool pigeon, 'an informer who elicits secrets in the guise of a friend or fellow inmate and reports that information back to the authorities'.[69]

Whatever way a spy or counterspy chose best and most conveniently to counterfeit a particular hand and signature in their attempt to fool their opposite numbers, there were other authenticating features left to conquer, and the one we turn to next also served to close a letter as well as to identify its author: the humble seal.

SEALED WITH A WAXY KISS

Seals served two purposes, authentification and security. The presence of a seal on a document showed that the document came with the authority of the seal-holder, whether an individual or an office. It could be placed next to a signature or be attached by a ribbon. When used to secure a document shut, however, a seal also served both to identify the sender and act as a visible layer of security – the presence of an intact seal ought to have guaranteed that the contents remained unviewed by third parties.

Seals came in various forms and materials. Sealing wax was a substance that became molten when heated, such that it could be dripped onto a letter, joining together two parts thereof when it solidified. Wafers were baked discs of starch which, if moistened, placed between two pieces of paper and the resulting sandwich pressed together, would join the pieces together. Yet, like many words, 'seal' has multiple meanings when used in an early modern context. It is variously, and sometimes simultaneously, the process through which a letter is secured (or sealed); the adhesive with which a letter is closed (wax, wafer); a design unique to an individual that serves to identify them (coat of arms, initials); and the thing that impresses the design into the adhesive (seal-stamp, signet ring).[70]

THE SEAL-STAMP

The seal-stamp is a device which bears a particular seal-design engraved into its surface. This design was chosen by its owner to serve as proof of their physical authority and it was by means of the stamp that it was to be transferred onto the document. Seal-stamps were made of metal, often brass, and bore the negative image of the desired impression – the image created was thus in relief, that is, it stood proud of the matrix in which it was created. They could be independent pieces or incorporated in a ring, known as a signet. Important seal-stamps such as the Great Seal or the Privy Seal were intended to represent the authority of the monarch and thus were suitably large and the seal-design they bore suitably ornamental. In purely physical terms, the seal-stamp was used to provide sufficient pressure to ensure that the chosen adhesive bonded well to the things to be joined together, and to create the seal-impression.

The seal-impression provided authentication in the form of a recognisable device that demonstrated the identity of the sender. Sometimes this device was playful in nature, or had a metaphorical resonance with its owner, such as Sir Thomas Roe's seal, which featured an image of a small deer, or Sir Nicholas Bacon's seal, which featured a boar.[71] John Donne went a little further, explaining why he replaced his familial sheaf of snakes seal (Fig. 9) with an anchor upon his ordination in 1615 in a poem: 'This seal's a catechism, not a seal alone.'[72] For Donne his new seal was a visual representation of his faith.

The seal-stamp would be used to create one of two types of seal: the exposed-/bare-seal (Fig. 10) or the papered-seal (Fig. 11). In both cases, the

Fig. 9: John Donne's 'sheaf of snakes' seal-stamp with the resulting
papered- and bare-seals.

adhesive might serve solely to carry the image of the seal-stamp or it might also serve to join two pieces of paper together as a security measure.

Each type of seal had its advantages and disadvantages when it came to deterring counterfeiting. The exposed-seal provided a much sharper image for the counterfeiter to work with, but it also demanded much better reproduction if it was to be successfully forged. The papered-seal was, by its nature, less precise in its outline, making it easier to get away with a less exact copy, but its imprecision made it harder to copy the image it carried. Fig. 12 shows a counterfeit passport in the name of Robert Gray, as forged by Thomas Douglas, aka Robert Gray, bearing King James's signature (Jacobus R[ex]) and further authorised with a papered-seal (both of which were illegally produced).

If one wished to forge a letter or document convincingly, it was necessary to include the seal-design of its supposed author. To create the seal, whether exposed or papered, required a functioning seal-stamp carrying the appropriate design. The options for acquiring this were simple: borrow, steal

Fig. 10: The exposed- / bare-seal: the adhesive (wax) is applied on top of the paper and the seal-impression is borne by the wax.

Fig. 11: The papered-seal: the adhesive (which may be wax or wafer) is placed between two sheets of paper, and the seal-impression is borne by the paper.

or counterfeit.[73] Borrowing or stealing perhaps required a proximity to the subject denied to the average spy or even counterspy. In most cases, therefore, the only viable option was to counterfeit. To counterfeit a seal, one had either to make a new seal-stamp or to cast the new seal directly from a negative impression taken of the exposed-seal.

Engraving a seal-stamp from scratch to replicate it was a common practice. All stamps in official use were meant to have been engraved by the warden of the Mint, but this requirement had been much neglected. Officials from the shires for whom a trip to the Royal Mint in the Tower of London was perhaps inconvenient were in the habit of re-making their stamps 'in house' to save themselves the time and trouble of such a journey. As a result, many such seal-stamps were effectively counterfeited, not by criminals or

Fig. 12: A forged passport in the name of Robert Gray. The use of a papered-seal allowed the forger greater leeway to get away with inaccuracy.

spies, but by the officials who used them. Around 1595, an order was there-fore made that county sheriffs should instruct all officers using seals to present them on a certain day at the Mint in order that they might be checked.[74] The problem was clear. If even government officials were using second-rate – or 'counterfeit' – seals ('counterfeit' on account of their not being produced by the Mint), then how could one safely tell if the seal on, for instance, a passport was in fact genuine? Technically counterfeit they may have been, but they would still have been made in the traditional fashion: engraved by hand directly into metal. This process was time-consuming and highly skilled, and thus of little use to the average spy.

What both spy and counterspy needed was a way to counterfeit a seal quickly and efficiently, so that they could replicate the seal's two functions – security and authentication – whenever and wherever necessary. For a spy, it might allow them to create a convincing passport or other official document, whereas the counterspy might use the counterfeit seal to replace the one they would likely break in the opening and reading of a letter before sending it on its way. To counterfeit a seal quickly meant working with wax.

COUNTERFEITING THE SEAL-STAMP

How to bypass the two functions of the bare-seal was not a problem unique to the early modern period, however. As far back as the second century CE, the Hellenic satirist Lucian included a passage on the subject in his treatise *Alexander the False Prophet*. Lucian's Alexander was a priest who acted as an intermediary between the gods and man. One of his particular 'gifts' was the ability to enlist divine assistance that allowed him to know the contents of sealed petitions given him by the people without opening them. Alexander was, of course, cheating. He had simply mastered the art of removing an exposed-seal and replacing it so precisely that his sleight of hand went unnoticed, and this was how he duped his followers. Lucian noted two of Alexander's techniques. The first involved melting the wax of the bare-seal at the point that it made contact with the scroll through deft use of a hot needle, thus preserving it intact while separating it from the document it was designed to protect.[75] Once its contents had been perused, it only took a little care and a naked flame to reattach the seal, thus rendering the document once more 'unread'. The second method was to take a negative impression of the exposed-seal with a substance that would later harden, and use this impression to either cast a new exposed-seal which could then be used to close the letter in question, or to fashion a new seal-stamp. Lucian detailed two formulae suitable for this purpose. The first mixture he described as a 'plaster . . . a compound of Bruttian pitch, asphalt, pulverized gypsum, wax, and gum arabic', while the second involved mixing marble dust with the glue used in bookbinding.[76]

A century or so later, Lucian's formulae were repeated by Hippolytus in his *Refutation of All Heresies*, with some additional information regarding quantities and some alternative mixtures: 'they also say that wax with pine resin has a similar effect, as well as a solution of two parts mastic, one part dry bitumen. But sulphur alone is reasonably effective, as well as gypsum powder soaked with water and resin. This especially works wonderfully for sealing molten lead'. Hippolytus did not merely describe how to forge a seal, but also suggested it was a relatively common process. The moulding substance would be made in large quantities and formed into 'the shape of little pellets'. These pellets would then be softened over heat in whatever quantity was required, while the seal-forgers, in order to prevent the resulting goo from sticking to the seal they were intent on counterfeiting and thus ruining their day, 'coat their tongues with oil, then use their tongue to smear the seal with oil'. Hippolytus also noted the relative insecurity of sealing wax, which was made primarily from beeswax and turpentine, a combination that created a relatively soft and pliable matrix which was easy to use, but just as easy to abuse.[77] He suggested that mixing 'pig fat and hair' with the wax would help to prevent the subsequent bare-seal from being compromised, though it is not entirely obvious how he expected this to help matters.[78] The counterfeiting of seals was something expected and to be prepared for, and any counterfeiter worth his or her salt would have the tools of their trade – from quills to inks to moulding putties and sealing waxes – close to hand at all times.

Fourteen centuries later, these classical texts were still being mined for information on how to defeat exposed-seals. Celio Calcagnini included a character who was virtually channelling Lucian's Alexander in his 1544 'Oraculorum Liber'. In the centuries that separated Calcagnini from Lucian (and Hippolytus), however, advances had been made in the formulation of sealing wax. A typical sixteenth-century sealing-wax formula looked something like this:

> Take a pound of fine rosin [i.e., solidified resin], a quarter of a pound of beeswax, a quarter of a pound of red lead [i.e., lead(II) oxide] and two ounces of oil or soft grease, boil the wax and rosin together, and then straw [i.e., sprinkle] the red lead and grease upon it and stir them together, and then put it into some cold water, and after temper it in your hand, and it will be good red wax.[79]

The rosin rendered the final product somewhat brittle – shellac, a resinous substance secreted by lac beetles, was used in many such recipes for the same reason – while the lead oxide produced the deep red colour most often associated with sealing wax of this period. Some recipes recommended a different substance to produce this colour, namely dragon's blood (not the blood of an actual dragon, but either a type of naturally red gum or cinnabar).[80] A seal made from a brittle substance offered increased security: it was much harder to keep such a seal intact while you persuaded it to relinquish its grip on a letter.

The increasing probability of a bare-seal failing to survive even the most carefully executed of letter-openings merely accentuated the need for the dark artificer to master a sure way of counterfeiting one. The change in wax formulation over the centuries most likely rendered the heated needle technique largely ineffective, even though Calcagnini still included it as one of the techniques Lucian had attributed to Alexander. The two moulding substances Calcagnini lifted from his classical reading may well have proved useful, especially because he adjusted the recipes, or at least the names of some of the ingredients, to suit his audience or perhaps the modern, brittle waxes: the first substance, which he named 'collyrium' (or kollurion), was now a mixture of 'Bruttian pitch, bitumen, ground glass [*lapide perspicuo*, which also translates as 'translucent stone', suggesting alabaster, a type of gypsum], wax and mastic [resin from the mastic tree]'. Both this and the putty based on bookbinders' glue apparently hardened immediately, with the latter 'becoming more solid than horn or even iron'.[81] Both of these substances thus promised the easy creation of a usable facsimile seal-stamp, and thus the simple re-creation of any seal, at least in terms of shape. Things were not as simple as these writers made out, however, and the process, while effective, could take several days – the dark artificer would still need to be able to mix wax in any colour, and also reproduce any other identifying feature, such as scent.[82]

EXPERIMENTAL METALS

Arthur Gregory spent countless hours in his 'poor house' experimenting with various spycraft techniques. One problem he was particularly keen to solve was the thorny question of how reliably to counterfeit a seal. Gregory, like Calcagnini, concentrated on developing a substance that would allow him to take an accurate impression of a bare-seal from which he could either create a convincing if counterfeit seal-stamp, or directly remould a new seal. It appears he found such a substance, but he was unable to demonstrate its efficacy to Walsingham, as he explained in a letter dating from February 1586: 'I prepared a singular piece of the usual metal with intent to show the same to your Lordship, but a sudden swelling in one of my eyes did prevent me.'[83] The ingredients with which he hoped to create his moulding substance were anything but inert, and in this instance they had caused one of his own eyes to bulge out of its socket. He thus decided that it was not safe to put his 'usual metal' into Walsingham's hands. This was no doubt a wise decision. Rather than demonstrating the counterfeiting of a seal in person, Gregory instead writes about his experiments concocting invisible inks, amongst other things (this would be the last time he listed actual ingredients in a letter). At this point, it seems that Gregory had not connected his attempts to formulate the perfect moulding putty with his sudden incapacitation, and so continued in his quest, considering the substance useful enough to warrant large-scale production: 'I am continually employing myself to bring my secret metal to the best perfection in great quantity.'[84]

A decade later, Gregory would write to Walsingham's successor, Robert Cecil, of his continued metallurgical investigations, admitting that 'with making of metal this last night I have gotten an unsteadiness in my hand which will not leave me in a few days'. Handling the magical moulding putty, he now realised, was a dangerous enterprise, and he now 'scarce dare keep it in my hands'.[85] Practice made perfect, however, and Gregory was soon convinced that he had finally solved the problem: 'That I might be the better able to perform that which I have promised your honour touching the safe making of my sealing metal without danger of hurt, I have so well practised therein that I can assure your honour to show you a way to work it cold in the nature of wax.'[86] Gregory, like many of those actively involved in the espionage business, was reluctant to put the details of his methods into writing, even in his letters to Walsingham and Cecil. This is not particularly surprising – why give away the secrets of your trade in a letter when you can demonstrate them personally and, for preference, remain *the* purveyor of them. Luckily for us, the secrets that Gregory was intent on preserving were not entirely his own.

Lacking the formula for Gregory's seal-moulding putty, it is difficult to be sure that he derived either the idea or the recipe from Calcagnini or della Porta's *Magiae Naturalis*, even though we know that the latter was the most common source for many of the spycraft techniques in use during the period. The rather damning, if circumstantial, evidence pointing to della Porta as his primary source is to be found in Gregory's physical symptoms. Gregory's swollen eye, his tremor and his reported exhaustion all point to his having poisoned himself.

The recipes that della Porta recommends for the counterfeiting of seal-stamps are, on the whole, quite different to those of his ancient forebears.[87] His first is based around sulphur and powder of ceruse (the white lead said to have been used by Queen Elizabeth I as a cosmetic face paint); his second is formulated from vinegar, vitriol and verdigris mixed with quicksilver; and his third consists of steel filings mixed with quicksilver.[88] The fact is that many of the ingredients used in these mixtures are poisonous, and, as with the recipe for sealing wax noted above, they were held in the maker's hand before use. Mercury is a dangerous toxin, especially when present in vapour form, and verdigris, ceruse and the red lead that was used to colour sealing wax are not only toxic but would have been supplied to Gregory in the form of eminently breathable powders. Sometime in February 1595, Gregory wrote to Cecil that 'I find my self utterly unfit to be a sudden counterfeit' on account of his developing an 'unsteadiness in my hand'.[89] Gregory was naturally worried that the result of his continued experimentation had rendered him useless in the short term – counterfeiting handwriting would not be possible with a shaking hand, and he might find his position usurped by another. Tremor is a common symptom of both copper and mercury poisoning. Gregory was quite literally working in a toxic environment, and he had been incapacitated by the ingredients he was using, likely at della Porta's behest, to formulate his 'secret metal'.[90]

While Gregory was sure that he had mastered the art of counterfeiting seal-stamps using his 'secret metal', and could finally do so without poisoning himself (or so he believed), there was still one particular part of the process that remained beyond his control. To make a perfect counterfeit seal-stamp, one needed a perfect seal-impression to work from: 'I am sorry that among so many seals upon the out cover there is no choice of one perfect print. I wish it had been better, nevertheless I will proceed as I may and do my best: But if your honour hath had any other letters that could help it, I humbly desire your honour to send the *bare-seal* for it importeth greatly.'[91] Not all seal-impressions were suitable for counterfeiting, as their condition could simply be too poor to take a viable impression from. The best seal-impression to work from was a bare-seal or exposed-seal, such as Gregory wished for, as these seals had a greater three-dimensional depth and finer features than papered-seals.

While a simple scroll was, as Lucian explained, extremely vulnerable to being invisibly penetrated, the flattened, folded paper that formed an early modern letter was increasingly likely to have its own, sophisticated, security system built in. This system is letterlocking, and it introduced yet another layer of complexity to the manipulation of letters. Before attaching their remoulded seal(s), the counterfeit letter needed to be folded in exactly the manner that the recipient expected – King Charles I, for one, wrote that he could identify the female author of one letter 'by the fowldings'.[92] It is to this technique that we turn next.

LETTERLOCKING

To understand letterlocking and the manner in which its use contributed to the security status of a letter, we must first remember that the gummed paper pouch we now call an envelope was not invented until the 1800s. Before this date, letters were folded in such a way that the piece of parchment or paper they were written upon formed its own delivery package. It is this process that is called 'letterlocking'. There were many ways to 'lock' a letter, some simple, some highly complex, and they each tell their own story.[93] Letterlocking was not an elite activity, nor one necessarily connected to espionage or any other nefarious activity. Anyone who wrote a letter would employ letterlocking to close it for delivery, even if that meant folding the letter and simply tucking one end into the other, the 'tuck and seal' method. The 'tuck and seal' may have been popular, but it offered little in the way of security to spies, diplomats, and others for whom privacy of communications was of greater importance. The more complex styles of letterlocking had security features such as 'anti-tamper' mechanisms (or 'locks') that were designed to show the recipient whether or not the letter had been opened by an unauthorised third party. Letterlocking could also, in some cases, serve to identify the sender. In this respect, it could serve the same two purposes as seals: security and authentication.

Charles I was adamant that he recognised letters sent to him by Jane Whorwood, the woman who began as his spy and ended as his lover, from the way in which she folded them; this had the great advantage that she could leave her letters unsigned. Locking a letter involved putting it through a certain amount of manipulations, the type, complexity and number of which bore a direct relationship to its ability to resist tampering. Each one of these manipulations were likely as unique to an individual as their manner of writing.[94] Letterlocking could thus also be used to make a point – receiving a letter from a queen which was not only written in her own hand but folded by it too was a powerful statement of intimacy. Naturally, if it was recognisable, it was also vulnerable to counterfeiting. Within an active secretariat this could be quite a useful feature, as we can deduce from the request by Thomas Lake, the clerk of the signet, that Robert Cecil return a set of letters to the court as Elizabeth I had changed her mind. If these letters were yet to be sent on their outward journey, she wished that Lake might have them 'folded in a small plight [plait] like those of her own hand and so sealed', a task he thought 'may well enough be done'.[95] Though we will see that this particular folding might have been a rather challenging one, it was not for nothing that Lake was nicknamed 'Swiftsure', but on account of his prompt and efficient manner of conducting business.[96]

Just as a monarch's hand, signature and seal were at the mercy of their secretariat, so was their style of letterlocking. And anything that a secretary could do was at the fingertips of a dark artificer. Letterlocking was just one more arena in which spies and their close cousins, the counter-espionage agents, might do battle. In seeking to open and refold letters so that they might be sealed 'like those of her own hand', Elizabeth I's signet clerk Lake was merely re-creating the actions of operatives such as Gregory, an acknowledged master of this particular art.

A badly locked letter was certainly an object of suspicion. In 1630, for example, William Boswell wrote to the Privy Council concerning a letter of recommendation he suspected 'surreptitiously and unduly gotten'. One of the reasons given for this suspicion of counterfeit was that 'the fold, and making up of this letter is much narrower than the ordinary manner observed in the said Office'.[97] Boswell was employed specifically to verify documents, and his success may have contributed to his later appointment as Stuart ambassador in The Hague, where his duties included intercepting the letters of Charles I's sister, Elizabeth of Bohemia. Party to both sides of the espionage coin, Boswell was worthy of the title 'honourable spy'.[98]

The repackaging skills that William Camden attributed to Gregory in the *Annales* are not to be underestimated, as the challenge in reconstituting security-based letterlocking styles was not merely in the foldings per se, but also in the locks that they used. One such style was the 'triangle lock', in which the lock took the form of a large, triangular piece of paper, the pointy end of which was threaded through a slit made in the letter-packet (Fig. 13). The fat end was then folded over the letter-packet, hiding the pointy end, and stuck down with an adhesive. The act of opening the letter destroyed the lock, thus advertising the letter's interception. Naturally, della Porta considered exactly this problem, explaining how one was to 'Open letters, and shut them without suspicion', even when they had locks threading through the paper:

> We use to seal letters, putting paper upon them, which goes through the letter on one side, and wax is put on the other side, where it comes forth, and there it is sealed. You shall open the letter thus: Break away that part of the paper, that is put upon the place, where it passeth through the letter, and the hole is, the letter opens presently: read it, and shut it again, and put the paper torn off, in its proper place: first, anointing the crack with gum-tragacanth, dissolved in water, for the paper will be so glued, that it will be stronger there then elsewhere; press it with a small weight, till it grow dry; the fraud cannot be discovered, because the glue is white, and is not known from the colour of the paper.[99]

One might think a reasonably competent interceptor would simply fashion a new lock, counterfeit the seal and reclose the letter, negating the need for della Porta's invisible gummy glue. This would be true if the letter-writer had not locked their letter with a triangle cut from the same piece of paper that the letter had been written upon – in this latter case, the recipient could try to match the triangular lock with the triangular gap in the letter as if they were two pieces of a puzzle.

The puzzle pieces could be matched because of marks left on the paper's surface by its method of manufacture. Paper in this era was made from linen rather than wood pulp. The linen was placed in a large tub where it was beaten and shredded until it formed a sort of paper soup, and the sheets of

Fig. 13: The security features of the triangle lock made it a very effective style of letterlocking, and it was a favourite of both Walsingham and his cryptanalyst Thomas Phelippes.

paper were made by scooping a thin layer of the waste out of the tub with a rectangular wooden frame containing a wire mesh. The wires running horizontally in the frame were packed close together, only a millimetre or so apart – the indentations they formed are known as 'laid lines'. These wires were held in place by another set of wires, often thicker and spaced 10 to 15 millimetres apart, which ran vertically within the frame and created the indentations known as 'chain lines'. Both laid and chain lines were slightly lighter in colour than the surrounding paper, as at these points the paper was thinner. Watermarks were created in the same fashion, by embroidering the required image onto the paper frame's wire mesh with yet more wire. The resulting paper, called a broadsheet, was then hung up to dry. These lines allowed the recipient of a triangle-lock letter to ask certain questions to check whether the letter had not been tampered with en route. Was the lock made from the same paper as the letter itself? Did the chain lines and laid lines match? If there was a partial watermark on the lock, did the parts match with a watermark on the letter? In similar fashion, writing on the lock itself could also provide such security: if the address was half-written over the attached lock, an interceptor would have trouble replacing it; if the triangular lock was cut from the body text of the letter itself, the text would only make sense by matching lock and letter.[100]

There was an extreme iteration of the triangle lock that was not only aesthetically pleasing but one of the most complex, and secure, letterlocking styles yet discovered: the so-called 'spiral lock', possibly the 'small plait' Lake made for Elizabeth. Different variants of this lock have been found in letters from Elizabeth I, Mary, Queen of Scots and Essex, to name but three.[101] It is a lock that would have taxed even the most nimble-fingered interceptor – even making it from scratch was like navigating a labyrinth. This in itself might persuade some that a queen such as Elizabeth or even Mary would be unlikely to lock their own letters in this manner. This would be to misunderstand the craft that lay behind such a lock – both the skills and the implements needed were similar to that most popular of pastimes for royal woman (especially those, like Mary, who had a lot of time on their hands): embroidery.[102] It is highly likely that Mary was taught the spiral lock at the French court by Catherine de' Medici, her Italian mother-in-law, before bringing it to Scotland with her in 1561.[103] Even the most difficult technique could be imitated, and while the spiral lock might have begun its life in the hands of the Italian or French aristocracy, it was soon being manipulated by a Scottish counterfeiter.

Fig. 14 shows a replica of an open spiral lock letter sent in 1604 to Sir Robert Cecil.[104] It clearly shows the lock's primary giveaways, namely the 'beak' of paper cut from the letter itself, and the multiple slits sliced through it. It was sent by James Stewart – a man unwise enough to have been caught counterfeiting his royal namesake's signature and his sign manual, actions that had constituted treason in England since 1554. Stewart's letter was a straightforward plea for clemency, and the fact that he did so with a letter locked in such a complex manner tells us not only that security technology was constantly evolving, but that it was equally constantly being challenged by those who sought to profit from it. Stewart presumably hoped that a beautifully locked letter would increase the chances of a favourable response, or was perhaps hoping to persuade Cecil that he possessed skills too useful to

Fig. 14: Opening a spiral lock letter was far simpler than closing it, but it left the dark artificer with something of a problem. Here are the stages of opening such a letter, and the paper detritus that is left behind.

waste on the scaffold – it may just as easily have led Cecil to conclude that Stewart was far too familiar with this format of royal correspondence. Stewart produced his spiral-locked plea for clemency while confined in the Tower. It was quite possibly his final action; impressive as it was, it failed to prevent his execution for treason.[105]

As you can see, the unfolded letter is covered in slits, has a long strip of paper missing from its middle, and there are three scraps of loose paper left over. The scraps are what is left of the long strip of paper, in the shape of a sword or a bird's beak, that has been cut from the middle of the letter. Just to make things extra awkward, this 'beak' only has the two long edges cut, and

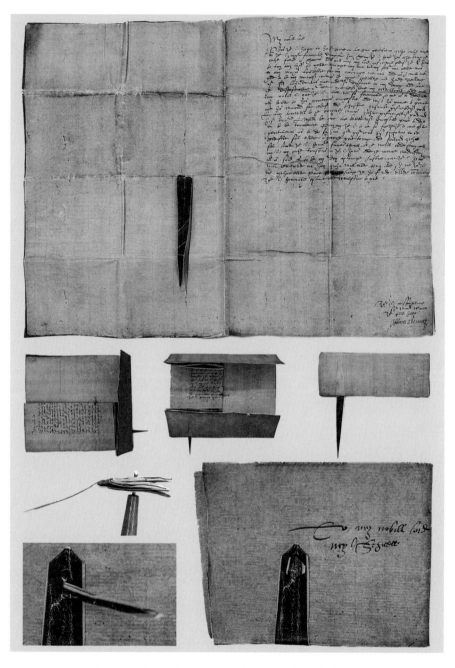

Fig. 15: The various stages of folding the spiral lock.

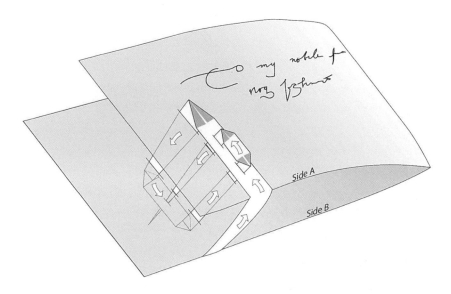

Fig. 16: Another indication of just how complex the finished spiral lock packet was, and just how difficult (if not impossible) it would have been to reconstitute once opened, is given in this exploded view – the arrows indicate the direction of threading; it is also depicted with a single fold of the letter itself for ease of comprehension – in reality, this letter would comprise several layers of paper.

so remains attached to the paper throughout the letterlocking process (Fig. 15). A series of slits are then cut through the entire letter-packet and the beak is carefully threaded through these slits and through itself before being finally tied shut. An unskilled letterlocker could quite easily tear it while threading it through the packet.

The spiral lock was extremely secure, but the sender could render it yet more so with a couple of simple additions. The first was to make the 'beak' even more fragile by wetting its points of entry and exit through the letter-packet with saliva: this would cause the paper to return closer to its original state of a bathful of free-floating linen waste, allowing beak and substrate to melt into one another, making their union all the closer when they dried. A second method was to apply adhesive in the form of wax to the area of the lock. This would seep through the layers of the substrate, making the delicate beak and slit areas not just more prone to tearing but to doing so in unpredictable ways, making the resulting damage even more difficult to mend invisibly.[106]

Creating a spiral lock was a complicated operation, one not to be undertaken lightly. Creating the slits through which the beak was to be threaded necessitated the use of a penknife or bradawl: this reminds us of certain truths that are difficult to comprehend, such as the fact that James Stewart plainly had a sharp object with him as he lay in prison awaiting execution. The typical penknife was not well-suited to homicide, however (the bradawl even less so), as its blade was short, rounded, and honed only along one edge. This blade was attached to a long, fine bone handle terminating in a point that could be used to punch holes in paper or help with the task of threading floss or paper through the holes cut during the locking process (see Fig. 1). There are a few instances of a prisoner attempting to prove that the penknife was mightier than the sword. One occurred on 8 March 1711, when the French double agent, the marquis de Guiscard, who was being examined by the English Privy Council on a charge of treason, assaulted statesman Robert Harley, 1st earl of Oxford and Mortimer, at a council meeting. Fortunately for Harley, Guiscard's penknife got caught in the ornamentation of Harley's waistcoat (or his collarbone, depending on which story you believe) where it broke. Clutching his now fractured blade, Guiscard managed a second thrust which succeeded in injuring Harley, but not fatally.[107]

Just as we have seen with the problems Arthur Gregory was caused by his experiments with materials to counterfeit seals, spycraft techniques could be dangerous to their user. Stewart's spiral lock variant would, after initial folding, have sixteen layers of paper needing to be penetrated for each slit (not counting the times the beak had to penetrate itself), and that could be a dangerous operation in itself.[108] The merest slip of the blade could spell trouble. Indeed, in 1575, Michel de Castelnau, sieur de la Mauvissière, the French ambassador in London, wrote to Burghley to explain that while he desired to 'kiss the hands of Her Majesty', he could not, as he had accidentally stuck the tip of a penknife into his arm while locking a letter, thereby touching a nerve and causing the arm to swell up.[109] Though it is not clear what kind of letter caused Castelnau to stab himself, it shows the dangers inherent to the epistolary life. We also can see that letterlocking was just another of the ways by which a letter-writer could inconvenience the counter-espionage agent: Gregory reported to Robert Cecil about one particular letter, 'the breaking of the covering & folding it often in other crests caused me to have much trouble'.[110]

JACK OF ALL TRADES, MASTER OF LETTERS

In a period when the letter was the most important mode of information transfer, the mastery of its various components could make all the difference – if the spy failed to fool the counterspy with their manipulation of letters, it might very well be the death of him. Mastery of a single device was simply insufficient. We know that each individual element was important because of the actions and words of the men (and women) who sought to gain advantage through use of a letter. When Charles II revoked the sanctions on religious nonconformity in 1672, a rush of personal letters flooded across the Narrow Seas, spreading the word to the Low Countries. This epistolary campaign was not the result of a groundswell of public opinion, however, but a purposeful act of spamming undertaken by just two men. In an attempt to conceal the common provenance of these letters, one of the counterfeiters wrote that he created them 'with all the variety of hands as I could write, with several seals; & several ways of folding up'.[111] Even the common people were sensitive to inconsistencies in a letter's presentation, and every letter had multiple potential red flags that might betray a dishonest nature were the counterfeiter careless or simply unskilled. The suspicions of Ambassador Boswell about the letter of recommendation mentioned above were not triggered by the unfamiliarity of the letterlocking style alone; he also noted that the letter's layout was incorrect, that it was written in two different hands, and that, while the seal *appeared* to have been made by Charles I's signet, there were suspicious anomalies: 'I conjecture by some parts of the wax, somewhat different in colour from other, & by some small rags of paper in it, hath been formerly upon some other letter, or writing. But when; by whom, or with whose notice it was put unto this letter in question, I cannot absolutely determine.'[112]

To be convincing, a counterfeit had to do more than read as though it were written by its apparent author – it had to be written in the correct hand, bear the correct signature and the correct seal, and present the correct method of folding. To create a convincing counterfeit was no mean feat. Without all these features in place, it could be difficult to trust that the letter in your hand was what it purported to be. Unfortunately for the would-be letter-forgers, there were other ways of guaranteeing that the message in front of you was genuine, ways which also served to secure these messages from prying eyes. One of these was the use of cipher and codes.

2

—◆—

CIPHERS & CODES

In March 1597, Thomas Phelippes found himself in the less than salubrious setting of the Fleet prison, in debt to the crown to the tune of £10,000 (something like £1.25 million in today's money). A decade previously, as right-hand man to the secretary of state Sir Francis Walsingham, he had been granted an audience with Queen Elizabeth I where she had thanked him personally for his key role in thwarting the most recent, and serious, conspiracy against her life, the Babington Plot. Walsingham's death had seen the end of Phelippes's permanent employment as an intelligencer, placing him on the road to debtor's prison. Nevertheless, the Cecils and Essex still called upon his talents as a codebreaker, albeit sporadically – he may have been a prisoner, but he was still indispensable. Having shivered his way through one of the coldest winters in recent memory, he once more found himself labouring away deciphering coded messages. No longer did he receive the approbation of the monarch, however, merely complaints that his work was too slow. His health was being slowly ruined by the proximity of his enforced lodgings to the filthy and disease-ridden river Fleet, and he could no longer access his records to assist him in his endeavours: he sent his wife Mary to retrieve papers now and again but, while she was an accomplished intelligencer, she was no cryptanalyst, and found locating the desired information amongst the piles of symbol-dripping sheets next to impossible.[1]

That same month, the queen and her 'elf', Robert Cecil, pressed Phelippes to decipher some Spanish papers they had sent him with greater dispatch. Try as he might, he could work no faster. He pointed out that the great Catholic enemy replaced their codes in 'such kind as will ask time to tread it out', reminding them that decoding the letter of the count d'Olivares, by which he uncovered the planned invasion that was the Spanish Armada of 1588, had 'held [him] twenty days in work'.[2] Their responses were unsympathetic. He was, and would remain, entangled in a mess of debt. More than ever, Phelippes found himself at the mercy of the cryptanalyst's most fearsome enemy, time. No one, he told himself, his wife, and those of his fellow prisoners who were willing to listen, truly understood his craft.

IN THE BEGINNING

The history of cryptography is the history of the evolution of communication, and as such its traces can be found in the classical writings of Virgil, Polybius and others, in sixth-century runic manifestations, and in early medieval works such as *The Reckoning of Time* by the eighth-century monk the Venerable Bede. Cryptology as an area worthy of study, however, was first developed in the Arab world, in *Kitab al-Muamma* (*Book of Cryptographic Messages*) by al-Khalīl (718–786), now lost, and *Risāla fī Istikhrāj al-Kutub al-Muammāh* (*On Extracting Obscured Correspondence*) by al-Kindī (*c.* 801–873).[3] While these men and others developed sophisticated methods for both encrypting and decrypting messages, the Western world ploughed its own, rather simplistic furrow. It was not until 1401, for example, that anyone thought to enhance the security of the monoalphabetic ciphers that had been in use since the time of Julius Caesar.[4]

The 'Caesar cipher' (aka the 'shift cipher') was used by both Julius and Augustus Caesar in the first century BCE, and is in itself perhaps the most famous cipher technique. It was a simple substitution alphabet formed by 'shifting' the alphabet by a certain number of degrees in order to find a substitute for each letter, such that with a shift of four degrees, 'a' in the original message (the plaintext) would be enciphered as 'd' in the crypto- or ciphertext, 'b' as 'e', 'c' as 'f', 'd' as 'g', etc. All the encoder needed was to count the degrees of shift desired, and the message could be enciphered easily. Naturally, it was vital that both sender and recipient used the same alphabet: to keep things suitably early modern, we will use the twenty-four-character English alphabet (in which 'i' and 'j' were interchangeable, as were 'u' and 'v') in all our examples, unless otherwise indicated. If we were to encode the plaintext message 'we are undone' with a shift of four degrees, the ciphertext would read 'zh dvh yqgrqh'.

The art of secret writing and its development in the West was indelibly associated with the diplomatic profession.[5] Ciphers were integral to the Venetian system of government by the sixteenth century, for example, and diplomats were required to write everything, even notes on scraps of paper, in cipher.[6] Official ciphers would be replaced if it appeared that they had been broken. Giovanni Soro had served the Council of Venice as cipher secretary for thirty-three years when he presented them with a treatise on ciphers in 1539, though little remains of it bar a few notes. Between 1546 to 1557, Florence had its own set of cipher experts such as Pirro Musefilo, count della Sassetta, who regularly received ciphers to solve from all over Europe. For some, such as the Argentis in Italy and the Rossignols in France, cryptography was a family business. Giovanni Battista Argenti and his nephew Matteo Argenti were not only employed as cipher secretaries by the Papacy in 1585 and 1591 respectively, but they also innovated: they were the first to use a mnemonic key, a recovery phrase, as a method of formulating and transmitting a cipher alphabet.[7] The Rossignols deciphered important Huguenot messages at the sieges of Réalmont (1626) and La Rochelle (1628) for Louis XIII, while Antoine Rossignol and his son Bonaventure designed an allegedly unbreakable 'Great Cipher' for his successor Louis XIV in the mid-seventeenth century.[8] Their office in Versailles in the 1660s was called the *cabinet noir*, its workings soon so notorious that the term 'black chamber' came to denote any international, organised espionage agency reliant on the combination of the interception of letters and codebreaking. Information had long been a vital part of diplomacy in peacetime, and was a potent weapon in times of war: ciphers promised a measure of control over it.

The English appear to have been a somewhat late arrival to the cryptographers' ball, as the first political dispatch using cipher in an English source dates from 1499.[9] In a world dominated by men, it is perhaps surprising that the dissemination of the art of secret writing in the British Isles was greatly assisted by those royal women of Europe who found themselves married to English monarchs. Katherine of Aragon is a case in point. As dowager princess of Wales, Katherine was officially appointed as her father King Ferdinand of Spain's ambassador to England in 1507, and as such was provided with a cipher key.[10] While the expectation may have been that she would have a cipher secretary to take care of such matters, Katherine had other ideas. In March 1507, Ferdinand sent his daughter a packet of letters. One of the letters contained within this packet was for King Henry VII of England (Katherine's once and future father-in-law), 'in answer to that which he wrote to me', in which Ferdinand referred him to a further message. This further message was contained in the body text of his letter to Katherine, and was written in cipher. Ferdinand instructed his daughter to 'have it separately deciphered by a trustworthy person' and to present it with his letter to Henry.[11] She was, after all, ambassador to the English court. Katherine later told her father's secretary, Miguel Perez de Almazán, that she had deciphered it 'without any assistance',[12] and her father that she had given his letter to the king, 'explained to him the cipher', and that he 'expressed himself much gratified'.[13] She also confessed to Almazán that she wished she were able to write in cipher as well. By that September, she had fufilled this desire.[14] This was how far England was behind the rest of Europe: a year after the Council of Venice had appointed Soro to the position of cipher secretary, the king of Spain's daughter was explaining how ciphers worked to the king of England. Katherine was not the only royal woman to personally wield ciphers: Mary of Guise used them with various French correspondents while she was regent of Scotland and her daughter, Mary Stuart, famously followed in her footsteps.[15]

The influx of Jesuit priests onto English soil in the 1570s and their machinations had forced Sir Francis Walsingham to catch up with this new technology – technology in which enemies of the state, Mary Stuart for one, were already well versed.[16] He thus recruited the cryptanalyst John Somer, who in the early 1560s had been involved in breaking the ciphers of Scottish regents while working for Sir Nicholas Throckmorton, the English ambassador in France.[17] In 1576, Walsingham also began to co-operate with a Dutch writer, statesman and codebreaker, Philips of Marnix, lord of Saint-Aldegonde, whom he met during the latter's embassy to England.[18] In 1577, Saint-Aldegonde shared a cipher used by Don Juan of Austria, half-brother of Philip II and governor of the Spanish Netherlands, with Walsingham; following the assassination of his father William the Silent in July 1584, Maurice of Nassau, the new stadtholder of Holland and Zeeland, also sent Walsingham several Spanish letters decrypted by Saint-Aldegonde.[19]

By 1578, despite this Anglo-Dutch codebreaking alliance (which would extend well into the seventeenth century), Walsingham had found himself in need of a new cryptographer. While Somer was still decrypting letters as late as 1584, he had climbed the diplomatic ladder and was often away on embassy.[20] Saint-Aldegonde had returned to the Netherlands, and was no longer close at hand. Walsingham's colleague, the other principal secretary, Thomas Wilson, identified an alternative: 'This afternoon I do send . . . a letter written in cipher, as you may see, wherein may be matter of great moment, being well deciphered. If Saint-Aldegonde cannot do it, nor Master Somer, then I would you did send the same to your servant young [Thomas] Phelippes'.[21] Phelippes had already mastered Latin, Italian, French, Spanish and German.[22] He was perfect for the job.

CHASING THE CODE

Cryptanalysts such as Somer, Saint-Aldegonde and Phelippes approached their work armed with a set of mathematical and analytical tools and a natural predisposition towards pattern recognition, often enhanced by a facility for speaking and writing multiple languages. They were aware, for example, that while a message enciphered using a simple substitution alphabet might appear impenetrable at first glance, the characters it used retained the exact same relationships that existed between the letters of the plaintext message. Primary amongst these relationships was the frequency with which each letter of the alphabet tended to appear in any particular language, and this meant that the first, and most powerful, of the tools a cryptanalyst employed was frequency analysis. This technique was both simple and effective, and it dealt a devastating blow to the security of the monoalphabetic cipher. When presented with a ciphertext, a cryptanalyst would first count the number of times each character occured, and then compare the results with their knowledge of the presumed plaintext language.[23] The most common cryptotext symbol was likely to match the most common letter in the plaintext language. Once this basic operation had been completed – that is, the characters in the cryptotext message had been counted and placed in order of frequency – the cryptanalyst could start to work on recognising other features.

The power of frequency analysis had been noted by the Arab scholar al-Kindī in the ninth century, but Western Europe had to wait until 1466 for it to be described, in the manuscript treatise *De Componendis Cifris* (*On Devising of Ciphers*) by the Genoese polymath Leon Battista Alberti.[24] *De Cifris* in its original Latin was perhaps read only by devotees of the art, but it nevertheless has foundational status in European cryptography. Alberti did not merely explain how to employ frequency analysis to break a cipher, but suggested various methods of frustrating its use. Amongst his recommendations for increasing the security of a cryptotext were new features such as 'nulls' (characters that represent nothing), homophones (using several different characters to represent the same letter), avoiding common letter sequences, using words without vowels, and including fake words and other red herrings.

Alberti's observations regarding frequency of letters and the various other patterns the cryptanalyst was to look for would later find themselves in one of the many books dedicated to the art of codebreaking, John Falconer's 1692 *Rules for Explaining and Decyphering all Manner of Secret Writing*, which summed up the manuals that had appeared over the previous 250 years.[25] Falconer's text sought to demystify the process of codebreaking for the layman, and provided a veritable checklist of features to look out for. Having identified the most frequent symbols in the cryptotext, and thus the probable symbols for the most common letters in the presumed plaintext message, the next task was to identify consecutive letters, with a view to distinguishing between vowels and consonants: isolated letters must be vowels, Falconer suggested; letters doubled at the beginning of a word are generally vowels (except, as he notes, in some English proper names such as

'Llandaff, Lloyd'); the frequency of characters in two-letter monosyllables is instructive; three-letter words beginning and ending with the same letter are probably consonant-vowel-consonant; the vowel 'e' is often to be found at the end of words; doubled letters in the middle of four letter words are usually vowels; doubled letters in polysyllabic words are usually consonants; and 'i', 'a' and 'u' are rarely used at the end of words, but often at the beginning. Other recurring groups of characters might occur in certain words, such as 'ion', 'ight', 'ck', and so forth.

Patterns represented weakness, and were a gateway for the cryptanalyst, but they also occurred at levels above individual letters and groups thereof. Correspondents often included standard formulae at the beginning and end of their letters, even when enciphering them (use of a cipher did not excuse bad manners). Many cryptanalysts, therefore, began their work by looking for information such as the date, or rhetorical flourishes in standard greetings or sign-offs such as 'I pray this finds you well' or 'your humble servant'. They might also use their knowledge of the message's context such as the suspected sender and recipient, and perhaps an idea of what they were liable to be talking about, to help give them an edge. All they needed was for the smallest crack in the cipher's defences to open up; frequency analysis, pattern recognition and hard work would take care of the rest. In this way, the cryptanalyst could methodically dismantle the cryptotext, exposing the message beneath. It was a laborious process, but it worked.

Alberti may have explained the use of pattern recognition and frequency analysis as tools for breaking ciphers, but his great innovation was an enciphering method designed to frustrate the use of these tools: the polyalphabetic cipher.[26] This was a different beast from the homophonic cipher, a cipher which gave several options for some if not all of the plaintext letters, as it used multiple substitution alphabets in the same message. Alberti had simply realised that with this technique, using a new substitution alphabet for every word or even character in the plaintext message, a cipher could be rendered virtually, or at least practically, unbreakable, making the job of the cryptanalyst hair-rendingly frustrating. He also realised that enciphering a letter in such a manner was something of a chore for the writer (as was

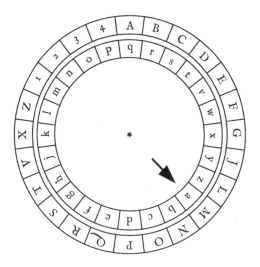

Fig. 17: A representation of Alberti's cipher wheel with adjusted alphabet on index wheel and pointer added for ease of comprehension.

deciphering it for the recipient). His solution was as elegant as it was simple: the cipher wheel.

Alberti's cipher wheel comprised two concentric dials (or 'volvelles'), each of which had letters inscribed around its circumference. All one need do to encipher a word is to turn the index (here the lower-case 'a' on the inner wheel) to a previously agreed or otherwise indicated position (here the upper-case 'M' on the outer wheel. We refer to this as 'index set at "M"') and then trace the letters of the message on the outer wheel – the adjacent letters on the inner wheel would indicate the enciphered letters, making up the cryptotext. The cipher wheel was a paper technology (though they could also be rendered in brass), and is easiest to understand in use; the inner wheel was intended to be drawn on a piece of paper, cut out and stitched to the outer wheel, which remained static on another piece.[27] The cipher wheel depicted in Fig. 17 is based on Alberti's, and has a truncated alphabet on the outer volvelle, along with the numbers 1, 2, 3 and 4 – some letters seem to be omitted because they do not appear in the Latin or Italian alphabet, while the numbers allow for a second method of enciphering, superencryption or superencipherment.[28] Alberti is clear that the characters on the inner wheel can be placed in any order (his 1568 editor chose a zigzag configuration), but we have rendered the alphabet in standard order for ease of comprehension.[29] It only remained for the sender to communicate the manner in which the recipient must calibrate their wheel to allow them to decode the message.

While the cipher was the beating heart of cryptographic technology, few relied on it alone – most combined it with a code, also called a nomenclator. The difference between a cipher and a code is as follows:

> A *cipher* is the method by which each individual letter of a message is replaced by a letter, number or symbol – this procedure (also known as an algorithm) may be a highly complex mathematical computation or as simple as a = 1; b = 2; etc.
>
> A *code or nomenclator* is a system in which whole words or units of meaning are represented according to a predetermined convention: King = *; Queen = ?; Prince = spaniel; and so forth.[30]

The early modern mind was quite happy to confuse the issue by conflating these two meanings, however, as the philosopher and statesman Francis Bacon noted: 'For CYPHARS; they are commonly in Letters or Alphabets, but may be in Words'.[31] The cipher and the nomenclator would often be combined into a 'cipher key' which supplied the user with the particular substitution alphabet to be used and a separate list of code words, which could include any amount of substitutes, from a mere handful to hundreds. Both cipher and nomenclator alike could be alphabetic, numerical or symbolic, so several combinations were possible, such as alpha-numeric, alpha-symbolic, numeric-symbolic, and so forth. A spy might also choose to give all their correspondents the same cipher alphabet but a personal nomenclator, or vice versa.

SPREADING THE CODE WORD

Alberti's Latin work, while groundbreaking, was disseminated very carefully in manuscript, and perhaps only amongst the true devotees of the mathematical and cryptographical arts at the most important courts in Europe.[32] *De Cifris* would not see print until 1568, long after Alberti's death, in an

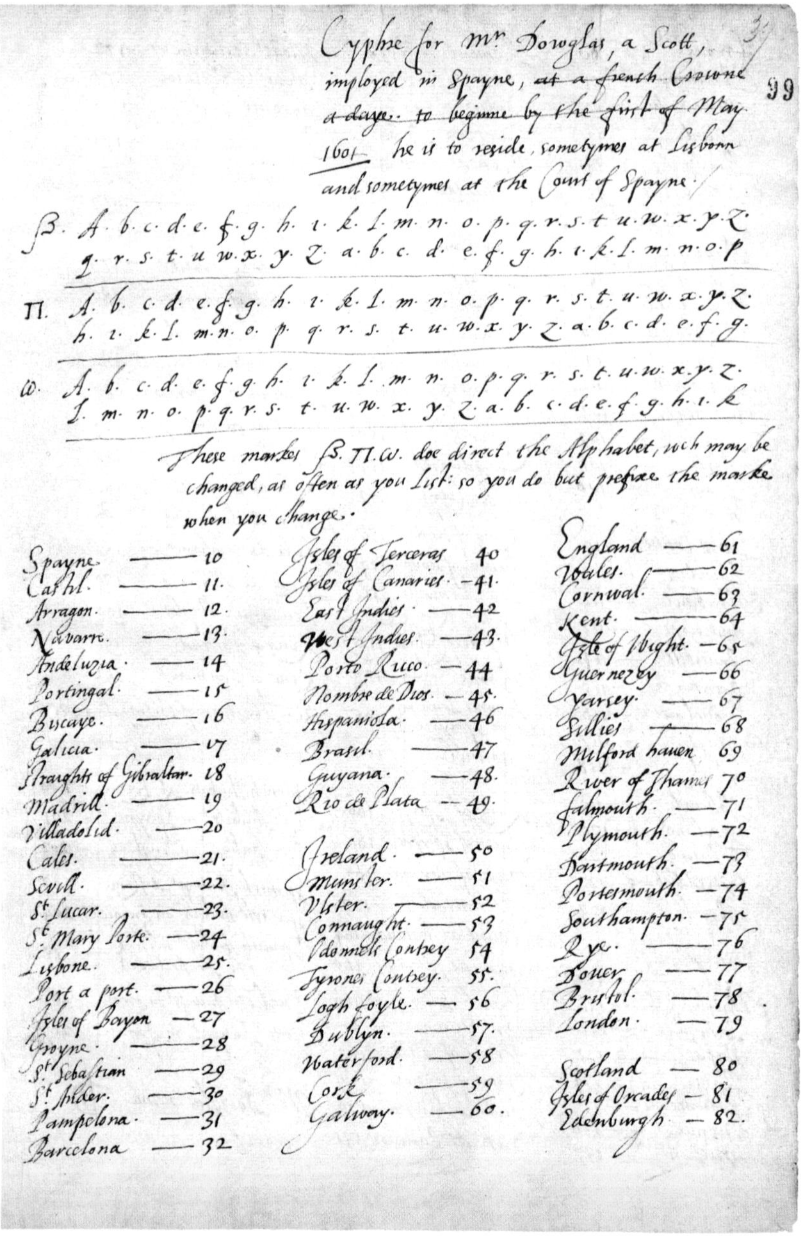

Fig. 18: This typical alpha-numeric cipher key has three substitution alphabets (ß, π, and φ), and a numerical nomenclator (numbers 83–207 are found on the verso).

incomplete version translated into Italian.[33] The first printed exploration of polyalphabetic ciphers was in the posthumous *Polygraphiae Libri Sex* by Johannes Trithemius, printed in 1518: this was a revised edition of his unpublished manuscript *Steganographia* (composed *c.* 1499) which had caused a minor scandal due to a mistaken belief that it relied upon supernatural forces such as angels.[34] It may be for this reason that the magus and mathematician John Dee made a manuscript copy of *Steganographia* in 1564 which he sent to William Cecil.[35] In *Polygraphia*, which lacked any reference to supernatural entities, angelic or otherwise, Trithemius favoured a more consistent, progressive encryption model than Alberti's, and devised a set of tables to aid both encryption and decryption which allowed for the reader to scroll easily through the twenty-four iterations of the Caesar cipher. (Dee may also have acquired a 1561 French edition of *Polygraphia*.)[36] As can be seen in Fig. 19, it is easy enough to use. To encode the letter 'e', first find the plaintext character in the table's left-hand, blue column (alphabet 'A'), and trace horizontally until the row intersects with the column that equates to the shift alphabet in use (alphabet 'm', for example; here rendered in green), and the character found at this intersection is the cipher letter, 'q'. To give an example, using substitution alphabet 'b', the pronoun 'we' in the phrase 'we are undone' enciphers as 'xf'.[37]

Trithemius also included a series of functioning cipher wheels in his book that imitated the workings of his tables, though they rather sacrificed usability at the altar of aesthetics.[38] The Trithemian table was perhaps more reliable if less straightforward to use than an Albertine cipher wheel, which was very easy to accidentally read backwards, confusing the entire process.

Trithemius's polyalphabetic enciphering procedure entailed advancing through the possible iterations of the Caesar cipher one at a time, as each character was enciphered. Alberti favoured a more random approach. One of his suggestions regarding how to indicate which substitution alphabet was being used was to include an upper-case indicator: a 'B' in the text indicated that the substitution alphabet now in use was the one beginning with the letter 'b'.[39] He also had another, more sophisticated idea that would not be published in print until Giovan Battista Bellaso's *La cifra del sig: Giovan* of 1553, and is often attributed to the French cryptographer Blaise de Vigenère:

A	b	c	d	e	f	g	h	i	k	l	m	n	o	p	q	r	s	t	v	w	x	y	z
B	c	d	e	f	g	h	i	k	l	m	n	o	p	q	r	s	t	v	w	x	y	z	a
C	d	e	f	g	h	i	k	l	m	n	o	p	q	r	s	t	v	w	x	y	z	a	b
D	e	f	g	h	i	k	l	m	n	o	p	q	r	s	t	v	w	x	y	z	a	b	c
E	f	g	h	i	k	l	m	n	o	p	q	r	s	t	v	w	x	y	z	a	b	c	d
F	g	h	i	k	l	m	n	o	p	q	r	s	t	v	w	x	y	z	a	b	c	d	e
G	h	i	k	l	m	n	o	p	q	r	s	t	v	w	x	y	z	a	b	c	d	e	f
H	i	k	l	m	n	o	p	q	r	s	t	v	w	x	y	z	a	b	c	d	e	f	g
J	k	l	m	n	o	p	q	r	s	t	v	w	x	y	z	a	b	c	d	e	f	g	h
K	l	m	n	o	p	q	r	s	t	v	w	x	y	z	a	b	c	d	e	f	g	h	i
L	m	n	o	p	q	r	s	t	v	w	x	y	z	a	b	c	d	e	f	g	h	i	k
M	n	o	p	q	r	s	t	v	w	x	y	z	a	b	c	d	e	f	g	h	i	k	l
N	o	p	q	r	s	t	v	w	x	y	z	a	b	c	d	e	f	g	h	i	k	l	m
O	p	q	r	s	t	v	w	x	y	z	a	b	c	d	e	f	g	h	i	k	l	m	n
P	q	r	s	t	v	w	x	y	z	a	b	c	d	e	f	g	h	i	k	l	m	n	o
Q	r	s	t	v	w	x	y	z	a	b	c	d	e	f	g	h	i	k	l	m	n	o	p
R	s	t	v	w	x	y	z	a	b	c	d	e	f	g	h	i	k	l	m	n	o	p	q
S	t	v	w	x	y	z	a	b	c	d	e	f	g	h	i	k	l	m	n	o	p	q	r
T	v	w	x	y	z	a	b	c	d	e	f	g	h	i	k	l	m	n	o	p	q	r	s
V	w	x	y	z	a	b	c	d	e	f	g	h	i	k	l	m	n	o	p	q	r	s	t
W	x	y	z	a	b	c	d	e	f	g	h	i	k	l	m	n	o	p	q	r	s	t	v
X	y	z	a	b	c	d	e	f	g	h	i	k	l	m	n	o	p	q	r	s	t	v	w
Y	z	a	b	c	d	e	f	g	h	i	k	l	m	n	o	p	q	r	s	t	v	w	x
Z	a	b	c	d	e	f	g	h	i	k	l	m	n	o	p	q	r	s	t	v	w	x	y
A	b	c	d	e	f	g	h	i	k	l	m	n	o	p	q	r	s	t	v	w	x	y	z

Fig. 19: A Trithemian table.[40] In this table: blue (vertical): plaintext; blue (horizontal): first letters of the substitution alphabets; green: the cipher alphabets: alphabet 'b', alphabet 'd', alphabet 'm'; orange: finding the ciphertext for 'w' and 'e'.

the keyword. The keyword was a simple way of demonstrating to the recipient which alphabet was in use at any one time. Say, for example, we pick 'SPYCRAFT' as our keyword. This means that the first alphabet we use from the Trithemian table (or from our Albertine cipher wheel) is alphabet 's', the second alphabet 'p', the third alphabet 'y', the fourth 'c', the fifth 'r', the sixth 'a', the seventh 'f' and the eighth 't'. After the eighth letter the sequence is simply repeated.[41]

Keyword ciphers had one weakness, however: they were repetitive. Because they simply reused the same combination of substitution alphabets over and over again, keyword ciphers tended to repeat particular combinations of cryptotext, especially when enciphering short words such as articles or conjunctions. These repetitions could present an observant cryptanalyst with a way to deduce the keyword from what would otherwise appear to be nothing more than a thick cipher soup, and thus allow them to render the message in plaintext. Vigenère may not have invented or even introduced the keyword cipher into the sixteenth century's pantheon of techniques, but he did fix this one weakness in his *Traicté des chiffres, ou secrètes manières d'éscrire* of 1586, and in the process devised what is now considered its apogee: the autokey cipher.

The autokey cipher still needed a keyword, but it only used it once: after the keyword had enciphered the first few characters, *the message itself* then became the key. In this way, if your cryptanalyst was unable to crack the cipher used by the first eight letters of the message (assuming the keyword is still 'SPYCRAFT'), the rest of the message would remain secret, too – and decoding eight characters, each of which has been enciphered using a different substitution alphabet, is practically impossible using pen and paper alone.[42]

A mathematical way to break Vigenère's autokey cipher was not proposed until two centuries later, but despite its first-rate security score, there is no evidence that it was ever used in the field during the sixteenth or seventeenth centuries. There were perhaps two reasons for this: first, it is extremely time-consuming to both encipher and decipher; and second, if even a single letter is either enciphered or deciphered incorrectly, the cipher rapidly becomes unreadable. Vigenère's autokey cipher was as unworkable as it was unbreakable. It is the perfect example of how theory and practice were not always comfortable bedfellows.

There was another way of presenting a cipher alphabet that made life more complicated for all concerned. While polyalphabetical ciphers using letter substitutions were highly effective, it was also possible to use symbols rather than letters.

WHEELS WITHIN WHEELS

In 1563, della Porta's *De Furtivis* introduced the symbolic cipher wheel. Aware that cryptography was far harder in practice than it appeared in theory, he followed Trithemius's lead in giving his readers the opportunity to fashion a working wheel by having three versions of the outer, static volvelle printed in the book's body text and a set of inner – or index – wheels printed on the endpapers.[43] They were not only simpler than Trithemius's coloured wheels, and thus far easier to use, but they were also cheaper, being monochrome woodblocks the reader was able to cut out and assemble themselves. Della Porta included some important updates to Alberti's original design. He placed numbers alongside the letters of the alphabet on the outer volvelle, used a symbolic rather than alphabetic cipher on his index wheel, and included nulls. His most complex wheel, for example, had an alphabet of twenty-one characters (omitting 'k', 'w' and 'y'), with a further seven blank characters for use as nulls (see Fig. 20). He also included a handy pointer, or manicule, to make orienting his wheel more straightforward. Quite apart from the utility of this 'cut-out-and-keep' piece of cipher technology, its use of symbols rather than an instantly recognisable alphabet was of particular importance. Not only would this at the very least compromise a cryptanalyst's pattern recognition skills, as the symbols were unlikely to be instantly memorable, but it also allowed for a seamless transition between cipher and code. Instead of an alphabetic cipher and a numerical nomenclator, which were easily distinguishable on the page, the two could be blended into one by the production of a symbolic nomenclator (Alberti's numerical superencryption was also designed for this purpose). The resulting symbolic stew would be liable to give even the hardiest cryptanalysts indigestion.

It is perhaps the hallmark of a true innovation that those who follow it augment rather than simply copy. And so it was with the cipher wheel. In 1587, the physician Timothy Bright produced a manuscript containing selected highlights of *De Furtivis* on behalf of William Davison, one of Queen Elizabeth's secretaries.[44] Davison then presented the manuscript to either Elizabeth or Walsingham, possibly in a bid to regain favour following his unfortunate part in the execution of Mary, Queen of Scots (Elizabeth blamed

Davison for the death of her Scottish cousin, asserting that he had not held onto the signed warrant of execution as ordered, but passed it on to Burghley instead).[45] Bright did not merely copy parts of della Porta's text, however, but also improved and commented upon it, including four cipher wheels, one more than della Porta. The manuscript now held in the Bodleian Libraries is a work of rare beauty, and some of Bright's innovations may have been encouraged by aesthetic considerations. He places his cipher wheels on recto and verso of the same leaf, thus avoiding obscuring or simply destroying text on the other side of the wheel with the string needed to hold it in place. Bright's final wheel takes della Porta's most complex wheel and adds new features (see Fig. 20).

Bright changes things markedly: his wheel's inner volvelle uses a twenty-character alphabet and eight nulls, while its outer volvelle has twenty symbols, one null and what he calls *otiosa litera*, 'idle letters': 'I', 'S', 'H', 'R', 'A', 'V' and 'C'. Setting the wheel to the appropriate position could be achieved either numerically, 'index set at XI', or symbolically, 'index set at ⚭'. Bright was well aware of the final destination of his work, and his copy thus presumably represents an attempt to improve the mechanics of enciphering and deciphering, though whether his extended wheel would have created better or worse ciphers than the unextended wheel is debatable.[46] The gift, astonishingly beautiful as it was, might have been of more use to the authorities had Davison presented it a year earlier.

FROM TEXTBOOK TO CASTLE

In 1587, the year that Bright presented his handcrafted *De Clandestino scripto* at court and Vigenère published his *Traicté des chiffres*, one of the most famous cipher-driven episodes in history had only just drawn to a close. While the ciphers employed in what was an existential struggle between Sir Francis Walsingham and Mary, Queen of Scots were far more sophisticated than is generally accepted – they were primarily symbolic substitution alphabets with symbolic nomenclators – they were superseded in terms of security by Vigenère's autokey system. The irony of Mary's downfall is that even if she and her secretariat had known of Vigenère's cipher, it would not have made the least bit of difference.

Fig. 20: Left: della Porta's second cipher wheel at page 79 of *De Furtivis*, which Bright also copied at fo. 19r.

Zipher.

Poterit hoc exaduerso fieri: vt latini characteres inferius, et ignoti superius designentur, seruato prædicto ordine; verum vbi extra limbum velis interserere, tales superflua notæ interserantur eis figuris, quæ cohærere debeant: nam sic interpres rotæ reuolutione inhibebitur, quo minus quæ scriptum sit intelligatur, dum otiosa litera potestatem frustra conatur aptare; otiosa litera tales sunto. I S H R A V C.

Quæstus hostis magnus est, & quæstus noster non minus est, hi plorant, & hi non rident, quid faciendum est nunciato.

Right: Bright's updated version at fo. 19v. Bright's other wheels, at fo. 13r and 13v, are almost exact copies of della Porta's wheels as found at pages 73 and 83 of *De Furtivis.*

In their battle for control of the information bridleway, Mary and her foot soldiers (her secretaries and her many supporters amongst the English noble classes, for example) placed their faith in the security afforded by their (actually rather sophisticated) manipulation of networks, postal services and ciphers. Their faith was not rewarded, however, but would instead be their undoing; Walsingham had measures in place which frustrated them at every turn – and silently to boot. It is through considering this battle that we will look at how cryptography was actually *used* in this period: knowing how to make and break a cipher or code was one thing, but putting this knowledge into practice on the front line was quite another.

THE UNSTITCHING OF MARY, QUEEN OF SCOTS

When the Catholic threat to England intensified once more in the 1580s, and Sir Francis Walsingham found himself in need of a good conspiracy to finally rid England of Elizabeth's Catholic cousin, he perhaps remembered the fiasco of the Casket Letters. Mary might have long abdicated her Scottish throne, and she may have continued living under house arrest, but she remained a powerful figurehead. Only her death would do, and that required unimpeachable evidence of treason. The Casket Letters might have served to sharpen the executioner's axe, but had also shown that mere forgeries alone would not legitimately allow Elizabeth to swing it. Walsingham decided that the best way forward was to manoeuvre Mary into betraying herself. He did this through careful and cunning manipulation of her correspondence.

Walsingham and the Queen of Scots had long clashed over matters relating to correspondence. When first placed under house arrest, Mary had been allowed to use the diplomatic mailbags of foreign embassies in London, but within two years she was complaining of being 'obliged to leave all my letters open', and by 1582 that all her correspondence was passing through Walsingham's hands.[47] Mary was either being disingenuous in order to convince Walsingham that this was the case or needlessly pessimistic, as many of the letters sent between 1578 and 1583 appear to have escaped his clutches.[48] The exposure of the Throckmorton Plot in 1583, which had shown that the Spanish were more than willing to collude with Mary to overthrow Elizabeth, had led to the banishment of the Spanish ambassador Bernardino de Mendoza. This left the French diplomatic mail stream as Mary's only official line of communication with her supporters. Unbeknownst to her, Walsingham had recruited a mole in the French ambassador Castelnau's embassy in the form of one of his clerks, Laurent Feron, who had kept the 'spymaster' supplied with copies of Mary's correspondence.[49] The Throckmorton Plot may have ended in the ignominious death of its eponymous leader, Francis Throckmorton, but 1584 also saw victorious Spanish armies in the Low Countries and the assassination of William the Silent in Delft at the hands of a Catholic. Burghley and Walsingham responded by drawing up the 'Bond of Association', which effectively enshrined in its signatories (the majority of the country's ruling classes) an obligation to protect Elizabeth and the Protestant succession from harm and conspiracy, by use of immediate force if necessary. The bond cleared a way through the thickets of law which had long hindered the crown from taking direct action against Mary (who was, ironically, also a signatory). Furthermore, Castelnau's involvement with Throckmorton allowed Walsingham to blackmail the French ambassador: he now promised to keep his secret safe in return for direct access to all of Mary's correspondence. There was no longer any need to rely on the subterfuge of a mole, as Castelnau simply shared all of Mary's communications with Walsingham directly.

Walsingham further tightened his grip on the Scots queen. He replaced her keeper, the rather too familiar Sir Ralph Sadler, with the austere and unforgiving Calvinist Sir Amias Paulet, and then had her moved from the unpleasant and malodorous Tutbury Castle to the more salubrious environs of Chartley Manor, a moated manor house (owned by Essex). In doing so he even appeared magnanimous: it had been alleged that the castle's environs were affecting Mary's health. The move also served a practical purpose. John Somer, who was onsite assisting Sadler, had complained that it was hard to control the queen's correspondence in Tutbury, as her household was scattered all over the sprawling residence.[50] With her new gilded cage came a new household, and new possibilities. Walsingham, aware that his blatant, if not absolute control of Mary's correspondence was hindering her from pursuing any conspiracy in which he could then ensnare her, adjusted his approach. He presented Mary and the new French ambassador, the vigor-ously Catholic Guillaume de l'Aubespine de Châteauneuf (who had replaced the compromised Castelnau in 1585), with an apparently golden opportu-nity to establish an entirely new, and seemingly very secret, line of commu-nication. The man at its heart was a new member of the Chartley household, a Catholic refugee called Gilbert Gifford. Mary had no reason to suspect Gifford of being anything other than loyal to her and the Catholic cause – he had been recruited by Thomas Morgan, whose association with Mary began when he joined the household of George Talbot, 6th earl of Shrewsbury, in 1568.[51] Unfortunately for the Catholics dabbling in epistolary subterfuge, Gifford was working for Walsingham.[52]

No stranger to clandestine communications, Mary had at her disposal a number of ways to smuggle correspondence both in and out of prison (which is what Chartley was, for all the pretensions to house arrest). This was not the problem. The problem was what happened when these letters made it into the outside world. Gifford is best known for his ingenious method of smug-gling letters in and out of Chartley, either placing them in 'a small watertight box that he slipped through the bung-hole of a beer cask where it floated on top of the beer', or in a space hollowed out of the bung which sealed the barrel.[53] As beer was only delivered once a week from Burton Abbey, and surreptitious letters plainly entered and left Chartley on a more regular basis, Mary's more familiar methods, which included smuggling letters hidden in the lace of girdles and in pairs of shoes, must still have been in operation.[54] It was the channel Gifford opened with Châteauneuf that was important, however, as no matter how these letters got themselves out of Chartley, they still had to get to the French ambassador for distribution – and Gifford ensured that they would first pass through Walsingham's hands. Elizabeth's secretary of state was ready to take action against Mary just as soon as the opportunity arose.

THE BABINGTON PLOT

Had the young and wealthy recusant Anthony Babington not appeared on the scene, Walsingham would no doubt have invented him.[55] Babington was not a complete stranger to Mary: he had delivered various packages to her while she was in the custody of the earl of Shrewsbury, whom he had attended as a page.[56] He subsequently fell in with a bad crowd in Paris, some of whom were Mary's agents, and by June 1586 this rather naïve young gentleman had assembled a motley crew of Catholic conspirators around himself. Together they hatched exactly the kind of plot that Walsingham needed to expose in order to condemn the Scottish queen – a poorly thought-out but treasonable plan to assassinate Elizabeth and place Mary on the English throne. Unfortunately for Babington, one of his 'co-conspirators' was Gifford. Walsingham was thus aware of the plot before any letters had reached Chartley, and had merely to follow it as it played itself out, collecting whatever evidence he needed on the way to achieve his goal: Mary's execution. Things got serious when Babington, encouraged by Mary's willingness to renew their acquaintance, sent her a long letter in which he first explained his plan and then asked her permission to carry it out. It was July 1586.

Babington's letter gave Walsingham the opportunity he needed to catch the queen in a treasonous act, but Elizabeth's secretary of state knew full well that everything depended on her response. Perhaps more importantly, it depended on the evidential trail with which he might convince a court that it was, indeed, *her* response: Mary had argued cogently (albeit at one remove) during the tribunal of 1568–9 that it was impossible to prove that the Casket Letters were her true voice, a defence Walsingham needed to circumvent. While Mary may have thought Gifford's new postal channels rather more secure than was, in fact, the case, she was no fool. Conscious of the need both to secure her communications from prying eyes and to distance them from her own voice, Mary ensured that the letters Gifford ferried between her and her supporters were written in cipher.[57]

CRYPTOGRAPHY, CIPHERS AND SECRETARIES

As we have seen, the process of enciphering a message is conceptually simple: you apply the rules that govern your particular system of secret writing to your plaintext message and you end up with your ciphertext or cryptogram.

To decipher the text, that is, to turn it from ciphertext into plaintext, you simply reverse the process. This means that the rules that constitute the cipher need to be available to both sender and receiver – and also that the security of the message relies not only on the complexity of your cipher, but also on no one else being in possession of these rules.

The labour-intensive and cumbersome task of enciphering letters into great strings of letters, numbers and symbols was seldom executed by the monarch. Secret script was instead the prerogative of the secretaries – in Elizabeth I's case, Cecil would underline any parts of a draft letter that were in need of enciphering, and then hand it to another secretary who would produce a fair copy in secretary hand and cipher for the queen to sign.[58] In Mary's case, as one of her secretaries pointed out during her trial, there was also far too much of it for someone unpracticed in cipher and codes to produce, let alone a queen, whom years of inactivity had rendered somewhat sickly: 'They cannot any way say it should stand with reason that the Queen did decipher and put in cipher her letters herself. For it appeareth that she dispatched more pacquetts ordinarily every fortnight than it was possible for one body weak exercised therein to put in cipher and decipher those sent much lesse for her being diseased, a Queen etc.'[59]

It was also part of secretaries' remit to store the cipher keys, as one of Walsingham's clerks, Robert Beale, suggested: 'A secretary must have a special cabinet, whereof he is himself to keep the key, for his signets, ciphers and secret intelligences'.[60] Secretaries, as the name suggests, were keepers of secrets. No mere penmen, they were a vital part of the business of government. They acted, according to Nicholas Faunt, another of Walsingham's secretaries, as his master's 'own pen, his mouth, his eye, his ear, and keeper of his most secret cabinet'.[61] A secretary enjoyed unparalleled trust, like no other servant or minister; Robert Cecil compared the counsels between prince and secretary to 'the mutual affections of two lovers, undiscovered to their friends'.[62] Such trust was not to be accorded lightly, logic suggesting that the wise man would 'let [his] secret services be known to a few'.[63] Secretarial manuals recommended employment of two secretaries, one for internal affairs, one for foreign affairs – the latter generally enjoyed more prestige, power and autonomy.

Mary had employed her two secretaries at Chartley, the Scot Gilbert Curle and the Frenchman Claude Nau, since 1568 and 1574 respectively. Nau, a Parisian lawyer, had been recruited on her behalf by the Guise family in France, and acted as her de facto foreign secretary, and thus as her primary keeper of ciphers. Curle, while the junior man, also enjoyed a great deal of trust, as Walsingham's cryptanalyst Somer suggested: 'Curle, [Mary's] Scots secretary . . . is not so quick spryted nor prompt as Nau (French-like), but hath a shrewd melancholy wit, not so pleasant in speech & utterance, suspicious enough. She maketh great accompt of him for his fidelity & secrecy'.[64] Curle was also deeply involved in the manipulation of ciphered texts. Walsingham's informers did not know that Mary also employed a third, secret secretary, Jerome Pasquier, her master of the wardrobe at Chartley (either he or his father had served as secretary to Castelnau), to carry out much of the labour-intensive work of enciphering and deciphering letters and keeping their various cipher keys organised and up to date.[65] Nau, as Mary's senior secretary, bore ultimate responsibility for all ciphered communications, however, and Curle and Pasquier worked under his supervision.[66]

TAKE A LETTER, ANTHONY

The famous ciphered letter from Babington to Mary that marked the beginning of the end for Elizabeth's cousin was actually an enclosure – a letter within a letter – sent to Nau at Chartley.[67] Its exact date is unknown, but it can only have been after a letter Curle sent Babington on Mary's behalf on 25 June.[68] Not long after Curle sent this letter, Walsingham was informed by his agents on the ground that Babington was ready to put his plan into action, and on 7 July the spy chief sent one of his best cryptanalysts, Thomas Phelippes, to Chartley. The master codebreaker arrived at the manor house two days later.[69] It is possible that Phelippes was sent to Chartley at this time to replace Somer, who had been at both Wingfield and Tutbury working with Sadler.[70]

In moving Phelippes from London to Chartley, Walsingham sought to ensure that his surveillance operation would not founder on the rocks of time. It was all well and good intercepting a letter, opening it, copying it, repairing it with fish glue and perhaps a counterfeit seal, and sending it on its journey looking as fresh as the day it was first locked, but if this letter took much longer than expected to reach its destination, the delay might cause an understandably skittish conspirator to run to the hills. Certainly, this was a constant worry, as Davison would later warn Phelippes in a way that suggests that neither he nor Burghley entirely trusted Phelippes to relock violated letters as convincingly as, say, Gregory might: 'The French ambassador hath written to my Lord Treasurer [Burghley] complaining of the apprehension & deferring of his packets . . . they should be made up ready to be delivered unto him but that you will first let your Lord Treasurer & me sight in what state the packets are before they be delivered.'[71] There was a good reason that most letters began with a formulation such as 'I received your letter of 10 July on 12th instant [i.e., of this month]': this would tell the recipient how long letters were taking to move from A to B – these formulations provided a sort of temporal security. Babington, at this point, was in Derbyshire, conveniently close to the brewery at Burton-on-Trent that marked the end-point of Gifford's beer-barrel postal service, and nowhere near London (sending a letter from Chartley to London could take up to four days, and even then it still had to be opened, decoded, closed again and sent on to its original destination, causing considerable delay).[72] Having Phelippes onsite also allowed the authorities to take immediate action should it be deemed necessary.

Unaware of the status of this new watcher, Nau wrote to Babington on 13 July informing him that Mary had received his ciphered letter the evening before: 'Yesternight Her Majesty received your letters and therein closed, which before this bearer's return cannot be deciphered. He is within these two or three days to repair hither again; against which time Her Majesty's answer shall be in readiness.'[73] Nau here demonstrates the importance of time – Babington was using a key sent to him by Curle (we will explain how we know this presently), but there was insufficient time to decipher Babington's letter before the secret bearer had to leave Chartley. Perhaps more importantly, Mary and her secretaries had to consider the contents of Babington's letter, craft a response in French (Mary's mother tongue), and translate it into what ran to ten pages of English prose before the letter could be enciphered.[74] Nau expected that the reply would be ready to send by the time the bearer returned to collect the next batch of letters, on 15 July at the earliest. Acknowledging this fact gives the lie to the idea that Mary prevaricated for a week before deciding on her course of action. Nau knew that it would take time to decipher Babington's letter, to write a response that would avoid directly incriminating his queen, have Curle translate it into English and, finally, encipher it. Mary was not dallying, uncertain of how to act. She knew her own mind. She merely waited for her secretaries' quills to catch up with her resolve.

The cipher key (Fig. 21) Babington used to encrypt his letter, and that Curle used for Mary's reply, comprised an alpha-numeric-symbolic alphabet, with five nulls, one dowbleth (indicating that the letter it follows ought to be repeated, thus avoiding repeating symbols that would make decoding easier in most languages: they would immediately indicate 'nn', 'll', 'tt', 'ee', etc.), and a thirty-five-word nomenclator. Each of these features was designed to slow the progress of decoding should the letters fall into the wrong hands. Even this cipher key, which was relatively simple, could be used to create a complex cryptotext that resisted easy decoding: it was hard enough to use when you had the key to hand. Fig. 22 shows a small part, roughly 5 per cent, of the letter Mary sent to Babington as it might have been enciphered.[75]

Though this is invariably called 'Babington's cipher', it was created and supplied by Mary's secretariat. Nau and Curle used two distinct types of cipher keys, what we will dub 'nursery' and 'mature' ciphers. When approached by a prospective correspondent, Mary's secretaries would send a relatively simple key with which they might make their initial epistolary advances. If Mary found their overtures compelling, they would be provided with a new key, one more suitable for the correspondence to come. This is what happened with Babington: the end of Mary's reply to him included the words 'I have commanded a more ample alphabet to be made for you, which herewith you will receive.'[76] This new, mature cipher was more complex than the nursery version hitherto used between the pair, and subsequently far more difficult to break.

In August 1586, in a search for more evidence, Walsingham's men ransacked Mary's apartments. In the process, they found fifty-three cipher keys, of which seventeen resembled the nursery cipher used for the initial correspondence with Babington, while the remaining thirty-six were more complex or mature ciphers.[77] The nursery cipher used by Babington was not

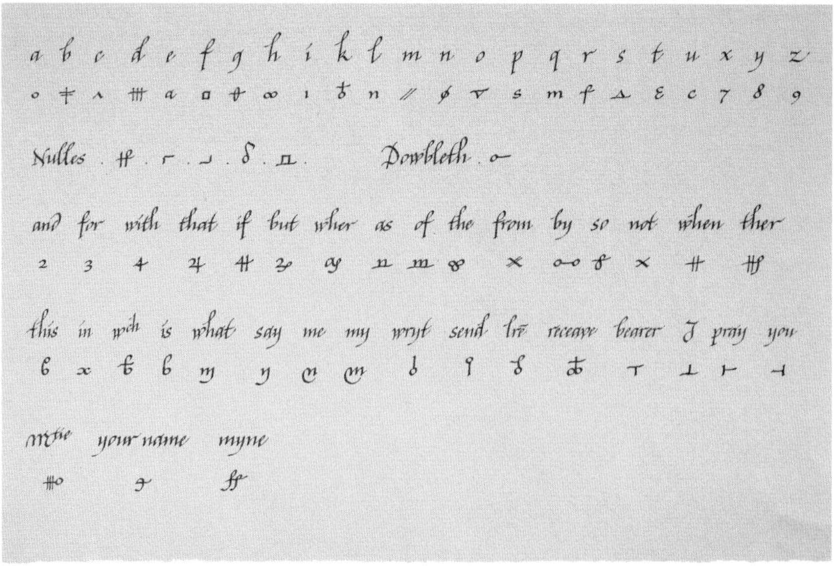

Fig. 21: A modern rendering of the cipher key used between Babington and Mary's secretariat.

discovered in this haul, but has survived in a copy made by the authorities at an earlier juncture, alongside two other cipher keys of similar construction (see Fig. 23). These three cipher keys have the same basic structure (an alphabet comprising twenty-three letters, five nulls, one dowbleth and a thirty-five-word nomenclator). The regularity of these cipher keys (including the number of symbols common to all three, and the omission of the letter 'w') suggest that they came from the same source; this source was most likely Mary's Scottish secretary, Gilbert Curle.

The simple truth is that, no matter what the history books say, Phelippes did *not* break Babington's cipher during this period. He simply did not need to – he already had the key. This fact is corroborated by a feature common to each of the three nursery ciphers: the nomenclator words 'your name' and 'myne' only make sense in a key sent by one individual to another. If Phelippes had deduced these keys, he would either have used the names of the individuals concerned, or, if he had yet to discover who the individuals at either end of the correspondence were, 'the writer's' and 'the recipient's'. The similarity

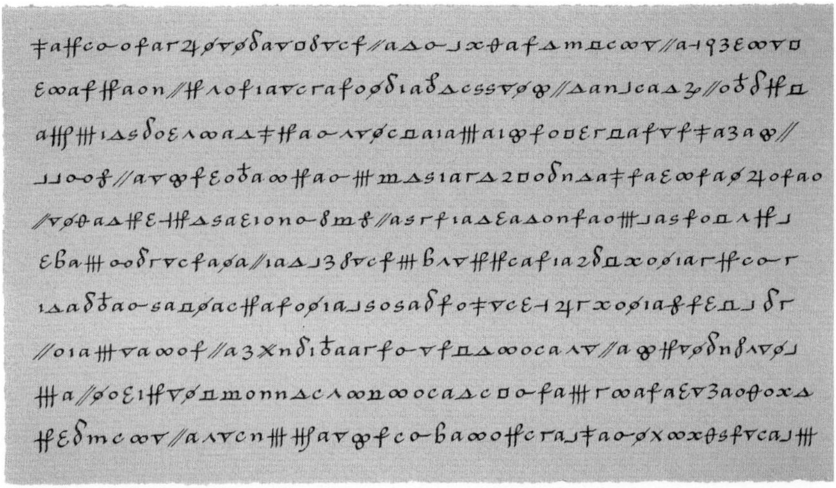

Fig. 22: Just as material conditions are crucial to understanding how the dark artificer might counterfeit a letter, so must we appreciate the amount of time it takes to encipher one. With this in mind, we recommend that you decipher this passage, which has been enciphered using the 'Babington' key, as seen in Fig. 21, and perhaps even re-encipher it.

between these keys may have acted to protect the identity of users, as it would have made it difficult to assign them to particular individuals until further contextual evidence had been collected. The authorities were plainly unsure – at least initially – which of these ciphers was used by Lady Ferniehirst, which by Dr Lewes and which by Anthony Babington, as each of these names has been assigned to different keys before being crossed out and reassigned.[78]

The messages sent during the Babington Plot using the nursery ciphers might well have thrown any cryptanalyst playing with frequency analysis off the scent, if only temporarily, as they might have reasonably assumed that such letters had originally been written in French, not English as was the case.[79] The mature ciphers took the same form as the nursery ciphers, but they were far more complex, increasing the number of features designed to confound the cryptanalyst. While the nursery ciphers featured an alpha-numeric-symbolic substitution alphabet, the mature ciphers took this one step further. Fig. 25 is a good example of this. It shows a fully homophonic

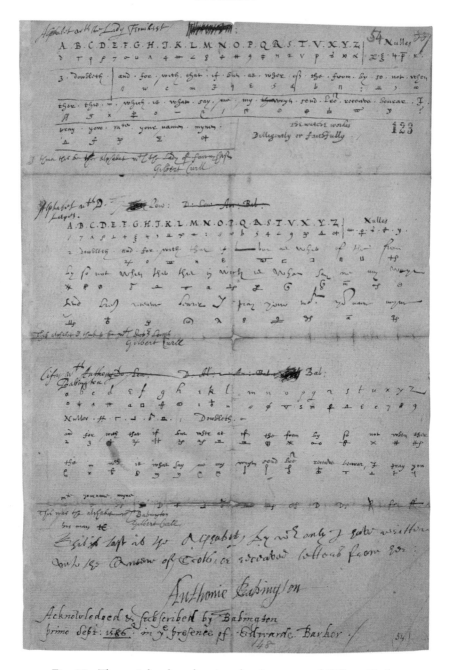

Fig. 23: Three cipher keys bearing the signatures of Gilbert Curle,
who matches them with their correspondents (two tentatively and
one certainly), and Anthony Babington, who confirmed the key he
used while writing to Mary.

symbolic alphabet, with each letter having four symbolic options available. Alongside the homophonic alphabet stand upwards of thirty nulls, as well as symbols serving to double and annul the preceding character, and symbols for punctuation. It also provides symbols for bigrams (sequences of two letters), trigrams (sequences of three letters), digraphs (a pair of letters which make one speech sound), and a much enlarged nomenclator of upwards of 150 entries, including phrases such as 'My good brother', names of individuals, countries and towns, as well as the months of the year, a rare feature for sixteenth-century cipher keys.[80]

The new, mature cipher that was sent to Babington was a far more intimidating beast than the nursery cipher it was intended to replace. It was also just as useless, as it was simply intercepted en route, copied and sent on its way. When Babington wrote a letter to Mary using this new key, Phelippes could decipher it as easily as he had the previous messages.[81] That these more complex ciphers were of Nau's design became clear in the subsequent trial, as Phelippes stated: 'The new Alphabet sent to be used in time to come between that Queen and Babington . . . is of Nau's hande.'[82]

When historians talk of 'the cipher code of Mary, Queen of Scots', what they mean is 'one of the many cipher keys formulated by her secretariat and used by one individual in their correspondence with the Scottish queen'. Similarly, when they talk of Phelippes 'breaking Babington's code', what they actually refer to is his *deciphering* of Babington's letter – as we have seen, he already had the key. This is no disparagement of the talents of Walsingham's first-choice cryptanalyst, of course, as he had already proved his worth in other campaigns. Even the best cryptanalyst needed time to break a cipher, however, and when it came to potential threats against the life of his queen, Walsingham could not afford to dither. In order to maintain control of the situation, he needed to know exactly what was being planned, preferably before the plotters themselves. This is why Gilbert Gifford's inveigling himself into Babington's circle was so important to Walsingham's plans. Gifford's efforts in ensuring that any letter, whether inbound or outbound, and no matter how secretly it appeared to be directed, passed through Walsingham's hands (albeit by proxy), meant that it was not only the messages between Mary and Babington that had been intercepted and copied, but also the key to understanding them. Phelippes would have begun to decipher Babington's letter before Mary had even received it.

MISUNDERSTANDINGS, MISAPPREHENSIONS AND FATAL MISTAKES

On 14 July, both Phelippes and Mary had read Babington's letter in which he explained his plans for placing Mary on the throne of England. It plainly improved both their moods, as on that day Phelippes wrote to his master of an encounter with the Scottish queen in which she acknowledged him as she was going out riding.[83] He wrote, 'I had a smiling countenance but I thought of the verse *Cum tibi dicit Ave sicut ab hoste cave*'.[84] The Latin translates as 'beware the hearty greeting, it may hide an enemy'. It presumably did not occur to Mary that his apparent good mood might have sprung from his understanding that it was Mary, not Elizabeth, who was now firmly caught in the jaws of a trap. Here the Latin phrase Phelippes uses becomes all the more interesting: it is only the second half of a well-known medieval couplet – the first line accuses Englishmen of having tails.[85] When it came to Mary, Phelippes had a tail hidden from her view – the tail of a rat who betrayed her with a smile, or that of a devil, damning her to a traitor's death. Phelippes was perhaps of the same mind as the duke of Gloucester: 'I can smile, and murder whiles I smile'.[86]

Mary may have been feeling too positive following her secretaries' deciphering of Babington's message to read his countenance in any other way than as friendly and encouraging. Certainly she had changed her tune regarding Phelippes. Barely four months earlier she had warned Châteauneuf off a man who had offered him his services: 'I suspect [this man is] one named Phelippes, Walsingham's servant, who about Christmas resided in this house upwards of three weeks, beware of committing yourself further to him, for, now that he has promised to do me service, I know that he plays a double game'.[87] She would soon cast him in a more positive light.

Two weeks after the silent exchange of glances with this slippery servant of Walsingham's who had suddenly reappeared at Chartley after six months' absence, Mary wrote to her friend Thomas Morgan describing a hooded man

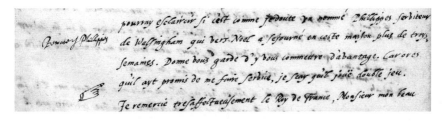

Fig. 24: Phelippes had deciphered Mary's letter to Châteauneuf, and not only written the words 'Beware of Phillippes' in the margin, but doodled a manicule pointing at the passage in question. By this drawing, he visually reiterated the message he had sent to Walsingham with his line of Latin verse: Phelippes was proud to be the undoing of the Scottish queen.

'of low stature, slender, every way dark yellow haired on the head and clear yellow bearded, eaten in the face with smallpox, of short sight, thirty years of age by appearance'. This man, she said, was Phelippes. While in her earlier letter to Châteaneuf she was certain that Phelippes was playing a '*double jeu*', by July she had returned to a prior conviction that he was a friendly mole, Morgan's man sent in her hour of need. She told Morgan that 'myself and some of mine have given him occasion to have declared himself at hunting and otherwise', but that she had thus far been disappointed.[88]

Phelippes's triumphalism did not go unnoticed. Several years later, when Mary's son had finally acceded to the English throne, his earlier threats to have revenge on those who took part in the murder of his mother must have loomed large in Phelippes's conscience. The cryptanalyst attempted to launder his part in the proceedings by asserting that he had only followed orders, and intimated that he would have been unable to assist the stricken queen in any case, even if he had wanted to: 'at Chartley he had as good watch set on him as there was on the imprisoned Queen's servants'.[89] This latter point is supported by Mary's correspondence. She told Morgan: 'it is true that he hath been looked to as narrowly as any of mine saving that without license he might go abroad [i.e., wander out of Chartley]'. In the deciphered transcription sent to Walsingham, Phelippes edited out this line, suggesting that if it was true that the watcher was himself being watched, he did not want his master to know that he knew.[90]

TRIAL AND TRIBULATIONS

Mary's response to Babington, sent on 17 July 1586, largely sealed her fate, containing as it did the words 'proceed in the [rest of the] enterprise'.[91] The letter, naturally, went directly to Phelippes, who immediately set about transforming the dense knots of cipher symbols into some ten pages of plain English. There was no need to go through the rigmarole of frequency analysis, as he already had a copy of the appropriate cipher key – but even with the key, this was the work of several hours. Before he sent the plaintext on to Walsingham in London, or so the story goes, Phelippes drew a gallows on the address leaf, an act which has led to this missive being termed the 'Gallows Letter' by historians, even though none of the extant copies features this macabre doodle. But this is likely a misreading of the material nature of post. Phelippes did not send a single letter to Walsingham but, as was common practice, a thick packet of letters. Walsingham, in his reply to Phelippes, refers directly to 'the gallows on the packet', not the gallows on the letter.[92] The packet also contained deciphered letters to the archbishop of Glasgow, Dr Lewes and Morgan. In his covering letter, Phelippes tells Walsingham that 'I hope she [Elizabeth] will hang Nau and Curle'. The gallows he drew were not for the Queen of Scots but for his vanquished opponents on the cryptological field of battle, Mary's two secretaries. It was not that he felt Mary deserved to escape punishment: he counselled that Mary's original enciphered letter to Babington, which he still possessed, ought to serve as 'evidence against her [Mary] if it please God to inspire Her Majesty [Elizabeth] with that Heroical courage that were needed for avenging of God's cause and the security of herself and this state'.[93] Phelippes was also well aware that, given Mary's status, she would be beheaded rather than hanged: this is why he specifically referred to Mary's letter as the 'Blody Letter' or the 'bloodye dispatche'.[94]

THE POSTMAN AND THE POSTSCRIPT

Phelippes sent his transcript, that is, a deciphered copy of the 'bloodye dispatche', to Walsingham on 19 July, two days after the ciphered original had been 'sent' from Chartley. It comes as no surprise that Phelippes, even though he was in possession of the relevant cipher key, could not produce his plaintext translation sooner – after carefully opening the letter, he would have deciphered each of the symbols one by one on a separate sheet of paper. With a letter such as this, which comprised some 10,000 characters, this would have taken quite some time. Finally, if he had time to spare before a private messenger bound to London was ready, he would have copied out the plaintext to make his scribbles more legible, and then sent this fair copy to Walsingham, accompanied by several other letters. In order to prevent disaster, Phelippes held on to the unscathed original.

In his accompanying letter, Phelippes argued that they might yet 'discover more particularities of the confederates' by sending the original onwards to Babington.[95] Walsingham's interest was piqued, but he stopped his servant from instantly releasing the original, and instead told Phelippes to come to London, and to bring the cryptogram with him. He was to receive thanks for his work from the queen herself, though Walsingham warned him that the other 'quaint devils', the 'practisers' as he called them, would be jealous of this honour, and in any case, the gallows doodle on the packet of letters itself had got everyone talking.[96] It was now five days since Mary had sent her response to Babington, and still her letter was caught in Walsingham's postal system.

By the time Phelippes arrived in London, Walsingham (or, potentially, Queen Elizabeth herself) had decided against arresting Babington immediately in favour of Phelippes's earlier recommendation. To increase the likelihood of Babington's revealing 'more particularities of [his] confederates', it was determined that a forged postscript be added to Mary's already extremely long message. This postscript was a simple request that Babington reveal the identities of the 'six gentlemen' who were to carry out the assassination. Walsingham knew full well that were such an addition to Mary's letter, which was 'very long and all in cipher fair written', to be poorly produced, Babington would spot this blatant attempt at entrapment and flee.[97] Phelippes may have been a master cryptanalyst, but his hand was somewhat scratchy, and certainly not 'fair'. Walsingham's operatives all had their own expertise, and he had handwriting experts in his little black book. Within it, he found a man 'expert in the *imitation* of hands; and could add, according to instruction, any postscript, or continuation of one, in the very form and turn of letters wherein the rest of the epistle was written, to draw out such farther intelligence as was wanted for a complete discovery, from the traitors themselves, of their treasonable intercourse'.[98] According to the eighteenth-century source cited here, the man Walsingham chose was the 'small writer' himself, Peter Bales, the man who had wowed Elizabeth with his micro-graphical skills a decade before.

Walsingham was mindful of his coterie of freelance operatives, however, as he knew that passions and jealousies were already running high. It was for this reason that he wrote to Phelippes on 30 July, the day after Babington had (finally) received the invisibly doctored letter, asking him to reassure Arthur Gregory that 'he shall not find me unmindful of him, as one that esteems both his sufficiency and his fidelity'.[99] Gregory, who also counted the imitation of hands as one of his particular skills, was presumably put out that the flamboyant and rather arrogant Bales had been selected for this task rather than he.

The postscript as delivered on 29 July was apparently perfect, as Babington never questioned its authenticity, but the twelve-day delay in its delivery had prompted the bird to fly. Walsingham, however, feared that it was the post-script that had lost him Babington, and with it the original, ciphered letter sent him by Mary. 'You will not believe', he wrote to Phelippes, 'how much I am grieved with the event of this cause [and] fear the addition of the post-script hath bred the jealousy [suspicion]'.[100] As it turned out, Babington had not only been completely fooled by this textual embellishment, but had even answered it: 'I wrote for answer . . . that so soon as any resolution should be taken I would inform her.'[101] Walsingham had risked everything for nothing, but while his operatives lost sight of Babington for a few days, no harm was done. The more Walsingham learned of Babington, the more clear it became that as a conspiratorial mastermind he was somewhat lacking – he could not tell Mary, or Walsingham, the names of 'the six' for the simple reason that they were yet to be chosen. If this postscript was truly the first instance of such a forgery in the history of intelligence, as Christopher Andrew suggests, it also has the dubious distinction of having been utterly pointless.[102]

Phelippes had been confident that Babington would not carry out Mary's final instructions, 'Fail not to burn this [letter] presently', writing to Walsingham that 'it is like enough for all her commandement her letter will not be soon defaced'.[103] There are several reasons why Phelippes might have thought that Mary's enciphered letter would survive for longer than its royal author might have wished, and this is besides the fact that, judging from the amount of letters surviving in archives bearing the same message, such instructions were often ignored.[104] For one thing, the letter was extremely long and would take no little time to decipher – and Phelippes did not know that Babington was not entirely comfortable with ciphers, and needed help from another conspirator, the poet Chidiock Tichborne, to finish the job. For another, Babington needed to be sure he understood and had memorised the instructions it contained before committing them to the flames. There is also the possibility that Babington, as a Catholic, would have a strong urge to keep the letter as a sort of 'relic' of Mary, the conspiracy and his glorious part within it.[105] History now records the burning of the letter as having taken place, even though Babington does not mention it in his confession.[106]

True, the enciphered letter with the added postscript does not survive, and not even a copy of this cryptogram was presented as evidence at the trial, but it is just as likely that Walsingham himself had destroyed it. For Walsingham, the fake postscript would have served as evidence that he and his agents had tampered with the letter. This might not have affected the outcome of Mary's trial greatly, but it would quite possibly have cast further doubt on its legitimacy and thus of her execution – and tempers across Europe were already frayed enough.

Whether or not the original was committed to the flames by Babington as ordered or burnt by Walsingham himself matters little, however. Walsingham had learned from the Casket Letters affair. As Mary made clear in her futile demand to see originals, an enciphered letter written neither in her hand nor even, when translated, in her first language was proof of nothing: the words 'proceed in the [rest of the] enterprise' could not possibly be connected to her through ink alone. The way to entrap Mary was not through documents in which her voice was not to be found anyway, but through her keepers of secrets, her secretaries.

Before Walsingham's men rifled through Mary's drawers in August, both the Scottish queen and her secretaries had been removed from Chartley. This gambit was a great success – the boxes of documents containing the fifty-three cipher keys that they discovered were soon in Walsingham's possession, safe from the attentions of any match-wielding queen or secretary. Walsingham returned Mary to her apartments in Chartley a fortnight later, on 25 August, but retained both her archive and its keepers, Nau and Curle. Walsingham finally had total control of the Scottish queen's secrets.[107]

Mary had placed her faith in the inscrutability of enciphered letters. Historians have suggested that Walsingham had a perfect facsimile of the original ciphered text produced to stand in for the letter Babington received (and burnt, according to this argument), and that it was this facsimile that Mary's secretaries identified as being the true and original letter. In this way, they suggest, Nau and Curle were tricked into giving the testimonies that ultimately condemned Mary. Such suggestions are not only speculative but make little sense.[108] For one thing, no such facsimile has survived. Second, any ciphered letter to or from an individual such as Babington (who at this point was still using one of Curle's nursery keys) would have looked much like another: Mary's secretaries were potentially communicating with seventeen individuals using twenty discrete but remarkably similar cipher keys. As such, the secretaries could only have testified to a plaintext letter, copies of which are not only extant, but are plainly the documents referred to in the court proceedings.[109] Curle, for example, testified that '[he] setteth down all the points of the Queen of Scots's letter to Babington in self same words that it is here formerly set down to be given in evidence against her', while Nau 'sayeth, that he took the points of the letter written by the Scottish Queen unto Anthony Babington . . . of the delivery, of the Scottish Queen's own mouth from point to point . . . these points contained in the Scottish Queen's letter to Babington were first delivered by the same Queen unto this Examinate by her own speech'.[110] There was no need to present the original cryptogram to convict Mary. Her secretaries, who were by profession the keepers of her closest secrets, had thrown her under both the coach *and* the horses. They testified that those treasonous parts of the correspondence with Babington they were shown during their interrogations had been dictated to them.[111]

That Walsingham did not rely on perfect facsimiles of the ciphered letters to extract confessions from Nau, Curle and Babington merely accentuates the fact that no matter how expertly one might counterfeit a hand, it only went so far. In a court of law, what mattered was the explicit testimony of those party to the conspiracy: it was not counterfeited letters that sank Mary, it was human testimony. While a letter written by a secretary was still assumed to represent the words of the employer, what truly mattered was not the physical artefact but the manner in which it was authenticated – Nau, Curle and Babington authenticated Mary's words, and her words were treason. Phelippes and Gregory, the latter of whom had recently arrived at Chartley, might have taken possession of all of the materials necessary to make convincing counterfeits of Mary's letters – they had her paper stock, wax, pens and possibly ink, not to mention a whole heap of cipher keys – but they did not need to take advantage of them. The only bit of counterfeiting that went on during the back and forth of the Babington Plot was undertaken in the postscript, and while Babington did not suspect it was anything but his mistress's ink and voice captured in symbols, it made no difference to proceedings: it posed a question he could not answer.

The fate of the Babington Plot revolved around the false sense of security given to its protagonists by cipher keys; it was foiled without a single letter exchanged between Mary and Babington being read through cryptanalysis, and Mary was condemned without recourse to any letter containing treasonous words in her own hand – Phelippes already had the cipher keys, and Mary's secretaries swore that the words they wrote and enciphered came directly from the mouth of the Scottish queen. Phelippes may have wished that Nau and Curle be hanged, but it was not to be: for betraying their queen, they were granted their lives. Babington was executed on 20 September 1586; Mary, Queen of Scots was beheaded on 8 February 1587.

UNPLEASANT REVERBERATIONS

Following Mary's execution, a passer-by stumbled upon Secretary Curle's wife Barbara, who was part of a Scottish train on their way to Fotheringhay Castle hoping to collect their mistress's body: she exclaimed that 'the young King can not be so graceless and monstrous in nature as to leave his Mother's death unrevenged', and that as a fellow secretary, Phelippes should intervene for her husband's release from prison. A friend assured Phelippes that he should 'build but little upon the speech because they carry but Womanish presumptions', but it made Walsingham's cryptanalyst decidedly uneasy.[112] In this he was uncomfortably prescient. The hard times that befell him following Walsingham's death were only to get harder. The combination of his inadvisable communications with Hugh Owen, who had created a web of agents for the Spanish that bore comparison with Walsingham's, the accession of Mary's son James VI to the English throne and the subsequent Gunpowder Plot led to a longer spell behind bars, and the rest of his life disappeared in a haze of court cases and unpaid debt.[113]

It is difficult to find much fault with how Mary, Queen of Scots and her secretaries wielded cipher and codes over the course of the Babington Plot. Her secretaries, Nau and Curle, produced two distinct levels of cipher keys for Mary's use, nursery and mature, which they assigned to her correspondents relative to the level of security required. The more complex or mature ciphers were extremely sophisticated, and demonstrated a keen understanding of the cryptanalytical techniques then in use – they were anything but simple, sharing several features with the 'Great Cipher' later created by the Rossignols.[114] If anything, the protection offered by these complex ciphers and her general faith in cryptography may have lulled Mary into a false sense of security. The oft-held view that she formulated her own ciphers and that they were particularly weak as a result, but that this demonstrates her independence of mind and is thus 'empowering', is not only patronising but completely ignores the fact that she used her secretaries Nau, Curle and Pasquier to encipher and decipher all her correspondence.[115] This, no doubt, was largely down to her education in France. By thirteen or fourteen, Mary had been trained to act secretly and divulge her secrets to few, and was keen to demonstrate how well she had internalised this lesson. She told her secretary that she wished to write to her mother, Mary of Guise, in cipher, in effect asking for a suitable cipher key. Not only was this request denied, but she was actively discouraged from undertaking such writing practices herself: 'her secretary advised her that there was no need as he was already sending her mother all sensitive information in code'.[116] While she was well aware of the importance of protecting her correspondence from prying eyes, there is no actual evidence that Mary practised the art of cryptography herself. She left such activities to her secretaries.[117] She understood full well that, in doing so, she set her correspondence at another remove from her voice. She had argued during the tribunal of

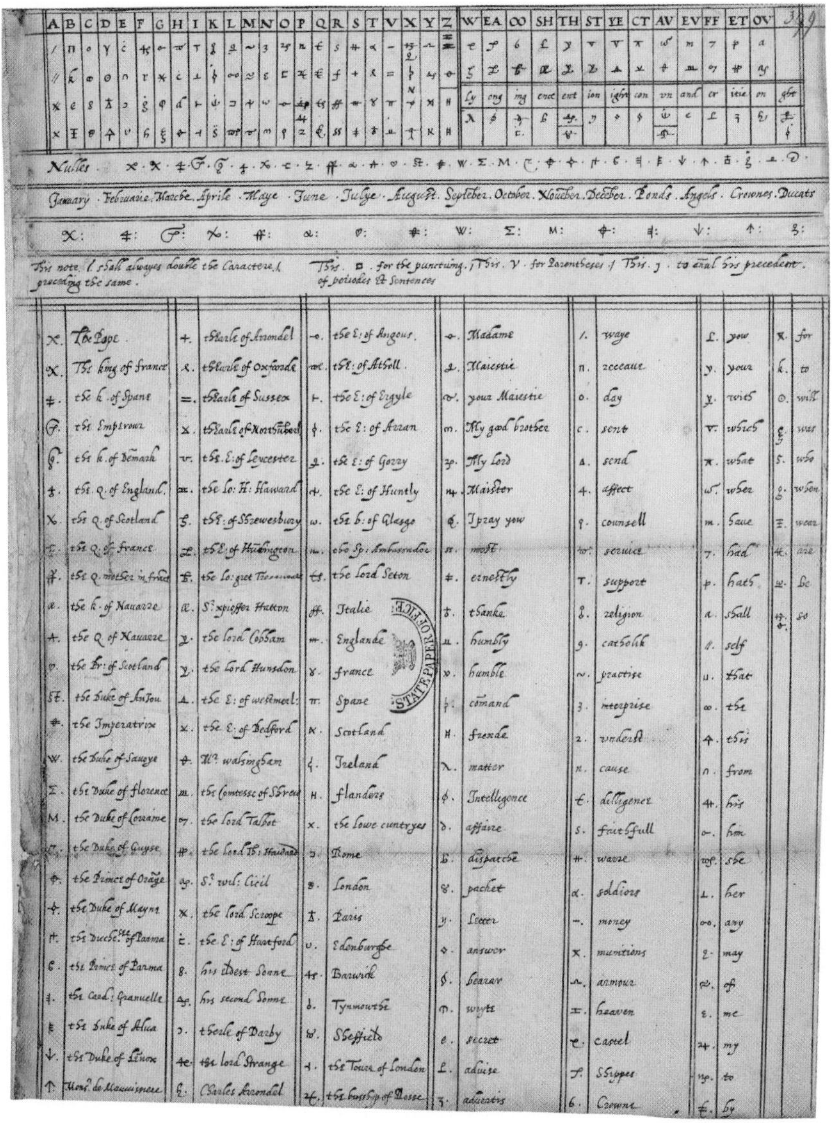

Fig. 25: One of the 'mature' cipher keys developed by the secretariat of Mary, Queen of Scots.

1568–9 that the Casket Letters were not in her hand, and thus could not be used in evidence against her. By having her secretaries encode English letters on her behalf, she ploughed this same furrow. Her mother tongue was French, despite her Scottish heritage, and enciphered English letters could thus hardly be used as evidence against her. While she was correct in her reading of the legal situation, she was defending herself against the wrong threat. It was, ironically, her secretaries and their facility with cipher and codes that were her undoing.

THE GENERATION GAME

Despite their failure to save Mary, Queen of Scots, cipher systems combining substitution alphabets and nomenclators remained the most popular and usable method of protecting one's correspondence for another two centuries or so. In 1589, for example, one of Burghley's spies, Thomas Fowler (whose code name was 'Fidelis' – the faithful), noted that the beautiful sister of the 2nd earl of Essex, Penelope Rich, had entered into a secret correspondence with the bereaved James VI of Scotland on her brother's behalf. She had fabricated a witty nomenclator as part of her correspondence, inventing 'nicknames for every one that is partaker in the matter': Elizabeth I was 'Venus'; James VI was 'Victor'; Essex 'the weary knight', and she herself 'Ryalta'.[118] While James was impressed by 'the fineness of her wit, the invention and well writing', he nevertheless required an interpreter, someone by whom 'the dark parts thereof [were] expounded to him'.[119] This need for assistance resurfaced in 1602 when James allegedly hired a tutor to instruct him in the art of secret writing, a type of intelligence with which he was neither 'acquainted nor accustomed'.[120] If Henry, Lord Howard, is to be believed, the tutor he chose was Francis, Lady Kildare, the woman who, in 1603, was appointed governess to James's daughter the Princess Elizabeth. James thus became the second monarch in England in a century to be taught cryptography by a woman. While Lady Kildare was quickly dismissed because of her husband's involvement in treasonous plots, she never lost the king's favour and was, for instance, invited to Elizabeth's wedding in 1613.[121] It is not clear whether or not Elizabeth Stuart learned the art of secret writing from her governess or her father, but she would spend much of her life surrounded by experts in the trade: her husband's uncle, Duke

August of Brunswick-Lüneburg, wrote the influential *Cryptomenytices* (1624) under the pseudonym Gustavus Selenus, for instance.[122] Unlike her grandmother, Elizabeth enciphered and deciphered her letters personally, even though she had a small army of secretaries at her disposal. It is hard not to reach the conclusion that Lady Kildare, if not her father, had counselled her in the danger of allowing secretaries too much access to one's secret correspondence. Nevertheless, the exiled queen did follow diplomatic convention inasmuch as she kept using the same cipher keys for several years, sometimes treating them like family heirlooms: denied the opportunity of giving her son Charles Louis the keys to Heidelberg Castle when he came of age in 1635 by the inconvenient fact of its being occupied by foreign powers, she gave him the cipher key she and her late husband had used from 1622.[123]

While Elizabeth Stuart was a more than capable cryptographer, she, like Walsingham before her, knew the value of having a specialised cryptanalyst to hand. This is perhaps one of the reasons she used her influence to help the Dutch polymath and poet Constantijn Huygens secure the position of secretary to the new prince of Orange in 1624.[124] It was a typically smart move. Huygens had studied cryptanalysis at the University of Leiden in 1616, and his secretarial salary was soon being enhanced to the tune of 100 Dutch guilders per month, the equivalent of £10 sterling, for the decryption of letters.[125] Huygens took his side hustle extremely seriously, and in his autobiography waxed lyrical on how his expertise had benefitted his master, the prince of Orange, during the wars with the Spanish: 'At every single siege, I proved my skills, anticipating the tricks of the enemy by means of my own knowledge of deceit (in times of war one is allowed to be deceitful). Even if the letters originated in Constantinople or were fantastically shaped, like griffins or other never before seen fable beasts, I managed to decrypt them.'[126]

The narrative of ciphers and codes always falling to cunning cryptanalysts is one spread largely by the cryptanalysts themselves, it appears. When Huygens wanted a pay rise, he and his friends reminded Amalia, the dowager princess of Orange, that he had been instrumental in securing the siege of Breda for her late husband.[127] In a private letter to Elizabeth, however, Huygens presented a very different image of himself and his ability to break Spanish ciphers. In one packet he sent letters from both the private secretary to Tommaso Francesco of Savoy, prince of Carignano, and the Spanish resident agent at Charles I's court, Juan de Necolalde, admitting in his accompanying letter that 'There remain several others in cipher, in which I hoped to be able to assist Your Majesty. But they are addressed to the king of Spain, whose ciphers have always been found more difficult to conquer than he.'[128] Phelippes, of course, would have agreed with him.

Sir Thomas Roe, Elizabeth Stuart's most loyal supporter and sometime Stuart ambassador in Constantinople, begged her to send him a cipher key with which they might secure their correspondence. Mindful that taking this need for a cipher into his own hands might be seen as insolent, given their relative stations, Roe waited four years before finally relenting and sending her a monophonic cipher alphabet and nomenclator, though they abandoned its use after two years.[129] A decade later, finding that once more 'there may be cause of secrecye', he again mustered the courage to send her a cipher of his own devising, this time a polyalphabetic shift cipher using four discrete alphabets and a numerical nomenclator of somewhere between 43 and 160 characters.[130]

Roe was aware of Elizabeth Stuart's love of instruments, with his friend Sir Dudley Carleton, the Stuart ambassador in The Hague, pointing out that the only gift she truly appreciated were 'fine and curious workes', such as astrolabes and clocks.[131] It is likely that Roe had enticed her to communicate in cipher with him once again by sending her a mechanical device, a cipher wheel, because the mistakes that she made while encoding her letters point strongly to her using such a device.[132] His new cipher employed neither Alberti's schemata of indicating the alphabet in use via the inclusion of an upper-case letter in the text, nor did it follow Trithemius's method of changing alphabet by one degree for each letter. Instead, it combined the numerical key used in both della Porta's cipher wheel design and in the Trithemian table found in Selenus's *Cryptomenytices* with Alberti's more random method.[133] A typical sentence would read as follows: 'I have had newes from K. 50. 6nfzn. 4kmyhq4. 4lmp. 5mnw last 4dkwzhu.'[134] Elizabeth did not encipher every word: Roe's new cipher, like any fully polyalphabetic cipher, was a lot of work, even if you had a Trithemian table or cipher wheel handy. Roe soon realised that it was too unwieldy: 'I find I have put Your

Majesty to too much trouble to read, and write my Cyphar, and because it is too busy to use all the letters, you may please to save the labour, unless it be for names, or words referred to figures. I sent it only to secure my errors, that they did no hurt; Your Majesty is safe, and out of danger.'[135] Elizabeth Stuart's brother Charles I made the same observation about the ciphered letters sent him by Lady d'Aubigny, namely that 'I do not think fit to stay this packet upon the deciphering of them; because it will cost more than a day's work.'[136] To be viable, a cipher had to balance security with usability: the next cipher Roe sent Elizabeth would be merely homophonic rather than fully polyalphabetic.

Most of the many treatises and books on the subject of ciphers were more concerned with the mathematical rather than the practical considerations of ciphers – some, such as Trithemius's work, were considered more demonological than mathematical. Selenus's *Cryptomenytices* ran to over 500 pages, many of which were taken up with seemingly endless tables. Falconer was not alone in his opinion of Vigenère's autokey cipher: not only did it require 'too much time to be put into practice', but it had other disadvantages, namely that 'by the least mistake in writing, it is so confounded, that the confederate with his key shall never set it in order again'.[137] Theory, as Mary, Queen of Scots discovered to her cost, was all well and good, but practice was another matter entirely – and this held whether your ciphers were too difficult to use in the field, or, as in Mary's case, the keys were known by your enemies all along.

Constantijn Huygens's library shelves groaned under the weight of the accumulated wisdom of Western cryptographers in various editions and languages. Vigenère's *Traicté des chiffres* nestled alongside Trithemius's *Polygraphie* (1561); della Porta's *De Furtivis* (1563), *De Occultis Literarum Notis* (1593/1606) and *Magiae Naturalis* (1558); Daniel Schwenter's *Steganologia & Steganographia: Geheime Magische/Natürliche Red-und Schreibkunst* (c. 1620, largely plagiarised from Trithemius); *Polygraphie* (1621), Dominicus van Hottinga's plagiarised edition of Gabriel de Collange's French translation of Trithemius's *Polygraphia*; Selenus's *Cryptomenytices* (1624); Pietro Maria Canepari's *De Atramentis Cujuscunque Generis* (1660); and Gaspar Schott's *Schola Steganographica* (1665). Despite being in possession of this formidable cryptographical resource, when he was asked to design a series of ciphers for English Royalists during the Civil Wars, he produced examples that Elizabeth Stuart's grandmother would have recognised and perhaps even dismissed as overly simplistic: homophonic substitution alphabets with an extensive nomenclator.[138] The fact of the matter was that despite the theoretical innovations, the ciphers that were used during the fifteenth, sixteenth and seventeenth centuries were those that gave the greatest balance between security and usability.[139]

3

DISGUISE & DISTRACTION

In *The Advancement of Learning* (1605), Francis Bacon wrote that ciphers were best when they fulfilled three criteria, namely that they 'be not laborious to write and read; that they be impossible to decipher; and in some cases, that they be without suspicion'. As we have seen, all of the cipher systems available, whether they used letters, numbers or symbols, visibly advertised their purpose. For Bacon, the 'highest degree' of cipher enabled the spy 'to write OMNIA PER OMNIA [all into all]'. He devised his solution to the thorny problem of how to write in a cipher that did not look like a cipher while serving under the English resident ambassador in Paris, Sir Amias Paulet. While Bacon had been sent to France in the latter half of the 1570s to gain a working knowledge of the French legal system, he appears to have taken the opportunity to learn from his colleagues in Paulet's secretariat, one of whom was Thomas Phelippes. Bacon, Phelippes and Paulet considered each other as friends for many years afterwards, and were in regular communication while Mary, Queen of Scots was being held in Chartley Manor.[1]

Bacon would wait a further eighteen years before he thought fit to explain what kind of cipher he had been describing in *The Advancement*, in an expanded and updated version of his 1605 work called *De Augmentis Scientiarum*, published in 1623. His method was avowedly steganographical, that is, it was a sort of 'hidden writing'. Steganography was the second branch of cryptology, cryptography being the first. Deriving from the Ancient Greek words *steganós* (cover, roof) and *graphia* (writing, drawing), it differed from cryptography as it sought to 'hide in plain sight', and thus conceal meaning imperceptibly. The primary purpose of steganography was to look like anything other than a secret message. In the world of spies and intelligencing, this technique was not restricted to writing. In a very real sense, steganography is the art of disguise – whether you are making a letter look like a boring discussion of your nephew's boils by starting and ending with descriptions of them (an interceptor confronted with dozens, if not hundreds, of epistles would tend to first scan the beginning and end of a message for suspicious phraseology and toss those letters lacking any obviously interesting matter onto the 'no action to be taken' pile), or hiding your true identity as a counterfeiter and fraudster behind the costume and authority of an ambassador, you are donning a disguise.[2]

Steganography became increasingly important in seventeenth-century England, not least in 1643 when Parliament, heartily sick of the large numbers of Royalists plotting against it using ciphers to keep their secrets to themselves, took the rather direct if draconian route of simply outlawing all cryptographic writings. By April of that year, possession of a ciphered letter or even a cipher key was considered proof of espionage, and was thus punishable by death.[3] To all intents and purposes, the government had equated cryptography with treason. To escape prosecution conspirators took cover behind a shield of steganography, and in doing so effectively rewrote themselves.

THE BACONIAN CIPHER

Bacon's invention had 'the perfection of a cipher, which is to make anything signify anything', and it used two distinct stages of encryption to achieve its goal of being 'void of all suspicion'. Stage one was to transform the original message into a set of *differences* – in this way, Bacon suggested, 'thoughts may be communicated at any distance by means of any objects perceptible either to the eye or ear, provided only that those objects are capable of two differences; as by bells, trumpets, torches, gunshots, and the like'. A message could thus be transmitted using, for example, two musical notes, two arm positions, or even a pair of hats – one red, the other blue. The letter 'A' was represented by the 'difference string' 'aaaaa' (or, if you prefer to visualise hat colour, red-red-red-red-red). The letter 'B' was represented by the 'difference string' 'aaaab' (in hats, red-red-red-red-blue), and so forth:

112

A = aaaaa	F = aabab	L = ababa	Q = abbbb	W = babaa
B = aaaab	G = aabba	M = ababb	R = baaaa	X = babab
C = aaaba	H = aabbb	N = abbaa	S = baaab	Y = babba
D = aaabb	I/J = abaaa	O = abbab	T = baaba	Z = babbb
E = aabaa	K = abaab	P = abbba	U/V = baabb	

To give an example, the plaintext 'BACON' would be enciphered as 'aaaab aaaaa aaaba abbab abbaa' (or red-red-red-red-blue red-red-red-red-red red-red-red-blue-red red-blue-blue-red-blue red-blue-blue-red-red). As each letter is represented by a string of five differences, the message as sent (the stegotext) is now five times longer than the plaintext. This technique is more than reminiscent of the binary mathematics introduced by Gottfried Wilhelm Leibniz's 1679 article 'Explication de l'arithmétique binaire' ('An Explanation of Binary Mathematics'), and encodes the alphabet using what we would now call 5-bit encryption.[4] All that the system required was for the medium carrying the message to have five 'differences' (or 'bits') for each individual letter of the message being carried. It was for this reason that Bacon wrote 'the infolding writing [the stegotext] shall contain at least five times as many letters as the writing infolded [the plaintext]'.[5]

The process of encoding the plaintext BACON into, for example, the stegotext 'Arthur Gregory, an English spy' is straightforward. The plaintext is first transformed into a series of 5-bit difference strings: BACON becomes 'aaaab aaaaa aaaba abbab abbaa' or, in terms of colourful hats, red-red-red-red-blue red-red-red-red-red red-red-red-blue-red red-blue-blue-red-blue red-blue-blue-red-red. Next, this string is enfolded into the stegotext 'Arthur Gregory[,] an English spy':

aaaab | aaaaa | aaaba | abbab | abbaa
Arthu | rGreg | oryan | Engli | sh spy

Bacon chose to do this not through colour, but through subtle differences in handwriting (script), somewhat akin to writing a message in two fonts rather than the usual one. Using, for example, Johnston Sans for the a-form and Calibri for the b-form, we are left with the following:

Arthur Gregory, an English spy

Bacon provided a handy table showing each letter of the alphabet, both upper and lower case, in a-form and b-form. Because his cipher relied on the difference between two letter types, he called it a 'bi-formed' alphabet (any method of differentiating the a-form from the b-form would work). The table he published in 1623 shows the differences between his letterforms quite clearly, with the b-form, when compared with the a-form, generally having an extra flourish (Fig. 26a):

Exemplum *Alphabeti Biformis.*

a. b. a. b. a. b. a. b. a. b. a. b. a. b. a. b.

A. A. a. a. B. B. b. b. C. C. c. c. D. D. d. d.

It does not appear that writing a message using these two indicative alphabets would prove particularly taxing. The same cannot be said for the table published fourteen years after Bacon's death in 1640 (and reprinted in 1670), as several of the letterforms, such as 'm', 'n', 'r' and 's', for example, appear remarkably similar in the 'a' and 'b' alphabets. By the time the magisterial edition of his works was published in 1870, the situation had worsened further: the 'a' and 'b' forms printed in the table are virtually indistinguishable – what was a difficult enough system to deduce from the original 1623 text had, over time, been rendered largely incomprehensible by the presumably accidentally enforced homogeneity of the printing press (Fig. 26b):[6]

Example of an Alphabet in two forms.

a	b	a	b	a	b	a	b	a	b	a	b
A	*A*	*a*	*a*	*B*	*B*	*b*	*b*	*C*	*C*	*c*	*c*
D	*D*	*d*	*d*	*E*	*E*	*e*	*e*	*F*	*F*	*f*	*f*

Figs 26a and 26b: Bacon's bi-formed alphabets from *De Augmentis* as printed in the first edition of 1623 and the Spedding edition of 1870.

JARGON: DROPPING THE CIPHER

A more literary mode of steganography was the wrapping-up of secret information within other genres of discourse, most notably mercantile. In 1584, a letter from 'William Wilbeck' to his 'cousin and most dear friend Thomas Wilbeck' was intercepted, copied and decoded: it was, in fact, from Gilbert Curle, secretary to Mary, Queen of Scots, to Thomas Baldwin, a servant of the earl of Shrewsbury. In this letter, Curle used a mercantile nomenclator to obscure its message – Elizabeth I was referred to as 'the merchant of London', Sir Francis Walsingham as 'the merchant's wife' and Mary, Queen of Scots as 'the merchant of Newcastle', and so on. It was not particularly successful, however, as within a month Walsingham had sent a copy of the letter to Mary's keeper, Sir Ralph Sadler, with the decoded text written between the lines. It was accompanied by the nomenclator, which also provided an example of how it might be used: '*Exempli causa:* If I will write the Scottish Queen shall not be removed, then to write the merchant of Newcastle shall not goe beyond the Sea'. Sadly, Walsingham did not tell Sadler what he thought about being downgraded to a mere 'wife'.[7] Baldwin was imprisoned in the Tower for his steganographic and libellous exchanges with Curle; for now the latter, as we have seen, was allowed to roam free so that Walsingham might catch bigger game.

While Curle also made extensive use of substitution alphabets, their great weakness, namely that their use shouted 'secrets enclosed', was part of their downfall. One way to hide the fact that you were using a substitution alphabet was to employ musical notation: the notes on the stave doubled up as cipher symbols. Considering the oft-held conflation of spies with musicians, it would seem appropriate that many cryptological writers, including Alberti, Trithemius, della Porta, Selenus and Vigenère, discussed ciphers based on music in their manuals, as did the papal cipher secretary Matteo Argenti.[8] Witnessing such ciphers in the field is rather less common, and one of the few examples of musical steganography in manuscript was a system developed by the Spanish general Marco Antonio Colonna in 1564 – a simple substitution cipher, it used a combination of pitch and duration to indicate individual letters.[9] The most famous English musical cipher, which was allegedly shared by Jane Lane and King Charles II, only exists in a nineteenth-century hand and is most likely a hoax.[10]

Letter-writers increasingly removed the substitution alphabets from their cipher keys, working instead primarily with linguistic lists, that is, word-nomenclators: the Royalist secret organisation the Sealed Knot referred to ambassadors as 'factors', to letters as 'merchandise', ammunition as 'spice' and money as 'tobacco' or 'wool'.[11] It comes as little surprise that the word 'trade' represented the gathering and distribution of information, and a clearing house or cover address would be referred to as a 'shop'.[12] Another Royalist circle had horses as 'English gloves'; frigates as 'Flanders' or 'lace'; and men as 'silk-stockings'.[13] Yet another had a treaty as 'marriage'; to make peace as 'to couple'; the English as 'the father'; the Dutch as 'the mother'; and the Dutch commissioners as 'the Lady's friends'.[14] With the latter list, it is not hard to see how one could easily write a letter seemingly full of domestic gossip that was in fact anything but.

The technical name for discourse constructed from such nomenclators was 'jargon', a word which had previously meant 'unintelligible, or meaningless talk or writing' or 'the inarticulate utterance of birds', but which had been given this new meaning in 1594 by Francis Bacon in his 'A True Report of the Detestable Treason, Intended by Dr Roderigo Lopez'.[15] Bacon described a letter that formed part of the case for the prosecution as being written in 'jargon or verbal cipher': 'This bearer will tell you the price in which your pearls are esteemed, and in what resolution we rest about a little musk and amber, which I am determined to buy'. One of the suspects indeed confessed that the sentence held a hidden meaning, explaining that the price of the pearls referred to the acceptance of Lopez's offer to poison the queen, while the provision of musk and amber referred to the king of Spain's decision on whether or not to put Elizabeth's ships to the torch.[16] By the 1650s, the term jargon was common enough for the Royalist Alan Brodrick to use it when describing the Sealed Knot's steganographic discourse.[17]

Such nomenclators were often designed to work in specific theatres of conflict, such as the pair meant for Francis Bolton and John Conyers for use in the Spanish territories. These nomenclators used Dutch names, presumably because the letters would have been sent via the Spanish Netherlands, where they might be intercepted – substituting the name 'Jan van Harpe' for the queen of England, or 'Nicolas de Witte' for the king of France, for example.[18] One particularly complex steganographic nomenclator was intended for a Master Briskett, probably in Ireland. This organised its nomenclator alphabetically with columns marked *vera* ('true') and *ficta* ('false'), including pairs such as 'abandon' and 'about', 'abide' and 'abbey', 'ability' and 'abridge' (the column for words starting with the letter 'a' alone ran to fifty-six entries).[19] Another set, this time intended for use in Scotland, drew its names from literature, listing the king as 'Endymion', the queen as 'Minerva' and, perhaps manipulating gender to good effect, the prince as 'Philomela' and the princess as 'Leander'.[20]

Literary nomenclators came back into fashion following the outlawing of ciphers in 1643, with Royalists in particular drawing code names from the romance genre. When discussing the retaking of Arundel Castle in 1643, Jane Bingley and her husband addressed letters to their daughter Susan, who had crossed the channel into France, by the names 'Philitia' or 'Amorella', while they assumed the names 'Fidelia' and 'Melidora'. This trick did not necessarily allay suspicion, of course – one letter of theirs which had been intercepted bears the annotation 'Fidelia to Amorella. Note! Some court ladies at Oxford took names out [of] romances'.[21]

Elizabeth Stuart, sometime queen of Bohemia, who was well versed in the prose romance genre, had used the names 'Astraea' and 'Celadon' from Honoré d'Urfé's *L'Astrée* (1607–27) when communicating with her husband Frederick V in the 1620s, and would later use the same technique when discussing the marital indiscretions of her son, Charles Louis, referring to him as 'Tiribaze', the satrap of Western Armenia mentioned by Plutarch, and his wife as 'Eurydice'. In these letters Elizabeth assumed the identity of 'Queen Candace' from Ben Jonson's *Masque of Queens* (1609). By the 1640s, under pressure from the ban on ciphers, Elizabeth abandoned cryptography altogether in favour of steganography, and began signing her letters with a cipher, a mirrored E (i.e., æ).[22] Where fashion led, espionage often followed, and while individual spies had long been referred to through numerical codes – Charles I's mistress and spy Jane Whorwood was referred to as '409' and '390', for example – they, too, adopted literary covers. Whorwood also used the name 'Hellen' (not entirely inappropriately, considering that on three separate occasions she arranged for a ship to spirit Charles away from the Isle of Wight, even if he failed to board a single one), while Aphra Behn and William Scott followed Elizabeth Stuart's lead in choosing 'Astraea' and 'Celadon' as code names in 1666–7.[23]

Code names could also be used to hide more than just a spy's identity. They could also silently transmit a substitution alphabet (for more reckless spies, the ban on possessing ciphers was no deterrent). There are three such code names attached to cipher keys found in the archives of Sir Edward Nicholas, the Royalist counterpart to John Thurloe. They included 'Profligantes', which was shared by George Morley and Lady Isabella Rich, 'Lycanthropus' for Sir Giles Talbot (the werewolf was perhaps drawn from Webster's *The Duchess of Malfi*), and 'Labyrinthus' for Richard Lane. These names suggest that, for all the deadly seriousness of their circumstances, the Royalists enjoyed the thrill of playing the spy – perhaps a hangover from the days when cryptography was more an expression of a shared social status and cohesion than a necessary evil during times of civil war.[24]

Assuming a female code name was indeed a common trick for male spies.[25] After all, everyone knew that women's letters were full of mere tittle-tattle and family business, and thus of no interest to intelligencers. One particularly active spy appears to have taken advantage of this prejudice, and assumed the names 'John Williams', the gender-neutral 'Jo. Harrison' and 'Jo. Warde' ('Jo.' could be an abbreviation for 'John', 'Joanna' or 'Joan'), but, most regularly, 'Margaret Smith' or 'Elizabeth Smith', while being referred to by John Thurloe as 'Blanck Marshall', the nameless agent. Either the famed Parliamentarian spy chief was keen to hide this particular agent's true identity from even his own side, or he simply did not know it.[26]

One of the downsides of all this disguise and dissimulation was that it was difficult to know who was or was not on your side if you did not already know them. William Waad suspected the Gunpowder plotters of communicating their allegiance through embroidered ciphers:

> send to the commissioners for a fair scarf that Rookwood made . . . by the figures or ciphers something may be gathered, and if that scarf which

Percy had could be recovered, it were well it were seen. I perceive there were very fair scarves made for diverse of them, and it were not amiss to learn of the embroiderers what scarves of such sort have been lately made, and for whom.[27]

It is certainly the case that some groups wore secret (or not-so-secret) signs to identify one another: supporters of Elizabeth Stuart wore locks of hair as earrings, members of the secret society of Béatrix de Cusance in Antwerp wore harpsichord pendants, and royals wore cipher jewels.[28] Following the regicide of 1649, Royalist sympathisers in both England and on the continent often wore specially designed rings: in appearance ordinary mourning rings, inside they hid a miniature portrait of the king. The allegiance of the Royalist wearer was hidden but ever present. Some followed the proto-scientist John Bulwer's recommendation of using hand signals to make up 'an alphabet of privy ciphers, for any kind of secret intimation'.[29] Other, more intimate techniques were developed, including secret handshakes: one conspirator, told that his escape would be organised by a priest, was to identify himself by taking him 'by the thumb with his little finger'.[30]

X MARKS THE SPOT: LADY BRILLIANA HARLEY AND THE CARDAN GRILLE

At the beginning of the English part of the Wars of the Three Kingdoms in 1642, support for each side was often geographically skewed. The Harleys, a noble family of some pedigree, were Puritans and committed Parliamentarians, unlike the majority of the Herefordshire gentry.[31] Sir Robert, the head of the family, spent most of his time in Westminster; his two sons, Edward and Robert, served alongside William Waller on the front line, fighting against the king for Parliament; their daughter Brill (also Brilliana, after her mother) was being educated by her great-aunt, Lady Mary Vere, in London.[32] Lady Brilliana, Sir Robert's wife, left alone in Brampton Bryan Castle, the family stronghold, found herself tightly moored in a tempestuous sea of Royalists. By July 1643, she was being actively besieged. Though the siege lasted a mere six weeks, Brilliana held back the Royalist floodtide with a force of just fifty musketeers, and her spirited resistance against what must have felt like insurmountable odds made her an unimpeachable heroine of the Civil Wars. Brilliana died in October 1643, but she left more behind her than just her reputation. She had been in regular correspondence with her husband, her namesake daughter and her son Edward (or Ned as she called him), often communicating vital intelligence in the process. Even though it would be another month before Parliament outlawed the use or possession of ciphers, in March of that year Brilliana chose not to protect her letters in that manner. Whether or not she had been informed of this upcoming ban by her husband, Brilliana chose a different method, one that was steganographic in nature. The technique she hoped would allow her messages to escape the attentions of the swirling Royalist menace altogether was at least 100 years old. It was the Cardan grille.

Named for Girolamo Cardano, the Italian polymath in whose work *De Subtilitate Libri XXI* (1550) the idea first appeared, the Cardan grille was simple to use, if perhaps a little cumbersome. In much the same manner as a cipher key, it relied on the recipient having a copy of the 'key'. While it was a paper technology like the cipher wheel, the Cardan grille was less an aid to enciphering than a spatial code itself. It was an overlay into which holes (or text boxes) had been cut. When placed onto the host message (or stegotext), the words that remain visible through the holes comprise the plaintext.

The grille could be used with print or manuscript works, and could reveal words or letters, as required. When used with a printed work, the grille's text boxes would be cut to reveal the appropriate words or letters on the page, and the recipient needed to have both the grille and the printed work in question to be able to read the message (which meant that organised correspondents might agree on the literary text to be used and merely send the grille once cut to order). Manuscript letters were approached slightly differently: the words were written into the boxes before the stegotext was wrapped around them. In other words, a pre-cut grille was first placed over a blank sheet of paper and the message which required hiding was written onto those parts of the paper revealed by the cut-outs. The grille was then removed and the gaps on the writing sheet filled in by hand, hopefully in such a way that the words of the plaintext did not stand out from those of the stegotext or host message. To do this imperceptibly took both literary skill and spatial awareness – to write a message into which the 'grilled' words fit snugly, both semantically and physically, was no simple task. In his works, della Porta included several examples of this type of grille, including a demonstration of the fundamental principle.[33] Timothy Bright included a grille in his copy of della Porta's *De Furtivis*, thus considering the technique useful for presentation to Walsingham or Robert Cecil.[34]

Whether Brilliana lacked the will or merely the time to create smooth literary and artistic epistolary messages is not clear, but she chose a simple and efficient way of preventing the grille from casting its shadow across her letters too darkly. Rather than packing the spaces left between the words of the plaintext to create a dense stegotext, she spaced out both the lines and the words so widely that the order in which they had been created was utterly obscured. She also sought to hide the tell-tale lack of literary merit or narrative flow by writing to her son that 'you will not marvell at this nonsense which I have writen to you' as she did so in order 'to make you merry'.[35] As we find so often, the ways in which these various message-hiding techniques were actually used show the fear of interception standing shoulder to shoulder with an almost blasé assumption that the technique used could hardly be suspected, let alone penetrated. It seems as though every type of cryptological technique represented the triumph of hope over experience, and quite possibly a deep-seated belief that 'this time it will be different'. It rarely was.

Having attempted to smooth away the evidence of her use of the Cardan grille through word-spacing and assertions of purposeful comedy, Brilliana immediately tells her son Ned – and thus any pair of prying eyes – how to read the letter: 'pin that end of the paper that has the cross made in ink upon the little cross on the end of this letter; when you would write to me make use of it'.[36] Of course, the grille must align properly if it was to function, and for Ned, X marked the spot. This was where he was to pin the grille she had sent him. She also comments on his own employment of the technique: 'I read your letter very well, . . . but if you would let the paper you write upon be of the same breadth of the cute [cut] paper, it would be much better' – that is to say, if the letter paper and the grille used to inscribe a message onto it were of different sizes, matters were liable to get confusing. Finally, she tells her son exactly when the grille should be used: 'From this place make use of the cut paper.'[37] Luckily for us, two of the actual grilles Brilliana used to read and write her letters to Ned survive, nestling between the pages of a letter-book bound in Victorian times and retained by the family. These two grilles, which are identical, are now 'attached' to the letters Brilliana sent on 1 March and 9 March so that they reveal the messages hidden within. Both of them show the peaks and troughs of having been folded independently of the letters to which they are attached, strongly suggesting that they have been sent as enclosures in another letter at some point in their lives.[38]

While the Cardan grille is often referred to as a cipher technique, it is actually steganographic in nature. It is designed to hide a message in plain sight. It was perhaps unfortunate that Brilliana's letters had several features that might serve to tip off the vigilant interceptor, from the instruction to lay a piece of paper over the letter, to the way in which the passages containing her stegotexts were written with completely different spacing in comparison to paragraphs of plaintext (Fig. 30).[39] How much this would have helped such an interceptor is another matter, as it is still extremely difficult to decode.

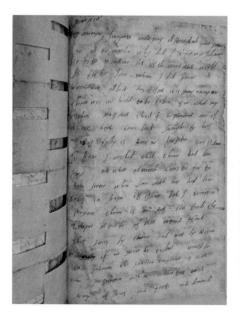 

Fig. 27: Brilliana's Cardan grille in action: the left image shows the letter unadorned, the right the letter with the grille overlaid to reveal the message.

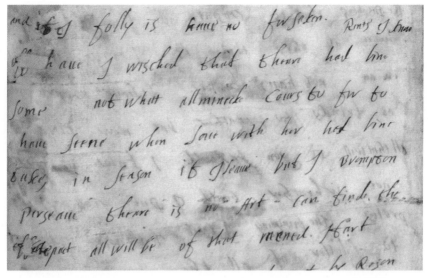

Fig. 28: Without the grille, the letter makes little sense: 'and if I folly is haue no forsaken rents, I know off haue I wisched that theare had bine some not what all mineche cours to for to haue seene when loue with her had bine take, in season If I leaue but I Brampton perseaue theare is no Art, can finde the [hole in ms] ~~xx~~pact all will be of that ruened Hart'.

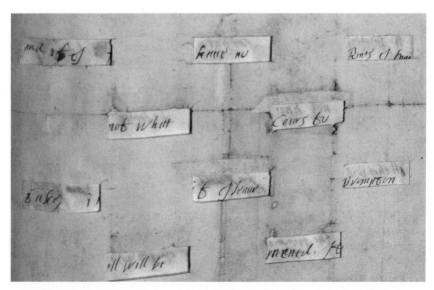

Fig. 29: Placing the grille on top of the letter, however, is nothing less than revelatory. The message now reveals that Brilliana is worried about her next move: 'and if I haue no Rents, I know not what cours to take, If I leaue Brampton all will be ruened'.

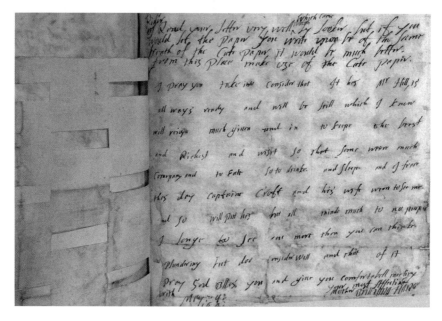

Fig. 30: Different line spacing for non-grilled and grilled parts of the letter. Brilliana's instruction in the letter itself, 'From this place make use of the cute [cut] paper', as well as her sudden doubling of the space between the lines, perhaps makes it obvious that she is using some sort of paper layover device.

THE POSTMAN ALWAYS CHECKS TWICE

There would have been no need to go to the lengths of using jargon or a technique such as a Cardan grille if letters could be carried from one place to another without fear of discovery, but this was easier said than done – especially if either the letter-writer or recipient was under siege. The Greek general Aeneas Tacticus discussed this problem as early as the fourth century BCE, in his manual *Poliorketika*, or *How to Survive under Siege*. One of the methods he recommended involved the use of a pig's bladder. First one wrote a message on an inflated bladder with 'glutinous ink', then deflated the bladder, stuffed it into an oil flask and filled it with oil. The message thus 'disappeared' into the flask. Once delivered, the flask was emptied and its bladder removed and inflated so that the message could be read. If desired, the message could then be wiped off, replaced with a new one and the flask returned.[40] Almost two millennia later sieges were still catalysts for the development of new methods of message-smuggling, though 'new' seems, as ever, to overlap with 'traditional' to no small degree.

In 1632, Horace de Vere's English regiment formed part of the Dutch army which lay siege to Maastricht, then in the hands of the Spanish. During the action, many women were caught in the act of smuggling letters both in and out of the beleaguered city on behalf of the Spanish. Some of them had gone to great lengths to hide their cargo of information. One soldier's wife, having been captured but found to be carrying no letters, was threatened with hanging (it was her second offence), upon which she 'confessed, that she had swallowed two copper-boxes, with two letters'. Whether she came to a sticky end or not, it is unlikely that her night in captivity was particularly comfortable, as the physician working for the Dutch 'gave her some pills which wrought so well with her that the next morning they [the copper-boxes] were found, washed, opened, and these letters found in them'. Luckily, there were less uncomfortable ways of achieving the same results. A few days earlier another woman, having been apprehended by the Dutch army in the same manner, confessed that 'she had swallowed down a bullet . . . which after a purge she voided, & the letter was found: the letter being wrapped together in a little hollow bullet, & baked in paste'.[41]

While della Porta noted that messages could be bound in musket balls, which were around the size of grapes and thus eminently swallowable, he suggested that instead these then be fired into the besieged city from a musket. A variation on the musket ball/bullet method which made good use of the relative malleability of lead was to hide the message in earrings, which could be made of 'thin [sheets] of lead, rolled up and worn in women's ears'.[42] The women of Maastricht were no doubt glad that those who bade them swallow their letters did not follow the Italian's prescription for smuggling messages in a dog by wrapping them up in meat and feeding them to the unfortunate hound: 'when he is killed, the letters may be found in his belly'.[43]

Charles I employed a willing stomach to smuggle a message to the governor of the besieged town of Newark during the Civil Wars in 1646, though the messenger in this case was male. Once he arrived, an emetic was administered and he soon coughed up his cargo, the message it contained having been written in cipher to provide an extra layer of security.[44] Such methods were not the prerogative of Royalist couriers alone; in 1650, Oliver Cromwell exchanged messages with Colonel John Hewson wrapped in balls of yellow wax which would traverse their own course through their carrier's digestive tract as he travelled between correspondents.[45] It was not always necessary to go to such lengths, however: the earl of Derby noted that messages encased in a protective layer of wax or lead could be carried about the messenger's person and only swallowed if capture appeared imminent (he had tested his methods during the siege of Lathom House). Before we congratulate the earl on the consideration shown for his messengers, we ought perhaps note that some sources suggest that once a message was sealed in its waxy tomb, it could also be placed into a 'green' (that is, a fresh) wound before smuggling.[46] Encasing letters within musket balls was of course limited to brief messages, much as it was when using an egg, another technique which, however ludicrous it may seem, actually works.

The eggy method was recommended by della Porta on the grounds that 'when prisons are shut, eggs are not stopped by the Papal Inquisition'.[47] Della Porta's method relied on writing a message on the egg's shell, but the polemicist Thomas Lupton's *A Thousand Notable Things* (1579) detailed how to insert a message into it. This involved soaking the uncooked egg in vinegar until the shell softened (this can take up to six hours), cutting a slit into the egg's shell and sliding the message, written on a slip of paper, into it. It was important to use eggs with white shells, as the vinegar dissolved the colour of, say, brown eggs. To harden the shell and seal up the slit, the egg merely needed to be soaked in cold water, and the message was ready to send on its way.[48] As with the musket ball method, any message so concealed would need to be very short, or in extremely small writing. Short, however, did not necessarily mean insignificant: in 1642, Sir Roger Twysden was detained by the Commons as they believed that he had 'carried intelligence of great consequence . . . subtly conveyed into Nutshells'.[49] This method also went back to the classics: in his *Naturalis Historia* of 77 CE, the Roman writer Pliny the Elder claims that Cicero once saw Homer's *Iliad* written in tiny script on a piece of parchment placed in a nutshell. When he was working as a clerk of the chancery, in 1587, Peter Bales left his calling card of miniature writing behind, which was displayed there for years after:

A most strange and rare piece of work brought pass by Peter Bales an Englishman, a clerk of the chancery, of the proof & demonstration of the whole Bible to be written by him every word at length within an English walnut no bigger than a hen's egg . . . And thus confesseth the proof: the nut holdeth the Book; there are so many leaves in his little book as in the great Bible and he hath written as much in one of them little leaves as a great leaf of the Bible containeth.[50]

Bales left but one clue as to his method: 'if you would write smaller, turn your pen a little more aside, and write with the lower nib thereof'.[51]

MICROGRAPHIA

The skill with tiny writing shown by Bales in his bejewelled 1575 gift to Queen Elizabeth I and his nutwork in chancery was no mere parlour trick. During the Eighty Years' War in the Low Countries, Constantijn Huygens was faced with the problem of how to get messages across enemy lines to his employer's wife, Amalia, princess of Orange. Amalia and Huygens both knew that, while her husband was acting as the general of the army, he was suffering from dementia. While she quietly took care of business during his absence from The Hague, neither she nor his secretary could afford for the Spanish to discover this weakness in the Dutch chain of command. Huygens 'had to invent every day new expedients and to exercise his eyes on a kind of small writing', and did so with such success that the resulting letter, once folded, did little 'exceed the tip of a quill, or the size of a pea, so that it could be hidden in some place by women or little boys', or attached to the leg of a pigeon. Amalia was unappreciative, as his tiny messages were naturally awkward to read, and ordered him to stop showing off. Huygens's feelings were hurt and he later wrote in his *Mémoires* that it was necessity, not vanity, that had driven him to write such tiny letters, to prevent them from being intercepted.[52]

Huygens was competing with the enemy: the Spanish might have been using micrographia as spycraft as early as 1586. In that year, the military officer Sancho Martínez de Leiva recommended the services of the Italian

Fig. 31: Micrographia – if enshrouded in wax and silk floss,
such tiny letters could, like musket balls, be easily swallowed
if the carrier was threatened with capture.

Carlos Fantino to the Spanish secretary of state Juan de Idiáquez. Martínez de Leiva enclosed two samples of Fantino's art attached to a sheet of paper with wax: one, measuring 2.8 x 2.1 centimetres, presented Canto 11.65 of Ludovico Ariosto's epic poem *Orlando Furioso* (1532) in Italian; the second, measuring 2.7 x 2.9 centimetres, bore most of the Latin text of the *Salve Regina*, an ancient Marian hymn.[53]

Size was not everything, and when no expert in micrographia was available, or the messages were simply too much to secrete inconspicuously, more capacious containers were necessary. Some have suggested that Mary, Queen of Scots recommended the soles of shoes as perfect hiding places for messages, but this is a misreading of her French. In fact, she suggests that packets of ciphered letters could be sealed with wax and substituted for the cork generally used to stuff high-heeled mules so that they kept their shape. It was the presence of such special stuffing that could be indicated by a mark 'on the sole above the heel'. Mary also suggested that letters might be unfolded and laid flat 'between the pieces of wood in the trunks and chests which you send' – a padlock would indicate the need for said trunks to be taken apart.[54]

In fact, any container that could be converted to surreptitiously convey letters was considered fair game. During the Bishops' Wars of the late 1630s, Gualter Frost, later a key figure in the Commonwealth's Council of State, transported letters in a hollowed-out cane.[55] In 1645, the governor of Cardiff was informed that Charles I had sent a messenger out of Oxford with letters for his supporters in the west of England: the messenger was to be a lame soldier. The unsuspecting bagman was subsequently captured and thoroughly searched, but his antagonists discovered no letters about his person; at least, not until one of them thought to investigate his wooden leg. Once removed, the prosthetic limb was found to have a secret chamber containing no fewer than eighteen letters.[56]

Had this soldier not been betrayed, he would no doubt have waltzed past the Parliamentarian patrols unmolested, as such a pitiful figure was unlikely to generate much suspicion. Certainly, it was normal to recruit such illicit couriers from those trades whose members were perfectly common sights on the highways and byways – apothecaries, midwives, musicians and itinerant booksellers, for example. Royalist physician Peter Barwick noted of the women employed by the bookseller Richard Royston to smuggle letters between London and Oxford that it was the 'mediocrity or rather meanness of their condition' which rendered them 'less conspicuous and more safe' for such operations. It was perfectly normal for such women 'frequently to travel on foot, like strowlers begging from house to house, and loitering at places agreed upon, to take up books . . . it was easy to sew letters privately within the cover of any book, and then give the book a secret mark, to notify the insertion of such letters therein'.[57]

Sometimes the wildly ostentatious trumped the drably invisible. When George Stewart, 9th seigneur d'Aubigny, was killed at the battle of Edgehill in 1642, his widow Katherine Howard, Lady d'Aubigny, was given a passport to Oxford so that she might deal with his estate. There she met Charles I, and promptly turned she-intelligencer (a contemporary term, originally used derogatively as women were neither expected nor supposed to engage in the dangerous trade).[58] Charles wished to mobilise his allies in London, and so sent 'a commission under the Great Seal' pertaining to provoking a rising against Parliament under Katherine's safekeeping.[59] The Great Seal was not known for its compactness, so it is perhaps astonishing that Lady d'Aubigny transported it 'made up in the hair of her head'.[60] Katherine's relative invisibility, in spite of what must have been a massive hairdo, came from a combination of her total rejection of subtlety and the fact that women were generally considered incapable of political thought: they were hardly likely to be smuggling letters left, right and centre. The women of Maastricht caught in the act by besieging English soldiers might have put the lie to this particular belief, but it persisted in the face of overwhelming evidence to the contrary, especially when it came to the higher classes – certainly it was accentuated by the social stratification in England, as lower-born men were very reluctant to interfere in any way with higher-born women. When Apolin Hunt, who used the code name 'Lady Hall', was imprisoned, for example, she was treated with due respect by her jailer until, following a concerted investigation, he discovered that her title was a mere contrivance; she was no 'Lady' but rather the daughter of an old, drunken and defrocked priest. His next message to his superior, John Thurloe, contained the suggestion that he might 'send the Slutt to Tynemouth Castle'. Disturbingly, Apolin subsequently disappeared from view, leaving no further traces in the archives, her class (or lack thereof) proving her undoing.[61]

This unwillingness to believe that women of note might, indeed, be smuggling letters to and fro often proved an advantage even when they were caught in the act, when their class also offered them some protection from being manhandled in the name of a 'search'. In 1647, Lady Cave was in the process of smuggling a letter to Charles I, at that point incarcerated at Holdenby House, when she was betrayed and subsequently arrested. Her captors wisely considered it best to have a pair of gentlewomen search her. Depite their efforts, however, nothing was discovered until 'some 2 or 3 days after (upon an accident) the letter was found behind an hanging, in the room where she was searched, where it seems she had put it, when she stood with her back to the hangings, and conveyed it with her hands behind her, whilst she talked with the gentlewomen'.[62] By 1658, the authorities had grown wise to the possibility that women such as Lady Cave might delay their being searched by simply distracting their guardians: when Lady Mordaunt was suspected of possessing incriminating letters, she was 'stript and search'd by women sworn to that purpose; and her hair pull'd about her ears to find papers', while her husband and his servants 'had all their clothes cut and opened'.[63]

Messages were regularly sewn into clothes, hats and other garments, as Tactitus recommended.[64] In 1597 Sir Thomas Chaloner suggested to Essex that a letter might be 'stiched in a doublet',[65] for example, while in 1572, a Cypriot spy who had been employed to deliver a message to the Venetian envoy in Constantinople, then under house arrest, was told to hide the message in a piece of cloth waterproofed with wax which was then to be 'stitched up as a secret compartment inside his clothes'.[66] Some letters, such as the diminutive folding sent by James Ségur-Pardeilhan to Lord Burghley in 1585, still bear holes which may well have resulted from their being stitched into place.[67]

There were other ways of using clothing to hide a message. In 1660, Charles II received a communication written on a piece of 'White Persian' cloth, for instance.[68] A letter written on paper could be folded into a very small package, but being hard and unyielding, it was thus vulnerable to a fingertip search. The same would obtain if one, for example, transported the paper letter unfolded and sewn into a garment's lining, as it would change the garment's feel. Linen, however, could be hidden within clothing and was

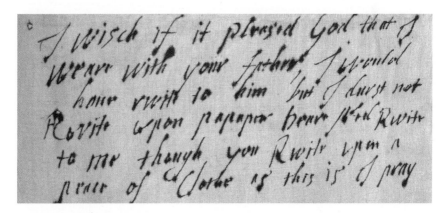

Fig. 32: Lady Brilliana wrote to her son of how she felt unable to write to his father. 'I would have rwite to him but I durst not Rwite vpon papaper', she told him, before asking him to 'Rwite to me though you Rwite vpon a peace of Clothe as this is I pray.' While linen was not the perfect medium for holding plain ink, as can be seen by the way in which the ink has spread on the material, it did have one great advantage over paper: flexibility.

only liable to discovery in the event of the garment concealing it being unstitched. It could also be scrunched up and hidden in places that paper letters could not, as well as masquerading as handkerchiefs and the like.[69] While under interrogation at the Tower of London following his arrest on suspicion of complicity in the Gunpowder Plot of 1605, the Jesuit priest Henry Garnett might well have taken advantage of these properties – he mentions handkerchiefs in two letters. His captors certainly felt that this was a possibility: his jailer was instructed 'to observe to whom he gives any handkerchers'.[70]

DISGUISED INTENTIONS

Spy-handlers sometimes found their own identities got in the way of secret work. As those men with their own intelligence fiefdoms were each well known to their antagonists, it was often too dangerous for a spy to meet with them in their usual place of business. As they were most likely under continual surveillance themselves, any visitor would have their cover blown. Samuel Morland, Thurloe's right-hand man, therefore ensured that there was always 'a convenient room or two in some private places in the city . . . hired by the year in another's name, on purpose to meet such persons in a disguise and receive their intelligance'. In this way, the venue's purpose was protected from prying eyes, as were its visitors, whether they were Thurloe himself or those agents he controlled. A similar trick was used to help agents abroad from giving away their allegiance by having to address their intelligence reports to Spy Chief John Thurloe, Westminster, England: false addresses. For instance, Thurloe's linguist Isaac Dorislaus was informed that an operative named 'Master Williams' (perhaps the elusive 'Blanck Marshall') would direct his letters to either of the two following addresses: 'To Zedekiah Hoskins Merchant in Milk Street, London', or 'To Master William Hanmer in Sheer Lane at the sign of the Sugar Loaf, London'.[71] Dorislaus, who was in charge of the day-to-day running of the Post Office, knew that any letter directed to one of these false addresses was effectively marked 'For the attention of Secretary Thurloe'.

Those who did not wish their letters to be intercepted purely on account of their expressed destination could also send them under a cover, through use of a clearing house. The technique was simple. The spy addressed their letter to an unsuspected third party, who then passed the letter on to its intended recipient. Sometimes, these third parties acted as unofficial sorting offices for entire spy circles. The same document that shows that Dorislaus was aware of the Milk Street and the Sugar Loaf addresses also suggests that there were clearing houses that he was not aware of. It states that Williams might also address letters to 'John Richards' at either the sign of the Harp or the sign of the Bell on King Street, Westminster, as the occupiers (presumably the innkeepers) were under instructions to 'carefully send them to me always'. It also contained a numerical cipher for use in communications with Williams. It is not clear who was hiding these clearing houses from Dorislaus, though likely candidates are Morland or Thurloe. The document now resides in the archives of Edward Hyde, secretary of state to King Charles II in exile: it was not only Thurloe who intercepted letters, it was his opponents, too.[72] What was sauce for the goose was sauce for the gander.

One of the Interregnum's more active postmen was Anthony Hinton, an apothecary (an occupation which not only allowed him both to pass far and wide, but also to receive all manner of individuals at his shop without raising suspicion) who also operated a clearing house for the Royalist secret society the Sealed Knot. Anyone who wished a letter delivered within this network first wrote, sealed and addressed their communication, using the appropriate code names – Edward Hyde to the exiled Charles Stuart, was 'Monsieur d'Esmond to Mrs Brown', for example – and then enclosed this packet in a wrapper addressed to Hinton. Hinton would open the packets and distribute the contents accordingly. The system worked well at first, but Thurloe soon cottoned onto the 'great number of subtle and sly fellows in and about the city . . . whose daily business is to go laden with intelligence, and instructions . . . and so to disperse them among their factious brethren'. Thurloe had plenty of men at his disposal, setting some to 'dog these expresses from house to house, and from place to place, till they were apprehended with all their packets'.[73] Hinton was amongst those arrested, and he soon betrayed practically everyone in the network – Thurloe's reputation for picking the 'locks leading into the hearts of wicked men' was more than enough of an incentive to talk.[74] For all their subterfuge and carefully constructed lines of communication, cover addresses and code names, the Sealed Knot was rendered toothless by the telling combination of manpower and intimidation.

The information held within a letter could be disguised through mercantile discourse or cunning methods of smuggling, just as the identity of an individual spy could be protected by adopting code names. Sometimes a letter simply needed to be safely stored until it could be collected, away from the prying eyes of the pursuivants. Rather than directing letters to a specific address that would thus associate an individual name with the network, some preferred to use 'dead drops', places containing convenient nooks and crannies in which letters could be hidden and picked up at a later date once the coast was clear. Dead drops also had the advantage of preventing the simultaneous apprehension of both spy and courier, thus helping reduce the risk associated with that most dangerous of times, when information is in motion. Dead drops were designed to preserve the anonymity of the user, much like the Venetian use of dedicated letter boxes in the shape of a lion's mouth ('*bocca di leone*') or the 'head of a stern bureaucrat' into which concerned citizens could post intelligence information.[75] The best were both obscure yet easy to use without drawing undue attention. One method was to make a drop while indulging in another, preferably common but unsavoury, action. Supporters of Parliament in Royalist Oxford found a suitably unpleasant way of smuggling information out of the city. One city street had a 'hole of a glass-window' in which letters could be left to be collected that same day and 'conveyed two miles off by some in the habit of town-gardeners, to the side of a ditch, where one or more were ever ready to give the intelligence to the next Parliament garrison'. The postbox had the perfect cover – it was in a street commonly used for public urination.[76]

Other dead drops were more complicated. In November 1587, for example, intelligencer Ingram Thweyng sent a letter from Calais to Hugh Owen explaining how he intended to retrieve information from an agent he was sending to England should their current method of smuggling it to the continent be compromised. On landing in Dover, the new agent was to take the master of the boat and find a nook in the cliffs suitable for concealing a letter. Thweyng would later send a boat to the same port, ostensibly to pick up his sister who was to be waiting at this very same place. In the remarkably likely event that she was not sitting under the cliffs waiting for a passing sailor, the boatman would find a letter in the nook which 'will declare the cause why she cometh not'. This letter was actually an intelligence report – if Thweyng did have a sister she was not involved in this process – which would then be returned to Thweyng via the boatman. Thweyng further suggested that in order to prevent any suspicion from falling on the drop itself, his agent should repeatedly visit the general area without using it, and thus (eventually) he might place his letter unobserved. The technique had the added advantage of keeping Thweyng removed from the action, and thus safe from immediate apprehension. As every pick-up was potentially hazardous, each letter was to include details of the date, time and position of the next drop. It was a clever way of ensuring as much security as possible for these exchanges, which were one of the times at which a spy was at his or her most vulnerable. The only mistake Thweyng made was in revealing his system to Owen. While Thweyng and his agent had to understand the process, Owen did not. Unfortunately for Thweyng and his network, the letter which explained everything bears the following endorsement: 'intercepted'.[77]

HIDING THE EVIDENCE

The 1580s was a busy time for pursuivants in England as they tried to hold back the tide of Jesuits flowing in from the continent. In the decade preceding the death of Mary, Queen of Scots, around 300 had entered the country, each fully prepared to give his life in what was the increasingly clandestine battle for the Catholic soul of Elizabeth I's country. Around half of these had failed in their mission: thirty-three had been hanged, around fifty languished in prison, where eight had died, and some sixty had returned to the continent. A decade later, as the number of Catholic-friendly houses swelled, so did the number of active priests, to over 300.[78] This increase was accompanied, or perhaps enabled, by the use of hides or, as they are commonly termed, priest-holes. The equivalent of a dead drop for an individual rather than a message, hides were designed to conceal the whole man, not merely his letters or paraphernalia, until the pursuivants had gone on their merry way and it was safe to allow the poor fellow out.

Before the hide became the go-to home improvement for recusant gentry, Catholic priests threatened with capture tended to secrete themselves in any available space, including trees, haystacks and in at least one case, an oven.[79] When available, caves were also popular, both for people and for the illegal printing presses that were used to manufacture illicit devotional materials that accompanied the Catholic mission in England. The first hides were relatively simple affairs, often mere extensions of hidden cupboards intended for the safety of valuables. The two most common types were the 'hole-under-the-garderobe' and the 'lath-and-plaster-hutch-in-the-roof'.[80] Both had rather grave disadvantages. The 'hole-under-the-garderobe' was effectively an enlargement of the space between ceiling and floor, and as garderobes (toilets) generally took the form of semicircular extensions outside the house, that such a space had been carved out was often obvious from the outside. The 'lath-and-plaster-hutch-in-the-roof' variety also had two particular problems. The first was that the roof was well known to be likely to hold such an addition – in 1606, Salisbury gave instructions regarding the search of Hindlip Hall that 'any double loft [or] loft towards the roof of the house . . . must of necessity be opened'. The second was that, being less than solid in construction, they lacked soundproofing and were easily exposed by tapping on suspicious walls or by 'fishing', the random thrusting of a sword through any walls or ceilings that looked suspicious.[81] It appears that on several occasions incumbent priests only narrowly escaped being wounded or even slain by such methods, never mind being discovered. In any case, pursuivants were known to bring carpenters and masons on their missions to ferret out hidden Jesuits. These simple shelters were simply insufficient.

The incorporation of these hides into the fabric of English country houses began around 1580, but it was not until the end of that decade that they were either numerous enough or clever enough to provide anything but very cursory protection. In 1588, everything changed. More than simply a high water mark in the shape of the attempted invasion by the Spanish Armada, 1588 was also the year that Nicholas Owen began his work as an interior designer and installer of bespoke hides for the dangerously recusant, work which continued until his arrest in 1606.[82]

Owen, or 'Little John' as he was known, was the doyen of the hide, building in escape routes, connections with other hides (including ways of getting food to the inconvenienced guests), and even hides within hides – the idea being that the first might be easily discovered and, as it was empty, promptly ignored, thus saving the priest in the inner hide from arrest, ignominy and probable execution. Owen preferred to burrow into masonry or brickwork wherever possible, making his hides impervious to detection by tapping, sword-fishing or through comparing a building's internal and external dimensions. Several examples of Owen's ingenuity still survive, in houses such as Oxburgh Hall in Norfolk, Braddocks in Essex, Sawston Hall in Cambridgeshire, Hindlip Hall and Harvington Hall in Worcestershire, and Baddesley Clinton and Coughton Court in Warwickshire.[83]

The building of hides diminished greatly after Owen's arrest and subsequent expiry in the Tower (where he was tortured so gravely that his body gave way), and within a few years, as Catholics became less of a threat and the religion more widely tolerated, it ceased completely. Just because there seem to have been no new hides built after around 1610 does not mean that they were not used, however. In 1651, following defeat at the battle of Worcester, Charles Stuart struck out with a band of loyal followers intent on escaping the country. He soon found that there were times when one simply had no choice but to hide. At Boscobel House, for example, a day spent hiding up a tree (the famous 'Royal Oak') was followed by a night in the house's garderobe hide (which was only 84 centimetres deep). He then travelled to a house in Moseley, where he passed another night in a hide. At Madeley Old Hall, however, it was felt unwise for him to use any of the house's many hides as they were all too well known. He passed the night in a barn instead. Sometimes, even kings could not be choosers.

DRESSING UP AND DRESSING DOWN

It was one thing to physically hide a message or to disguise its contents or recipients with mercantile discourse and code names, or to secrete a turbulent priest in a hole-in-the-wall, but quite another to physically hide an individual's identity. Dressing up, or indeed, dressing down (see Fig. 33), was a time-honoured practice amongst those who wished to remain anonymous, though it carried about it more than a faint whiff of moral danger. Clothing was generally believed to affect the wearer, just as it provided vital clues to one's status. While the sumptuary laws which once matched man and material had been toothless long before they were finally repealed, wearing clothing 'beyond one's station' was still generally frowned upon. Waad, for example, saw fit to comment on the Gunpowder plotter Ambrose Rookwood's possession of a 'very fair Hungarian horseman's coat, lined all with velvet, and other apparel exceeding costly, not fit for his degree'.[84]

Donning the luxurious apparel of someone far beyond one's own position in society was thought to render the wearer vulnerable to 'sinful behaviours such as lust, avarice, envy and generally lax prodigality'.[85] A similar connection was made with make-up. In 1628, the she-intelligencer Lucy, Lady Carlisle, lover of the 1st duke of Buckingham and later a 'guest' at the Tower, was the subject of much gossip and jealousy, particularly from the female members of the duke's family.[86] 'She hath the Queen's hart above them all, so as in comparison she valleweth them at nothing', complained one correspondent, but that was far from her worst crime: 'she hath already brought her [the queen, Charles II's mother] to paint & in time she may by her example be led unto more debauchedness'.[87] Wearing make-up was an essentially dishonest undertaking.

Some attempts at disguising an individual's identity seem to have been doomed from the outset, such as that reputedly made to protect Anthony Babington from capture following the dismantling of his plot to assassinate Elizabeth I in 1586. Having cut off his hair, his co-conspirators 'besmeared his face with the husks of green walnuts'.[88] Such simple attempts at transitioning an individual from instantly recognisable to bland anonymity were fraught with difficulty. In 1623, Prince Charles and court favourite Buckingham travelled to Madrid, intent on securing the Spanish Match, James's plan to marry his son and heir to the Spanish infanta. Wishing to remain incognito, the men donned false beards to hide their identities, beards they had allegedly tried on during court masques.[89] Rumour had it that their disguises were rather less successful than the one adopted by Charles I's brother-in-law, the sometime king of Bohemia Frederick V, in

Fig. 33: Having fled to Whiteladies following his defeat at Worcester, Charles II is disguised as woodcutter 'William Jones' by Richard Penderel, a local farmer's son. Following a rough haircut with a pair of shears (perhaps into a 'Babington'), the beleaguered monarch's transformation was completed with a loan of Penderel's doe-skin doublet and a pair of his breeches.

1622 during the Thirty Years' War (1618–48). He had both shaved off his beard and adopted the role of servant to his wife's secretary, Sir Francis Nethersole, as they made the dangerous journey to his ancestral lands, the Palatinate, a journey that took them directly through enemy territory. Sometimes, of course, disguise was in the eye of the beholder – in 1621,

Frederick had been captured by imperial forces, but they had released him on account of his looking so young and insignificant.[90]

Many men who wished to avoid drawing unwelcome attention to themselves went to somewhat greater lengths than donning false beards or besmirching their good looks with a rough haircut and a smudge of unripe walnuts. Well aware that women were less liable to being challenged while carrying surreptitious letters, dukes and generals alike took to the dressing-up box and presented themselves as women, all the better to slink unnoticed past enemy lines. Several used the technique to aid their escape from incarceration of one kind or another. Having been committed to the Tower after fighting on the losing side at the battle of Worcester in 1651, for example, Royalist general John Middleton subsequently absconded from prison and escaped to the continent 'in his wife's clothes'.[91] The Parliamentarian soldier Colonel John Lambert, who had himself been sent to the Tower having attracted the opprobrium of his masters, effected his escape by substituting his prison maid, Joan, for himself by dressing her in his nightcloak and having her occupy his bed while he made use of a conveniently situated rope. Not long afterwards, he took matters a little further when the house at which he was hiding in Millbank was 'beset with soldiers to take him'. Aware of the danger, he 'dressed himself in woman's clothes and a mask, [and] gave [£10] to a neighbour to break a wall to pass through the house', where a coach was waiting to bear him away into the misty streets of London and beyond.[92]

Fig. 34: A lady's vizard mask like that possibly worn by Lambert. The bead in the mouth opening was held between the teeth, thus keeping the mask in place.

Perhaps Lambert had been inspired by the antics of George Booth, leader of the eponymous uprising, who, having fallen foul of Lambert in a skirmish near Northwich, Cheshire, on 19 August 1659, made his escape dressed as 'the Lady Dorothy'. Booth was captured after stopping off at Newport Pagnell after his companions, 'having called in a barber to shave them, tried to buy his razor' in an attempt to avoid exposing that Lady Dorothy was no sort of lady at all.[93]

Borrowing a woman's clothes was one thing, but convincing your peers you actually were a woman required a little more dedication. In April 1648, with his father King Charles I imprisoned and his elder brother safely abroad, the fourteen-year-old duke of York swapped captivity in St James's Palace for freedom and exile in Holland less by dressing as a woman than by becoming one, albeit temporarily. The first part of the subterfuge, as with Lambert, was the relatively simple matter of escaping his immediate environs: Lambert had exited the Tower by means of a handy rope, while the young duke was handed a 'cloake and periwig' by Colonel Bampfield – notorious turncoat and, at this point at least, Royalist spy – as he took a turn around the gardens. His identity thus occluded, if not entirely hidden, the duke hurried to a boathouse where a second conspirator, Anne Murray, later Lady Halkett, promptly 'dressed him in the woman's habit that was prepared; which fitted His Highness very well & was very pretty in it'. Anne's account of the duke's new clothes not only mentions the fabrics used, 'a mixed mohair of a light hair colour & black & the under petticoat was scarlet', but also that the tailor chosen to make the disguise 'had never seen any woman of so low a stature have so big a waist'.[94] At a time when dressing in women's clothes was, for a man, something of a last resort, it is instructive to note how Murray does not so much dress the young duke as transform him. Another source notes that this transition was achieved with the help of 'black patches', that is, highly fashionable self-adhesive beauty spots, and that the only hiccup in the plan occurred when Bampfield attracted the suspicions of the boatman transferring them to the ship that would bear them both to safety. He began 'tying the duke's garter' while still on the boat: it was – and still is – unusual behaviour for a man to hitch up a lady's dress in public and start adjusting her underwear.[95] For spies such as Anne Murray and Bampfield, a convincing

Fig. 35: The seventeenth century was a time when spies explored the various possibilities afforded by the donning of disguise. This was writ large in items such as this 'dressing-up with Queen Henrietta Maria' game. Comprising a base miniature portrait and up to twenty-four sheets of mica (a translucent silicate) with disguises painted onto them, it allowed the user to turn the queen into a masked, cloaked figure or statesman, amongst other possibilities.

disguise plainly relied on getting the details right. By way of contrast with this litany of mid-seventeenth-century cross-dressing men, in 1584, Charles Paget advised Mary, Queen of Scots to do the opposite: 'Me thinketh there were no way so sure to escape as to clothe yourself in man's apparel and to have one woman so clothed to attend you, and so may Your Majesty be conveyed to any place of England to pass the sea either to Scotland, Spain or Lorraine.'[96]

At times, all this cross-dressing and donning of disguises resembled something of a pantomime, if not a farce, and perhaps nowhere is this made more clear than in the confessions made by the various members of the Babington Plot. Babington at one point told his interrogators that no decision had been made as to who would carry out the assassination of Elizabeth I. This was both true and not true, as it appears that every member of the conspiracy was ready to do so. John Savage is often identified as the intended assassin, but it appears he may simply have been the next conspirator off the block, so to speak: 'After [the priest John] Ballard was apprehended, the same day Babington (fearing his present danger to be discovered) moved Savage first (whom he presently apparelled to go to court)'. This need for appropriate clothing is reinforced throughout the confessions, and Babington's subsequent apprehension 'moved Savage to a present execution of that attempt against Her Majesty's person, which he promised to do accordingly, & was thereupon in haste suited with new apparel to go to the court for that purpose'. Elizabeth's courtiers were not known for their sartorial conservatism, and one can only deduce that any would-be assassin who failed to sport the very latest fashion would draw so much attention to themselves that they would find it impossible to carry out their mission.[97]

As the conspiracy fractured, its members were advised to 'disguise & sever themselves, & so fly'. Even in flight, the conspirators were conscious of their appearance, and swapped outfits repeatedly: 'Savage lent Babington his apparel to fly away in, & put upon him Babington's apparel & came to [John] Charnock's chamber in the same & told Charnock of the same & there put off Babington's apparel & borrowed Charnock's apparel & put it upon him.' If it is unclear what Savage hoped to achieve by first wearing Babington's clothes before swapping them with another conspirator, it is quite evident that one of the conspirators feared that at least part of his customary outfit was far too recognisable: '[Edward] Jones sayeth that upon the request of Payne the servant of [Thomas] Salusbury to change his cloak with Howlet the said Jones his servant because Payne's own cloak was better known, the said Jones willed his servant to deliver the said Payne his cloak'.[98] Clothing was certainly one of the first identifying traits referred to when pointing out a suspected spy to a colleague, and elaborate descriptions of a suspect's appearances were part and parcel of observation methods practised by informers.[99] For instance, a letter sent from Saint-Malo in Brittany to Dartmouth, via Guernsey and Plymouth to prevent interception described two 'traitors', who were soon to cross the channel into England, by way of their dress. One had 'a green cloak and a cut doublet of fustian, with lace like a merchant, and has a hare lip' while another 'has a grey cloak. But all these marks may be altered'.[100] It should come as no surprise that the term 'turn-coat' for someone who has changed sides comes from exactly this action: 'In the last you wrote to me that, if I undertook the voyage for His Majesty's title, that it would be thought there I had turned my cloak and had become French.'[101]

Even though the sumptuary laws had been repealed in the first decade of the seventeenth century, clothing was, for most people, a prime indicator of identity. Any attempt at sartorial manipulation was, therefore, an act of steganography: it sought to render an individual's status invisible in plain sight, to not only obscure identity, but to hide the fact that it was doing so. This was certainly a lesson taken to heart by the Jesuits who came to England in the late sixteenth century. They were not only permitted to eschew their traditional priestly apparel on the grounds that it was likely to interfere with their mission, but were provided with a new set of clothes before setting off to England.[102] Merely by changing one's wardrobe, identity could be rewritten. As with all attempts at disguise, however, familiarity tended to reduce effectiveness. In 1608, Thomas Howard, 3rd Viscount Howard of Bindon, wrote to Salisbury concerning a Jesuit recently apprehended in Lyme Regis who had 'hidden in the lining of his cloak two several testaments for his better credit with dangerous English miscreants'. His initial misfortune was that he had been 'attired in the manner of Jesuits when they come into this land'.[103] Just as Howard was not to be hoodwinked by a mere cloak, there was more to maintaining a convincing illusion of being 'Lady Dorothy' than simply donning a dress, a wig and a beauty patch or two.

THE COUNTERFEITING OF ROBERT GRAY

Thus far we have considered disguises, whether of words, letters or people, in terms of avoiding suspicion, of replacing true identity with something innocuous such that the item or person in question might remain hidden in plain sight. There is, of course, another aspect to disguise – that of making something appear grander or larger than it is in reality. Such physical sleights of hand might include misinformation, such as Elizabeth Stuart, sometime queen of Bohemia, sending a letter describing the duke of Buckingham's calamitous attempt to sack the port of Cádiz and plunder Spanish treasure ships in 1625 as a qualified success to a friend in the sure knowledge that it would be intercepted by the enemy.[104] This type of disguise could also be reproduced on a personal scale. Perhaps the most audacious example of this was carried out by Thomas Douglas, a Scotsman who, apparently aggrieved at his lack of preferment, unleashed a series of events that saw him counterfeiting rather more than a few letters.

At around the same time that Christopher Porter was arrested for counterfeiting the signature of Robert Cecil, the secretary of state numbered the glibbery Thomas Douglas amongst his intelligencers.[105] Douglas was nephew to a notorious forger, the parson of Glasgow Archibald Douglas, a man thought by some to be involved in the murders of David Rizzio and Henry, Lord Darnley, respectively the secretary and husband of Mary, Queen of Scots. Many believed him responsible for the Casket Letters of 1567. He was certainly behind a series of forgeries that 'implicated Esmé Stewart, Duke of Lennox, in popish plots'.[106] He had also served as a spy for Walsingham in 1583, and soon after was appointed Scottish ambassador in London. While Archibald had died in poverty in 1602, his nephew Thomas might be forgiven for believing that, with a late but infamous ambassador for an uncle and an influential employer in the shape of Robert Cecil, the accession of King James VI of Scotland to the throne of England in 1603 would be the making of him.[107] Cecil appears not to have held his Scots intelligencer in particularly high esteem, however, considering some of his 'intelligence' to be arrant nonsense, while allegedly dismissing him as 'an open-mouthed fellow, and apt to lie'.[108] He thus employed him solely at the grittier end of business. When the expected smooth and graceful slide into a position at court through which he might enrich himself failed to materialise, Douglas took matters into his own hands. He fell in with two other disaffected Scots, James Stewart and Robert Wood, and the trio promptly pooled their resources in order to seize what they considered their just deserts.

Thomas was already, like his uncle before him, an accomplished counterfeiter.[109] In January 1604 the three men set about forging documents granting the bearer the right to provide a particular set of goods or services, which they promptly sold to a merchant for the tidy sum of £300 (around £40,000 today).[110] Such highly lucrative licences were granted by the crown, and often represented a thank-you for services rendered. These letters were authenticated by the monarch's sign manual and the signet.[111] Unfortunately for the intrepid trio, the Treason Act of 1554 had made the counterfeiting of the sign manual and the signet as dangerous as counterfeiting the Great and Privy seals. Douglas, Stewart and Wood were now guilty of treason.[112] On hearing the news that the merchant who had bought their forgeries had not only been arrested for possessing counterfeit papers but had immediately declared that he had received them 'from a Scot', Douglas and Wood decided that they ought take a protracted sojourn to Calais in the interests of their continued good health.[113] Stewart either elected to remain in London or was arrested before he was able to flee. In any case, he was subsequently tried and executed for treason, while Wood and Douglas were exiled in absentia.[114]

While this foray into the dark side had netted Wood and Douglas considerably more money than Christopher Porter might have hoped to clear in even a year of dedicated and flawless forgery using his signature-stamps, the risk assumed had also been somewhat greater: while the act might well have endangered Porter's ears, forging Cecil's signature was not treason.[115] It was from his temporary base in Calais that Douglas promulgated a far more audacious act of forgery. Rather than counterfeiting a mere document,

Fig. 36: The introductory letter of 'Robert Gray', as forged by Thomas Douglas and presented to Oldenbarnevelt. It remains in the archives of the Dutch States General, without any indication that it is, in fact, a counterfeit.

Douglas counterfeited himself, and in doing so would almost bamboozle an entire continent.

On 2 August 1604, a man 'of medium height, wearing a light beard, sharp-featured, and with prominent eyebrows, and lacking several teeth' presented the grand pensionary of the Dutch Republic, Johan van Oldenbarnevelt, with a letter from the new king of England, James I, in favour of one 'Robert Gray, a Gentleman of our Bedchamber' (Fig. 36).[116] The letter was as fake as the man who presented it. 'Robert Gray' was the invention of Thomas Douglas.[117] Nevertheless, it appears that Oldenbarnevelt was impressed with this new 'sharp-featured' face at court, to the point of offering the Scot a commission in the Dutch army. Douglas, or Gray as he now presented himself, had not come all this way to be a soldier, and so returned to Calais where he promptly offered his services as intelligencer to the port's governor, Dominique de Vic. Douglas had already planned his next trip, to the heart of the Spanish Netherlands, and he thought de Vic might forward him some money in return for information gathered there. Douglas appears to have been a persuasive individual, as while de Vic refused his kind offer of possible secrets in the future in return for ready cash in the present, the Scot still managed to convince the governor's son that a loan of £10 was perfectly safe. And so, coffers bolstered, and armed with another letter of introduction, Douglas once again assumed the identity of 'Robert Gray, Gentleman of the King's Bedchamber', and made his way to Brussels.[118] On his arrival, he suggested to Archduke Albert, who ruled the Spanish Netherlands alongside his wife Isabella Clara Eugenia, that he might help enlist Scots and English soldiers to support the Spanish in their campaign against the rebellious Dutch – not something that would have pleased his new friend Oldenbarnevelt. While Douglas did not in the end carry out this task, the trip was hardly a failure, as he returned to Calais clutching 100 gold pieces, a token of friendship given to him by Blasius, Archduke Albert's secretary.

Having tested his handiwork in The Hague and Brussels, and thus convinced that his credentials were sufficient to persuade Protestant and Catholic powers alike, Douglas upped his game. Using a new set of letters that introduced him as a special envoy of King James, he embarked on an embassy to the courts of the German Electors, the four princes and three bishops who were responsible for choosing the Holy Roman Emperor – the emperor-in-waiting was traditionally installed as such by having the title 'king of the Romans' conferred upon him. Even though Douglas appears to have suggested that his mission was very hush-hush (presumably in order to explain why an ambassador would turn up at a European court with no retinue), flying below the radar did not mean he did not need to look the part, and alongside his letters of introduction and his undeniable chutzpah, he sported a grand-looking ambassadorial chain stolen from the son of the Polish ambassador in London.[119]

The first port of call on the whistle-stop tour of 'Robert Gray, ambassador to the newly installed king of England' was the seat of the archbishop of Cologne. The simple act of undertaking the 250-mile journey perhaps in itself suggests the measure of Douglas's seriousness, and on arrival he not only found his expenses defrayed and his arms laden with gifts, but it appears

148

that he so beguiled the senators that they wrote to James by way of response to the message he brought. As it happened – and whether by chance or design is something of a mystery – there was another prestigious visitor in town, the papal nuncio. Hearing of Gray's presence, the nuncio invited him to a formal banquet, where the two of them discussed the possibility of King James being elected to the imperial dignity.

At first glance this seems a ludicrous idea, but rumblings of discontent were stirring. The current emperor, Rudolf II, had instigated a war with the Ottomans which was hurting many of the Electors where they felt it most deeply, in their purses. The fact that his younger brother Matthias, who was most likely to replace him, was particularly anti-Protestant did not help matters either. Matthias had not, however, been officially elected king of the Romans, so technically there remained a way of saving the situation. However unlikely it might have seemed, James was already considered to favour peace over war as a general principle, and, while a committed Calvinist, was known for his toleration of Catholics in general. What was more, he had already been in contact with the Pope in the run-up to the death of Elizabeth I (though he denied it, naturally, and his secretary Sir James Elphinstone had been made a scapegoat for the rumours). Indeed, both Spain and France had allegedly promised to support his claim to the English crown should he promise tolerance of Catholics once he ascended the throne. Had negotiations reached up to this level, then they would certainly have involved Cecil, who was working for both Elizabeth and James in the months before the succession question was rendered absolutely imperative by the English queen's death. Douglas would later assert that Cecil knew all about his mission. Spreading such a rumour was certainly within Cecil's ambit, but it seems more likely that there was an amount of wishful thinking going on. As Francis Bacon sagely observed, 'man would rather believe what he wishes to be true'.[120] Wherever the idea had come from, it appears that Douglas had, in a heartbeat, moved from counterfeiting an ambassador to counterfeiting England's geopolitical strategy.

Douglas's visit to Cologne was successful on many levels, not least financially – he set out on the next leg of his embassy in a coach lent to him by the papal nuncio and accompanied by a new luxury alongside the many gifts he was now laden with: three newly hired servants. At a mere 18 miles, the journey to see the archbishop of Trier in Bonn was somewhat shorter than his trip to Cologne had been, which must have come as some relief: it also proved rather less successful. The archbishop of Trier treated 'Gray' with enough suspicion to make him move on almost immediately to Aschaffenburg (a journey of almost 125 miles), where he spoke with the next spiritual Elector on his list, the archbishop of Mainz, who 'entertained me sumptuously, gave me presents and provided me with a coach and lackeys'.[121] Whether or not Douglas was serious in his ministrations, truly believing that he was well on the way to securing the four electoral votes that would guarantee James's election as king of the Romans, or whether his treatment in Cologne and Mainz had made him overly ambitious, the wheels were about to come off his (borrowed) coach.

The fourth – and final – leg of Douglas's journey saw him travel to Heidelberg, the seat of the Elector Palatine. Explanations differ as to exactly what it was that made the Calvinist Friedrich IV suspicious of this Catholic ambassador purporting to come from England's new king, but familiarity doubtless played a part – unlike the Catholic Electors, who had seen no good reason to engage with the Calvinist king of a relatively minor European country, Friedrich had dealt with James when he was only king of Scotland. Whatever the reason, Friedrich saw enough in the ambassador's documents to believe that they were not what they seemed, and promptly threw the Scotsman into jail, sending a message to James asking whether he should send the miscreant back or deal with him in situ. Much to the prisoner's chagrin (Douglas begged Friedrich to instead send him to fight the Ottomans, a move perhaps only marginally less likely to result in a grisly demise), James wanted him back, possibly in order that he could better scotch the rumour that he desired the imperial crown. (This was not the last time that James's friends in Europe would help him; Friedrich would later repeat the favour when William Baldwin, a man thought complicit in the Gunpowder Plot, turned up in the Palatinate but was also sent home to meet his fate.)[122]

Douglas eventually made three confessions, two in the dungeons of Heidelberg and one in London's Tower. These confessions are as slippery as the man himself, and tell different stories. Douglas first takes responsibility for writing the letters himself, before changing his story and insisting that 'they were written to his dictation by a poor Frenchman lodging "in an alehouse near the tennis court in the Blackfriars"'.[123] He first blamed the conveniently disembowelled Stewart (whose spiral-locked plea for clemency had proved unsuccessful) for the initial counterfeiting of the king's signature, suggesting that he obtained the Privy Seal of Scotland with which he had provided the final authorisation by borrowing it from his brother James, who worked for the Scottish secretary Elphinstone. Eventually, he confessed that 'in truth he caused the said Privy Seal to be counterfeited, and therewith sealed six letters, unto six Princes of Germany [i.e., all the Electors bar the king of Bohemia], counterfeiting the king's hand to every one of them'.[124] Wherever the truth lies, it seems that the successful counterfeiting of documents was a joint enterprise – clumsily counterfeited documents could slip through unnoticed if the official checking them either lacked familiarity with their usual form or simply could not be bothered (or did not desire) to inspect them fully.

The story of Thomas Douglas shows that the counterfeiting of documents was no mere matter of petty fraud or even exposing conspiracies. In the wrong hands, it could potentially change the course of history. Douglas left England in June 1604, and spent much of the next seven months living it up as 'Robert Gray', his one-man embassy blazing a trail through some of the richest courts in Europe, negotiating (if he is to be believed) for King James to accede to the imperial throne. At the end of January 1605, Gray had arrived in Heidelberg, where his embassy juddered to a halt. By the end of May, he was being escorted back to England, Thomas Douglas once more. On 24 June, he was committed to the Tower, his fate all but sealed. After a brief trial, Douglas was found guilty of treason and other 'prancks', and put to death.[125] His brief time in the spotlight shows us something of the sheer power and authority the royal sign manual carried with it, especially when wielded by a man who must have possessed no little charisma. It is no hyperbole to say that Robert Gray, ambassador to King James, was a disguise Thomas Douglas created with a signature, a seal and outrageous self-confidence.

4

---◇---

INKS & INVISIBILITY

In 1584, Mary, Queen of Scots wrote to the French ambassador at Elizabeth I's court, Michel de Castelnau, on the subject of invisible ink. She informed him that 'the best and most secret writing is alum dissolved in a little clear water twenty-four hours before you want to write'. The invisible writing could then be revealed, hopefully by the intended recipient, by dipping the paper in a bowl of water: the writing would appear white and could be read until the paper dried, when it would disappear once more. Alum writing could also be revealed by heat, though this would leave the secret message permanently exposed.[1] Alum, or potassium aluminium sulphate, was commonly used for pickling food and was thus found in most pantries, and it also had a more industrial use as a mordant (or fixer) for dyes in the textile trade. Its use as an invisible ink – or white ink, as it was commonly termed – was no great secret, however, and can be seen in many contemporary recipe books and miscellanies,[2] such as this example written in the last decades of the sixteenth century (Fig. 37).

By the beginning of 1586, however, Mary appears to have changed her mind, writing from Chartley to Guillaume de l'Aubespine de Châteauneuf, Castelnau's successor, that 'writing with alum is very common, and easy to be suspected and discovered'. Nevertheless, Mary did suggest that it could still be used in certain ways, such as on deliveries of 'white taffeta or a similar cloth', possibly because water revealed alum writing on fabric with great speed and clarity, especially when compared to the heat reveal on paper.[3]

It is unlikely to be a coincidence that in this very same month, the dark artificer Arthur Gregory wrote to Sir Francis Walsingham on the same subject, from his 'poor house': 'the writing with alum is discovered diverse

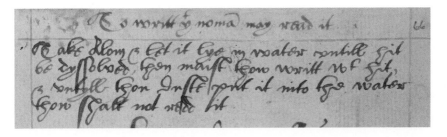

Fig. 37: 'To writt y.ᵉ no ma[n] may read it. / Take Alom & let it lye in water vntill hit / be dyssolved, then maist thou writt w.ᵗ hit, / & vntyll thou duste put it into the water / thou shalt not redd hit.'

ways; with fire & with water, which they use; but most apparently by rubbing of coal dust thereon which bringeth it forth white'. Walsingham had read both Mary's letter extolling the virtues of alum as well as her conclusion that it was too easily discovered (these letters survive in the archives as copies produced by Thomas Phelippes). Perhaps mindful of Walsingham's many responsibilities and the value of his time, Gregory included a helpful post-script running up the letter's left-hand margin: 'If your honnor rub this powder within the black lyne the letters will appear white' (Fig. 38). Historians have suggested that Gregory included a small package of coal dust with his letter.[4] It seems much more likely that he expected Walsingham to source his own 'dust', however, as it would be readily available from any nearby fireplace. In either case, what this letter truly shows is Gregory's understanding of the power of direct experience (see Fig. 39).

Ever mindful of incriminating himself when displaying his mastery of the darker arts of subterfuge, considering the generally felt connection between dissimulation, dishonesty and things demonic, Gregory went to great lengths to protect himself from accusations of impropriety: 'in my trying that ever was required to be done, I never failed or made default, & voluntarily protesting, before the face of God, that I never put pen to paper, nor did any other thing for practice, but on so sudden executed that which I have been commanded unto by authority abhorring and detesting all knavish use of whatsoever'.[5] In essence, Gregory was reminding Walsingham of the lengths to which he was going in order to improve his technical mastery of the cat-and-mouse game of invisible inks, writing of his 'trial of many ways to

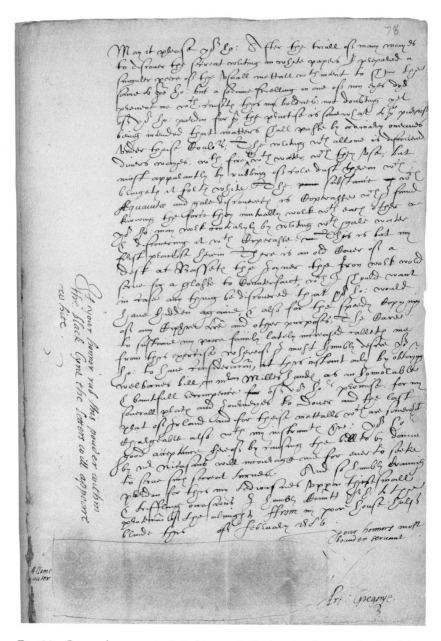

Fig. 38: Gregory's postscript is in his own italic hand – the main body of the
letter had been written by a secretary. Writing in one's own hand
communicated intimacy, appropriate when dealing with secrets, and it
allowed him to demonstrate his skill with invisible inks.

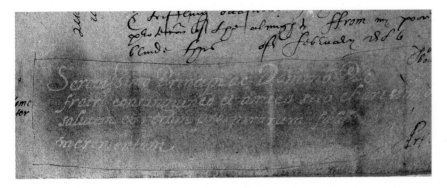

Fig. 39: Detail of Fig. 38. Someone, whether Walsingham himself or a servant, has dutifully rubbed coal dust into the area delineated by Gregory, as instructed, thus revealing the hidden words. The actual Latin message is a formulaic message of goodwill.

discover the secret writing on white papers', which also included another type of invisible ink: 'The substance which Aquavita and gall discovereth is copperas which I find knowing the force they mutually work with each other and Your Lordship may work contrarily by writing with gall water & discovering it with copperas: This is but my first practise herein.'[6]

Gregory was not breaking new ground here so much as retreading it – as was the case with many other technologies, Europe staggered blindly in the rather more secure footsteps of the ancients and the Chinese when it came to writing. In the third century BCE, Philo of Byzantium had recommended using gall-water as an invisible ink on human skin or clean fabric (such as a 'new hat') with copperas applied with a 'sponge' acting as its reagent ('a substance used in testing for other substances, or for reacting with them in a particular way; (more widely) any substance used in chemical reactions'),[7] and revealing the hidden message.[8] Walsingham may already have been aware of the use of coal dust as a substance that could reveal invisible writing – some two centuries after Philo, the poet Ovid commented on its use in revealing secret messages written in new milk, a technique favoured, he asserted, by milkmaids writing love letters.[9] For their part, the Chinese were not only manufacturing paper long before the continental Europeans, but they were also aware of the white ink properties of alum in the twelfth century, though on at least one occasion considered it akin to magic.[10]

The combination of gall-water and copperas mentioned by Gregory had two particular advantages. The first was that it was reversible (as Gregory had discovered in his home laboratory): you could use copperas as your ink and gall-water as your reveal, or, vice versa, use gall-water as your ink and copperas as your reveal. The second was that its ingredients would not look out of place on any writing desk, as the two substances comprised a standard black ink recipe.[11] This property ensured that whichever substance was used for the white ink, the application of the other was, to all intents and purposes, the act of mixing black ink on the paper itself.

Given the common usage of these ingredients, one might expect the gall-water–copperas invisible ink combination, and particularly its reversible nature, to be rather more widely known. And yet, some seventy years after Gregory's letter, we find a Royalist member of the marquess of Ormond's circle suggesting that this pairing was, if not unknown, perhaps largely forgotten: 'the secret that I. Ogilby gave (namely the powder of gall in water, to be washed over with the powder of calcined copperas) is not discovered, but may be safely used'.[12] (Another in the same circle simply referred to 'the English Nunn's powder', suggesting that a woman had introduced them to the secret.)[13] This apparent loss of collective memory might simply be attributed to the relative rarity of surreptitious letters being sent on a regular basis over a protracted period of time by the same people.

Whether or not the simple convenience of gall-water–copperas invisible ink was forgotten, recovered and promptly forgotten again, it is certainly true that if it was a secret, it was not a particularly well-hidden one. An indication of just how easily these recipes could be found, and yet how secret those who used them believed them to be, can be seen in the memoirs of Anne Halkett, an active member of a Royalist spy ring in Edinburgh in the 1650s (when she was still Anne Murray). This spy ring counted the exiled Charles II amongst their correspondents, and used a type of invisible ink they believed was known only to them. One of the circle, Sir George Mackenzie, happened to be perusing the wares of a Scottish stationer when he found the recipe for 'their' secret ink staring back at him in black and white from the pages of a book. His fellow conspirator, Sir Robert Moray, suggested that this visibility might be an advantage. As Halkett put it, 'the only hopes he had was, that if that book came into their English hands they would not believe any thing so common as to be in print would be made use of in any business of consequence'.[14]

Not only were these formulae scattered amongst the manuscript miscellanies or recipe books that were to be found in many households, and in any number of the so-called Renaissance books of secrets that flew off the presses in the fifteenth and sixteenth centuries, but from 1589 they were included in the second edition of Giambattista della Porta's bestselling *Magiae Naturalis*. The recipes and techniques listed by della Porta were not unique to him – like many early modern writers, he was perfectly happy to crib his techniques from any source he could uncover.[15] While most miscellanies and ancient works that mentioned invisible writing contained just a handful of recipes, della Porta's *Magiae Naturalis* boasted an entire chapter devoted to the art. It was by far the most comprehensive collection available.

While an English translation of della Porta, entitled *Natural Magick*, would not hit the stands until 1658, the playwright and one-time spy Ben Jonson's epigram 'The New Cry' suggests that by 1610 the Italian's work had become a must-read for the would-be politiques and scoundrels of the day, and that they could find a veritable cornucopia of espionage techniques between its pages: 'They all get Porta for the sundry ways / To write in cipher, and the several keys / To ope the character. They've found the sleight / With juice of lemons, onions, piss, to write, / To break up seals and close 'em.'[16] In terms of invisible inks, Jonson mentions only sour and stinking liquids, possibly because he was intent on satirising those who saw conspiracies everywhere, but lemon juice was the substance that people remembered. Thirty years after Jonson, lemon juice and white ink were practically synonymous, so much so that Abraham Cowley, the spy, poet and cipher secretary to Queen Henrietta Maria, could write a poem entitled 'Written in Juice of Lemmon' and feel comfortable that everyone would know what he meant.[17] Lemon juice is particularly flexible as it reveals in water or heat. In water the words become visible (albeit not with the clarity of a heat reveal) and disappear as the paper dries: once dried, the paper will not reveal its message again. When the first reveal is achieved through the application of heat, however, the message is permanently scorched into view (the acidic nature of

Fig. 40: It was common to end a secret letter with the words 'burn after reading'. When using heat to reveal a white ink, one had to be careful not to burn the letter *before* reading.

the juice causes the inked paper to oxidise quicker than the surrounding areas when exposed to heat).[18]

The lemon juice–heat reveal method first became popular in sixteenth-century Italy, but it was soon disseminated more widely: an anonymous Dutch recipe book, *Dat batement van recepten* (1549), cites an Italian work from 1525 when describing lemon juice as suitable for use as an invisible ink.[19] The first documented use of lemon juice as the basis of an invisible ink, however, is to be found within an Arabic manual for secretaries, *Subh al-Ashā* (1412), by al-Qalqashandī, but it did not use a direct heat reveal.[20] Al-Qalqashandī's recipe called for an equal amount of fried 'black [i.e., dried] lemon with colocynth root (a strong laxative sometimes called bitter apple or bitter cucumber) in olive oil', a mixture that could then be thickened using egg yolk. This formula required a very simple reagent that was rarely available to a conspirator: time. The mixture appears to have had an affinity for mould, as in time 'hair was supposed to grow where the writing had been'.[21]

Jonson's satirical poem may have suggested that by the early seventeenth century practically everyone knew that to make invisible writing required a lemon or an onion – assuming one had limited access to urine – and had got this knowledge from *Magiae Naturalis*, but this may be somewhat over-stating the case. Della Porta's perennially popular tome was somewhat more comprehensive than Jonson allowed, as it also included alum, the gall-water–copperas combination and several more besides: altogether he lists fourteen substances that can be used as discrete invisible inks (vitriol, gall-water, alum, orange juice, lemon juice, fat (of several kinds), urine, sour grape juice, services (fruit of the sorb tree), ammoniac salt, gum, fig-tree milk, milk of tithymalus and vinegar), seven mixtures (burnt straw in vinegar, galls in wine, cherry juice and calamus, vinegar with egg white and quicksilver, gum with salt, gum and lime, and goat's suet with turpentine) and even two ways to write on a stone (gall and vitriol powder plus gum juniper – the reveal is achieved with vinegar).[22]

If there was a tendency towards repeating old prescriptions, albeit not entirely uncritically, there was also a place for invisible ink amongst those involved in experimental science. Robert Boyle, the Irish natural philosopher and chemist, not only subjected recipes such as gall-water and copperas to experimental scrutiny, investigating quantities and how, for example, ink might be erased and even its colour changed, but also considered new possibilities. One of these, though, it must be said, hardly the most practical, was the serum of human blood (the clear fluid left after blood has coagulated). In his Appendix to the *Memoirs for the History of Human Blood* (1684), Boyle wrote of how he first hypothesised and then tested a potential invisible ink experi-mentally: 'Having formerly had occasion to observe, that man's urine would tolerably well serve for what they call an invisible ink; and having considered (when I remembered this) the great affinity that is supposed to be between urine and the serum of blood, I thought fit to try, whether the latter might not be employed like the former, to make a kind of invisible ink.'[23] Boyle's mention of the 'great affinity . . . between urine and the serum of blood' brings to mind

Gregory's earlier mention of the 'mutual force' worked between gall-water and copperas, and how this knowledge led him to the understanding that they made a reversible ink, suggesting that Gregory's experiments were not quite the undirected stumbling in the dark they might at first appear.[24] Certainly, investigation into the nature of things, along with the desire to work from experience rather than simply to regurgitate past authors, would lead some to consider recipes that might be thought somewhat fanciful: 'That which is written with the water of putrified willow, or the distilled juice of glow-worms, will not be visible but in the dark, as Porta affirms from his own experience.'[25] The sixteenth-century Italian naturalist Ulisse Aldrovandi attributed the creation of an ink that could be read at night but not during the daytime to his contemporary, the Dutch physician and classical scholar Hadrianus Junius.[26] The idea itself derived from the mythical *liquor lucidus*, a liquid light source prepared from glow-worms (and sometimes fish scales) and which was alleged to possess great luminescent qualities, the history of which stretched back at least as far as the thirteenth-century German philosopher and theologian Albertus Magnus. In 1658, Thomas Muffet's *Theatre of Insects* recorded several methods of creating this liquor, the commonest of which involved burying the glow-worms in manure for several days or mixing them with mercury, and sometimes distilling the liquor that resulted, though he was quite clear in stating that it did not work.[27]

NOW YOU SEE ME (NOW YOU DON'T)

Simply knowing what might serve as an invisible ink was not enough to enable secret communication, of course. Invisible ink is of no use if the recipient cannot render the message visible. Well aware of this fact, della Porta usefully categorised his inks by way of their reveal, that is, how the invisible was to be rendered visible – not all invisible writing gave up its secrets at the merest hint of a naked flame. There were three primary categories: those that were revealed by application of liquid; those that became visible through exposure to heat or fire; and those exposed by the application of dust (by which he generally means carbon powder, or coal dust). Furthermore, della Porta counted five liquids amongst those that acted to reveal invisible writing – vitriol, water, solution of litharge (lead(II) oxide), vinegar and gall solution – each of which acts as a reagent when introduced to its partner ink. The same process was true of a heat reveal – the proximity of heat causes a chemical reaction to occur (or accelerates it) within the substance used for the ink (in lemon juice, for example, this reaction is oxidation). Other reveals occur for more straightforwardly physical reasons – fat repels water, so on soaking a stone that has been written on in goat fat, the untreated areas of stone will change colour, rendering the letters visible, for example.[28]

While the proliferation of books and recipes for invisible ink were a major boon for the prospective dark artificer, they did not automatically transform one into a master of the art of invisible writing. Recipes could, and did, fail, often because they included information that was simply incorrect. John Cotgrave's *Wits Interpreter* (1655), for example, included several recipes taken directly from della Porta that appear to have been badly translated.[29] Cotgrave's version of the gall-water–copperas invisible ink would, if followed directly, have disappointed the casual experimenter: 'Take Chalcentum [copperas] and dissolve it in water, then take some galls, and gently bruised, put them in water letting them stand so a day and a night, then strain it, and with the water write your mind on a piece of white paper, and send it to your friend, when you would have them seen dip the letter first in water.'[30] Plain water, of course, would do absolutely nothing in this instance. As della Porta had suggested, the letters needed to be dipped into 'the first liquor', that is, the copperas solution, to render the writing visible.[31] Whether Cotgrave's error was introduced by a translator, writer or compositor, it clearly shows how easy it was to get things wrong. Della Porta was careful to indicate when he had tried a technique himself, such as when he noted of Africanus's famous technique of writing on eggs that he 'could do nothing of it'; he did report success in lighting rooms with the liquid of glow-worms, so perhaps even he was not infallible.[32]

Getting a recipe wrong was potentially disastrous, as using an inappropriate reveal could render the message unreadable forever. Dipping a lemon-juice letter in water, for example, might reveal the message, but only temporarily, and once the letters had faded, they could not be coaxed back into life – the reveal would effectively wash the white ink away. In a similar fashion, a few short swipes of a gall-water-infused cloth over a message already written in gall-water would render the entire message unreadable, as subsequent use of the correct reveal, copperas, would now merely produce inky smears where once were words. It is for this reason that Robert Bowes, the English ambassador to Scotland, approached suspected letters, blanks which bore signatures but no other writing (one was signed by the spy William Herle), with caution and some anxiety: 'sundry of these blanks are filled & be written with ink of white vitriol prepared. Which I shall shortly (by God's grace) try & discover'.[33]

Arthur Gregory had good reason to remind first Walsingham, and later Robert Cecil, of the effort and experimentation that was involved in acquiring his expertise, not to mention the effects mixing poisonous recipes had had on his health, as he attempted to consolidate what little patronage he had already acquired. The dark artificer needed skills beyond the merely chemical if he was to catch any would-be conspirator in the act.

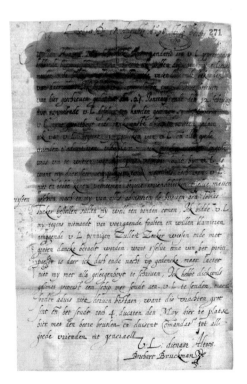

Fig. 41: It paid to be careful when handling potential invisible ink letters. In his overzealous search for invisible ink between the lines, this letter's interceptor has rendered the first few lines of the letter illegible.

WHERE BE THE INVISIBLE WRITING?

It was all well and good having a list of the various invisible inks available, quite another to identify when and where they were being used. A dark artificer such as Gregory would have had to infer the presence of invisible writing in the first place from whatever clues were available, and space was, of course, one of the most important prerequisites. Della Porta interspersed his invisible ink recipes with handy hints on their employment: 'So we may bring forth letters written between the verses, and in the close setting together, or larger distances of syllables. Let the Epistle contain some void space, that the letters may not be seen; and if this be intercepted, it will hardly be read.'[34] Hiding invisible ink messages 'between the lines' was certainly a common technique, as in the message from Arnault Backer to Sir Robert Williamson shown in Fig. 42.[35] A letter's interceptor might thus infer the presence of invisible writing from any suspiciously empty space, as della Porta suggested, while the letter itself might contain instructions as to where to find or include

Fig. 42: Here, Dutch lines in black, plain ink are interspersed by English lines in (revealed) invisible ink. The invisible ink is either copperas or gall-water, and has been revealed by its 'partner' ink.

163

invisible writing. When Lord Inchiquin wrote to Catherine Grey in Paris in August 1659, for example, he did so following a series of letters showing that they both used an invisible ink recipe made from an unnamed but apparently expensive and poisonous white powder – a recipe so complicated that having burnt it in order to avoid being found in possession of such incriminating evidence, he realised he could not remember how it worked. When the time came to use this invisible ink, he approached the subject from an obtuse angle: 'I pray neglect not now to use the powder', he wrote, before informing his correspondent to 'apply it as well between the Ribbs [jargon for 'lines']'.[36] He thus hid his instructions under a cloak of medical discourse. In another letter, Edmund Wyndham chastises the recipient for failing to follow instructions: 'I wonder that you had forgotten the directions I gave you how to give notice when you made use of the powder, which was to give a dash after your name as I have done. & if you can by that discover mine, I shall by the same discover yours, & therefore I pray try this which you now receive.' This time, his correspondent understood the message perfectly, and, having spotted the dash that came after Wyndham's initials, revealed the invisible ink message that lay hidden between Wyndham's lines with a few careful wipes of his reagent-infused cloth or sponge.[37] Back in 1586, Mary, Queen of Scots had suggested that if Châteauneuf were to send her messages in alum, they would be best hidden in quires (collated foldings of manuscript) sent to her by his secretaries, with the presence of invisible ink indicated by the addition of a piece of green string to every volume so extended. There was no further need to indicate where in the booklet the secret writing was inserted: 'always write on the fourth, eighth, twelfth and sixteenth page and so on, proceeding by fours', Mary instructed her correspondent, 'so there is no need to make a mark to know where something has been written'.[38]

There was, of course, always the option of simply trying a reveal to see what happened, even though such an action might prevent the letter from being sent on its merry way (see Fig. 43). While Gregory had previously informed Walsingham of his work on the 'many ways to discover the secret writing on white papers', he would direct Cecil to this same expertise some twelve years later: 'May it please your honour I have tried all parts

Fig. 43: Sometimes the dark artificer was left searching for letters on an empty page.

of the letter to satisfy your honour's desire but could find nothing I durst have assured your Lordship without trial that there should be nothing, beside my knowledge of the letter's manner of spacious writing.'[39] For all his expertise, Gregory was not able to reveal invisible writing that was not there, no matter how much Cecil wished it to be. This letter not only shows that Gregory was quite diligent in his searches, but also that he had faith in his hard-won experience – something for which there was no substitute, whether you were a conspirator or counter-espionage operative. Sadly, neither Gregory nor any other left a clue as to how one might spot the presence of invisible writing without trial and error. It should come as no surprise, however, that in the aftermath of the Gunpowder Plot, when imprisoned suspects were known, or at least suspected, of using invisible ink in their communications, the man whom Cecil turned to was Arthur Gregory. His skills would be tested to their utmost, as he was to first reveal, and then counterfeit, the correspondence between Henry Garnett and Anne Vaux.

INVISIBLE INKS, VISIBLE SIGNS

Forging the various parts of a letter was anything but easy, even when one had clear examples of the hand, the signature, the seal and the style of locking to copy – and plenty of time in which to do it. Add the complication of hidden messages written in invisible ink and the task became all the more difficult. Arthur Gregory was no one-trick pony. While his talents are generally seen to begin and end with the imperceptible opening and closing of letters, he was something of an innovator in spycraft techniques, as he would regularly remind both Sir Francis Walsingham and the Cecils, William and Robert, over the final years of the sixteenth century. This notwithstanding, his employment by the state was somewhat ad hoc, and he appears to have retired from active duty in 1601. It took a national crisis to lure him back into the fray, a crisis which finally brought Gregory the recognition, and the financial reward, that he felt he had deserved all along. The year was 1606, and his actions in 'deciphering A Letter in the GunPowder Treason' won him a pension of £400 per annum.[40] Gregory was not noted for his skill as a cryptanalyst, however, and nor do those ciphered writings connected to the Gunpowder Plot seem significant.[41] In any case, Walsingham's top cryptanalyst, Thomas Phelippes, was still available for such duties, even if he was at this point languishing in some dank prison cell or other.[42] As we have seen in other instances, 'deciphering' could also simply mean the ability to read or make legible, but Gregory's real contribution was rather more impressive.[43]

Gregory had been called in to help tidy up the ragged edges of the conspiracy, and his 'secret services' this time involved a little more than the standard 'intercept, copy, reseal and forward' rigmarole, as he explained to Sir Robert Cecil: 'Your Lordship hath had a present trial of that which none but my self hath done before, to write in an other man's hand, & discovering the secret writing, being in blank; to abuse a most cunning villain in his own subtilty, & leaving the same at last in blank again; wherein though there be difficulty, their answers show, they have no suspicion.'[44] Gregory had taken letters written with invisible ink, revealed their secrets, and rendered them invisible once again. He did not mean this literally. The only white ink which could fade back in and out of invisibility was alum, and this would only occur if it had been revealed with water (once dried, it could be revealed permanently with heat). Using a water reveal in these circumstances, namely when white and black ink messages were written onto the same piece of paper, could cause problems: while the white ink message might fade away once the paper dries, the process might well damage the paper itself, betraying that someone had been searching for invisible ink. Whatever reveal a dark artificer might use would prevent the original letter from being forwarded on to its addressee after its sojourn on his desk: the water reveal would most likely leave evidence on the paper, while the heat reveal's message would not fade away. What Gregory means by the words 'leaving the same at last in blank again' is that he re-created the original letters, white ink and all.

The letters received by the correspondents in question – the Jesuit priest Henry Garnett and his acolyte Anne Vaux, a recusant gentlewoman – were thus counterfeits. By reproducing those passages written in white ink, Gregory kept the correspondence alive while his superiors watched and waited to see if Garnett and Vaux would share any new information about the Gunpowder Plot. Gregory's counterfeit letters were presumably destroyed, cast by Garnett and Vaux into the very fire that had revealed them. The original letters, their invisible passages revealed and annotated for use as evidence, remained in the possession of the authorities, and thus are now to be found in Hatfield and The National Archives at Kew. While, in the end, these letters proved of little use to Cecil and company, they tell us much about the practical problems invisible inks posed for both conspirator and counter-espionage operative alike.

CAUGHT UP IN THE AFTERMATH: HENRY GARNETT

Having finished his training at the Jesuit seminary in Rome, Henry Garnett entered England in 1586, a mere two years after the passing of an act banishing all Roman Catholic priests from the country. Within a matter of months he had become England's Jesuit superior, his continued freedom dependent on the goodwill of the sympathisers and recusants who both sheltered him and accommodated his performances of the Catholic Mass. Having evaded the authorities for some twenty years, he fell victim to the anti-Catholic fervour that had gripped the country following the abject failure of the Gunpowder Plot, and was apprehended in February 1606. The plot, also known as the Powder Treason, was designed to place a Catholic on the throne of England. In order to effect this change of regime, Robert Catesby and his band of desperadoes sought to dispose of the incumbent monarch, the Protestant James I, and his heir, Crown Prince Henry, in spectacular fashion – by blowing up Westminster during the state opening of Parliament on 5 November. The plot was discovered, with Guy Fawkes famously captured on the evening of the 4th as he hid, matches at the ready, beside thirty-six barrels of gunpowder in an undercroft attached to the House of Lords. As the highest-ranking Jesuit in England, Garnett was well aware of Catesby, his supporters and their desire to foment rebellion – desires he had repeatedly and pointedly counselled against. He had also been told of the existence of this particular plot by Catesby's confessor, Oswald Tesimond.[45] It mattered little, however, as Garnett was ruled by his conscience: the information had come to him via the sacred act of confession, so Garnett felt unable to inform the authorities as was his duty under law. When news of the plot's ignominious failure spread, Garnett went to ground in a bid to escape the inevitable fallout, and even wrote to the English Privy Council declaring himself innocent of any involvement.[46] It was all to no avail, as on 15 January 1606 he was declared an accessory and a warrant was duly issued for his arrest. His lair, perhaps predictably in such times, was betrayed. Following a tip-off and an intensive search, Garnett was finally discovered, filthy and barely able to walk, in one of the many squalid priest-holes that had been built into the walls of Hindlip Hall in Worcestershire to hide men such as he. He had shared his hiding place with another Jesuit, Father Oldcorne, while their two servants, Nicholas Owen and Ralph Ashly, had squeezed themselves into another of the hall's secret refuges until lack of victuals forced their surrender. Garnett was committed to the Gatehouse, one of London's many prisons. His stay was short, as he was transferred to a jail that perhaps facilitated his close observation rather better, and certainly one which better indicated his eventual fate: the Tower of London.

The Tower was much more than a prison. It housed an armoury, a menagerie with menacing lions – Cecil appears to have been rather excited by the arrival of two cubs in July 1605 – and the Royal Mint, as well as playing host to those individuals unfortunate enough to be introduced to the Duke of Exeter's Daughter (as the chiropractic torture device the rack was known) and her sadistic gang of friends.[47] The parts in which the Tower's involuntary inhabitants found themselves incarcerated were effectively self-service – if you wanted anything more than the bare essentials, you had to pay for it. Friends might come with food, wine and extra clothing, while your spouse might grace you with the occasional conjugal visit. High-status prisoners such as Henry Percy, 9th earl of Northumberland, who had been arrested in November suspected of complicity in the Powder Treason, took full advantage of this. Known as the 'Wizard Earl', he installed both a library and an alchemical laboratory in the Martin Tower, the better to while away the long hours between prison visits.[48]

Nevertheless, a prisoner in the Tower was often the subject of continued subterfuge, and Garnett, once committed, was placed under close, albeit subtle, observation: the Privy Council encouraged his keeper, a Mr Carey, to feign an interest in the Catholic faith and thus gain the new prisoner's confidence. Soon convinced of Carey's sincerity, or at least of his usefulness, Garnett used him to send a gift to his nephew, Thomas, who at that point was languishing in Garnett's previous lodgings, the Gatehouse, also under suspicion of complicity in the Gunpowder Plot.[49] The gift was a pair of spectacles, but what Henry really wanted Thomas to see clearly was their protective wrapping, a piece of paper which bore the words 'I pray you lett these Spectacles be set in Leather, & with a Leather case, or lett the fould be fitter for ye nose. Y^rs for ever H.G. Henry Garnett.'[50] The wrapping was not there simply to protect the package's contents. The contents were there rather to provide Garnett with an excuse to send his nephew the wrapping paper – they were the cover under which he smuggled a message out of his cell. The wrapping paper bore a second, hidden message, written in invisible ink (see Fig. 44).

Garnett's story is told in his own letters and in the writings of another Jesuit priest, Father John Gerard, who had famously escaped from the Tower in 1597, and would also escape the crackdown on Catholics that had led to the arrest of his superior. Considering the continent a somewhat safer and more comfortable refuge than a rancid priest-hole squeezed between the floors of a Worcestershire manor house, Gerard fled England. He subsequently wrote his

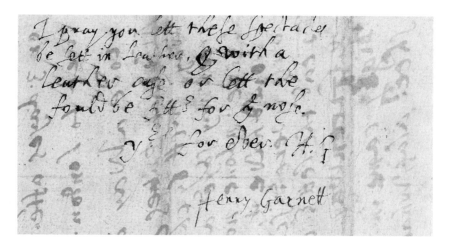

Fig. 44: Only the black ink of Garnett's endorsement would have been visible – the light brown script is the invisible ink on the other side of the paper which has been 'revealed' by the application of heat.

Narrative of the Gunpowder Plot (c. 1607), which not only tells Henry Garnett's story but also provides vital information about the Jesuit mission, while in Rome. Gerard shows us that Garnett's technique of hiding a message on a wrapper ostensibly used merely to protect another object was not one of his own devising. It is difficult not to think of a Jesuit as carrying out a type of theological espionage, engaged on a secret mission in very hostile enemy territory – they certainly faced the same penalty as a spy, execution, if caught. We know that they were provided with clothing to help them blend in, so it seems highly unlikely that they would have been sent on such a mission without at least some idea of how to keep themselves, and their communications, safe from prying eyes. It comes as no surprise to find that, almost a decade before Garnett wrapped up a pair of spectacles, Gerard was doing exactly the same thing, sending two boys to St Omers, a Jesuit seminary in Saint-Omer, France, which specialised in the education of English Catholics, with letters written 'so that the writing was not visible on the paper. In the paper itself I wrapped up a few collars, so that it might seem that its only use was to keep the collars clean'.[51]

The technique had a flaw, of course – the recipient(s) needed to know that the paper was more than it seemed. Gerard solved this by instructing his delivery boys to tell the priests who awaited them to 'steep the paper in water, and they [the priests] would be able to read what I had written'.[52] Gerard's subterfuge was thus at the mercy of his messengers, who might simply lose confidence and confess, both possibilities enhanced by the threat of duress from the authorities, or be simply untrustworthy. Garnett chose an apparently safer path by cutting out the weak link represented by messengers: the spectacles themselves were a code telling the recipient that there was more than could be seen with the naked eye. The text, once revealed, read as follows:

Fig. 45:

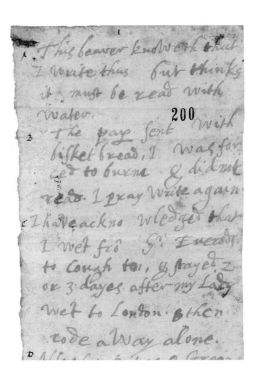

A.   This bearer knoweth that I write thus, but thinks it must be read with water.

B.   The pap[er] sent with bisket bread, I was for ced to burne & did not read. I pray write again.

C.   I have ackno wledged that I we[n]t fro[m] S.ʳ Euereds to Cough ton, & stayed 2 or 3 dayes after my Lady we[n]t to London. & then rode away alone.

Garnett's first paragraph, helpfully marked as 'A' by Attorney-General Sir Edward Coke, who annotated the intercepted letter in preparation for any forthcoming court action, suggests that Garnett trusted his keeper Carey to deliver the letter, but not necessarily to leave it unread. He therefore took out insurance against this possible betrayal, letting Carey think that the message to his nephew would reveal in water – any attempt to reveal it by this method would not only fail (as we will see), but would probably wash away enough of the invisible ink that was on the paper as to render it resistant to any subsequent attempt at a heat reveal.[53]

At 'B', Garnett's message also tells us that the efforts being made to smuggle letters into his cell, albeit unsuccessfully, were once more under the cover of an innocent object – here his 'bisket bread', which presumably came wrapped in another conveniently blank piece of paper.[54] The letter also states that he was almost caught in the act of revealing the bisket bread message, and cast the wrapping into the fire rather than allow its secrets to be spread abroad, illustrating another advantage of the heat reveal: if you were caught holding your bread wrapper up to the fire, you could act as if you were simply tossing it into the flames rather than revealing secret messages.

Fig. 46: Secretively revealing a message by candlelight.

Finally, at 'C', Garnett informs his nephew of what he has told his interrogators: vital knowledge if they are to get their stories straight. Gerard states that in his letters to Thomas, Garnett used 'ordinary ink', but wrote 'besides in the margin and in the free parts of the paper some other things with the juice of orange, which could not be seen without holding to the fire'.[55] The condition of the paper of Garnett's wrapper confirms that the reveal was indeed carried out by heating – a quality shared by several other white inks, as we have seen.[56]

Garnett was right to distrust Carey, as his jailer was neither sympathetic to Catholics nor the only individual perusing these messages, as the lieutenant of the Tower, Sir William Waad, was overseeing the entire process. With the benefit of distance and a little hindsight, Father Gerard realised exactly what had transpired, and he subsequently set this down in his *Narrative*:

> When this letter was thus read by warming at the fire, because it could not then be delivered to the Priest, they therefore counterfeited the Father's hand and sent it to Mr. [Thomas] Garnett in the Gatehouse, to deceive him also and to make him return answer to the Father [in the Tower], that so he might think himself secure, and be emboldened to commit yet further trust unto this false messenger [Mr Carey].[57]

Gerard understood that reading an invisible ink letter rendered it useless for anything but evidence, and that the Garnetts had been fooled by counterfeits. Corroborating evidence tells us that their letters were taken directly to Waad, who then passed them on to Arthur Gregory, who promptly revealed the messages that lay hidden by invisible ink.[58] Gregory was sufficiently skilled not only to counterfeit hands well enough to fool both Garnetts, but also to rewrite those parts originally written in invisible ink. The correspondence Henry and Thomas Garnett had convinced themselves was both private and secure had been neither: it had been controlled from the outset by the authorities in the form of William Waad and, or so it appears, Arthur Gregory. In this sense, the Garnetts made the same mistake as Mary, Queen of Scots: they underestimated their opponents. As with Mary, it was not a mistake from which they might easily recover.

This was not the first time that Waad found himself dealing with a Jesuit priest with a penchant for invisible ink – the Tower's lieutenant had encountered Gerard when the Jesuit was incarcerated at the Clink, the notorious Southwark prison, and, as clerk of the Privy Council, it was Waad who confronted Gerard with the 'collar wrapping letters' that had been intercepted en route to St Omers. Gerard, naturally, denied all knowledge, at which his interrogator 'dipped the paper in a basin of water, and showed [him] the writing, and [his] name subscribed in full'.[59] Despite having made the perhaps rather naïve error of signing his name to these letters (an act which, ironically, demonstrated his absolute faith in his subterfuge), Gerard maintained his innocence, insisting that the message was forged. Later, he would blame his undoing on his use of lemon rather than orange juice as his invisible ink:

> For I never wrote now with lemon-juice, as I once did in the Clink; which letter was betrayed to the persecutor Waad, as before I related. The reason of my doing so then was because there were two letters there, which had to be read in one place, and then carried to another. Now lemon-juice has this property, that what is written in it can be read in water quite as well as by fire, and when the paper is dried the writing disappears again till it is steeped afresh, or again held to the fire. But anything written with orange-juice is at once washed out by water, and cannot be read at all in that way; and if held to the fire, though the characters are thus made to appear, and can be read, they will not disappear; so that a letter of this sort, once read, can never be delivered to any one as if it had not been read.[60]

He may state that he used lemon juice in the St Omers letters because he needed the letters to be revealed, read, hidden and revealed again, but no matter how much he insists on the matter, lemon juice does not behave in this fashion. Gerard is perhaps getting his invisible inks mixed up. Lemon juice will reveal once in water (albeit not brilliantly), but once the paper has dried it will not reveal again, either in water or by heat. This passage has even been interpreted as showing that letters made with lemon juice will fade even after a heat reveal, and can subsequently be revealed again.[61] This is not the case. Gerard may, in fact, have been using an altogether different substance as invisible ink: alum. One of the properties of a message written with alum is that it will reveal on paper when wetted and fade again as the paper dries. The message can then be revealed once more (albeit permanently) through heating. The Jesuit may have unwittingly reinforced the almost indelible association of invisible ink with citrus fruits when it seems likely he was using one of the several other varieties of white ink that were available. The letters sent between Garnett and his nephew were not where the interests of Waad, Cecil, Coke and Gregory lay, however. They were seeking more bountiful prey, the wider network of recusants under whose protection Jesuits such as Garnett had flourished.

KEPT CLOSE AND SECRET

Anne Vaux (pronounced, in typically English fashion, Vawkes or Vorx) was a well-known, wealthy recusant gentlewoman who, along with her elder sister Eleanor, regularly gave succour to Jesuit priests such as Garnett in spite of the severe penalties for doing so.[62] Garnett referred to them as 'the virgin' and 'the widow' respectively, and they rented safe houses for him and his ilk across the country (one of these houses, Whitewebbs in Enfield Chase, would later become infamous as the place where the Gunpowder Plot was hatched). When Garnett went to ground following the plot's failure, he did so at Hindlip Hall, the house of a friend of Anne's named Mary Habington. In her later confession, Anne Vaux would admit that she and Mary had left Hindlip only a few days after the man who had discovered Garnett hiding within its walls, Sir Henry Bromley, the sheriff of Worcestershire, had set off for London with his prize.[63] Anne Vaux may have been deeply embroiled in the illegal act of harbouring Jesuits, but she appears to have had no difficulty in avoiding arrest, even though she was staying at Hindlip for the entire time that Bromley and his men were searching for Garnett within its walls. The authorities were aware that Vaux had communications with the Gunpowder plotters, and she had been interviewed by Coke in London in December 1605, but they saw no reason to detain her.[64] Much greater interest was shown in the disappearance of a 'Mrs Perkins' (the woman who, amongst other things, had rented Whitewebbs). Thomas Wilson, Cecil's man, had interviewed one of the servants, James Johnson, in an attempt to discover the whereabouts of his absent mistress, but to no avail.[65]

Anne Vaux was a committed Catholic, and she was particularly committed to Henry Garnett. She was also the spider at the centre of the web of communication that connected the English recusants, and so, when Garnett was taken to London, she felt compelled to follow him so that she might keep this web intact. Aware of the dangers to which she exposed both herself and those who harboured her, such as her friend Mary in Fetterlane, she took to changing lodging every two or three days.[66] It was Garnett who unwittingly betrayed her whereabouts. The authorities were not merely intercepting his letters. His companion in Hindlip's priest-hole, Father Oldcorne, had also accompanied Garnett to the Tower, and the two Jesuits had been placed in chambers which allowed them to speak with one another through a small gap in the walls. On 23 February, Garnett spoke with his one-time cellmate in hushed tones. 'I think Mistress Ann is in the Town,' he said, directing his words through the fissure. 'If she be I have writ a note that my keeper may repair to her near hand and convey me any thing unto her who will let us hear from all our friends'. Neither man considered the possibility that a third party might be listening. This was quite an oversight. That night, their assigned eavesdropper was John Locherson, a man who also happened to be Salisbury's secretary.[67] Yet another secret had leaked out.

Time, it appears, was also working against them. Two days later James Johnson, the servant from Whitewebbs, would be interrogated again; this time, however, in a somewhat more intimidating setting, namely the Tower. Johnson duly confessed that, contrary to his earlier statements, he had known for the past three years that 'Mrs Perkins' was none other than Anne Vaux.[68] This information transformed Anne's status overnight. No longer was she eliminated from enquiries; she held a ranking position on the 'most wanted' list. Unaware of Anne's unmasking, Garnett decided to reach out. He did so via the 'safe' corridor of communication he had opened up with his nephew Thomas.

On 26 February, Henry Garnett thus wrote another letter to his nephew Thomas at the Gatehouse, this time thanking him for various items of linen, requesting some socks, and noting that he wanted money as he had yet to pay his fees – yet another reminder of the Tower's status as part prison, part hotel.[69] Those experienced at eluding the authorities knew full well that two channels of communication were better than one, and the Catholic underground was aware that alum made an excellent white ink when used on linen.[70] We may thus consider the possibility that Henry's letter was rather more than the dull litany of thanks it purported to be, and indicated acknowledgement of messages received, though none survives.

Fig. 47 shows the once-invisible writing as far lighter in colour than the normal, black ink writing.[71] The scorch marks meanwhile confirm that the white ink was revealed by the application of heat. Garnett's invisible message again concerns what he had so far told his interrogators, not least that he had admitted no particulars 'but of Mrs. Parkins, & the meeting of Catesby & Winter [i.e., Wintour] in Queen Eliz's time'. The letter's final (invisible) words, written upside down at the top of the letter, were as follows: 'My very louing sister Adieu. More hereafter: Do not indanger yourself. But if you have any to bring you to [m]e by the Cradell To[we]re you mayst.'[72] These final words indicate that the true recipient of this letter was not Thomas, but Anne, and it was duly forwarded to her. Garnett was unaware that Anne's alter ego 'Mrs Perkins' had been discovered, and thus that his talk of her during his interrogation had put her in greater danger. Approaching the Tower complex so that she might see him close to the Cradle Tower, where his chamber was located, was not the wisest of moves. Further instructions followed.

'You shall know my mind more fully if you or any friend repair to my keeper's mother as you shall know directions', wrote Garnett on 3 March. 'But come not hither except with good guides and when Waad is abroad, for he is often with me or in the Gallery hard by, you may see me, but not talk'.[73] Unlike in the Babington Plot, when Mary's letter to Babington had left plenty of space in which Phelippes and Bales could insert their famous (if pointless) postscript, Garnett's letter to Anne was already full. There was no room for Gregory to add a specific visiting time onto this letter to lure the elusive 'Mrs Perkins' into his trap. That she appears to have received one nonetheless, presumably by word of mouth, simply reinforces the feeling that Garnett and Vaux were entirely at the mercy of the authorities. When

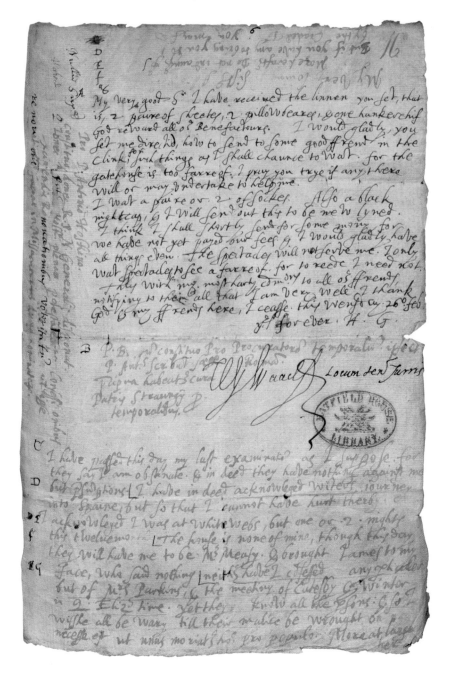

Fig. 47: Henry's letter about socks also contained the following line: 'The Spectacles will not serve me. I only want spectacles to see a farre of, for to reede I need not'. Mention of spectacles could only mean one thing to Thomas: invisible ink. Note that it has been signed by Waad '*locumten turris*', or 'in the Tower', presumably to indicate it has been passed fit for delivery.

Anne arrived at the Tower under cover of darkness sometime around 11 March, Waad's men were waiting for her. Not entirely naïve, she spotted her would-be captors and fled, but to no avail: 'with some rough usage they carried her back unto the Tower . . . and there committed her prisoner, which is a very unwonted place for women to be committed in'.[74] Garnett cannot be accused of unnecessarily enticing Anne to come to the Tower and see him – indeed, it seems more likely that Waad had given her false instructions via Carey's mother – and the priest later expressed his regret at her capture, writing that 'I had hoped Mistress Anne Vaux would have kept her self out of their fingers.'[75] This late-night rendezvous of recusants was engineered not by the Catholic correspondents, but by the controllers of their illicit conversation.

SLIP OF THE PEN

Anne's first surviving letter to Henry, written when she was still at large, is extremely difficult to read and must also have been difficult to forge. Those parts which are legible suggest that it was written in response to Garnett's letter of 26 February, as it not only includes the apology 'But that you did write in Latin which I cannot read' but also the words 'I will come to the garden . . . if I may see you it will please you to appoint the time' in reply to his semi-invitation to the Cradle Tower.[76] Anne's script betrays its invisible application: lines run across one another and odd gaps and misspellings are numerous. Historians have suggested that she had trouble with her eyes, or even that she was next to illiterate: in 1953, Godfrey Anstruther argued that 'the letters' illegibility reveals that she was near-sighted and not accustomed to writing', while a decade later Philip Caraman wrote that 'her letters are difficult to read, ill-punctuated and in places obscure'.[77] This is most likely a mix of casual misogyny (her punctuation is no different from any of her male contemporaries) and a lack of appreciation of just how difficult it was to use invisible ink when unaccustomed to its vagaries.

When you write in invisible ink, you cannot see the letters and words as they are formed on the page, which makes it extremely hard to keep one's place, both physically and within a sentence's unit of meaning. These

Fig. 48: Anne Vaux's invisible ink letter, barely legible without the use of UV light.

difficulties may be accentuated when the writer is under duress, which you may consider to be every time they put invisible ink to paper. Lack of practice may also compromise legibility – especially when using fluids such as lemon or orange juice, which are very light and would in ideal circumstances need to be thickened with gum arabic or something similar. Too runny an ink will bleed through the fibres of the paper, also affecting legibility. This will only be apparent to the recipient, however.

Anstruther and Caraman were not the only ones who found Anne's first stab at wielding the white ink problematic: Garnett's response included the words 'Your last letter I could not read, your pen did not cast ink'.[78] Garnett, of course, was actually reading a forgery of Anne's letter which was attempting to be as faithful to the original as the other letters were – if Gregory could not read Anne's words, he would still have to produce *something*, or the game was up. Garnett might have complained about Anne's technique, but, experienced as he plainly was, even the Jesuit made mistakes such as repeating words he had already written: 'He did it to draw draw'.[79] Now safely ensconced within the thick stone walls of the Tower, and their correspondence literally signed off by their captors, invisible ink was all the more important.

The next letter of Anne's that has survived shows that while she had not completely mastered the use of invisible ink, her technique was very much improved, and she only makes the occasional mistake, such as in Fig. 49. It is unclear why this letter is endorsed in plain ink in secretary hand rather than Anne's usual italic (as used in the invisible writing), but the words themselves are something of a giveaway: 'I pray you prove whether these spectacles do fit your sight.' It could, of course, be that both the italic and secretary hands here are Anne's, as women did use secretary hand, but there are no other letters of hers extant with which to make such a comparison. What this endorsement does show is that someone knew exactly what this letter entailed. Perhaps Anne had wrapped the usual pair of spectacles in blank paper, and the endorsee wanted to ensure that Garnett got the message, or had simply given her a piece of paper thus endorsed and otherwise blank to suggest to her that invisible ink was still a viable and safe method of communication. Whatever the truth is, the contents of Anne's letter do leave us with the tantalising possibility that Garnett was using a hitherto unsuspected substance for his invisible writing: 'On Saturday at supper the attorney said that when you were in examining, you feigned yourself sick to go to your chamber and coming and coming [*sic*] thither you seem to take

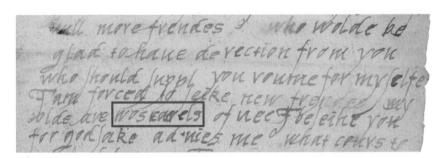

Fig. 49: Writing with invisible ink is tricky – you cannot see what you have just written, so a momentary lapse of concentration can be problematic. Here, Anne Vaux writes 'most' and 'carels [careless]' over one another.

some *marmalade* which even then was sent you and burned a letter which your keeper seeing did tell and you being examined said'.[80] When captured at Hindlip, it was reported that Garnett had a jar of marmalade, that is, orange juice in a concentrated and unperishable form, in his possession. It is quite possible that Garnett wrote his letters not with orange juice but marmalade.[81]

By the time Anne wrote her letter, Garnett had been put to torture, and within days he would be tried, found guilty of 'misprision' in the Gunpowder Plot – that is, of not revealing his knowledge of the conspiracy – and sentenced to death. This unfortunate if wholly predictable turn of events cast something of a pall over his correspondence, and when Garnett next wrote to Anne, again in invisible ink, he set her free of obligation to him: 'the vow

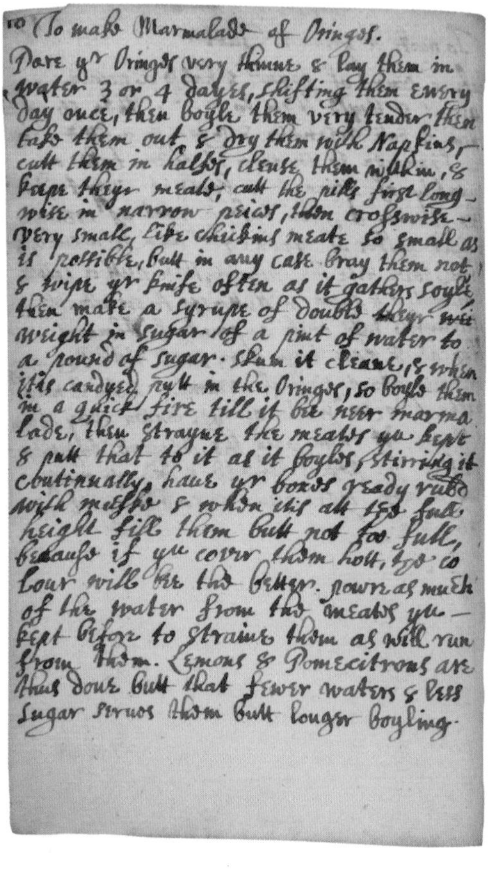
10 To make Marmalade of Oringes.
Pare yr Oringes very thinne & lay them in
water 3 or 4 dayes, shifting them every
day once, then boyle them very tender then
take them out & dry them with Napkins,
cutt them in halves, cleanse them within, &
keepe theyr meate, cutt the pills first long-
wise in narrow peices, then crosswise
very small, like chickins meate so small as
is possible, butt in any case bray them not,
& wipe yr knife often as it gathers soyle,
then make a syrupe of double theyr weight in sugar & of a pint of water to
a pound of sugar. Skum it cleane, & when
it is candyed putt in the Oringes, so boyle them
in a quick fire till it bee neer marma
lade, then strayne the meates you kept
& putt that to it as it boyles, stirring it
continually, have yr boxes ready rubd
with muske & when it is att the full
height fill them butt not too full,
because if you cover them hott, the co
lour will be the better. powre as much
of the water from the meates you
kept before to straine them as will run
from them. Lemons & Pomecitrons are
thus done butt that fewer waters & less
sugar serves them butt longer boyling.

Fig. 50: 'To make Marmalade of Oringes'. While quince paste was also commonly called 'marmalade', it is not necessarily good for invisible ink. Orange marmalade works, however, and only needs a little dilution.

of obedience ceaseth, being made to the Superiors of this Mission; you may upon deliberation make it to some there'. His letter finished with the words 'Let all I write out be very secret.'[82] Vaux's reply began with the words 'Good father. I have received your spectacles.'[83]

'A NEST FOR SUCH BADD BIRDDS'

In his final letter to Anne Vaux, written on 21 April 1606, Henry Garnett used black ink to tell her of the problems that had beset him, because he now realised that all the subterfuge and marmalade had been useless, as 'our confessions & secret conferences were heard; & my letters taken, by some indiscretion abroad'.[84] Despite their greatest efforts, they had been outwitted. Henry Garnett was hanged, drawn and quartered at St Paul's Churchyard on 3 May 1606.

Anne Vaux was released the following August, and lived for another thirty-one years. If Henry Garnett got one thing right, it was his estimation that 'she shall have no hurt for it . . . & Master Lieutenant said she was dogged by a seminary Priest. She was not taken for me, but for Whitewebbs'.[85] The house at Whitewebbs, which had seen so much skullduggery, had not finished with its association with Anne Vaux, however, as a correspondent wrote to Salisbury: 'Watson that owns the house . . . purposeth (as the report goeth) to let it again to Mistress Vaux which kept before by the name of Mrs Perkins, when she comes out of the Tower, This I tell your Lordship because it is next neighbour to Theobalds, and unfit it should be again a nest for such badd birdds as it was before.'[86] Salisbury presumably needed no reminding that Whitewebbs neighboured on his own Hertfordshire residence, Theobalds, but these birds did not come home to roost; Anne and her sister flew north, and took up residence in Leicestershire instead.

In his handling of Henry Garnett and Anne Vaux, William Waad had directed a quite brilliant piece of counter-espionage, one which relied heavily on the skills of Arthur Gregory – specifically, on his ability to counterfeit letters even when written in invisible ink. Gregory's letter to Robert Cecil made it plain exactly what he achieved, namely 'discovering the secret writing, being in blank ... & leaving the same at last in blank again'.[87] Gregory convincingly imitated the hands of Henry Garnett and Anne Vaux, exposed the writing they had sought to conceal by the use of marmalade and orange juice before reproducing these same letters complete with their invisible ink messages, thus keeping the correspondence open while holding on to the original letters.

Invisible inks were hard enough to use at the best of times – it is very difficult to keep track of the words you write when you cannot see them being formed, and every time you remove pen from paper to recharge it with ink you risk more confusion. Such problems simply multiply if you are trying to reproduce another piece of invisible ink writing, especially under time pressure. Gregory, however, appears to have solved this problem in a manner that was not only ingenious, but potentially ground-breaking.

COPYING THE INVISIBLE

Arthur Gregory's 1586 letter to Walsingham is often cited on account of its active inclusion of invisible writing in alum along with the instruction to reveal the message with coal dust, and rather less so for its description of how gall-water and copperas may also serve as invisible ink. This same letter, however, also provides an insight into how Gregory set about copying the Garnett–Vaux correspondence with such apparent accuracy: 'There is an old cover of a desk at Bassette the joiner, the ironwork would serve for a glass to counterfeit, which I should want in case any thing be discovered that your Lordship would have hidden again, & also for the speedy copying of a ciphered letter and other purposes.'[88] If he is to counterfeit a letter that includes invisible ink messages, or perhaps make a quick copy of a letter written in cipher, Gregory writes that he will need this 'cover of a desk' with its ironwork. That is, Gregory wants a piece of technology that he can use for this task. Typically, he is less than forthcoming about what this desk actually is, or how it operates. It does appear that it facilitates the making of facsimiles, however. Della Porta suggested that a letter may be copied using backlighting, the words traced onto a blank piece of paper laid over the original, but this technique is unlikely to allow for the copying of (revealed) invisible ink writing – even if the light source used were powerful enough, revealed invisible ink is, as can be seen from the various figures, much fainter than black ink.[89]

Gregory's reticence regarding its actual design is perhaps not surprising given his constitutional aversion to giving away valuable secrets, but a decade later he would give more clues in his letters to Robert Cecil: 'Your perspective glass with the box is in hand & shall be finished with expedition. The crystalline is most fair and large – I could not find such an other.'[90] What was earlier a contraption attached to a desk, the ironwork of which 'would serve', and which used a 'glass' or mirror 'to counterfeit', had now developed somewhat. Gregory now spoke of a 'perspective glass with the box', noting that it also uses a 'crystalline' or circular lens. The perspective box was constructed specifically to facilitate the easy copying of documents. Typically, Gregory's offer of a new technology is wrapped up in a promise of demonstration: 'I will most frankly discover [display] the depth of my skill & deliver unto your honour the Box with the perspective glass finished with all these subtleties, & instruct your honour in the secret use thereof.'[91] The development of Gregory's perspective box was plainly beset with teething troubles, and after asking that he be 'excused the intolerable delay of the workman in your box for your crystalline glass, which now I am promised presently' his pen fell silent on the matter in 1596.[92]

A decade later Gregory wrote to Cecil not with promises of what he could achieve, but with reminders of what he had achieved in the case of Garnett and Vaux – that is, 'discovering the secret writing, being in blank . . . & leaving the same at last in blank again'.[93] It was in a pair of postscripts that Gregory revealed his intentions. In the first, he wrote that 'Mr Lieutenant [Waad] expecteth something to be written in the blank leaf of a Latin Bible which is pasted in already for the purpose. I will attend it and whatsoever else commeth.' It is unclear who has possession of this Bible, but it may well be the Bible Garnett mentions in his letter to Anne Vaux of 3 March, which would suggest that Gregory was already in the Tower by this point, and had begun his work.[94] The blank page is prepared for a message, one which Waad and Gregory fully expect will be written in invisible ink. The second postscript sees Gregory's intention of reintroducing his perspective box: 'I have a box with a desk which I prepared many years since for your Lordship the crystal is broken but I will find a new: it may serve to excellent use.'[95] The use Gregory refers to is counterfeiting letters written in invisible ink. Waad and Gregory were anticipating the use of invisible ink, and already purposed to intercept, reveal and reproduce any letters that used it. It was for this task that the dark artificer had resurrected his perspective box.

Gregory's perspective box was probably a rather clever variation on the well-known contraption, the *camera obscura*. As with much contemporary technology, the *camera obscura* (literally 'dark chamber') was developed over centuries following the observation of a natural phenomenon, namely that if light is allowed into a darkened room through only a small hole or aperture, images of the outside are projected onto the wall opposite the aperture. This phenomenon was being commented upon as early as 300 BCE, with experiments being carried out to understand it in the centuries that followed. By 1545 the first illustration of a *camera obscura* had appeared in print.[96] The use of a glass disc or lens was described in Cardano's *De Subtilitate* in 1550, and in 1558 della Porta's *Magiae Naturalis* included an *obscurum cubiculum* as an aid to drawing.[97] The name '*camera obscura*' was coined by Johannes Kepler in 1604, and in 1620 he would tell Sir Henry Wotton, Stuart ambassador in Vienna, that the device allowed him to produce drawings '*non tanquam pictor sed tanquam mathematicus*' ('not like a painter but like a mathematician'). Kepler's camera was portable, and made use of 'a long perspective trunk' (also a common name for the telescope) with convex and concave glasses (mirrors) such that the 'visible radiations of all the objects without are intramitted falling upon a paper which is accommodated to receive them'. Wotton described the device to the then lord chancellor Francis Bacon, 'because I think there might be good use made of it for chorography [mapmaking]'.[98] (Mapmaking was another of Gregory's services; he reminded Walsingham in 1586 of 'my several plans and journeys to Dover and the last plan of Ireland'.)[99]

The *camera obscura*, however, projects an inverted image. This makes it perfectly good for mapmaking, but rather less useful for copying letters. A device called the *camera lucida* solved this problem: it creates the illusion of an uninverted image projected onto paper when the user looks through its primary mechanism, a prism. Generally considered to have been invented by William Hyde Wollaston in 1807, the *camera lucida* appears to date back to at least 1652 and the development of Sir Christopher Wren's 'perspecto-graph', a '*camera lucida* equipped with a sight . . . moveable along a mechanical track or pulley system', if not to 1596 and Gregory's perspective box.[100] Both Wren's perspectograph and Gregory's perspective box were themselves preceded by della Porta's description of how to use a 'concave glass' (in this instance, a lens – the word glass was used for both lens and mirror) to make an image appear as if 'hanging altogether in the air', such that it can be seen by none but 'those that stand over it'.[101]

As an active dark artificer, Gregory understood the value of being able to make quick and accurate facsimiles of documents in the field, and this impelled the creation of his perspective box. It seems likely that he inferred his instrument from della Porta's discussion of 'pyramidal glass' and how to fit various lenses into 'some table, or iron', in such a manner that it will 'shew you many diversities of images', specifically 'the right side will show right, the left the left, whereas the nature of plain glasses, is to show the right side as left, and the left side as right'.[102] While della Porta considered that the method of projecting an uninverted image in this manner was 'a great secret: many have tried it, but none could obtain it',[103] Gregory's facility in copying invisible ink letters strongly suggests that he succeeded where others failed.

Gregory's perspective box most likely comprised one or more crystals fitted into a wooden box and positioned by some sort of metal frame. All that remains of it are these few, epistolary fragments and their corroboration in a book we know he read. With access to such technology, and a little care, anything could be copied, and considerably faster and more accurately than by a scribe working freehand. Furthermore, copying in invisible ink would also be not only possible but relatively simple. The great advance was that the scribe did not need to take their eyes from the paper on which they wrote. Gregory saw the potential of such a device.

The battle waged between Arthur Gregory and the correspondents Henry Garnett and Anne Vaux was one of competing technologies. Unfortunately for the Jesuit and his co-conspirator, Gregory's ingenuity made it something of a David and Goliath affair, only this time, Goliath won, and comfortably so. Garnett and Vaux relied on marmalade, fruit juice and talk of spectacles to keep their secrets from view, Gregory on advanced optics, control of the postal channels and no little imaginative skill to reveal them. It really was no contest.

5

—◇—

STILETTOS & STORYTELLING

In 1565, a ship's barber-surgeon found himself taking direct orders from the commander of the Venetian fleet concerning a patient of his, a Turkish privateer recently taken captive. He was told in no uncertain terms to poison the man. What he did not know, however, was that this order had not come from the commander himself, but directly from the Council of Ten, the Venetian state security council. They wished to rid themselves of the privateer on a permanent basis, and for it to appear that he had died from the injuries sustained during his capture. To prevent the Turks from apprehending the true reasons for the privateer's demise, the Ten also requested that the commander return the letter containing their instructions. This was not unusual behaviour: state-sanctioned assassination, while part and parcel of the everyday working lives of the Ten, was not something to be routinely communicated to the enemy. That any trace of such orders still exists in the archives is astonishing, perhaps a sign that in Venice filing had turned into an unsuppressible and habitual obsession. The insistence on their operatives using a particular method to dispatch foreign spies was not unusual, either. Keen to do away with Mustafa dai Cordoani, a legate of Mehmet Pasha's whom they were convinced was in fact a spy, they asked Marchio Viladrino, a physician and professor of botany at the University of Padua, to concoct a poison specifically for the purpose. When Viladrino's confection proved anything but toxic (it failed twice), they approached another physician, one Comasco, to finish the job. Comasco's contribution also failed, and Mustafa lived to eavesdrop again – at least, until, having returned to Venice a few years later, he was found dead in the street. The official cause was the plague, but the Ten knew better: they had instructed the latest assassin, whose code name was 'Captain Trec', to ensure that the corpse resembled a plague victim's.[1]

Poison was not the only weapon wielded by Italian counter-espionage operatives, though it was the most difficult to detect, and thus often the most politically useful. Venice itself was home of the infamous *bravi*, a group of killers-for-hire who were, according to the travel writer Thomas Coryate, most associated with 'a little sharp dagger called a stiletto [or 'little steel']'.[2] The association between Italy and the stiletto was reinforced by the weapon's repeated mention in official intelligence reports, and on the stages of London's theatres.[3] Its use was also reported by later travel writers, such as John Raymond, who noted the pugnacious nature of Italians who, should they end up in a fight, knew that 'if in the contest their stiletto should do mischief, the next church may be their asylum, where no law or violence can attempt them'. This posturing went deep, he suggested: 'the common mode of the scholar is to go arm'd with a pair of pistols, and a stiletto by his side'.[4] Like the pistol, the stiletto had but one purpose: to kill. After penetration, the blade was to be moved around inside the victim, causing maximum damage.[5] The expectation appeared to be that a stiletto would most likely be used on an unarmed opponent – there seems little other explanation for why a popular 1536 manual of combat techniques written by the Italian fencing master Achille Marozzo, *Opera Nova*, included several pages detailing how an unarmed man might defend himself from an attacker brandishing such a blade.[6] A bladed weapon required strength, courage and no little skill to wield effectively, however, and was only effective at close, if not intimate, range. Any attempt to assassinate a well-known individual might well prove to be a suicide mission: such a target would invariably be accompanied, at the very least by courtiers, who would be likely to take instant and bloody revenge.

In English eyes, the depravity of Catholic Rome, Italy, poison and the stiletto were often conflated, as we see recycled in an incendiary polemic written after the Papal Bull issued by Urban VIII in 1627. Here Henry Burton raged against Catholics in Italy, calling stilettos and poisons their 'usual weapons'.[7] While the Venetian Council of Ten were quite happy to engage chemists to mix new poisons and put them to use, engage the stiletto-wielding *bravi* and even specifically request that an individual be strangled if

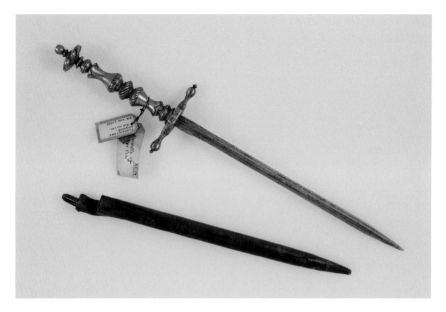

Fig. 51: A stiletto, or 'little steel'. An evolution of the poniard, it was developed to deliver the coup de grace to a beaten yet armoured opponent – the blade's shape concentrated the user's force into a small area, allowing it to pierce armour or chainmail, or to prey on vulnerable areas such as the eye slits.

the assassin thought fit, assassination played little part in English espionage and counter-espionage policy until the Interregnum.[8] Officially, at least – it was rumoured that one of Cecil's spies, Robert Poley, had assassinated the bishop of Armagh in the Tower of London with poisoned cheese.[9] Assassinations may have been rare, but simple murders were less so. Life was cheap in sixteenth-century England, and Poley would later bear witness to the playwright and one-time spy Christopher Marlowe receiving a fittingly metonymic dagger in the eye in a Deptford tavern.

Fear of the assassin hiding in the shadows did not merely derive from the hyperbole of attention-seeking travel writers and polemicists, however. Queen Elizabeth I and her advisors were particularly afraid of any threat they could not see, and this included any weapon that could be easily concealed until needed. The danger was perceived to be very real, not merely because of the specific threats made against the queen and, latterly, her successor James. While poison may have been their greatest fear, there were other surreptitious weapons that could give the spy or conspirator the upper hand: one of these came in the shape of the handgun, or 'dag'.

WHAT'S UP YOUR SLEEVE?

The assassination of the Scottish regent James Stewart, 1st earl of Moray, on 23 January 1570, was perhaps in itself no great shock, considering the state of Scottish politics in the latter half of the sixteenth century – some might consider that he received his just deserts, considering that barely two years previously he had attempted to have Mary, Queen of Scots assassinated by proxy with the Casket Letters. That his murder was carried out by a Catholic, James Hamilton, was thus also unsurprising. Most of the high-level assassinations executed during the late sixteenth and early seventeenth centuries – including those of the Huguenot Admiral Gaspard de Coligny (1572), William the Silent (1584), Henri III (1589) and Henri IV (1610) of France – were carried out by Catholics. This rather skewed statistic can largely be attributed to theology.[10] A Catholic could not only be convinced that they were doing God's work by removing a heretic from his earth, but could be sure that such an act would secure them a place in heaven. A Protestant, however, whose faith denied salvation through works, could be secure in no such conviction, and neither could they be absolved of all sin through an act of intercession (though this did not preclude their ever carrying out actions). The assassins themselves were often disgruntled soldiers, and almost always fanatics. Naturally, many were also persuaded to a course of action by financial inducements: Philip II of Spain was quite public in placing a bounty of 25,000 crowns on the head of William the Silent, and allegedly offered the royal physician Roderigo Lopez 50,000 crowns to murder his own patient, Elizabeth I.

What troubled many observers was the weapon that Hamilton used to murder Moray: an arquebus. Moray himself had seen the dangers of the increasing proliferation of firearms throughout the public domain, especially weapons such as the arquebus (which required less skill to operate than more traditional projectile weapons such as the longbow), and had attempted to ban their public carrying by royal proclamation two years before he met his untimely end.[11] The arquebus possessed a dangerous combination of range, accuracy and destructive potential, but it lacked one property crucial to the assassin: subtlety. It was big, cumbersome and required some effort to conceal, not least because it was fired by the application of a smouldering taper to the gunpowder charge (also known as a matchlock), with all the obvious problems that presented. Hamilton had the luxury of being able to conceal his weapon in a first-floor room of a house that Moray was due to pass by on horseback. While effective, an arquebus was hardly convenient. What the assassin needed was an easily concealable weapon that could be operated with one hand; this was found in a lethal technology that would revolutionise the business of targeted, high-level assassinations, the wheellock pistol.

The wheellock was a complicated mechanism that created its own spark by grinding a steel wheel against a sparking material (usually iron pyrite) which would, in turn, ignite the gunpowder charge in the pan and thus fire the weapon. The wheellock could be carried primed and ready to fire, and thence operated with one hand, a major advantage over the matchlock. On the downside, its mechanism was fiddly and unreliable, and required a separate key to 'wind up' the spring to ready it for action. While more expensive and less reliable than a matchlock – like a watch, it needed constant attention to function at its best – the wheellock rapidly became the weapon of choice for cavalry units, in themselves a social and military elite, on account of its particular advantages.[12] Wheellocks came in different sizes, from the long, powerful weapons wielded in battle to smaller versions such as the one shown in Fig. 52. That they came in such a relatively diminutive size and lacked a smouldering taper meant that these weapons, known as 'dags', 'could readily be hidden in a pocket or sleeve'.[13]

Many governments saw the danger presented by the proliferation of such easy-to-conceal yet destructive weapons; dags were described as 'diabolical', 'destructive' and even 'impious', and were banned from Habsburg territories by the emperor in 1518.[14] By 1541, the English Parliament had 'little shorte handguns and little hagbuttes' and their use in 'detestable and shameful murders' in its crosshairs. A new law was drawn up, including a clause stating that a demi-hake (the equivalent of a pistol) ought be no shorter than 2 feet 3 inches (around 70 centimetres).[15] Prescribing a minimum length was

Fig. 52: A 1577 portrait of the privateer Martin Frobisher showing the promising ratio of handgun to sleeve. Fashions of the time perhaps enabled the concealing of a weapon larger than one might expect, and a cloak one larger still, at least for a short time.

intended to make concealment virtually impossible. The same problem was being acknowledged across Europe: in 1542, the Venetian state, ever cognisant of the technologies that fuelled illicit activities, outlawed any firearm diminutive enough to be hidden in a sleeve.[16] Fear of dags was inversely proportional to their size. In England, therefore, further legislation was devoted to controlling the 'pocket dag', a smaller and somewhat easier-to-hide variant, and in 1549, Edward VI issued another proclamation prohibiting them from being carried within 3 miles of court.[17] This did little to prevent sixteenth-century men from showing off their wheellock dags in portraiture as a symbol of their wealth and status.[18]

All this legislative paranoia was as well justified as it was useless, as Moray discovered to his cost, and it was not long before a wheellock pistol was used in a successful assassination, one which sent shockwaves around the courts of Europe. Moray may have been the first head of state to be assassinated with a firearm, but he had met his maker while on horseback on a public road. William the Silent would be the first head of state to be killed with a handgun. What is more, it was the weapon's relatively diminutive size that allowed his assassin to execute his commission in the place where William ought to have been at his most secure: his own court.

SILENCING WILLIAM

When William of Orange became stadtholder of the provinces of Holland, Zeeland and Utrecht in 1559, Philip II thought he had found himself a loyal man who would support Spanish rule in the Netherlands. Matters did not proceed as he expected, however. Philip clashed repeatedly with William, leading to the latter's removal from his positions in 1568–9. By 1580, William, known as 'the Silent' on account of his ability to keep his political strategy close to his chest despite his well-known tendency towards loquaciousness, had become such a thorn in Philip's side that the Spanish king issued a proclamation exhorting loyal Catholics to assassinate him. A bounty of 25,000 crowns, lands and titles awaited the successful assassin.

In 1582, an eighteen-year-old from Bilbao, Juan de Jáuregui, who was working with the knowledge of the Italian cardinal Alessandro Farnese, pulled a dag on William during Sunday lunch. Overcharged with powder, Jáuregui's weapon misfired, removing his thumb as it did so. The unfortunate Jáuregui was promptly stabbed to death by William's men.[19] While his life had been saved by this misfire, William was badly injured, with some reports suggesting that the shot passed through his tongue while the discharge of gunpowder set light to his beard. Rumours of his death spread rapidly. William, now physically incapable of speech, was in no condition to rebut them, though his staff did so immediately.

Perhaps inevitably, two years later, on 10 July 1584, a second attempt was made on his life. This time, there would be no mistake. Balthasar Gérard,

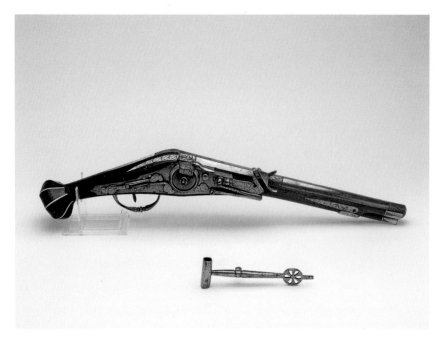

Fig. 53: A wheellock dag, with key for priming its spring.

William's successful assassin, was by all accounts a spy recently recruited to provide information on Spanish troop movements. It was through this employment, and his judicious use of forged documents declaring him to be one François Guyon, that he had managed to worm his way into the stadt-holder's entourage.[20] Having been appointed to serve on a diplomatic embassy to France as a lowly servant, Gérard eventually gained an audience with William at his Delft residence, the Prinsenhof, where he revealed his dag and fired. Gérard had loaded it with three bullets to increase its destructive power and reduce the possibility of missing his target – the bullets were connected with wire, in imitation of the naval chainshot used to tear through a ship's rigging. This new payload did shorten the dag's effective range, but it was still considerably further than the arm's length demanded by a stiletto. As the ability to launch an assault from even 5 metres from the target might make the difference between the instant and deadly retaliation of the target's companions and the assassin's escape, the attraction of the dag becomes clear. Three bullets were enough to ensure a lethal outcome. William died almost instantaneously; two of the bullets passed through his body before lodging themselves in the wall of the Prinsenhof, while the third remained in its target.[21] Unlike his predecessor Jáuregui (who, one imagines, was rather too shocked by his own injuries to flee before William's men put him to the sword), Gérard managed to escape the scene of the crime. Even though he had discharged his dag at close range, he made full use of the few feet that had stood between him and his target and the small headstart this gave him over William's guards. His freedom was short-lived, however, as he was soon captured. When interrogated, he swore that he had acted alone and out of religious fervour (as well as a desire for the 25,000-crown reward promised by Philip II). He stuck to this story even after being put to torture. Gérard possibly regretted having not suffered Jáuregui's fate, but he nevertheless showed great determination, enduring several hours of public torture before his eventual disembowelment and quartering.[22] Assassination was a dangerous business for all concerned.

EUROPEAN REVERBERATIONS

The shockwaves following William's death were palpable: Gérard's triple shot wheellock had upped the ante. Within a week of the assassination, the English ambassador in France, Sir Edward Stafford, warned Walsingham that there were three 'practisers' ready to do to Elizabeth (amongst others) what had just been done to William, and that within the next two months. Noting his suspicion that the information had been fed to him by a Spanish agent anxious to curry favour with the queen, he nevertheless concluded that the threat could not be ignored: 'there must no doubt be had that she [Elizabeth] is a chief mark they shoot at'.[23] Given the penchant for uncovering plots that reinforced the government's worst fears, it is no surprise that two such 'conspiracies' to do away with the English queen using handguns were subsequently, and very publicly, foiled.

The first was a rather unlikely plot allegedly formulated by the mentally unstable twenty-three-year-old John Somerville of Warwickshire. Somerville declared to all and sundry that he 'meant to shoot her [Elizabeth] through with his dag and hoped to see her head to be set upon a pole for that she was a serpent and a viper'.[24] He had forgotten the first rule of the successful assassin: tell no one. Along with his in-laws, Somerville was promptly arrested for 'the most wicked and desperate act by [him] intended'.[25] He had forgotten the second rule, too: be inconspicuous (he wore 'buttons of gold on his cape and doublet', gifts, he proudly alleged, from Mary, Queen of Scots).[26] Two months later Somerville was condemned to death and moved from the Tower to Newgate, where he was found strangled in his cell. No cheese was found at the scene; the official cause of death was suicide. His father-in-law was executed as a traitor the next day.[27]

The second plot was far more intelligently organised, but equally dubious. It revolved around William Parry, who worked for Walsingham, and yet the reporting of the case accentuated his dealings with Thomas Morgan, a known agent of Mary, Queen of Scots.[28] His first plan was to assassinate Elizabeth while she walked in the garden. Having been told that he could not 'carry a dag without suspicion', Parry replied 'as for a dag . . . I care not: my dagger is enough'. Alternatively, he suggested, the queen might be set upon in St James's by a group of men: 'it is much . . . that so many resolute men may do upon the sudden, being well appointed with each his case of dags'. He would not suffer Gérard's fate, however: 'those that shall be with her, will be so busy about her, as I shall find opportunity enough to escape', not least as his co-conspirator was charged with readying a barge to receive him.[29] Parry was more than aware of the opportunity that the dag presented, as even a small headstart over one's pursuers could prove vital if one wanted to escape.

Amidst all this bluster, in which the 'handgun stood for the ever-present threat of Catholicism reaching out into the heart of Protestant England to snatch the life of the monarch', the English Privy Council were clearly rattled.[30] The most recent proclamation against firearms, from 1579, had reiterated that dags and other such weapons were 'only meet [i.e., suitable] for thieves, robbers and murderers'. No one was to discharge a weapon or even carry one 'charged with shot and powder' other than 'at and in the places that are or shall be appointed for common Musters', nor were they to be used within two miles of any place occupied by the queen. Furthermore, the houses of anyone suspected of possessing or selling any 'small Dags, called pocket Dags', were to be searched, and any weapons found immediately seized. Finally, no one was to make, mend, import, sell 'or otherwise to utter any such small Pieces as are commonly called pocket Dags, or that may be hid in any Pocket, or like place about a man's person, to be hid or carried covertly'.[31] There was nothing more to be done. In 1610, Waad wrote to Salisbury of a gunmaker called Baker (aka John Tomkins) who, he asserted, had sold upwards of forty dags by May of that year.[32] As was so often the case, the law hung grimly on to the coat-tails of common behaviour for as long as it could, but was eventually shaken off and left bruised and battered by the side of the highway. The authorities were fighting a losing battle, and despite further proclamations in 1613 and 1616, when King James was spooked by rumours of another Spanish armada and a new shipment of pocket dags arriving from Spain, the impossibility of controlling such weapons was finally recognised. In any case, the wheellock was gradually being replaced by the cheaper and more reliable flintlock mechanism: the dag was here to stay.[33]

By the middle of the century, dags could be made that fitted into the palm of the hand. John Raymond took note of a particularly cunning contrivance during a trip around Italy in 1646–7, writing that 'At Venice I saw a pocket Church Book with a pistol hid in the binding, which turning to such a page, discharges. A plot (I conceive) to entrap him you hate, whilst you are at your devotions together, when there is least suspicion.'[34] It may well be that this was the same mechanism that was delivered to Francesco Morosini, doge of Venice at around the same time, though this dag-bible was fired by pulling on the ribbon that served to mark the owner's place (presumably Romans 12:19, 'Vengeance is mine').[35] Raymond had a particular interest in secret or silent weaponry, noting three further spy-adapted contraptions, namely 'a pocket stone-bow [a cross between a catapult and crossbow that fired pellets rather than bolts], which held under a cloak shoots needles with violence to pierce a man's body, yet leaves a wound scarce discernable', a walking staff that 'will jet forth a rapier with force enough to kill at a yard's distance', and a gun 'charged with wind', which was fatal from 'six paces' yet made almost no sound.[36]

Ultimately, fear of the dag was due less to its firepower and its effectiveness at ranges beyond those of stiletto or sword than the ease with which it

Fig. 54: This late eighteenth-century dag, concealed in a book of hours from 1627, was bought on the Rialto in Venice in 1810. It does not take much imagination to conclude that the buyer was on his Grand Tour, and returned home convinced that he had stumbled upon a piece of history, 'a bookgun once owned by Morosini'.

could be concealed, largely a function of the technological advance that was the wheellock. Less intimate than the stiletto, the wheellock pistol still required that the assassin remained in position until the very moment that they released their murderous cargo. It did not, however, demand anything like the blind courage required to plunge a dagger into the heart, temple or eye of a target who was quite probably in armed company. At the moment of truth, however, all pretensions to stealth were abandoned, and the assassin's chances of escape might very well hang on those few, valuable metres afforded him by the wheellock pistol's greater range.

There was, however, a weapon as silent and invisible in operation as the very best spy, one which allowed the assassin to make good their escape before the moment of truth. It was also a weapon that relied on planning and cunning rather than physical strength or training for its success. Furthermore, given the right support, it was the most egalitarian of murder weapons, as it allowed for the employment of the most inconspicuous of co-conspirators such as servants and housemaids. This weapon was poison.[37]

FOOD POISONING AND UNICORNS

While Mary, Queen of Scots had watched her Italian secretary, David Rizzio, stabbed to death in front of her while a pistol was allegedly held to her belly, it was neither fear of the blade nor of the pistol that kept her awake at night: it was fear of poison. This fear, while it perhaps blossomed beyond the bounds of reality, was not entirely unfounded: in 1551, while she was living at the Château Royal d'Amboise in France, a plan to lace her favourite dish of 'frittered pears' with poison was only narrowly thwarted. How much this episode affected the eight-year-old Mary is unclear, but it caused her mother enough anxiety to postpone her own return to Scotland.[38] In later life, Mary took any mention of poison seriously. In December 1570, the Spanish ambassador to England wrote to his master: 'It is true she [Mary] is not well, and is in much greater fear for her life than formerly, in consequence of a warning that she has received from a doctor, astrologer and sort of conjurer, to the effect that they are going to give her poison in her food, and who even goes so far as to indicate the day when it is to be done.'[39] Mere months after the astrologer's prediction, and despite being incarcerated in Sheffield Castle, Mary received news that her son's regent, the earl of Lennox, had told Monsieur Verac, once *valet de chambre* to the French king and thence an active agent for her cause in Scotland, that her life was to be taken by poison.[40] She wanted to gather evidence of Lennox's evil intent, and began by asking whether Verac could testify in writing that the rumours were true. Lennox discovered Mary's letter amongst Verac's papers, and was so incensed that he had the Frenchman locked up. He then made him write, presumably under no little duress, that her apprehensions were false: 'I . . . assure you, madam, as the truth is, that he [Lennox] has not spoken to me, nor held any proposal that might threaten your life, be it by poison or otherwise, and I cannot think who has given you this intelligence.'[41] Whether or not Mary believed Verac's testimony, her men shot Lennox dead during a raid on Stirling Castle not nine weeks later; perhaps she had been unwilling to give her son's regent the benefit of the doubt.

Her fear of poison would not relent: 'I am not out of danger if my food is not closely watched', she wrote to the archbishop of Glasgow in 1574, '[I must] have recourse to . . . a bit of fine unicorn's horn, as I am in great want of it'.[42] Unicorn horn, in its solid state, was supposed to indicate the presence of poison by effervescing; in its powdered (or 'fine') form it was considered a cure for many ailments, including poison. It had, of course, nothing to do with unicorns, being rather the tusk of the narwhal – nor did it actually work.[43] While Mary was bemoaning her lack of this wonder substance, Sir Francis Walsingham was shutting down an underground postal channel run by the travelling bookseller Henrye Cockyn of Fleet Street.[44] Walsingham's interrogations revealed unexpected information, namely that Mary was not merely sending and receiving ciphered letters enclosed in Cockyn's books, but also more substantial fare in the form of mithridate.[45] Named for the king of Pontus, Mithridates VI (132–63 BCE), who, legend had it, rendered himself impervious to poisons, mithridate was a rare and expensive substance believed to act both as prophylactic and antidote. Various recipes were available, each of which comprised some fifty-four ingredients, and all of which were supposed to derive from the king's original formulation.[46]

The mithridate delivered to Mary took a suitably convoluted route: Cockyn was given a half-pound tin of the substance by Nicholas Jude, the 'French ambassador's man', who had received it from the apothecary Humphrey Wymmes, who had been ordered to deliver it, along with various other items, by Dr James Good. For his part, Wymmes insisted from his accommodation in the Tower that he had no knowledge of the good doctor's being 'privy to their [mithridate or treacle] being sent to the Scottish Queen', nor that he himself had knowingly delivered such substances to her via Nicholas. (The second substance, 'treacle', or 'theriac', was another multi-ingredient antidote). Wymmes and Good diverged slightly in their estimation of who paid for the delivery: the former suggested the French ambassador's servant; the latter the ambassador himself, Michel de Castelnau.[47] To further muddy the waters, Cockyn stated that Good had told Mary that the mithridate in question came from Frances Newton, Baroness Cobham. One of Elizabeth I's chamberers in 1558, Cobham had eventually risen to lady of the Bedchamber.[48] Betrayal came from within.

The fact that Cockyn, ostensibly the mere 'postman' in the underground network, seems to have known exactly what each of the individuals who comprised his 'postal round' wrote to one another seems, on the surface, rather odd. It is in Dr Good's examination that we find the answer. Cockyn was no mere go-between: he acted as de facto cipher secretary for those outside Sheffield Castle to whom he delivered messages, both deciphering them and enciphering the resulting replies, using a key he had presumably memorised to ' "engleishe" such words in the same as were in cipher'. Good swore that he received neither alphabet nor cipher 'from the Scottish Queen or from any other', and, having none of his own, did not know 'of any cipher but Cockyn's'.[49] Cockyn, naturally, saw things differently, but if there was one constant within this, or any other circle of conspirators, it was the instinct to shift the blame onto someone else. In any case, having enciphered Good's letter, Cockyn knew that the doctor had written to Mary that the mithridate had come from Lady Cobham, whom he had earlier tried to keep out of his testimony.[50]

Not long before the failure of the Babington Plot a decade later, Mary wrote to her old friend, the by then compromised French diplomat Castelnau: 'I cannot but bethink me . . . of the practices and divers attempts which have been made against my life since I have been in this country, sometimes by violence, sometimes by poison, some of which I have already made known to the said Queen, with the names and surnames of the instigators and actors'.[51] Whether or not it was the mithridate and theriac smuggled into Mary's many and various jails that foiled the alleged poison plots or simple cunning, it is tempting to speculate that Walsingham's keenness to uncover their source may have resulted from his sheer frustration concerning Mary's continued existence. Certainly, rumour had it that he was intent on poisoning her following her 'final' arrest – presumably to avoid another farcical show-trial like the tribunal of 1568–9.[52] Mary did not, perhaps, expect that she would be poisoned by the testimony of her own trusted secretariat – when Walsingham imprisoned Nau and Curle he might have remembered Cockyn, and reflected further on how a cipher secretary often sat in the centre of each conspiratorial web, his knowledge of all the actors serving as venom enough. Walsingham might also have viewed the discovery of a new source for mithridate and theriac, both rare and expensive substances, as timely: there were rumours originating from Bruges that Lord Burghley would be poisoned.[53] Perhaps Mary's supplier could get her hands on more?

Mary was not the only queen who feared the silent judgement of the poisoner's art: her great rival and cousin Elizabeth I had precautionary measures against such an eventuality built into her daily routine. In 1568, one of Walsingham's Italian correspondents delivered a warning: 'the advices [Elizabeth] has recently received are not by any means to be despised, and begs her to exercise great watchfulness over her food . . . lest poison should be administered to her by secret enemies'.[54] The 'advices' to which he referred were most likely 'Certain Cautions for the Queen's Apparel and Diet', one of which read as follows: 'that it may please Your Majesty to take the advice of your physician for the receiving weekly, twice, some preservatiff *contra pestem & venena* [against pestilence & poison]'.[55] It is not clear what manner of 'preservatiff' Elizabeth was encouraged to take, but given Walsingham's particular interest, mithridate and theriac were presumably leading candidates – the French surgeon royal Ambroise Paré recommended they be taken in the morning for just this purpose, next to a 'conserve of roses, or the leaves of rue, a walnut and dry figs', and, not to be forgotten, 'a little draught of muscadine or some other good wine'.[56] It may have been this regimen that gave Elizabeth the confidence to eat the sweetmeats Mary sent her in the late 1570s, ignoring Walsingham's warning that they might be poisoned.[57]

Despite his desire to uncover the source of Mary's prophylactics and antidotes, Walsingham still had his own contacts: one of these was the French apothecary Nicholas Cabry, whom he had known since the St Bartholomew's Day massacre of 1572 (Cabry, along with several other Protestants, had taken refuge in Walsingham's Parisian residence during the first days of the massacre; Cabry never forgot this sanctuary).[58] In one delivery, Cabry sent

Walsingham 'unicorn's stone' from Constantinople, which he suggested might be tested on animals that had already been given arsenic, but neglected to include 'Metridec treacle', as he assumed Walsingham already had enough.[59] His next delivery included '½ oz of unicorn's stone, which I have tried', as well as some of the ingredients for making 'the mithridate of damocrat'.[60] Two years later, Cabry wrote to his friend: 'as you are curious about rarities, I send you word that I have got two boxes of treacle of Cairo, the seed of true ammonium, very aromatic, of which I send you a little box. Also a piece of Oriental unicorn horn, weighing seven crowns, much more certain than the common which we use daily'.[61] Cabry's reference to unicorn 'stone' as well as 'horn' points to another material commonly considered proof against poison, the bezoar. Bezoars form in the stomachs of ruminants in much the same way as ambergris in whales and pearls in oysters: indigestible, small irritants such as the beak of a squid and a piece of sand are enough to start the process in the latter beasts, while a bezoar may form around a hairball or other foreign object. Amongst their many supposed properties was the ability to render poison inert, and the bezoar taken from the stomach of a unicorn was, naturally, the most prized of all.[62]

Like her secretary of state, Elizabeth I was a firm believer in the bezoar. When a package of jewels was delivered into the care of Mary Radcliffe, a gentlewoman of Elizabeth's Privy Chamber, it included a 'Bezoar stone set in gold hanging at a little bracelet of a flagon chain', which was 'the most part . . . spent'.[63] This stone, clasped in gold and dangling on the end of a chain, would have been in prime position to be dipped into whatever beverage the queen had in her goblet, thus neutralising any poison present. That it was 'mostly spent' suggests that Elizabeth trusted few of her drinks. This was perhaps wise, seeing as even Lady Cobham, a lady of her Bedchamber and donator of mithridate to Mary, Queen of Scots, apparently cared more for the continued health of Elizabeth's enemy than for that of her own mistress.

While Walsingham's men were ransacking Chartley for incriminating evidence following the uncovering of the Babington Plot, they found more than just letters and cipher keys. Listed in an 'Inventory of jewelry, silverware and other small objects' belonging to the beleaguered queen were several items of precautionary ware: objects carved from rock crystal including cutlery handles (rock crystal was believed to shatter or change colour on contact with poison), a bezoar set in silver, 'a black stone, for use against poison, the shape and size of a pigeon's egg, with a protective covering of gold', boxes brimming with other prophylactics including 'coral, terra sigillata, mummy, powder of pearls', and a slice of unicorn horn set in gold on a golden chain.[64] This final piece is a reminder that unicorn horn was a status symbol as well as a valued medicinal tool: like Elizabeth's bezoar, Mary's piece of unicorn horn was attached to a golden chain. Following Mary's execution, her physician carefully guarded a 'little bottle of silver containing a stone medicinable against poison', perhaps the 'piece of an unicorn's horn with a little pendant of gold' bequeathed to her son, King James.[65] Some, such as Paré (who had also served as physician to Mary's *first* late husband, the French king François II), questioned the efficacy of both bezoar and unicorn horn.[66] Such doubts did not stop new pretenders to the panacean throne being regularly mooted: Lancelot Browne, physician to Elizabeth, James and Anna of Denmark, for instance, reported the gallstones of the porcupine (known as 'Lapis Malaccensis, or the stone of Malacca'), as 'preferred far before either bezoar stone or unicorn's horn' in India.[67] The fact that Robert Cecil archived Browne's report carefully amongst his papers suggests that such 'knowledge' was seen as useful intelligence.

Fig. 55: The 'Danny Jewel', an example of a piece of unicorn horn in eminently dippable configuration: it has been suggested that the scratch marks on the back indicate that it saw active service.[68]

POISONS ON TRIAL

While there were many, many substances known to be poisonous, the reasons *why* they were so was much in dispute. Medical knowledge and techniques may have been advancing continuously, but understanding of the efficacy of both poisons and their antidotes was still caught in the twilight zone between magic, tradition and what we now call science. As poisons were also thought to cause diseases, especially plague, panaceas such as mithridate and bezoars were regularly tested in the field, along with other promising elixirs, and reports of their efficacy circulated widely. In 1563, Claudius Richardus, surgeon to the Holy Roman Emperor, Ferdinand I, carried out several experiments on the use of bezoar stone as a treatment for illness, following which he pronounced it 'a kingly medicine'. Successes such as these were published in books such as *Dos libros*, the 1565 treatise on antidotes by the Spanish physician and botanist Nicolás Monardes. Richardus also took part in several poison trials, a practice resurrected by Pope Clement VII in 1524 at the start of his papacy. Keen to establish the potency of a new antidote oil created by the surgeon Gregorio Caravita, Clement 'gave' his physicians two condemned men on whom they might conduct a simple experiment. The pair were robustly dosed with wolfsbane (*Aconitum napellus* or *Aconitum lycoctonum,* the former also known as Monk's-hood) and, once it began to take effect, one of them was anointed with the antidote while the other was left to his fate: the untreated prisoner died in agony. A similar test, also successful, was undertaken on a prisoner who had been given arsenic. A pamphlet was soon published trumpeting the virtues of Caravita's new panacea. These successes kicked off a whole series of human trials in Bologna, Modena, Florence, Prague and Vienna. Other poison tests were carried out on condemned criminals, notably by Paré in 1566, not all of which were successful. Often, when antidotes failed (as in a 1561 trial in Prague where the supposed panacea, which had earlier proven efficacious against arsenic, was powerless against wolfsbane), this was put down to their having lost their potency through age, or to their being counterfeit.[69]

Panaceas were also tested at home. Sir Kenelm Digby, the natural philosopher and diplomat who dabbled in alchemy, was a great believer in the medicinal power of the viper, the only venomous snake in the British Isles.

The 'quintessence' of viper was considered both a remedy and a preventive measure, such that it 'preserveth from Gray-hairs, reneweth Youth, [and] preserveth Women from Abortion'.[70] Digby was well aware that the viper's therapeutic properties were intimately bound to its more poisonous nature, and thus doubtless took great care in preparing the viper wine his famously beautiful wife, Venetia, drank with enthusiastic regularity. When Venetia died suddenly in 1633, most likely of a cerebral haemorrhage, Digby was convinced that his wine had been the culprit. Others thought the same, but rather than it being an accidental death caused by an error in dosage or preparation, they were convinced that Digby had purposely and slowly poisoned Venetia with the noxious liquid, presumably out of jealousy. These rumours were doubtless tied to Venetia's great beauty – surely such a woman must be obsessed with her looks, and thus irredeemably vain and untrustworthy? Certainly, her habitual partaking of what was plainly a dangerous concoction served as proof of this vanity. Digby's wine became tainted: while he had once proudly shared his recipe with the royal physician Theodore Mayerne, he would later restrict his championing of the viper as a panacea to its use in the form of a *powder*. He sent his preparation of powdered viper to William Cavendish, marquess of Newcastle, suggesting that it would not only act as an aid to fertility but also a potent stimulant to help him satisfy his wife Margaret, his junior by thirty years. The marquess was disgusted by the hairs mixed in with the powder, which according to Digby were pieces of bone – he presumably would have found Digby's wine equally repellent.[71] The union produced no children other than Margaret Cavendish's many 'paper bodies', her written works. Digby never stopped searching for panaceas, and his book on the so-called 'weapons salve' by which wounds could be cured by anointing the blade that caused them, *A Late Discourse . . . Touching the Cure of Wounds by Powder of Sympathy* (1658, trans. White), which explained how to effect this cure 'naturally and without any magic', went into twenty-nine editions.[72]

It was not merely antidotes that were tested, however. In the late sixteenth century, a small quantity of suspected poison was 'carefully secured' by one intelligencer, who had intercepted it from a suspected poisoner and offered it to the authorities for testing.[73] Such behaviour was not rare. In 1609, another

Fig. 56: Venetia Digby on her deathbed. She was thought to have been poisoned by viper wine. The recipe for viper wine circulated in textbooks such as John French's *The Art of Distillation*: 'Take the best fat Vipers, cut off their heads, take off their skins, and unbowel them, then put them into the best Canary Sack; four or six according to their bigness into a gallon: Let them stand two or three months, then draw off your Wine as you drink it.'[74]

small phial brought in by one of Robert Cecil's informers was presented to a group of English doctors who proceeded to compare it with other substances found in an apothecary's, using taste, smell and visual inspection (they were presumably quite confident that it was harmless in the first place). Having deduced that it was 'natural balsam of Peru, and no other thing', they put it to one final test, giving some to a small dog which they then kept fasting all night. The dog was unharmed, though had it been poison it was enough, they thought, to have 'killed 5 great dogs, not only one little cur'.[75]

Another instance of animals being used to test for potential poison also serves as an excellent demonstration of the deep-reaching fear of the substance. On 5 October 1607, Paolo Sarpi, a Venetian lawyer, historian and prelate (a brother of the Servite Order), was walking home via the Rialto with two companions, a servant and a patrician, when the group were set upon by five stiletto-wielding *bravi*. The men had allegedly been hired on behalf of the Papacy after Sarpi had weighed in on an argument between Rome and the Venetian state. Sarpi survived the attack, something of a minor miracle as, by his own account, each of the three stiletto wounds he suffered, one of which was to his temple, penetrated 'more than four fingers'.[76] One source records the final thrust as entering his right temple and exiting between his nose and cheek with such violence that not only did it break his upper jaw but the stiletto's long, thin blade was bent in the process. The assassin, unable to remove it, fled the scene, leaving his 'little steel' embedded in Sarpi's skull. Having survived the initial assault, thoughts turned to the possibility of the blade being poisoned, but, once it was removed, Sarpi himself observed that the stiletto lacked the grooves in which he assumed any poison would be secreted (ironically, perhaps, such grooves – missing in this case – were most likely a technique known as cannellation, which served to strengthen a blade, making it less liable to breaking or bending).[77] The Senate were not willing to leave Sarpi's recovery to chance, so decided to send the weapon to a chemist for testing. The chemist stabbed a dog and a chicken with the stiletto removed from Sarpi's skull, and as neither died from their wounds, declared him free from risk of poison.[78]

SPREADING THE POISON

In his *Institutes of the Lawes of England*, the great lawyer Edward Coke listed four ways in which poison might be administered to a target: '*Gustu*, by taste . . . *Anhelitu*, by taking in of breath . . . *Contactu*, by touching: and lastly, *Suppostu*, as by a glyster [i.e., enema] or the like.'[79] The last method was rare but had been used in the murder of Sir Thomas Overbury in 1613. Coke had been deeply involved in the subsequent trial, which is presumably why it makes an appearance here despite its uncommon nature. Taste, scent and touch were vehemently guarded against, however. The 'Certain Cautions for the Queen . . .' did not merely recommend the regular ingestion of prophylactics, and that only food hailing from inside the court, or with spotless provenance, was to be consumed, but sought to shut down other pathways to the monarch. 'Your Majesty's apparel [i.e., clothing], and specially all manner of things that shall touch any part of Your Majesty's body bare' were to be carefully inspected and handled only by trusted individuals. Naturally, it was difficult to control every gift brought for Elizabeth, but a compromise was suggested: 'no manner of perfume either in apparel or sleeves, gloves or such like, or otherwise, that shall be appointed for Your Majesty's favour, be presented by any stranger, or other person, but that the same be corrected by some other fume'.[80] That is, perfumed gloves or sleeves given as gifts should be fumigated – gloves were routinely perfumed to counteract the stink of stale urine impressed on the leather during the tanning process, and the suspicion was that these fresh scents might do rather more than simply mask the stench: they might serve to conceal poisonous intent. The queen had taken this seriously enough in 1563 to give her personal perfumer John Wyngard a 'steel perfuming pan' with both 'lock and key' so that nobody but he could handle it.[81] In France, Catherine de' Medici, the Italian wife of King Henri II, was gaining a reputation as having something of a poisonous influence on the French court. Named in libels as 'Madame la Serpente', she, alongside her ladies-in-waiting, was held responsible for several political poisonings in the late sixteenth century (though such accusations seem to be more the result of misogyny and xenophobia than of any actual evidence).[82] One of her entourage considered especially bad company was the Florentine perfumer René Bianchi, a specialist in scenting gloves who was widely suspected to be an expert with poisons. Poison, perfume and gloves were linked by an intelligence report, which suggested that poison applied to gloves took effect not by direct contact with the hands, but by the victim's 'smelling' the fashionable handwear.[83]

The fear of gloves may have been well founded. The method had certainly reached the shores of England by July 1595, when the physician Dr Wood was imprisoned and lost his ears for the forgery of a document – handwriting, signature, seal and all – that provided him with an annuity on the death of his employer, Gilbert Talbot, 7th earl of Shrewsbury. Wood was confident of Shrewsbury's imminent demise: egged on by the earl's brother Edward, he planned to effect just such an event through 'works of darkness being done in secret', in this case by poisoning the earl's gloves.[84] The dark hand of the poisoner was seen lurking in every shadow, and when even the very air Her Majesty breathed was potentially dangerous, times were bad indeed. The fear was so great that poison and perfume were regularly conflated.

'God forgive me if I judge amiss', wrote one man in 1584, 'in seeing Charles Arundell [recusant and suspected spy for the Spanish only recently released from the Tower] provide gloves & sweet savours at a new perfumer's house in Abchurch Lane of late, if I did not fear some poison towards Her Majesty. She having her senses of smelling so perfect, & delighted with good savours.'[85] In 1587, Robert Dudley, 1st earl of Leicester, received a letter in which the imprisoned sender boasted of his knowledge of making 'mortal poisons and perfumes'.[86] Paré knew of a man who had put a 'secretly poisoned' pomander to his nose; his 'face swelled' and he would surely have died were it not for the remedies provided.[87]

A more detailed and direct report of the possibility of poisoning through breath was provided by Robert Wayland in 1599, buried within the litany of accusations he made against Sir Walter Leveson of Lilleshall Abbey, MP for Shropshire and latterly Newcastle-under-Lyme. Though hardly a spy, Leveson was a guest at the Fleet debtor's prison. According to Wayland, Leveson had 'put in practice a perfume to be made that would poison these that should smell thereof as they should lie in their beds', noting that the distillation apparatus had melted during the manufacturing process and fumes from the resulting chemical spillage had almost poisoned 'Richard Swanton, one of Her Majesty's messengers'.[88]

Wayland was prevailed upon to purchase various such 'things of venomous quality as the powder of glass, ratsbane [arsenic], or Seneca [presumably hemlock]'. Meanwhile, Leveson's solicitor and apparent tutor in all things poisonous, George Shepherd, encouraged him to buy books such as 'Arnaldus de Villa Nova's *de Historia Plantarum*', 'his 9 books de Venemin . . . better to understand how to put in execution his ungodly practices'. Leveson, intent on becoming self-sufficient in such matters, planned his own poison garden using 'diverse roots and seeds' given him by Shepherd, as well as plants such as 'conitum' (most likely wolfsbane), 'carula' (probably *Passiflora caerulea*, the passion flower, which contains cyanogenic glycosides that can lead to cyanide

poisoning) and 'mandray' (mandrake, a poisonous, hallucinogenic plant associated with witchcraft), as well as 'certain [other] things to make a perfume of
a venomous quality'.[89] Another of the reasons that perfumers, with their secretive ways and distillation equipment, were often conflated with poisoners was
the common distaste felt for the use of anything that masked one's true nature,
such as cosmetics – this common understanding presumably exacerbated the
accusations made against Digby following his wife's demise. Medicine, by way
of contrast, was thought to work by balancing the four humours (yellow bile,
blood, black bile and phlegm, which in turn represented the four qualities,
namely heat, cold, dry and wet), thus returning the body to its 'true' state.[90]
There were other forces at work, however.

A TOAD, BY ANY OTHER NAME

One of the mechanisms thought to be behind the operation of antidotes
were the occult virtues of sympathy and antipathy. Sympathy was a natural-
philosophical concept which described the inner links between all things, a
sort of mutual attraction that could be put to use in magic or healing.
Antipathy was, quite reasonably, its opposite; a mutual repulsion. An antidote which relied on antipathy worked by repelling the poison, and once
taken internally would expel it from the patient's body; one relying on
sympathy attracted the poison, so when applied externally would draw it
from the body. The manner in which your antidote worked was thus of no
little importance. An antidote that worked through sympathy, for example,
ought not be taken internally, as this kept the poison from leaving the body,
with predictably disastrous results. Sources sometimes disagreed on which
antidotes worked through which quality, however. The powers of sympathy
also explained those situations in which a substance could work both as a
poison or as a cure, depending on situation and patient. Theriac, for example
(a prime ingredient of which was viper flesh, which, as Sir Kenelm Digby
could attest, seemed as dangerous as it was beneficial) would itself act as a
poison if administered erroneously.[91]

The close relationship between some poisons and their antidotes was writ
large in the humble toad which, in common understanding, provided access

to both: as Duke Senior remarks in Shakespeare's *As You Like It*, 'Sweet are the uses of adversity, / Which, like the toad, ugly and venomous, / Wears yet a precious jewel in his head'.[92] The 'jewel' thought to reside in the toad's head was precious not least because it was reputed to act against poison. In 1569, the French humanist Pierre Boaistuau, for instance, wrote that 'In another country of the *Indians* is found a stone in the heads of old and great toads . . . which some affirm to be of power to repulse poisons'.[93] Paré disagreed: 'the vulgar opinion is false, who think that the toadstone is found in their heads, which is good against poison'.[94] This 'vulgar opinion' was still being aired by Thomas Lupton in 1579, however, who cited the Dutch physician Levinus Lemnius when writing 'A toadstone . . . touching any part [that] be venomed, hurt or stung with rat, spider, wasp, or any other venomous beast, ceases the pain or swelling thereof.'[95]

Opinions varied as to how a toad might be invited to relinquish its precious cargo. Lupton recommended placing a lightly bruised toad in an earthenware pot and burying the pot in an anthill: the ants would eat the toad's flesh, leaving the stone behind.[96] Edward Topsell suggested a rather more polite method – the toad would happily give up its stone if placed on a cloth 'the colour of red scarlet', he stated, though care must be taken to prevent the toad from immediately re-ingesting it. A true toadstone, Topsell suggested, would change colour in the presence of poison or, if held in the hand, would burn it. He also provided another handy test to ensure a stone's authenticity: 'the probation of this stone is by laying of it to a live Toad, and if she lift up her head against it, it is good, but if she run away from it, it is a counterfeit'.[97] That toadstones were, in fact, the fossilised, button-like teeth of long-extinct fish did not stop them from being made into rings or amulets.

Fig. 57: A ring from the Cheapside Hoard, which could easily be mistaken for a toadstone, as it shows one of the features noted in Topsell's *History of Four-Footed Beasts*, namely its having 'naturally engraven the figure of a Toad'.

Fig. 58: A 'frog pouch', a fashionable item of the latter half of the seventeenth century, easily attached to a she-intelligencer's dress. Designed to hold fragrances (the mouth's opening only allows for the tip of a little finger), they may well have borrowed the toad's aura: scent, like the toadstone, was held to protect against poisonous fumes. Six of these toad-sweet bags have been identified in museum collections, all with an English provenance: they closely resemble other *English* needlework styles despite the foreign origin of the silk materials.[98]

While the toadstone and its supposed powers as a panacea were some-what overstated, it was certainly true that a poison could be extracted from the warty amphibians, one which, according to Paré, saw its victims 'taken with a sudden *vertigo* . . . they fell into a swoon, intermixed now and then with convulsions. But they stammered with their lips and tongues becoming black; a froward and horrid look with continual vomiting, and a cold sweat, the forerunner of death, which presently seized upon them, their bodies becoming exceedingly much swollen'.[99] Of the many misdemeanours Wayland placed at Leveson's door in 1599 was his facility for extracting the toad's poisonous virtue. He told of how Leveson would 'put a toad called Rubata into the cup' which he would then heat, drawing the poison from the toad such that 'whoever drank of the same cup should be poisoned' (a tech-nique that might have been familiar to Shakespeare's Hamlet). Wayland detailed another technique – again framing the luckless toad as some sort of familiar by naming it (he presumably confused the Latin word for a type of poisonous toad, *rubeta*, with an actual toad, or might have been taking a sly dig at Robert Cecil) – which involved poisoning salt 'by putting the Toad Rubata in a bag amongst salt and drying it, at the fire, she being in the bag'.[100] It is a reminder that toads, like the mandrake in Leveson's garden, were also associated with witchcraft.[101] Following Juan de Jáuregui's botched attempt on the life of William the Silent, rumours were spread that the failed assassin had not merely been armed with a handgun, but also carried both dried toads and poison about his person.[102]

Knowledge of poisons and antidotes was based largely on ancient authority, notably Pliny the Elder's *Naturalis Historia* and more dedicated texts such as the sixth-century Greek physician and philosopher Galen's *De Antidotis*, and *De Theriaca ad Pisonem*, of contested authorship, published in 1531. According to Galen, poisons such as mandrake, opium and hemlock had natures which were opposed to that of the human, and had their effect because their 'specific form', or 'total substance', as it was known, changed the human body when administered.[103] This reaction differed from disease, which was the result of an imbalance of the four humours, though symptoms of poison and disease might resemble one another.

For Paré, symptoms themselves could be traced to the 'manifest and elementary qualities' of the poison itself. Arsenic, mercury sublimate and verdigris, for example, caused 'in the stomach and guts intolerable pricking pains, rumblings in the belly, and continual and intolerable thirst. These are succeeded by vomitings, with sweats some whiles hot, somewhiles cold, with swoonings, whence sudden death ensues' – indications of an excess of heat aligned with a corrosive quality. Hemlock, henbane, opium and the like worked through coldness, and would thus 'induce a dull or heavy sleep, or drowsiness . . . cold sweats, their faces become blackish or yellowish, always ghastly, all their bodies are benumbed, and they die in a short time unless they be helped'.[104]

Other than Leveson's seed catalogue, another list of poisons commonly in use was provided by Coke, and it was remarkably similar to the litany of substances thought to have been administered to Overbury: 'powder of Diamonds, the powder of Spiders, Lapis causticus (the chief ingredient

Fig. 59: A poison ring. Though more commonly meant for relics such as the hair of a loved one, the secret compartment also made them perfect for surreptitiously delivering poison into a glass or other receptacle. A seventeenth-century musician found a way for the two uses to work in harmony: 'get a ring that is hollow made, either of metal or red Horn, then take a piece of Snakes-Skin, that has been steep'd in the juice of Nightshade . . . and draw it into the hollow of that ring, as you would do hair, and whoever wears it, will be in love with you, by a secret and magnetic power'.[105]

whereof is Soap), Cantharides, Mercury Sublimate, Arsenic, Roseacre, &c'.[106] Paré, on the other hand, organised his lists not by recent use, but by source: 'Minerals or metals are either so taken forth of the bowels of the earth, or else from furnaces. Of these many are poisonous, as arsenic, sublimate, plaister, ceruse, litharge, verdigris, orpiment, filings of iron, brass, the lodestone, lime, and the like.'[107]

Paré's apparent obsession with poisons was perhaps related to the fact that in both his home country, France, and in Italy, birthplace of Catherine de' Medici, poisoning was practically a national pastime. In Italy, traveller Raymond noted the expertise of the natives and their 'curious (yet illegal) tricks in poison, some mortal by smelling so, others that given now, shall have no operation till many months after'.[108] A few years after Raymond's sojourn, a group of five women in Rome began selling poison to wives who wished to rid themselves of their husbands, leading to the death of dozens of men before the cabal was broken. Legend has it that the poison recipe they shared was called 'Aqua Fontana', but in the 1,450 pages of confessions the women merely referred to it as 'aqua'. To make it, one said, take 'two ounces of arsenic and one grosso [either 10 grams or a few pennies' worth] of lead and grind them together. Then fill a new water jar that holds a little more than [0.75 litres] and add the ground arsenic mixed with the lead bird shot'. Another revealed the secret ingredient, boiled toad, and the antidote, vinegar.[109] In France, several decades later, the fortune-teller and poisoner Catherine Deshayes, aka 'La Voisin', and her associates caused havoc at the French court.[110] In England, however, fear of poison far outstripped its actual use.

POISONOUS PLOTS, AGENTS PROVOCATEURS AND TALL TALES

The final decades of the sixteenth century and the first decades of the seventeenth were, as we have already suggested, prime years for the development of English espionage in both theory and practice. With the country seemingly beset by enemies – besieged by Catholics abroad and infiltrated by Catholics at home – plots, conspiracies and counter-espionage were writ large in English life. While poisons and their antidotes could be discovered in medical textbooks, once they had been bought in the apothecary's shop or foraged in the wild and suitably prepared, they still had to be administered. Most of the ways in which they were thought to be delivered to their target were explained in interrogation reports.

While the carefully worked exposure of the Babington Plot had provided Walsingham with all he needed to finally dispose of Mary, Queen of Scots by way of the legal system, the continued presence of French ambassador Châteauneuf (Castelnau's successor) remained a thorn in his side. France was unlikely to allow England to execute a member of its royal family without protest, and Châteauneuf was in a position to make such a move diplomatically impossible. To ensure that the upcoming trial would be Mary's last, Burghley and Walsingham needed to get the French ambassador out of the way. The method they chose was poisonous, but rather than actively poisoning Châteauneuf, they sought instead to implicate him in a conspiracy to murder by poison, one they could promptly, and publicly, foil.[111] All they needed was a suitable individual to carry out their plans.

In 1585, Walsingham had received a letter from Dieppe in which the writer thanked him for 'excusing me unto my mother'. It is unclear why this man was so grateful, but grateful he was: 'there is no man living to whom I am beholding but yourself. If I should live to see my blood shed in your honour's cause I should think it but some recompense for the great good I have received at your hands'.[112] He was William Stafford, the eponymous 'villain' after whom the subsequent plot became known. Walsingham's man through and through, it was time to repay his debt.

In December 1586, Stafford paid Châteauneuf a visit, presenting himself as one disaffected with the English (and, by implication, Protestant) authorities – he had, he explained, become rather unpopular with Leicester, who also happened to be Elizabeth's favourite. Not wishing to live under such a cloud of opprobrium, Stafford suggested that he join the retinue of visiting diplomat Monsieur Pomponne de Bellièvre and thus enjoy safe passage to France. The French ambassador, sensing an opportunity, asked Stafford whether there was 'nobody that for renown will do an exploit?' On asking what exploit he referred to, Châteauneuf replied directly: 'to kill the queen'.[113] Stafford said that he knew of such an individual, namely his brother's man, Michael Moody, then luxuriating in Newgate on account of debt. Persuaded there was still hope for such a mission, and that with one last, brave roll of the dice they could turn the tables on Walsingham, the Frenchmen wandered into his trap.

Unfortunately for Châteauneuf, Stafford was an agent provocateur, and promptly took the ambassador's secretary, des Trappes, to Newgate prison, where he introduced him to the would-be assassin. The ambassador was past the point at which he could hope to protest his innocence. In Newgate, Stafford asked Moody how, exactly, he proposed to assassinate Elizabeth, recounting the answer in his later examination: 'with poisonings of her stirrup, poisoning her shoe, for sayeth he "I am very well acquainted with her shoemaker", or by laying a train of gunpowder where she lieth to blow up the chamber and all that be in it . . . they were pretty devices'.[114] Pretty or not, they were theoretical – Stafford poured cold water on Moody's more explosive idea on account of his mother being one of Elizabeth's ladies of the Bedchamber, but that was more performative than practical, as he already had the ambassador hook, line and sinker; the sting was complete. In what was perhaps a final irony, however, Moody's 'pretty devices' may well have hailed from across the channel.

The *Workes* of the French surgeon royal Paré, published in 1575, contain much information about poison. In the section dealing with poisons delivered via the air (against which the best defence was, apparently, 'not to smell them'), Paré noted reports of substances that 'if you but anoint the stirrups therewith, they will send so deadly poisonous a quality into the rider, through his boots, that he shall die thereof within a short time'. The fact that they did not touch the skin was of no matter, as nature provided its own example, namely the 'Torpedo', a fish which could transmit 'a narcotic, and certainly deadly force' into a fisherman when they were connected only by the net.[115] It does not take a great leap of imagination to conclude that Moody's plan to do away with Elizabeth 'with poisonings of her stirrup' or by 'poisoning her shoe' came directly from a textbook.

Stafford was committed to the Tower, and while one might have expected a man who had admitted to leading a conspiracy to assassinate the queen to quickly lose all connection to his innards, he was released without charge some eighteen months later. Once again, Walsingham had created a plot in the absence of a conveniently real one. The Stafford Plot not only provided the final justification for the execution of Mary, Queen of Scots, namely that she had 'conspired with Her Majesty's subjects to have had her murdered, in the field, in the Chamber, in her bed, with daggers, with pistols, with poison or any other ways', but also allowed for the temporary incarceration of Châteauneuf and his secretary, thus neutralising any potential French protest or retaliation.[116] They were released two months after Mary's execution.

Concocting plots and conspiracies involving poison was not only useful when seeking to remove a problematic individual such as Châteauneuf; it was also good for demonstrating one's dedication and utility to Her Majesty. Walsingham finally passed on to the great spy network in the sky in 1590, leaving the 2nd earl of Essex and Burghley in a frantic race to fill his shoes. Burghley, however, was in the process of stepping back from public life, leaving his son, Robert Cecil, increasingly in charge of affairs of state, much to Essex's chagrin. Having acquired some of Walsingham's most valuable intelligencers, including the Bacon brothers and Thomas Phelippes, Essex, who had been appointed privy councillor in 1594, decided to take matters into his own hands. After all, he had married Walsingham's daughter Frances, the secretary's only surviving child, so doubtless felt this was his late father-in-law's legacy, justly claimed. It was time to engineer a political coup. At the centre of his scheme was Roderigo Lopez, Elizabeth's personal physician and, as luck would have it, a *converso*, that is, a Portuguese Jew who had converted to Christianity. How better to prove one's worth than by foiling a threat to the queen from within her closest circle?

The initial ammunition against Lopez was provided by a correspondence with Spain intercepted by Phelippes, and by the arrest and interrogation of the couriers who enabled it. Once they had implicated Lopez, Essex immediately crowed that 'I have discovered a most dangerous and desperate treason. The point of conspiracy was Her Majesty's death. The executioner should have been Dr Lopus. The manner by poison. This I have so followed that I will make it appear as clear as the noon day.'[117] Once Essex had turned against him, the matter was as good as settled. A brief trial followed, during which much was made of Lopez's Jewish roots.[118] Found guilty, he was hanged, drawn and quartered alongside his three supposed 'co-conspirators' at Tyburn in June 1594. The evidence against Lopez may have been slight, but Essex's need for a public 'win' was great.

While the Lopez affair was not a confection in the manner of the Stafford Plot, as it had its roots in opportunism rather than straightforward entrapment, it suggested that Essex had learned something from his father-in-law with regard to the efficient use of fear, and especially fear of poison. To add to the weight of import, Essex's intelligencer Francis Bacon wrote 'A True Report of the Detestable Treason, Intended by Dr. Roderigo Lopez'. While it remained unpublished until 1667, its original intention was clear: to make public the depth of the conspiracy Essex had foiled, and so add to his reputation and authority as a new master of intelligence. Poison, or the fear of it, was once more a weapon wielded to win reputation and promotion rather than one actually used to effect assassination. This was a lesson Robert Cecil took to heart, and when, a few short years later, bereft of a solid conspiracy with which to further discredit his queen's Catholic enemies and prove that only he, not Essex, could fill his father's shoes (Burghley had died in August 1598), he immediately concocted one, the Squier Plot.[119]

NO GREATER THAN A BEAN

On 29 January 1598, Sir John Stanhope, Elizabeth I's treasurer, received a bill of £4 18s for 'the diet, lodging and other expenses' pertaining to a seven-week stay in the Compter prison, Wood Street, by Edward Squier. Squier's sojourn had ended when he was transferred to the Tower, and he was subsequently 'executed for some lewd & notorious practice pretended by him against Her Majesty's person'.[120] The court gossip John Chamberlain told his friend Dudley Carleton that Squier, 'being in Spain . . . [with] one [Richard] Walpole, a Jesuit', had gone 'with the earl [Essex] in his own ship the last journey, and poisoned the arms or handles of the chair . . . as likewise he had done the pommel of the queen's saddle', but in vain.[121]

It had all started when the Protestant Squier joined an expedition by Sir Francis Drake, then was captured and taken to Spain. It is unclear whether he converted, or whether in return for his release he peddled tales; he in any case promised Jesuits in Seville that he would return to England and there turn assassin. Squier might have had no previous experience as a poisoner, but he soon told his Jesuit handler Richard Walpole of his skill in making perfumes, recounting how he had 'read in Tartalia [i.e., possibly, Nicolo Tartaglia] to make of a ball, the smoke whereof would make a man in a trance & some to die'. Considering this method overly convoluted, Walpole suggested that 'to apply poison to a certain place is the convenientest way'. Squier was given a recipe to follow, and advised to take care not to raise suspicion by purchasing all of the ingredients together. Perhaps overly careless of being discovered, or simply lazy, Squier 'bought 2 drams of opium & 5 drams of mercury water at a pothecaries shop in Paternoster Row towards the further end near Doctor Smith's house'.[122] He then sourced the other three ingredients (which he described as 'such as might be beaten to powder; . . . called by Latin or Greek names; . . . the whole composition was not above the bigness of a bean', and as costing 8 pence all together) in 'a potecaries in Bucklersbury at the Plowe' and in 'a potecaries shop in Newgate

Market'. He mixed the poison, left it to cure as instructed, and tested it on 'a whelp of one Edwards of Greenwich'. As he never saw the beast again, he presumed it had died.[123]

Squier's first target, or so the story goes, was Queen Elizabeth, for whom he abused his position as one of her equerries. Before the queen went riding, he approached her horse, and 'laid his hand on the pommel of the saddle and out of a bladder, which he had made full of holes with a big pin he impoisoned the pommel & the saddle being covered with velvet by brushing the poison in it through the holes of the bladder with his hand and soon after Her Majesty rode abroad that afternoon'. Assuming the poison would soon be transferred to the queen's mouth as planned, Squier set off to the Azores with Essex, this time carrying his poison in a 'little earthen pot of a zell [i.e., even] colour glazed within, with a narrow mouth, which he stopped with cork' in 'his portmanteau'. Within days he had applied the poison, 'clammy as it would stick to the pommel of the chair', rubbing it 'where he [Essex] did use to sit & lay his hand' using a piece of parchment. Squier was arrested on his return from the Azores, after a journey during which Essex had remained stubbornly impervious to the parchment poison which had presumably remained on his pommel throughout.[124]

Following Squier's execution, an anonymous pamphlet entitled *A Letter Written out of England to an English Gentleman Remaining at Padua* was published detailing the whole affair. It received several responses from exiled Catholic writers, including Martin Aray, whose *The Discoverie and Confutation of a Tragical Fiction, Devysed and Played by Edward Squyer* (1599) not only exposed the entire plot as a fiction, but also identified the author of *A Letter* as 'Master Smokey Swine's-flesh', that is, Francis Bacon. Bacon's 'letter' was no such thing; it was rather a piece of propaganda intended to smooth the creases from the government's handling of the case and lay the blame squarely on Spain and the Jesuits.[125] Squier was most likely innocent of the charges laid against him, the plot contrived by Robert Cecil to assert his authority following the death of his father.[126] Just because the Lopez and Squier affairs saw poison used as propaganda did not mean that it was never actually put to nefarious usage, however. One of the most notorious poisonings to take place in England was that of the poet Sir Thomas Overbury in 1613.

POISONOUS FAVOURITISM

Overbury was a close friend of Robert Carr, favourite of King James (who made Carr privy councillor and Viscount Rochester in 1611, and 1st earl of Somerset in 1613). When Carr began an affair with Frances Howard, wife of the 3rd earl of Essex, Overbury initially appeared in the role of Cyrano. His facilitation soon turned to disapproval once the possibility of Frances being granted a divorce so that she might marry Carr reared its adulterous head. His presence in court proving a barrier to a union much desired by Carr, Frances Howard and her family, and having refused an offer of an ambassadorship, Overbury was committed to the Tower. Five months later, he was dead, but not before he had been wracked with fevers, fits of vomiting and a raging thirst. It would take two years before rumours that his death had been illicitly procured became loud enough to see the lieutenant of the Tower Sir Gervase Elwes, the jailer Richard Weston, the physician James Franklin and the lady's maid Anne Turner accused of poisoning him. They had done so, it was alleged, at the behest of Frances Howard. Frances, by now married to Carr, was countess of Somerset. This was no spurious accusation.

Franklin gave testimony that Mrs Turner had asked him for 'a poison, that should not kill a man a presently, but to lie in his body for a certain time, wherewith he might languish away by little and little'. He procured some aqua fortis (nitric acid) which she tested on a cat. It 'languished, and pitifully crying for the space of two days, then died', so the countess deemed this method too violent. Franklin said the same of arsenic, so she sent him to buy some powder of diamonds.[127] Eventually, he bought 'many poisons, that is to say, aqua fortis, mercury water, white arsenic, powder of diamonds, lapis cosmatis, great spiders and cantharides'. There followed, he confessed, a concerted attempt to do away with Overbury, primarily by adulterating his food. When Overbury requested pork for dinner, they 'provided him a pig, and in the sauce they put white arsenic', but their victim 'did eat neither broth nor sauce for the most part'. Next they tried lacing his salt with arsenic, but that also failed, so when he was served partridge with water and onion sauce, 'cantharides, being black, was strawed therein instead of pepper'.[128] Though he began to ail, Overbury stubbornly refused to die; he was perhaps aware of Paré's warning that 'such as fear poisoning, ought to take heed of meats cooked with much art, very sweet, salt, sour, or notably endued with any other taste'.[129] Finally, so the confessions alleged, an apothecary's boy was contracted to administer the coup de grace, the indignity of a fatal enema performed with mercury sublimate.[130]

The four non-noble conspirators were executed; the earl and countess of Somerset lost their reputations, but held onto their heads. Doubts remain as to whether Frances truly intended to murder Overbury, or, indeed, whether his untimely and unpleasant death was the result of poison or chronic ill-health exacerbated by the less-than-clement lodgings and poorly considered self-medication. The timing may have been coincidental, but, within two years of the court case, measures were taken to assert better control over the supply of the sorts of substances used by poisoners – substances that were, of course, also put to therapeutic use. In 1617, King James approved the creation of the Worshipful Society of Apothecaries, and the following year saw the first publication of *Pharmacopoeia Londoniensis* (*The London Dispensary*) by the Royal College of Physicians. The *Pharmacopoeia* was a list of all known drugs, setting out their effects and use – if it was not listed in the *Pharmacopoeia*, it was licensed neither for use nor sale. In 1649, Nicholas Culpeper published an English translation, *A Physical Directory*, which included uses of the various preparations, making this knowledge far more easily available. Culpeper even included a recipe for theriac or treacle. The Royal College was not amused with this threat to their monopoly of pharmaceutical knowledge.

TOXIC RUMOURS

In his *Institutes of the Lawes of England*, Coke wrote that of all the ways in which murder might be prosecuted, poison was 'the most detestable of all, because it is most horrible, and fearful to the nature of man, and of all others can be least prevented, either by manhood, or providence'. For a short period in the sixteenth century, the punishment for such an offence in England was particularly brutal, even for an age not noted for its squeamishness: 'This offence was so odious, that by Act of Parliament it was made High Treason, and inflicted a more grievous and lingring death then the Common Law prescribed, viz. That the offender should be boiled to death in hot water.'[131] As the offence was thus considered graver than other modes of murder, it gave the authorities licence to pursue suspected poisoners more vigorously.

For all the manuals such as the *Pharmacopoeia* and experiments by men such as Paré, poison never quite shook off its devilish reputation. One informer told of a preventive measure that would literally work like a charm: simply utter the word 'Egaldarphe' three times before taking a sip of wine, and if it were poisoned the glass would break; if the cup were silver, it would 'froth or fume'.[132] This claim encapsulated all that was feared about poison – its readiness to adopt the form of any substance it was mixed with made it difficult to detect, and one's best chance of avoiding it may very well have been witchcraft and occult knowledge. These same qualities meant that fear of poison was endemic, and could be whipped up by the Walsinghams of the world in order to justify their less-than-savoury actions; invisible until actually used, poison was the perfect substance to place at the centre of an equally invisible conspiracy which could then be very publicly foiled. Through subterfuge, misinformation and a little judicious torture, poisonous confessions could be extracted from prisoners in order to further a spy chief's political ends: the fear and revulsion poison plots attracted offered an invaluable way to assassinate an individual's character. Later in the century, the public caught on, and used similar unfounded accusations to damage the reputation of first their king and then the royal favourite. Many suspected that the death of Prince Henry in 1612 was due not to typhoid, but to an unknown poison administered by his father, King James VI and I; the death of King James of old age and decrepitude in 1625, meanwhile, led to loud mutterings that his end had been hastened by the duke of Buckingham's poisonous, and unseemingly personal, attentions.[133]

Dangerous as it was, poison's true efficacy as a spycraft technique may well have been in the opportunity it presented to lay claim to the narrative rather than in its utility as a fast, efficient and practically invisible tool of *actual* assassination. Poison may have been an excellent tool for a spy, but fear of poison was the perfect paranoia to put to use in counter-espionage operations. For a trade that dealt in subterfuge, dissimulation and double-crossing, poisonous whisperings were second nature, and these whisperings would often continue long after death, and needed nothing so solid as evidence to support them. Like all truly effective invokers of fear, poison's power to invoke paranoia lay in the simple fact that poisons existed and could be found and administered with relative ease, if one had a mind to do so. The power of poison to create waves of fear in the public also had the spy chiefs themselves terrified, however. Walsingham wanted unicorn horn as badly as Mary, Queen of Scots.

CODA: THE BLACK CHAMBER

The act of spying is perhaps more associated with the ethereal than the physical – the world it conjures is one of snippets of overheard conversations and shadowy figures disappearing into the mist. The currency of the spy was information, and while eavesdropping was probably the most common method of gathering such material, there were safer and more efficient ways than hiding behind the doorways of taverns frequented by people of suspicion. Information was always at its most vulnerable when in transit, and the most common method of communicating over distance was through the humble letter, and the letter was anything but ethereal – what appear so often as flattened, featureless sheets of paper were in truth multidimensional items. Writing a letter in the sixteenth and seventeenth centuries was a relentlessly physical activity. It involved manipulating paper, quill and ink, folding techniques and seals; counterfeiting a letter could also incorporate the imitation of handwriting, the use of ciphers, codes, disguises, invisible inks, cunning methods of delivery, and even poison. As the letter was the most important artefact produced by spies, it was also the artefact most targeted by counterspies. Mastery of the letter's physical characteristics could therefore be the difference between the success or failure of a conspiracy or counter-espionage operation – it is no hyperbole to suggest that the spy's ability to manipulate these features could mean the difference between life and death.

The story of (English) spycraft from 1558 to 1660 is one of missed opportunity, of a movement away from the patronage-based systems of the sixteenth century and its encouragement of competition – rather than co-operation – that had led to innovations such as Gregory's perspective box fading into the mists of time, rather than changing the face of counter-espionage. It is also the story of the rise of a new style of intelligence office, the so-called 'black chamber', which presented an opportunity for these techniques to be committed into an institutional memory, and for the establishment of a more co-operative and effective secret service.

THE BLACK CHAMBER

Despite Arthur Gregory's repeated pleas for a more settled place of operations such as a desk in a room in the Tower, counter-espionage in the late sixteenth and early seventeenth centuries was a largely peripatetic occupation. Dark artificers such as he were sent to where the action was – Gregory was dispatched to join Phelippes at Chartley during the last spasms of the Babington Plot, for instance. This was because when correspondence was intercepted by the authorities it was generally at source, taken directly from its supposedly foolproof hiding place, stolen by an embassy mole, or perhaps handed over by an outwardly sympathetic jailer. If time permitted or expediency demanded, experts were consulted. When Walsingham or the Cecils found themselves in need of Gregory's delicate touch with a seal, they found him at his 'poor house' in Whitechapel, or else sent him the seals to counterfeit. When they needed a hand imperceptibly imitated, they might have sent for Peter Bales at his scrivener's shop in the Old Bailey district. When they needed a cryptanalyst, they sent for Phelippes – latterly, Robert Cecil sent whatever ciphers were in need of cracking to whichever debtor's prison his choice cryptanalyst was at that point gracing with his presence (in a way, Phelippes's incarceration was quietly convenient for the secretary of state). Counter-espionage operations were conducted on an ad hoc, mission-to-mission basis, and generally coalesced around high-value individuals, such as Mary, Queen of Scots or Henry Garnett. While this mode of operation worked reasonably well, and occasionally agents provocateurs were used to construct conspiracies as entrapment, it was at heart a reactive system: it only swung into action once a conspiracy had been discovered. It relied, therefore, on traditional espionage techniques such as betrayal and infiltration. The various competing spy chiefs were always chasing the game.[1]

By the 1630s, a system that made better use of counter-espionage resources such as Gregory and Phelippes had developed in Brussels, the heart of the Spanish Netherlands, though it was aimed at reaping secrets for financial rather than political gain. Alexandrine of Rye-Varax, countess of Taxis, was employing a new method of monetising her family's monopoly of the continental postal service. The Taxis family (later Thurn and Taxis, whose descendants still run the German postal system) were appointed as postmasters of the Holy Roman Empire by the Catholic Habsburg Emperor and commanded most of the postal routes in Western Europe, including those from the continent to England. When Alexandrine was widowed, she took over the family business in her son's name, and transformed some of her postal offices into spy hubs. This kind of intelligence unit would much, much later come to be known as a *cabinet noir*, or 'black chamber'.[2] A black chamber was, in effect, the place where letters were interrogated – the information gleaned from these interrogations was then stored in order that it might be referred to later, whether in a legal court or otherwise, by way of comparing ciphers, cross-referencing suspicious names, and so on. A black chamber created its own papertrail. The individuals who worked within this hidden office were polymaths, scribes, cryptanalysts and technicians, each of whom had their own, particular task – copying at speed, translation, code-breaking, mixing inks, or forging the various marks that authenticated a document (seals, handwriting, signatures, letterlocking). Whereas Gregory and his ilk protected their secrets jealously, and thus almost always worked alone (indeed, Gregory's teaming up with Phelippes at Chartley had been a rare occurrence and was not repeated), this team of at least a dozen individuals worked in tandem and in the same room, much like a modern production line. Their task was to quickly open, copy, refold and reseal scores of letters before releasing them back into the postal stream, their recipients hopefully remaining ignorant of the violation their letters had undergone. Meanwhile, Postmistress Alexandrine sold the information she uncovered to the highest bidder.

One of the reasons that this more centralised mode of espionage operation developed on mainland Europe earlier than in England was the demand for information caused by the Thirty Years' War. In England, the conclusion of peace with the Spanish in 1604 reduced the necessity for a fully fledged intelligence system gathering and storing information to use against its enemies (the Gunpowder Plot notwithstanding), and by the 1630s its secret services were largely reduced to a modus operandi of 'irregular opportunism'.[3] Few in the three kingdoms, even diplomats and ministers, expected their letters to be opened.

It is perhaps hard to comprehend, but if you were not an incarcerated deposed queen or a similarly indisposed suspect in the Gunpowder Plot, you would not necessarily consider that someone might actually dare intercept your letters. The sanctity of the mail was considered absolute – even the Jesuit Henry Garnett was surprised when he realised that not only had the letters between himself and Anne Vaux been intercepted and read, but that they had then been counterfeited so well that neither he nor Anne suspected foul play. In 1633, the Stuart agent in Brussels, Balthazar Gerbier, complained that someone within the Taxis postal service had 'kidnapped' his 'sacred' packets of letters and robbed them of their innocence: his horror would be all the more visceral when he realised that this violation had occured at the behest of a woman and that she had instituted a whole system purely to carry out such abuses systematically.[4] This negative reaction to postal violation was a recurring theme of the mid-seventeenth century, so much so that King Gustavus Adolphus of Sweden somewhat disingenuously gave the interception and publication of some of his letters to the prince of Transylvania as a reason for his joining the Thirty Years' War.[5] The Taxis postal system was subsequently dismantled in those areas of the empire the Swedes conquered (though the Swedes used the opportunity thus presented to begin intercepting the mail themselves, even that of their allies).[6] In England, a similar squeamishness was still present in 1642 when Lucius Cary, 2nd Viscount Falkland and Charles I's secretary of state, argued that the opening of private mail was 'a violation of the law of nature that no qualification by office could justify a single person in the trespass'.[7] Edward Sackville, 4th earl of Dorset and lord chamberlain, also found his thoughts regarding the practices of the king's enemies conjuring up images of sexual ravishment: 'In these licentious times, no rules of common honesty are obeyed, and shameful rapes made, even of letters, between men and their wives, fathers and children, friends and friends. No traffic nor intercourse is safe, nor any man or woman secure whom malice, rage and fury subject to the unlimited actions of some too potent men, to do evil.'[8] The onset of civil war meant that nothing was sacred. Charles discovered this when his former Latin secretary and crypt-analyst, the German Georg Rudolf Weckherlin, was recruited by the Parliamentarians and subsequently opened, deciphered and published some of his former master's letters in the pamphlet *The King's Cabinet Opened* (1645). Even then it led to questions being asked in Parliament.

The Civil Wars changed the nature of counter-espionage. Parliament worked to overhaul the traditional system, in which individuals operating through patronage-based relationships acted as autonomous and sometimes self-appointed spy chiefs, not least as this often ended up with them strug-gling to exert their positions over each other as much as over the supposed enemy. It introduced a series of committees such as the Committee of Safety (later replaced by the Derby House Committee) and the Committee of Examinations to oversee matters of intelligence. The chairmen of these committees were authorised to open the letters of whomsoever they thought fit, and during this time men such as Thomas Scott and latterly John Thurloe would find themselves at the helm of an increasingly bureaucratic intelli-gence operation.[9]

In 1655, a mere six years after the execution of Charles I, the lord protector Oliver Cromwell took a leaf out of Postmistress Alexandrine's book and appointed his then head of intelligence John Thurloe as postmaster general. His reasoning became clear two years later, when he declared that, as letters were the primary mode through which spies might communicate secrets, they ought therefore to be thoroughly interrogated. By this measure, the founding of 'one general Post Office', he hoped to ensure that Thurloe and his successors might 'discover and prevent many dangerous, and wicked designs . . . the intelligence whereof cannot well be communicated, but by letter'.[10] By this one simple move, Cromwell established the Post Office as an organisation whose prime purpose was the surveillance of correspondence rather than its delivery.[11]

Thurloe's Post Office was a relatively organised system of eaves-dropping, but one which added a bureaucratic slant to this classic spycraft

Fig. 60: A 1650s portrait of John Thurloe, taking his gloves off.

technique – instead of only sending spies to listen in on the conversations of suspects, it also sent their papery conversations to an office where they could be panned for the intelligence gold that lay hidden behind their wax seals, letterlocking, ciphers and other security mechanisms. This was eavesdropping from a distance.

Thurloe's unit was not the result of a dazzling moment of inspiration; he was simply following on from the work of his predecessors in gathering experts in all the techniques described in *Spycraft* under one roof in Whitehall, and he did so in the former chambers of Henrietta Maria, then simply known as 'the Queen's closet'.[12] The true change was in ambition – rather than cherry-picking correspondence or operating a sort of 'pop-up black chamber-lite' in the style of Somer at Tutbury, Phelippes at Chartley or Gregory in the Tower, the whole of the post was directed through Whitehall. In this way, Thurloe's operatives were placed where they could best be co-ordinated, controlled and exploited: in the middle of a stream of letters.

By concentrating a group of dark artificers in one place, Parliament had also taken a giant step towards the institution of a secret service no longer reliant on individual geniuses such as Arthur Gregory, but which operated more like a machine. In Gregory's time there was no 'spy school'. Individuals would learn part of their trade through what were effectively intelligencing apprenticeships such as that which Francis Bacon undertook in the embassy of Sir Amias Paulet, or that which Thomas Phelippes's younger brother would later undertake in Bacon's household.[13] These arrangements were based around family contacts and patronage relationships, and were thus not easily accessible. If an intelligencer such as Gregory failed to take on an apprentice, their particular skills and techniques would likely die with them. By concentrating several skilled operatives in one room, the black chamber encouraged a steady cross-fertilisation of ideas and expertise, and ensured that the demise of one individual rarely meant that their particular specialism would suddenly be uncatered for. John Wallis, for instance, was a celebrated mathematician and Parliament's go-to cryptanalyst, whose skills were, if anything, even more rarified than those his predecessor Phelippes had acquired. But just as John Daniel learned the art of counterfeiting a hand by watching the writing master Bales at his work in his shop, so Scott was instructed in the art of cryptography by observing Wallis – one contemporary commented that Scott was soon able to 'unriddle any cipher that was ever made'.[14]

Thurloe's black chamber did not appear out of thin air, as Scott had already thought to employ multiple individuals alongside each other. Thurloe merely expanded and rationalised the chamber in line with his newly acquired powers as postmaster general. It was one thing to inherit some of a predecessor's network, but a fully functioning intelligence service needed the sense of continuity that could only come with documentation. Scott complained bitterly that he was not given any guidance regarding the operation of the secret services that had come before him. He could not get his hands on a single document. This was no new complaint: previous secretaries of state such as William Cecil and his son and successor Robert spent much of their lives trying to take control of the state's papertrails.

When Thurloe began his tenure as Cromwell's spy chief in 1653, he immediately seized every scrap of official documentation he could get his hands on.[15] When with the Restoration the government changed once more, Thurloe finished what he had started, and ran off with its archive, hiding it in a false ceiling at his chambers at Lincoln's Inn. He had also kept a 'black book' full of names and used this to blackmail those of the new regime who wished to dispense with him. (Royalists such as Edward Hyde and Joseph Williamson tried to locate and neutralise this dark archive, but without success.)[16] Not all was lost, however, as Thurloe reckoned without a key feature of the black chamber: institutional memory. The chamber had become a process as much as a collection of spycraft specialists, and one of its members, Samuel Morland, had not only mastered several of its 'departments', but had been working as a double agent since 1659. He, along with the Dutchman Isaac Dorislaus, simply continued to be employed in the chamber as those around them disappeared in the usual frenzy of political bloodletting that accompanied a change of government. Thurloe may have appropriated the archives of the secret services, but Morland remained, in effect, the archive of its techniques.

In many ways, Morland was a man cut from the same cloth as Gregory. He had his fingers in many technological pies, even inventing an early version of the pocket calculator. In 1664 he gained the ear of the secretary of state Henry Bennet, soon to be Lord Arlington, and won an audience with the restored monarch Charles II to show him his 'models in little of several engines and utensils'. These were a series of devices designed to help replicate the counterfeiting skills Gregory and others had previously mastered. It was impossible to distinguish counterfeits made with Morland's 'engines and utensils' from the original letters, so the king ordered that his methods be put to work.[17]

IMPROVING THE BLACK CHAMBER

One technique that was vital to an efficient counter-espionage operation was the speedy production of accurate copies of the intercepted letters. This did not merely allow a letter to be sent on to its original destination without an overly suspicious delay, but was also of vital importance to effective code-breaking, and the more accurately transcribed letters a cryptanalyst had, the better. This was a truth long realised. Thomas Phelippes had once complained of the poor quality of the copies of ciphered letters he was expected to work from – Robert Cecil was reluctant to give him originals, not least when his cryptanalyst was incarcerated at the Fleet in the mid-1590s. Elizabeth's secretary of state was asking the impossible, unless Phelippes was to rely on some manner of divine intervention: 'I hope her Highness will not expect I should do more than a man can do upon an ignorant body's transcript unless I were a Daniel that could tell the dream that was forgotten.' Phelippes felt his time was being wasted: he suspected the original letter was a forgery meant as misinformation. Having none of his own collection of papers to hand, and lacking access to the original, he could neither compare cipher systems nor handwriting to ascertain whether the Spanish had sent a fake cipher to deliberately send the English authorities down rabbit holes.[18] Morland said that he had developed a way to provide accurate copies of documents, allowing for both accurate decoding and also for several individuals to be able to consult them simultaneously. Gregory had asserted the same some seventy years before. Their respective solutions, though strikingly different, provide a glimpse of what was to come: an intelligence unit that functioned via a host of easily replicable actions rather than relying on the artistry of the true dark artificer.

Gregory's perspective box allowed even a relatively unskilled draughtsman to copy any letter quickly, even if it was written in invisible ink or cipher. The idea probably occured to him while he was assisting Phelippes at Chartley, confronted by page after page of cryptotext in need of copying. Even for a man with his command of a quill, reproducing hundreds of cipher symbols accurately was fiendishly difficult and time-consuming, and too many errors made breaking a cipher more challenging than necessary. His was a game-changing piece of technology, but its success was short-lived, as the secret to its construction (and, it appears, even of its existence) subsequently lay hidden for many years in the archives it may have helped to create.

Morland's method also took the creation of multiple exact copies of documents out of the hands of the specialist scrivener. Whereas Gregory's perspective box was a variation of the *camera lucida*, Morland's innovation seems to have been much more akin to that mainstay of the modern office, the photocopier. Its inventor claimed that with it he could not only copy documents 'in under a minute' – no scrivener could work at such speed – but also revive ink that had faded.[19] Morland left no further clues as to how his machine might have worked. Others have surmised, however, that it was effectively an early incarnation of the copying machine patented by James Watt a century or so later, and that Morland may have developed it from an even earlier innovation by noted intellectual Samuel Hartlib.[20] According to the diarist and founding Fellow of the Royal Society, John Evelyn, Hartlib had 'an ink that would give a dozen copies, moist sheets of paper being pressed on it, and remain perfect; and a recipe how to take off any print without the least injury to the original'. (Hartlib also informed Evelyn that there were German stoves which could 'discharge excellent perfumes about the rooms', furnaces which secretaries and spy chiefs under Elizabeth I would no doubt have seen as all their nightmares come true.)[21]

Watt's device worked by pressing a thin piece of moistened paper onto the document to be reproduced, and thus transferring its image from the original to the copy paper – what is known as offset printing. The real work was done by the ink, however. Watt provided a recipe for the ink with which the documents to be copied ought to be written, and also a solution to moisten the copy paper. The two recipes are rather familiar; the former fundamentally gall-water–copperas ink, the latter simply gall-water. When pressed against the document, the gall-water in the 'copy paper' was activated by the copperas in the document ink. Watt's copying machine, and by inference Morland's, was in effect a very targeted invisible ink reveal.[22]

The copying machine was but one of a number of devices designed by Morland that would make the black chamber work more smoothly while demanding less expertise from its operatives. In 1666, he published a treatise entitled *A New Method of Cryptography*. Though short at a mere twelve pages, it included several hand-coloured copperplate engravings printed on a roller press installed in his cellar.[23] Morland stated that his *New Method* differed from other systems by being 'wonderfully facile and practicable', and that it took no more time than copying a letter by hand in a letterbook for administrative purposes as all statesmen were prone to do anyway. He also boasted of its great security, claiming that no cryptanalyst would be able to unravel the secret message 'through all the turnings, windings, and dark passages of so many cryptographical meanders', unless they used 'the Black Art'.[24] As ever, he appears to have been over-egging his pudding, and opinions of the usefulness of his treatise vary.[25]

Morland was ever mindful of those who had 'oft times occasion to hide a word, or short sentence, and not a whole page or letter', that is, the occasional cryptographer. To facilitate easy and quick encryption and decryption, therefore, he 'thought it convenient . . . to publish the description and use of a small portable, and low-priz'd [cheap] Machina, very useful for that purpose'.[26] This little machine was an updated version of Alberti's cipher wheel which used three wheels instead of two.[27] As well as describing it on paper, he also had a super-deluxe customised version of his cipher wheel made in silver for Charles II at the cost of £14 (cast from brass moulds he had made at the Royal Mint in the Tower, plain versions of his wheel in wooden boxes came in at a mere 10 shillings a piece). Developing these new devices cost £272 (around £30,000 today), but the king was more than appreciative of this sort of machinery (perhaps a taste inherited from his aunt, Elizabeth Stuart, who often gave watches as gifts and was fond of automata).[28] Like Gregory before him, Morland understood the power of demonstration; and how better to effect this than the rendering of a paper treatise into a tactile, user-friendly 3D working model? He even included a small aid to his wheel's operation, a 'digital index . . . which is to be put on the third finger of the right hand, that so he may not be constrayn'd to lay down his pen, at every motion'.[29] Morland was intimately acquainted with the process of enciphering and deciphering letters as it was part of his job, and this knowledge informed his devices. His machines were designed both to enhance performance and to save time.

Of the various devices Morland created for the black chamber, only the calculating machine appears to have survived, and this may well be due to the fact that most of his 'engines' had only seen the light of day in 1666, the year of the Great Fire of London. In 1689, Morland recounted how his copying machine was used 'at the General Post Office until at the Fire of London the apparatus was destroyed and was not set up again'. Morland himself surmised that the chamber was not reconstructed due to the necessary money being syphoned off by corrupt officials.[30] There is no evidence of how successful Morland's copying machine was, as only two examples of his process are extant, and of these only one (which bears on its reverse the words 'Sir S. Morland's proposal copied in a minute') is accompanied by what appears to be the original. The copied text is fainter than the apparent original and appears as if it was copied by mirror writing, as one would expect from a technique which relies on taking a direct impression.[31] On flipping the image, however, it is plain that copy and document, while containing the same words, are subtly different.[32]

Morland was a great believer in the importance of surveillance and of the part the Post Office could play in this, writing that

> a skilful prince ought to make watchtowers of his General Post Offices of all his kingdoms, & there to place such careful sentinels, as that by their care & diligence he may have a constant view of all that passes of any moment throughout the universe but more especially a true account of the various tempers of his own subjects, & of the first ferments of all factions, without which it is morally impossible for him long to sit safe on his throne . . .[33]

It was for this reason that he made his proposals for 'the King's Secrett Service', which he sent to Major John Wildman, the new postmaster general, at some point between 1689 and 1691. In it Morland listed its desiderata, which included the following:

> To counterfeit all hand writing so dextrously that upon occasion of State the King may send the copies and keep the originals of any letters, dispatches or other papers, till any designs be ripe for conviction.

To copy any number of whole sheets of paper close written on both sides in as many minutes time, with the advantage that it will be impossible for the copies to be erroneous.[34]

Morland was trying to rekindle interest in his copying machine, and thus his vision of a black chamber as an egalitarian surveillance system fuelled less by personal expertise than by easily replicable actions aided by cunning machines. For a short period Wildman acquiesced, and Morland set about hiring some sixty workmen to rebuild his machines at Lombard Street.[35] Feeling hard done by as a result of an unpaid pension, Morland suggested that the new king, William III, employ him on the upcoming waterworks at Hampton Court as 'a fair pretense to cover the secrecy of intelligence', under which he might continue to work on his spycraft machines.[36] It seems likely that this final proposal was not taken up: when in 1695 secretary of state Charles Talbot, 1st duke of Shrewsbury demanded to know of Morland, now blind and ailing, 'where those instruments and utensils' he had once shown to Wildman 'were disposed', Morland refused to answer and appears subsequently to have hidden them.[37] The new regime, for all the pretensions to modernity it professed, with institutions such as the Royal Society laying claim to a new vision of progress based on co-operation and merit rather than the individualism of the past, had begun to lapse back into the same corrupt systems of patronage that had once persuaded Gregory to keep his spycraft secrets to himself.

UNLOCKING THE SECRETS OF SPYCRAFT

Espionage is a messy and unpredictable business, and spies are slippery and elusive characters, but it is by concentrating on its physical manifestations that we can uncover not only the constant battles being fought between spies and counterspies but also highlight the all-too-often invisible actors in the best-known stories, the dark artificers such as Arthur Gregory. It might appear as though Gregory, for all Camden's praise of his ability to reclose packages imperceptibly, left little in the way of a technical legacy hidden amongst his letters other than a tendency towards self-aggrandisement: 'I have in myself to do Her Majesty especial service in such sort as all our engineers never dreamed of.' He also presented a 'portable counting house fit for all chambers', to Robert Cecil as a gift. It may well have been a boon to the cryptanalyst making use of frequency analysis, as access to a calculator of sorts would have sped up decoding.[38] We will never know, as neither he nor Cecil described the machine or its workings in greater detail, and, unlike Morland's calculator, there is no surviving example. For all Gregory's innovative genius, he, like Morland, made no long-term contribution to the English secret services, because he kept his techniques to himself. By piecing together his epistolary remains, however, we can still deduce that Gregory counted amongst his many innovations a method of rapidly counterfeiting seals, making it a viable option within such a time-sensitive operation as interfering with the post – if a letter took too long to arrive at its destination, suspicions would arise that it had been tampered with. Della Porta's isinglass method was good for 'lesser seals', or for those counterfeiters happy to wait three days for their gypsum to dry and then to send off a letter sealed with mere smudges and splodges; Gregory, instead, wanted a substance that could reproduce seals quickly, in 'large quantities', and with its features as sharp as a first impression. Gregory may have begun by deducing many of his techniques from 'books of secrets' such as della Porta's *Magiae Naturalis*, but he moved far beyond the shaky methods presented on the printed page to fashion techniques that survived exposure to the pressure-cooker environment of counter-espionage work. Gregory's experiments, of which we only have fragmentary reports, still epitomise the continuing quest to master the faithful reproduction at speed of all the authenticating devices then available (paper, quill, ink, folding, seals and handwriting), a search that continued to be necessary to professionalise the secret services.

In examining the physical remains and travails of spycraft techniques, we can not only reread some of the era's most crucial episodes, but can expose those all-too-invisible technicians whose actions and skills propelled them. By understanding the way in which cipher and codes were actually used in the field – as opposed to their presentation in textbooks – we can see that it was the royal consorts who introduced the technique into England. In relation to one of the more famous plots of the era, we can see how the undoing of Mary, Queen of Scots was not by the hand of Babington but by those of Claude Nau, Gilbert Curle and Jerome Pasquier. Not only did these secretaries play a crucial role in exposing a woman who fully understood the nature and ramifications of communicating by cipher, but they also allow us to see that the so-called 'Gallows Letter' has been misunderstood for hundreds of years. The doodle of the gallows was never on a single letter, but on a packet, and in any case did not refer to Mary's fate, but to that of her secretaries. Phelippes called another letter, the one which truly was the undoing of Mary, 'the Bloody Letter'. Phelippes knew full well a condemned queen would not swing from the gallows, but he hoped that his true opponents, the secretaries, would do so. The real battle in this plot was not between Walsingham and Mary, nor even Walsingham and Babington, but between Phelippes and Mary's secretaries, actors who remain peripheral characters in nearly all of the queen's biographies. The Babington Plot was not defeated by cryptanalysis, but by Walsingham's cunning shifting of the field of conflict. By employing Gifford to syphon off Mary's correspondence while allowing her to believe that it was going on to its destination unhindered, and in the process intercepting several cipher keys, Walsingham gained crucial hours if not days in which to fully frustrate Mary and her secretariat.

The increase in surveillance over the course of the seventeenth century was accompanied by a growing understanding of the need to disguise one's intentions, or even one's identity. Use of steganographical techniques such as mercantile discourse increased, as did attempts to hide identities through counterfeiting hands. The use of steganography is difficult to spot in early modern letters, as its primary security feature was not complexity, which usually advertised itself through use of mystifying symbols or numerous folds, but invisibility. By fully understanding how techniques such as the Cardan grille might actually have worked in the field we can, for example, not only show that a woman, Lady Brilliana Harley, was an important exponent of the art (and thus far its only identified practitioner), but show how other letters might betray the use of such a grille. This will allow us to discover other users in the future.

The ultimate steganographical technique was the use of invisible inks. As with all spycraft techniques, invisible inks were more difficult to use effectively than is generally appreciated, and also came in more varieties than generally accepted. Each white ink had its pros and cons, and presented particular challenges to the counterspy. By exploring a famous incident which revolved around invisible inks, we not only spot the use of unusual substances such as marmalade, but again see the actions of usually invisible agents. When imprisoned in the Tower following the Gunpowder Plot, Henry Garnett and Anne Vaux were hoodwinked by the genius of Arthur Gregory and the Tower's then lieutenant, Sir William Waad. Waad's man Carey intercepted their letters, and Gregory revealed the messages they had hidden with their particular choice of inks. This, naturally, rendered the original letters unusable for anything but evidence. Using his perspective box and no little skill, Gregory counterfeited their letters – invisible ink and all – so that these incriminating communications might continue until enough evidence was gathered. This leads us to the conclusion that neither Garnett nor Vaux read the letters that they sent each other. Instead, they read the letters forged by Gregory. The letters in the archives were those inter- cepted, opened and read by the authorities – we do not, and never will, know what was received by either Garnett or Vaux. The letters in the archive available to the researcher do not so much illuminate the events, as they illuminate the workings of the surveillance system.

And finally, the weapons used to effect the last resort of the spy, assassina- tion, reflect the conclusions reached about letters – an assassin was at their most vulnerable immediately after carrying out their mission. Weapons such as stilettos and handguns had their advantages, but both had to be used from relatively close range – in the case of the stiletto, intimately so. Poison was the spy's true weapon – it was not just the last resort of wronged women. As insubstantial as it was terrifying, poison displaced the assassin into a different space and time from their victim, and could be administered without the blind courage or training demanded by the use of stiletto or pistol. A truly egalitarian weapon, poison could be used in such a way that at the moment of truth, the assassin would be long gone. This quality, along with the lack of medical consensus over the use, cure or even nature of poisons, meant that poison was a weapon that perfectly fitted the spy's aim of asserting political action through manipulation of information – there was often no need to poison anyone, as fear of poison was enough to get the job done. Our exploration of its use has brought clearly into focus the horror of the regime whose rival spy chiefs framed naïve conspirators such as Edward Squier – and innocent physicians such as Roderigo Lopez – simply to further their own careers.

Ultimately, *Spycraft* shows us that the true fingerprints these spies left behind are in the techniques they used to carry out their missions, techniques that were developed by the Gregorys and Morlands of the era. It is in the archives that we may catch these spies and dark artificers, and through the physical remains of their interventions that we can best understand their nature. When it comes to those invisible actors in the dangerous trade, we truly may 'know them by their foldings'.

—◇—

LESSONS: THE SCHOOL OF SPYCRAFT

The following section concerns the practical application of some of the techniques discussed in *Spycraft*. These lessons may be experiments carried out by ourselves and others, step-by-step explanations of how certain ciphers functioned, or simple tables containing lists of ingredients and their modern equivalents. It is worth pointing out that if there is one thing that we have learned about spycraft techniques in general, it is that they do not always work as advertised: they often need some coaxing to achieve the best results.

The information in this book is provided for entertainment and historical purposes only – responsibility for its use resides with the reader and the reader alone. Neither the authors nor the publisher accept any legal responsibility or liability for any use of the substances listed in *Spycraft*, and we do not endorse the use of any ingredients that are toxic or otherwise harmful to beast or human (whether in liquid, powder, plant or amphibious form) by the reader.

1. FRAUD & FORGERY

Lesson 1.1. Counterfeiting Seals: A Gypsum-Based Method[1]

Ingredients

Anhydrous gypsum powder
Water
Gum arabic
Olive oil
Shellac solution
Glycerine

Process

— Apply olive oil to wax seal
— Mix 2 parts water to 1 part anhydrous gypsum powder and apply mixture to cover as much of wax seal as possible
— Allow to dry for at least 1 hour
— Apply 1 part water to 1 part anhydrous gypsum powder mix to completely cover the wax seal
— Let dry for approximately 1 hour
— Mix 1 part water to 1 part anhydrous gypsum powder (with 5 per cent gum arabic) and use this mixture to apply strengthening material (such as fabric) to the reverse of the gypsum cast
— Allow to dry for between 2 hours and 2 days
— Carefully release gypsum cast seal
— Cover gypsum cast with shellac
— Let dry for at least 5 minutes
— Screw gypsum cast into screw stamper (see Fig. 9)
— Cover gypsum cast with 1 part glycerine to 1 part olive oil mixture
— Apply hot wax to letter
— Apply gypsum cast to wax
— Allow wax to cool
— Remove cast
— Retouch wax seal as necessary

Notes

Extreme care is necessary here; there are several points at which things can go wrong:

1. if oil gets on the paper around the seal it may alert the recipient that subterfuge has taken place
2. as the first water–anhydrous gypsum powder mix is quite watery, it is liable to drip onto the paper, again potentially alerting the recipient

3. failure to add enough strengthening material can lead to the cast breaking, while having too much (especially if it takes the form of a piece of fabric) makes it liable to leaving traces on the final seal
4. the seal cast may well break when being removed from the seal
5. adding support to the cast in the form of a screw stamper and/or a plate to support the whole reduces breakage
6. the cast must be sealed with shellac and oiled to prevent gypsum residue remaining in the final seal.

Conclusions

This process is far more complicated and delicate than della Porta and company make out. It also takes quite an investment in time: to make a good counterfeit could take anywhere from two days to a week. An experienced and skilled operator can, however, make seals that are indistinguishable from the original, and, as Gregory suggests, it is important that the seal to be cast from is as good an impression as possible.

Lesson 1.2. Counterfeiting Seals: Other Recipes

While the gypsum recipe is perfectly safe, the other recipes mentioned by della Porta are not so, as they use ingredients that are toxic. Here are the basic processes that are at work:

Sulphur + Ceruse

This recipe from della Porta combines sulphur and ceruse (lead carbonate and lead hydroxide) to create a soft cast of a wax seal. Depending on the sulphur used – potentially sodium sulphide, sodium sulphate or atomic sulphur – the resulting cast compound might be lead(II) sulphide, known as galena, or lead(II) sulphate, known as milk white (see della Porta, *Natural Magick*, 351).

Vinegar + Vitriol + Verdigris + Iron + Quicksilver

This recipe from della Porta is more complicated in its method and materials. The combination of vinegar and vitriol, or acetic acid and sulphuric acid, with verdigris, either copper(II) carbonate or copper(II) acetate, creates a corrosive environment for the iron plates. With the addition of quicksilver, or mercury, a casting compound is created, potentially mercury(II) sulphate, mercury(II) acetate, mercury sulphide (known as cinnabar), or some combination thereof (see della Porta, *Natural Magick*, 351).

Steel + Quicksilver

This recipe from della Porta combines steel and quicksilver to create a metal cast of a wax seal (see della Porta, *Natural Magick*, 351).

2. CIPHERS & CODES

Lesson 2.1. Homophonic Ciphers

If we take a simple substitution alphabet like so:

a	b	c	d	e	f	g	h	j	k	l	m	n	o	p	q	r	s	t	u	w	x	y	z
u	w	x	y	z	a	b	c	d	e	f	g	h	j	k	l	m	n	o	p	q	r	s	t

and use it to encode the phrase 'cloak and dagger', we end up with 'x f j u e u h y y u b b z m'.

A homophonic cipher is simply a cipher that provides more than one possibility for some letters of the alphabet. If, therefore, we add a single homophone for just three of the more common letters (namely 'a', 'e' and 'o'), like so:

a	b	c	d	**e**	f	g	h	j	k	l	m	n	**o**	p	q	r	s	t	u	w	x	y	z
u	w	x	y	**z**	a	b	c	d	e	f	g	h	**j**	k	l	m	n	o	p	q	r	s	t
η				δ									γ										

'cloak and dagger' can now be encoded in thirty-two different ways, including, for instance, 'x f j u e η h y y u b b z m', 'x f γ u e η h y y u b b z m' and 'x f γ u e η h y y u b b δ m'.

If we add another homophone for these three letters, so that a = u, η or ρ; e = z, δ or π; o = j, γ or σ, the number of permutations shoots up to 243. With three or more possible homophones for common letters such as 'a', 'e', 'i', 'o', 's', 't', etc., things stand a fairly good chance of getting severely out of hand!

Lesson 2.2. Mnemonic Cipher Keys

Argenti's mnemonic key used a keyword to reorder the alphabet, which was then represented numerically. After the keyword gives the substitutions for the first few letters (here we use 'spycraft'), giving us the first eight letters of our substitution alphabet, the remaining letters are listed in order, giving us a complete alphabet as follows:

1	2	3	4	5	6	7	8	9	10	11	12	13	14	15	16	17	18	19	20	21	22	23	24
s	p	y	c	r	a	f	t	b	d	e	g	h	i	k	l	m	n	o	q	u	w	x	z

The above, converted into a usable encoding table, gives us:

a	b	c	d	e	f	g	h	j	k	l	m	n	o	p	q	r	s	t	u	w	x	y	z
6	9	4	10	11	7	12	13	14	15	16	17	18	19	2	20	5	1	8	21	22	23	3	24

Encoding 'cloak and dagger' thus gives us either '41619615618101061 212115' or '4.16.19.6.15.6.18.10.10.6.12.12.11.5'.

Lesson 2.3. Mnemonic Code-Name Keywords

BL, Egerton MS 2550 contains three cipher keys in which the spy's code name also serves as a mnemonic code-name keyword, providing each individual with a personal, non-contiguous substitution alphabet.[2] The code names are Profligantes, Lycanthropus and Labyrinthus. To turn a code name into a complete substitution alphabet, write the unused letters of the alphabet in order underneath the code name, like so:

p	r	o	f	l	**i**	g	a	n	t	e	s
b	c	d	h	k	**m**	q	v	w	x	y	z

The matching letters are now taken as plaintext to cipher, such that plaintext 'p' is enciphered as 'b' ('b' is the first letter of the alphabet that does not appear in 'profligantes'), while plaintext 'i' is enciphered as 'm'. A full, unalphabetised table of this substitution alphabet would look like this:

p	r	o	f	l	i	g	a	n	t	e	s	b	c	d	h	k	m	q	v	w	x	y	z
b	c	d	h	k	m	q	v	w	x	y	z	p	r	o	f	l	i	g	a	n	t	e	s

An alphabetised table of this substitution alphabet would look like this:

1	2	3	4	5	6	7	8	9	10	11	12	13	14	15	16	17	18	19	20	21	22	23	24
a	b	c	d	e	f	g	h	i	k	l	m	n	o	p	q	r	s	t	v	w	x	y	z
v	p	r	o	y	h	q	f	m	l	k	i	w	d	b	g	c	z	x	a	n	t	e	s

The phrase 'cloak and dagger' would thus encode as 'rkdvlvwoovqqyc'.

The same process produces different substitution alphabets for the spies Lycanthropus and Labyrinthus:

l	y	c	a	n	t	h	r	o	p	u	s
b	d	e	f	g	i	k	m	q	w	x	z

l	a	b	y	r	i	n	t	h	u	s	c
d	e	f	g	k	m	o	p	q	w	x	z

This type of mnemonic cipher key also appears in the folium holding the so-called 'Babington cipher' along with those for Dr Lewes and Lady Ferniehirst (see Fig. 23) in the phrase 'The watch words [are] diligently or faithfully'. These two words, 'diligently' and 'faithfully', function perfectly as mnemonic keywords in their own right:

d	i	l	g	e	n	t	y	a	b	c	f
h	k	m	o	p	q	r	s	v	w	x	z

f	a	i	t	h	v	l	y	b	c	d	e
g	k	m	n	o	p	q	r	s	w	x	z

Alternatively, they can be used together to form a single mnemonic keyword, 'diligentlyfaithfully' (one simply leaves out the 'or'):

d	i	l	g	e	n	t	y	f	a	h	u
b	c	k	m	o	p	q	r	s	w	x	z

Lesson 2.4. The 'Great Cipher'

This innovation was formalised by the great French cryptographer Antoine Rossignol, and was used in the mid-1600s. Rossignol had noticed that most nomenclators were built up in a logical (and thus predictable) manner. A list of names, for example, would most likely follow a strict hierarchy of import-ance, whereas words were extremely likely to be listed alphabetically.

Rossignol sought to remove these parallel relationships between plaintext and (numerical) code to increase the security of his ciphers.

For example, if one wrote, as most did, one's list of names in order of importance, one might end up with 1 = King James, 2 = Queen Anna, 3 = Prince Charles, 4 = Princess Elizabeth, 5 = Lord Buckingham, and so forth. Having ascertained that 1 = King James, one could easily deduce that 2 might be Queen Anna. In similar fashion, numerals replacing words or word-partials would invariably be listed alphabetically, such as 88 = when, 89 = where, 90 = which, 91 = who, 92 = why.

These internal relationships gave the cryptanalyst an extra way to recover the plaintext. Rossignol's idea was to mix the relationships up. The nomenclator above (1 = King James, 2 = Queen Anna, 3 = Prince Charles, 4 = Princess Elizabeth, 5 = Lord Buckingham, 88 = when, 89 = where, 90 = which, 91 = who, 92 = why) would be reorganised (e.g. 1 = which, 2 = Lord Buckingham, 3 = why, 4 = Queen Anna, 5 = who, 88 = when, 89 = Princess Elizabeth, 90 = King James, 91 = where, 92 = Prince Charles). Removing the parallel relationship between plaintext and code also made the life of both sender and receiver far more difficult, so the nomenclator would be written in two forms: the first was the encoding table, in which the plaintext was organised in standard (ie, hierarchical/alphabetical fashion); the second was the decoding table, which arranged the code in logical fashion.

Encoding Table		Decoding Table	
King James	90	1	which
Queen Anna	4	2	Lord Buckingham
Prince Charles	92	3	why
Princess Elizabeth	89	4	Queen Anna
Lord Buckingham	2	5	who
. . .		. . .	
when	88	88	when
where	91	89	Princess Elizabeth
which	1	90	King James
who	5	91	where
why	3	92	Prince Charles

See also the nomenclators employed by Elizabeth Stuart in her communications with Sir Thomas Roe in the late 1630s, which are expressed in varying degrees of logic, alphabetical or hierarchical (e.g. 1 = do, 2 = can, 3 = be, 4 = could . . . 45 = at, 48 = never, 51 = her . . . 116 = Sir William Boswell, 118 = [null], but 160 = England, 161 = His Majesty, 162 = the King, 163 = Scotland . . . 233 = agreement, 234 = agent, 235 = ambassador . . . 246 = aid, 247 = affairs, and so on).[3]

Lesson 2.5. Alberti's Cipher Wheels

To construct your own cipher wheel, simply visit https://yalebooks.co.uk/book/9780300267549/spycraft/ and print out one of the two outer volvelles (either 1. with the numerals for superencryption or 2. with a twenty-four-character early modern alphabet), and an index wheel (3. Alberti's original, 4. early modern English, or 5. uninscribed – make your own cipher!). Attach the index wheel to the outer wheel and cipher to your heart's content.

To give an example using Alberti's cipher wheel (Fig. 17), 'we are undone', the message we enciphered on p. 69 in the alphabet indicated by the wheel's configuration, becomes 'jv qfv jbtcbv'. The encryption is obviously compromised by the lack of a 'w' in Alberti's outer alphabet, but the message is enciphered using a single substitution alphabet (a monoalphabetic cipher), and is thus relatively simple to break – that is, 'v' is the most common letter, so probably equates to 'e' (as is, indeed, the case). Moving the cipher wheel one character for each of the message's letters, however, and we have a polyalphabetic cipher, and the message becomes rather harder to conquer: 'js ncp dvmtl'.

Lesson 2.6. Superencryption: Building Alberti's Numerical Nomenclator

The four numbers included on Alberti's cipher wheel (Fig. 17) were designed to be used with a numerical nomenclator. They can be arranged in many different combinations, from 1 to 4444, like so:[4]

Using one number gives us four options: 1, 2, 3 and 4.
Using two numbers gives us another 16 options: 11, 12, 13, 14, 21, 22, 23, 24, 31, 32, 33, 34, 41, 42, 43 and 44.
Using three numbers gives us a further 64 options: 111, 112, 113, 114, 121, 122, 123, 124, 131, 132, 133, 134, 141, 142, 143, 144, 211, 212, 213, 214 . . . up to 441, 442, 443, 444.

And using four numbers gives us a whole heap more: 1111, 1112, 1113, 1114, all the way to 4441, 4442, 4443 and 4444.

In total, there are 340 possibilities.

Each number combination would be assigned to a person, country, activity, thing, etc. These numbers could then be combined with the substitution alphabet when writing the cryptotext. In Alberti's clever system, the nomenclator numbers were also converted into the appropriate substitution alphabet, thus providing a second level of encoding, also known as super-encipherment or superencryption. Nomenclators were usually committed to paper, as in Fig. 25, but a short enough nomenclator could be committed to memory instead, adding another level of security. Take this example:

1 = The King	11 = London
2 = The Queen	12 = Paris
3 = The Prince	13 = Antwerp
4 = The Pope	14 = Madrid

To encipher the message 'The King and Prince must leave London for Antwerp', we first use the nomenclator, giving us the following semi-ciphertext: '1and3mustleave11for13'. If we then encipher the message monoalphabetically using Alberti's wheel (index set at 'M'), we are left with 'mqftoajgh&vmjvmmxcfmo'. Any cryptanalyst applying frequency analysis to this message would doubtless conclude that the ciphertext letter 'm', being the most frequent letter in the message, represented the plaintext letter 'e', leading them down a fruitless and time-consuming rabbit hole. Other ways of helping disguise the existence of a nomenclator within a standard cipher alphabet included representing it with a letter prefix, giving you 'ka', 'kb', 'kc' to 'la', 'lb', 'lc', etc., as necessary.[5] In general, however, nomenclators would most often use straightforward numbers.

Lesson 2.7. Numerical Polyalphabetic Cipher Indicator

Another way of indicating a polyalphabetic shift cipher was using a numerical indicator at the beginning of the message. The numerals accord to the degree of shift, with 1 meaning a = a, 2 meaning a = b, etc. The number 436, for example, would mean using the alphabets D, C and F from the shift table in Fig. 19 (horizontal blue), repeating the sequence until your ciphertext is complete:

key/index	4	3	6	4	3	6	4	3	6	4	3	6	4	3	6	4	3	6	4	3	6	4	3	6
plaintext	w	r	i	t	e	y	o	u	r	m	e	s	s	a	g	e	l	i	k	e	t	h	i	s
cryptotext	a	u	o	x	h	e	s	x	x	q	h	y	w	d	m	i	o	o	o	h	z	l	l	y

So the plaintext 'write your message like this' will encode as '[436] auoxhesxxqhywdmiooohzlly'.

Lesson 2.8. The Keyword Cipher

The keyword could be agreed in advance or included in the ciphertext itself (though the latter makes it rather susceptible to breaking by a canny cryptanalyst). Here we encode a message using the keyword 'SPYCRAFT' that begins with the words 'destroy the fathers' using shift ciphers as indicated in the keyword. This can be achieved using a Trithemius table or an Alberti wheel:

key/index	S	P	Y	C	R	A	F	T	S	P	Y	C	R	A	F	T	S
plaintext	d	e	s	t	r	o	y	t	h	e	f	a	t	h	e	r	s
cryptotext	w	s	q	w	i	o	d	n	a	t	d	c	l	h	k	l	l

Your message will read 'wsqwiodnatdclhkll'.

BL, Egerton MS 2550 shows one spy practising (albeit not always successfully) encoding and decoding two phrases – 'God save King Charles' and 'this is midsommer' – with the keyword 'robertus', using this exact tabular form.

Lesson 2.9. The Autokey Cipher

The weakness of the keyword is especially apparent when shorter keywords are used. Encoding the message from *Lesson 2.8* with the keyword INTER, for example, gives us a ciphertext of 'mrmyfal nmw oanmwaf'. The fact that the TER of the keyword coincides with 'the' in this message twice, even in this short extract, is obvious from the (here underlined) repetitions in the ciphertext: 'mrmyfal nmw oanmwaf'.[6] The autokey cipher fixes this weakness by removing the repetition of the keyword: in an autokey cipher, the keyword is used only once, with its job of dictating the shift alphabet in use then taken up *by the message itself*. The key for our message now becomes 'spycraft destroy the fathers':

autokey/index	S	P	Y	C	R	A	F	T	D	E	S	T	R	O	Y	T	H
plaintext		d	e	s	t	r	o	y	t	h	e	f	a	t	h	e	r	s
cryptotext		w	s	q	w	i	o	d	n	l	i	y	t	l	w	b	l	a

Your message will now read 'wsqwiodnliytlwbla'. The underlined letters in the cryptotext of this autokey example are the same as in the keyword example in *Lesson 2.8*; after this the two cryptotexts diverge markedly.

Lesson 2.10. The Message Decoded (Fig. 22)

Beware that none of your messingers quhome you send forth of the Realm carie anie letters vppon themselves but make ther dispatches bee conveied either after or before them by some other Take heed of spies and false brethren that are amongst you spetially of some priestes alreadie practised by our enemies for your discoverie and in anie wise keepe never anie paper about you that in anie fort maie doe harme for from like errors haue come the only condemnation of all such as haue suffred heretofore againnst whome could there otherwise haue been nothing proved.[7]

4. INKS & INVISIBILITY

Lesson 4.1. Invisible Ink Forms from della Porta's Natural Magick, *340–3*

Recipe	Reveal
Vitriol dissolved in boiling water	Gall
Burnt straw in vinegar	Unclear
Sour galls in white wine	Unclear
Gall-water	Diluted vitriol
Solution of alum (for linen/rag)	Water
Lemon juice	Litharge in water and vinegar
Goat's fat on stone	Vinegar
Citron, oranges, onion, almost any sharp thing	Heat

Sour grapes	Heat (reveal as black)
Services	Heat
Cherry juice added to calamus	Heat (reveal as red)
Sal ammoniac solution	Heat (reveal as black)
Vinegar, egg white and quicksilver	Heat (reveal as white)
Ceruse and traganth gum	Candlelight
Vinegar or urine on skin	Soot or burnt paper
Fat, gum, fig-tree sap, milk of Tithymals	Coal dust
Gum arabic or traganth in water, write on glass	Soot or burnt paper
Smear goat fat and turpentine on paper, write with iron stilo	Soot only (not fire or water)
Beat an egg, write with liquid, blacken the paper	Scrape off the black, letters will appear white
Writing on an egg (3 techniques):	
1. Wrap eggshell in wax, scrape letters with iron stilo, soak egg in 'waters of depart' (nitric acid), remove wax	Crack egg and hold the shell to the light
2. As above but boil egg first; after writing in wax soak egg in a mix of alum and powdered gall, then in sharp vinegar	Remove shell, message will appear on the white of the egg
3. Mix alum and galls with vinegar, use this to write on the egg. Dry egg in the sun, place in 'sharp pickle'	Reveal as above (This is Africanus's method. Della Porta was unsure of what was meant by 'sharp pickle' but 'put it into vinegar, and could do nothing of it')

Lesson 4.2. Ingredients for Inks, Invisible or Otherwise

Name	Modern Equivalent	Description
Alum	Potassium aluminium sulphate ($KAl)SO_4)_2$)	White powder, used in pickling foods and as a mordant (fixer) for dyes

Calamus	Calamus	Cane plant aka sweet calamus/ Sweet-scented lemongrass of calamus
Cervices	Services	Fruit of the service or sorb tree
Chalchantum		Synonym for vitriol
Cinnabaris (aka dragon's blood)	Cinnabar/Mercury sulphide (HgS)	Toxic ore used in alternative medicine, originally used as a pigment due to its deep red colour
Dragon's blood	N/A	'Bright red gum or resin, an exudation upon the fruit of a palm, *Calamus draco*' (*OED*, 'dragon's blood', n.)
Gum	Gum	'Viscid secretion issuing from certain trees and shrubs, which hardens in drying but is usually soluble in cold or hot water, in this respect [often] differing from resin' (*OED*, 'gum', n.2)
Gum, arabic	Gum arabic	Gum made from the hardened sap of the acacia tree, used as a stabiliser and emulsifier in foodstuffs and a binder for pigments
Gum, juniper	Sandarac	Gum made from resin of the cypress pine (*Callitris quadri-valvis / Tetraclinus articulata*)
Gum, traganth/ Gum-dragon	Tragacanth	Water-soluble gum made from milkvetch or mallow, shrubs of genus *Astragalus* or *Sterculia*
Litharge	Lead(II) oxide (PbO)	Toxic reddish powder used in gilding – when mixed with linseed oil it makes a hard, waterproof cement

Quicksilver	Mercury	Highly toxic and reactive metal, liquid at room temperature
Sal ammoniac/ Ammoniac salt	Ammonium chloride (NH_4Cl)	Salts used in breadmaking
Tithymals/ Tithymalus, milk of	Sap of spurge	Spurge, from genus *Euphorbia*, used as a purgative
Turpentine	Turpentine	Spirits made by processing resin from pine trees, used as a solvent for making paint and varnishes
Vitriol, blue (vitriol of Cyprus or Romish vitriol)	Copper sulphate ($CuSO_4$)	Toxic crystalline substance used as fungicide
Vitriol, green/ copperas (vitriol powder)	Iron(II) sulphate ($FeSO_4$)	Crystalline substance used as a mordant (dye fixative) in the textile industry and to blacken leather in the tanning industry; can be distilled to make sulphuric acid
Vitriol, oil of	Sulphuric acid (H_2SO_4)	Highly corrosive acid
Vitriol, white	Zinc sulphate ($ZnSO_4$)	Crystalline substance used as a mordant and preservative for leather

Lesson 4.3. Testing Inks, Invisible or Otherwise

#	Invisible ink	Material	1st Action	1st Reveal	1st Reveal permanent?	2nd Reveal?	2nd Reveal permanent?
1a	Lemon	Paper	A	Heat	Permanent	N/A	N/A
1b	Lemon	Paper	L	Water	Fades	Heat	Yes
2a	Orange	Paper	L	Heat	Permanent	N/A	N/A
2b	Marmalade	Paper	O W	Heat	Permanent	N/A	N/A
3a	Alum	Paper		Water	Fades	Water	No
3b	Alum	Paper	T	Water	Fades	Heat	Yes
3c	Alum	Linen	O	Water	Fades	Water	No
3d	Alum	Linen	D	Water	Fades	Heat	Yes
3e	Alum	Paper	R Y	Coal dust	Temperamental	N/A	N/A
4a	Copperas	Paper		Gall	Permanent	N/A	N/A
4b	Blue vitriol	Paper		Gall	Permanent	N/A	N/A

Testing by Laura James and Jana Dambrogio at MIT with Nadine Akkerman.

Lesson 4.4. Video Resources

There are several explanatory videos online, produced by Nadine Akkerman and Jana Dambrogio of MIT, that may be of interest. They include how to fold the triangle lock, how to make a tiny spy letter, how to hide a message in an egg, demonstrations of invisible inks including gall-water and copperas, alum and artichoke juice, and even how Elizabeth Stuart may have gone about decoding a letter. Go to https://vimeo.com/channels/secretwritingtechs to watch.

5. STILETTOS & STORYTELLING

This section comes with a warning: the substances listed here are poisonous. Do not handle, consume or otherwise use them.

Lesson 5.1. Organic Poisons

16th-/ 17th-Century Name	Modern Name	Connected to Whom in *Spycraft*	Notes
Wolfsbane / Monk's-hood or conitum	Aconite, *Aconitum napellus*; in Europe the name wolfsbane is usually reserved for its white-flowered relative *Aconitum lycoctonum*	Richardus; Wayland	Highly toxic blue-flowered herbaceous plant; active ingredient, aconitine, is a potent alkaloid toxin; can be absorbed through the skin
Hemlock, Seneca or conitum	Hemlock, *Conium maculatum*	Culpeper, *A Physical Directory*, 35, 48; Galen; Paré; Wayland	Causes dizziness, vertigo, sleepiness and death; primarily administered by mouth but the toxin coniine can also be absorbed through the skin; small amounts can be fatal within thirty minutes
Mandray	Mandrake	Culpeper, *A Physical Directory*, 13, 44; della Porta, *Natural Magick*, 9; Galen; Wayland	Root of Mandragora; hallucinogenic narcotic often associated with witchcraft and used in medicine

Carula	Passion flower, *Passiflora caerulea*	Wayland	Leaves and roots are toxic
Henbane	Stinking night-shade, *Hyoscyamus niger*	Culpeper, *A Physical Directory*, 41; Paré	Hallucinogenic and narcotic; leaves can be dried and then used in drink or burnt; boiling the leaves in oil creates henbane oil; often cited as the drug taken by witches to give them the sense of flying
Opium	Opium	Culpeper, *A Physical Directory*, 48; Galen; Paré	Derived from the opium poppy; narcotic and hallucinogenic
Toad	Bufotoxin	Paré; Wayland	Toxic substance secreted by many toads, including the common European toad, *Bufo bufo*; similar in effect to digitalis, which derives from the foxglove
Cantharides	Cantharides, Spanish fly	Coke; Culpeper, *A Physical Directory*, 28; Franklin	Derived from crushed blister beetles; cantharidin causes blistering and is highly toxic; sometimes unwisely used as an aphrodisiac
Powder of spiders	N/A	Coke; Franklin	N/A

Lesson 5.2. Chemical Poisons

16th-/ 17th-Century Name	Modern Name	Connected to Whom in *Spycraft*	Notes
Ratsbane or white arsenic	Arsenic trioxide (As_2O_3)	Franklin; Paré; Wayland	Arsenic is a semi-metallic element which occurs naturally and as a by-product of the copper smelting industry
Orpiment	Arsenic trisulphide (As_2S_3)	Paré	Often used as a pigment for painting as it is a deep yellow colour
Roseacre or realgar	Arsenic tetrasulphide (As_4S_4)	Coke	Also known as ruby sulphide; used as red pigment
Mercury water	N/A	Franklin	
Mercury sublimate	Mercury(II) chloride $(HgCl_2)$	Coke; Paré	White powder
Lapis causticus or lye	Caustic potash or potassium hydroxide (KOH)	Coke; Franklin	Highly corrosive alkali commonly used in the period to wash clothes and in the tanning process
Ceruse	White lead $(2PbCO_3 \cdot Pb(OH)_2)$	Paré	Sometimes used as a cosmetic
Litharge	Lead(II) oxide (PbO)	Paré	Used to make sealing wax red

Verdigris	Copper carbonate ($CuCO_3$)	Paré	Made by reaction of acetic acid (vinegar) on copper; used as a colouring agent
Aqua fontana	Contained arsenic, lead, boiled toad	female Italian poisoning ring	
Aqua fortis	Nitric acid (HNO_3)	Franklin	

Lesson 5.3. Physical Poisons

16th-/17th-Century Name	Modern Name	Connected to Whom in *Spycraft*	Notes
Filings of iron	Iron filings	Paré	Injures the intestinal tract
Powder of glass	Powdered glass	Wayland	Injures the intestinal tract
Powder of diamonds	Diamond dust	Franklin	Injures the intestinal tract
Filings of brass	Brass filings	Paré	Injures the intestinal tract

Lesson 5.4. Poison in Culpeper's A Physical Directory

16th-/17th-Century Name	Culpeper's Comments	Page no.
White hellebore	*Ellebori, Veratri, albi. nigri.* Of Hellebore white and black. The root of white hellebore . . . kills rats, and mice being mixed with their meat: it is but a scurvy, churlish medicine being taken inwardly, and therefore better let alone than used.	9

Mandrake	*Mandragoræ.* Of Mandrakes, a root dangerous for its coldness, being cold in the fourth degree, the root is scarce, and dangerous for the vulgar to use therefore I leave it to those that have skill.	13
Hemlock	*Cicuta.* Hemlock, cold in the fourth degree, poisonous.	35
Henbane	*Hyoscyamus &c.* Henbane . . . the black or common Henbane and the yellow, [are cold] in the fourth [degree], they stupify the sense and therefore not to be taken inwardly.	41
Mandrake	*Mandragora.* Mandrakes, fit for no vulgar use but only to be used in cooling ointments.	44
Nightshade	*Solanum.* Nightshade, very cold and dry, binding, it is somewhat dangerous taken inwardly.	53

Lesson 5.5. Prophylactics in Culpeper's A Physical Directory

Substance to Treat	Culpeper's Recommended Antidote	Page no.
Cantharides	*Atriplex, &c.* Orach, or Arrach . . . they help such as have taken cantharides.	28
Opium, Hemlock	*Origanum.* Organy, a kind of wild Marjoram, hot and dry in the third degree; helps the bitings of venomous beasts, such as have taken Opium Hemlock, or Poppy.	48
General	*Ruta.* Rue, or herb of grace: . . . This I am sure of, no herb resisteth poison more. And some think *Mithridates*, that renowned king of *Pontus*, fortified his body against poison with no other medicine.	51

	(See also della Porta, *Natural Magick*, 9: 'Much Rue being eaten, becometh poison; but the juice of Hemlock expels it; so that one poison poisoneth another.')	
Pestilence, poison, bitings of venomous beasts	Therica Diatessaron: This is a gallant Electuary, like the Author . . . it resists the pestilence, and poisons, and helps the bitings of venomous beasts.	177
Poison, filthy medicine	Mithridate. *Damocrates*. It is good against poison, and such as have done themselves wrong by taking filthy medicines.	179–80
Poison, bitings of venomous beasts	Andromachus *his Treacle*. The virtues of it are, it resists poison and the biting of venomous beasts.	183

—◇—

ENDNOTES

PRELUDE: THE SKELETON KEY

1. Camden, *Annales Rerum Anglicarum* (1616), 429. Translation taken from Camden, *Annales* (1625), sig. T1r.
2. Fuller, *The History of the Worthies of England*, 284.
3. Powell, 'Secret Writing', 38. In Fig. 1, the painter Samuel van Hoogstraten also includes two of his own plays, a pair of spectacles, and the medal he was awarded by Emperor Ferdinand III for a trompe l'oeil, celebrating his mastery of the art of deceit.
4. The late medieval author and diplomat Philippe de Commynes blurred the lines between messenger, diplomat and spy: Arthurson, 'Espionage', 134. The sixteenth-century Italian thinker Giovanni Botero added secretaries to the mix: Botero, *The Reason of State*, 48. See also Blakeway, 'Spies', 84.
5. Arthurson, 'Espionage', 142.
6. Keens-Soper, 'Wicquefort', 88–105.
7. The gentlemen quote is a father's advice to his son in 1673, cited in Marshall, *Intelligence* (2023), 141; Das, Melo, Smith et al., *Keywords*, 'Spy', 237. Iordanou, *Venice's Secret Service*, 161, points out that the emblematist Cesare Ripa regretted 'that more noblemen, rather than the plebs, practise spying'.
8. *The Statutes*, 443 (5 Eliz. c. 13, 14).
9. 'List of certain intelligencers', TNA, SP 12/265, fo. 207r. See also Shaw, 'Thinker', which examines the intelligence activities undertaken by the lieutenant of the Tower, Sir John Peyton.
10. Marshall, *Intelligence* (2023), 64.
11. Szechi, 'Introduction', endnote 1, mentions that the term 'dangerous trade' 'is so ubiquitous as, apparently, to have no single source'.
12. Jonson, *Epigrams*, 141: Epigram 59, 'On Spies'.
13. Webster, *The Duchess of Malfi*, act I, scene I, sig. C. We are indebted to Marshall, *Intelligence* (2023), 9, which uses the quote; see also ibid., 189. The suggestion that there were no spies derives from Burke, 'Early Modern Venice', 393.
14. Shapin, 'The Invisible Technician', 554.
15. On medieval spying practices, see, for instance, Arthurson, 'Espionage', and Allmand, 'Information'.
16. Works that describe the history of espionage from ancient to modern times tend to devote considerably more attention to the modern period. The primary focus of Kahn's seminal work, *The Codebreakers*, with its ambitious subtitle *The*

Comprehensive History of Secret Communication from Ancient Times to the Internet, for instance, largely considers the Second World War. The early modern period is discussed relatively succinctly: around 60 of 987 pages are devoted to it.

17. See Iordanou, *Venice's Secret Service*, 194.
18. For Scotland's sixteenth-century spy networks, see Blakeway, 'Spies', 83. For James VI's use of spies, see McInally, 'Scholars and Spies'.
19. See, for instance, Malcolm, *Agents of Empire*. Spain also had a more advanced system: see Perez, ed., *Ambassadeurs*.
20. The translation of Ripa's Italian text is contemporary: see Fig. 290 in Ripa, *Iconologia*, edited by Tempest. The first edition of Ripa's *Iconologia* was published in 1593, but 'the spia' emblem did not make an appearance until 1613 (see Iordanou, *Venice's Secret Service*, 160; Ripa, *Iconologia*, 253), although it always included 'Gelosia', another figure with a cloak of eyes and ears. In the 'Rainbow Portrait', *c.* 1602 (Hatfield House), tentatively attributed to either Marcus Gheeraerts the Younger or Isaac Oliver, Elizabeth I wears a cloak much like that of the anonymous Italian spy: her body is wrapped in the eyes and ears of the intelligence gatherer. The painter presumably combined several early emblems from Ripa – 'Gelosia' and 'Intelligenza' – to come up with the design (Fischlin, 'Political Allegory', 191, 203).
21. Gregory to Elizabeth I, not dated, no place given, Hatfield, CP Petitions 853.
22. 'Paper found in Arundell's Chamber', 21 April 1597, Hatfield, CP 50/35.
23. Gregory to Cecil, 28 February 1594[/5], 'From my poor house', Hatfield, CP 25/52.
24. Keblusek, 'Introduction', 13; Szechi, 'Introduction', 13. Actual expenditure on intelligencers was remarkably stable through the first half of the seventeenth century, at approximately £1,400 per annum through the Jacobean period, £1,400 per annum under the Caroline regime, and peaking at between £1,200 and £2,000 per annum under Cromwell: Marshall, *Intelligence* (2023), 73, 192.
25. 'Treasury warrant of the payment of £20 to Arthur Gregory, engineer of the works of Upnor Castle', 22 October 1599, West Sussex Record Office, Add. MS 18006; letter patent, King James, 1 June [1603], Devon Archives and local studies service, 281MZ16; customs book of Arthur Gregory, TNA, E 122/123/26, 1604–6.
26. Marshall, *Intelligence* (2023), 56.
27. The *OED* dates the term's first usage to 1943, but Alan Marshall has traced it to 1680: see Marshall, *Intelligence* (2023), 18, 22, 39 n. 54.
28. Scribal copy, Elizabeth to Leicester, 19 July 1586, TNA, SP 84/9, fo. 38r.
29. Hatton to Elizabeth, 17 June 1573, TNA, SP 12/91, fo. 116r. We do not know, however, whether Elizabeth ever addressed him as her eyelids, because none of her letters to him survive: Doran, *Elizabeth I*, 148.
30. Marshall, *Intelligence* (2023), 57.
31. Gregory to Reynolds, [September 1596?], no place given, Hatfield, CP 186/49.
32. Gregory to Robert Cecil, 28 February 1594[/5], 'From my poor house', Hatfield, CP 25/52.
33. Marshall, *Intelligence* (2023), 141, 143; Marshall, ' "Secret Wheeles" ', 194.
34. Loomis, ' "Little Man" '; Croft, 'The Reputation'.
35. Marshall, *Intelligence* (2023), 150.
36. Loomis, ' "Little Man" ', 138–9, citing Raleigh, 'Maxims of State', *The Works of Sir Walter Raleigh*, viii.23 (1829). Marshall, *Intelligence* (2023), 152, has 'beagles'

as 'under-officers'. It was Anthony Bacon who called Burghley 'old fox' in a letter, while Edmund Spenser referred to the Cecils as 'the fox' and 'the ape' respectively in his poem *Mother Hubberd's Tale* (1578–9).

37. Holograph, Elizabeth to Cecil, [summer?] 1598, Hatfield, CP 133/187. Robert told his father that the queen addressed him as 'Pigmey' and that his answer was carefully framed to give the impression that 'I may not find fault with the name she gives me, yet seem I only not to mislike it because she gives it' (Robert Cecil to his father, 16 February 1588, Dover, TNA, SP 15/30, fo. 156r).

38. 'Words spoken by John Mylles of Redborne, servant to the Earl of Essex in office of a pastler [a pastry cook], in derogation of Sir Robert Cecil, secretary to the Queen's most excellent Majesty', [before 25 February 1601], Hatfield, CP 83/53; Loomis, ' "Little Man" ', 138.

39. Gregory to Robert Cecil, 28 February 1594[/5], 'From my poor house', Hatfield, CP 25/52.

40. Gregory to Salisbury, undated, [1606], no place given, TNA, SP 14/24, fo. 67v.

41. Gregory to the lord treasurer, [on or prior to 1598], BL, Lansdowne MS 113, no. 67.

42. Eamon, 'A Theater of Experiments', 14, 23. The first edition of della Porta's *Magiae Naturalis* was translated from the original Latin into the major European languages French, Italian and German, before a much enlarged second edition (again in Latin) was published in 1589. This, too, was widely translated, though the first English translation, *Natural Magick*, did not hit the booksellers until 1658.

43. Zik and Hon, 'Giambattista della Porta', 46.

44. The natural philosopher – and by 1617 lord chancellor – Sir Francis Bacon demonstrated somewhat mixed views on the subject in 1620. He denigrated the 'labourers in the vineyard of natural magic', and wanted to dispense with the 'superstitious stories . . . and the experiments of ceremonial magic', while simultaneously hoping to restore the good name of magic as a way of controlling nature through knowledge: Bacon, *Novum Organum*, 139, 215, 459.

45. For the Chinese, see Macrakis, *Prisoners*, 14; for Philip II, see Budiansky, *Her Majesty's Spymaster*, 144.

46. Eamon, 'A Theater of Experiments', 24.

47. Eamon, *Science and the Secrets of Nature*, 201–3.

48. Zielinski, *Deep Time*, 75, citing *De Furtivis*, 2.

49. Morison, ed., *Prerogative Court of Canterbury*, 46; Gregory to Michael Hickes, [c. 1604–1606], BL, Lansdowne MS 91, fo. 129r (no. 61). Gregory may have been 'claiming to be the inventor of the viol strung with sympathetic metal strings': Hulse, 'The Musical Patronage', 33–4, 38.

50. Hogge, *God's Secret Agents*, 377–8, is a notable exception, though her discussion is limited to a couple of sentences.

51. For early moderns realising the importance of archives, see, for instance, Soll, *The Information Master*; de Vivo, *Information*; Head, 'Knowing Like a State'.

52. Boxall to William Cecil, 19 November 1558, St James's Palace, TNA, SP 12/1, fo. 8r; C.S. Knighton, 'Boxall, John', *ODNB*. Clarencius was lady-in-waiting Susan White, widow of Thomas Tonge, the Clarenceux King of Arms.

53. *OED*, 'ceringe', v.2c.

54. Beale, 'A Treatise', 431. Half a century or so later, some of Walsingham's papers and alleged secrets were printed, making it possible for Thurloe to cast 'the Moor' as his role model: see Marshall, *Intelligence* (2023), 58, endnote 56 refers to *Arcana Aulica, or, Walsingham's Manual* (London, 1652); *Scrinia Sacra; Secrets of Empire* (London, 1654).
55. Stewart, 'Familiar Papers', 243, citing Burghley's will.
56. Ibid., 244, citing a 1617 letter of Wilson to the king.
57. Ibid., 249–50.
58. For the Venetians and archives, see de Vivo, 'Archival Intelligence'.
59. For the historian as spymistress, see Akkerman, *Invisible Agents*, 3.
60. See, for instance, Andrew, *The Secret World*; Kahn, *The Codebreakers*; and for the early modern period specifically, Szechi, ed., *The Dangerous Trade*. Studies of specific early modern countries and territories can be found in notes throughout.
61. We are far from the only people adopting this course. Láng, *Real Life Cryptology*, 13, for instance, situates Hungarian cryptological systems 'not only as a scientific technology, but rather as a complex system of social practices [which] will enrich the traditional "internalistic" approach to this branch of the history of science and will situate it in the context of social history'. See also Allison and Kim's introduction to their edited collection *A Material History of Medieval and Early Modern Ciphers*.
62. For an image of Kircher's 'Panacousticon', see Zielinski, *Deep Time*, 129 (his Fig. 5.12).
63. Shelton, *Tutor to Tachygraphy*, A3r.
64. See Brewerton, ' "Several Keys" '.
65. Bales, BL, Harley MS 675, fos 3v, 12r–v.
66. Mazzola, *Learning and Literacy*, 50. As is so often the case, desire trumps interpretation – in this case, the desire to see women as active she-intelligencers when the evidence does not support the theory.
67. See Malay, 'Jane Seagar'.
68. See, for example, the intercepted letter to a nobleman, unaddressed, signed 'A.C.', 8 January 1655, Bod., Rawlinson MS 21, 448–51, which uses ciphered writing in invisible ink.
69. Marshall, *Intelligence* (2023), 65.

1. FRAUD & FORGERY

1. The silver casket in which these papers were purportedly discovered was bought for £1.8 million by National Museums Scotland in 2022. For an excellent discussion of the sonnets, see Dunnigan, 'Scottish Women Writers'.
2. Shrank, 'Manuscript', 202.
3. Guy, *My Heart*, 429–36, specifically 433.
4. For manuscript references to the Casket Letters, see ibid., 541.
5. An individual's handwriting was widely, though not universally, believed to present a true representation of what was in their heart: Shrank, 'Manuscript', 210–13.
6. Blackwood, *History*, 82.
7. Gregory to Robert Cecil, 1 August 1596, no place given, Hatfield, CP 43/36.
8. The commissioners for Essex to Robert Cecil, 22 July 1602, Chelmsford, Hatfield, CP 184/48.
9. Blackwood, *History*, 82.

10. Henry, Lord Cobham, to Robert Cecil, 8 February 1602[/3], Blackfriars, Hatfield, CP 91/109.
11. Bales, BL, Harley MS 675, fos 3v, 12r–v.
12. Ibid., fos 1r, 3r, 10v. Secretary hand had its own specific alphabet (see, for instance, Fig. 7) that was very different from Roman or Italian hands, which closely resemble modern letterforms.
13. Evelyn, *Numismata*, 268.
14. Lucy Peltz, 'Bales, Peter', *ODNB*. Peltz gives no source for this claim. The fate of the ring is unknown.
15. Bales to Burghley, 1 July 1591, BL, Lansdowne MS 99, fo. 161r (no. 59), endorsed by Bales as 'servant to my Lord Chancellor'.
16. The Herald's College, 1595, Hatfield, CP 37/6.
17. Bales to Burghley, [*c.* 1591], BL, Lansdowne MS 99, fo. 271r (no. 102), which opens with the words 'Since it hath pleased God to call my Lord Chancellor, My good lord and master'. Chancellor Hatton died in November 1591, hence the tentative dating of this letter. Our emphasis.
18. Bales, BL, Harley MS 675, fo. 19v. For Bales's possible secret services see Chapter 2, pp. 99–100.
19. Woudhuysen, *Sir Philip Sidney*, 32–3 (Woudhuysen quotes Middleton's *Father Hubbard's Tales*, ll. 494–5); Coatalen and Schurink, 'A Tudor Translator at Work', 260.
20. Lucy Peltz, 'Bales, Peter', *ODNB*.
21. W. Sterrell to Phelippes, 2 January 1592, Raglan, TNA, SP 12/241, fo. 4r. For the fullest account of this episode, see Gordon, 'Material Fictions'.
22. Chesters, 'John Daniel', 2.
23. Essex to the earl of Derby, 24 November 1590, 'from your lordship's house', TNA, SP 46/53, fo. 125r.
24. [Hugh Owen] to [Phelippes], [*c.* March 1594], [Brussels?], TNA, SP 12/248, fo. 126r (no. 53).
25. Essex to the dean and chapter of Christ Church, Oxford, 25 August 1594, Greenwich, TNA, SP 12/249, fo. 139r (no. 83).
26. Gordon, 'Material Fictions', 106–7.
27. Woudhuysen, *Sir Philip Sidney*, 35; Anthony Bacon to Anne Bacon, 19 October 1593, Twickenham Park, LPL, MS 649, fo. 337r; also quoted in Gordon, 'Material Fictions', 103. For the difference between Roman and its cousin Italian (or italic), see Wolfe, 'Women's Handwriting', 22–3, who also points out that Bales conflates the definitions of these two scripts. For an analysis of Anthony Bacon's intelligence network, see Tosh, *Male Friendship*.
28. For example, Elizabeth Stuart was known for her ability to 'decipher' difficult handwriting (or 'hands', as they were known): see Akkerman, 'Enigmatic Cultures', 77.
29. Rabbards, as quoted in Woudhuysen, *Sir Philip Sidney*, 34. Rabbards edited Ripley's *The Compound of Alchemy* (1591).
30. Bales's confession, 31 July 1600, TNA, SP 12/281, fo. 73r (no. 34).
31. Bales, *The Writing Schoolemaster*, Q2r–v. A hone-stone was a 'rock of which whetstones are made': *OED*, 'hone', n.3. Bales presumably feels that the whiter the stone, the finer its grain and so the sharper the knife: he was plainly a better calligrapher than he was a poet.

32. The Editors of *Encyclopaedia Britannica*, 'quill', *Encyclopedia Britannica*, 20 July 1998, https://www.britannica.com/science/quill-feather; accessed 3 October 2023.

33. 'Stanchgrain' was a powder made from one part burnt alum to two parts powdered rosin, used in preparing paper and parchment, especially to prevent colours from penetrating through the substrate: *OED*, 'stanchgrain', n.1. It most likely fills one of the tubes seen in Fig. 1. Bales also discusses parchment, which was generally used for official documents rather than letters, but his main advice here was to avoid it if it was too greasy, as there was no way of fixing this: Bales, *The Writing Schoolemaster*, Q4v.

34. Ibid., R1r. Using an uncharged quill to practise particular letterforms resembles a technique called 'dry point' mostly used by women to write in miscellanies (collections of poems, recipes, bons mots, etc.) and similar works, in which words were scratched into the paper's surface using a stylus (a pointed metal object such as a needle, hairpin or suchlike) without the brazen display of ink. In this period, women's writing was still considered unseemly, so this technique allowed women to express themselves on paper while retaining a suitable humility: see Powell, 'Secret Writing'.

35. Other vitriols included blue (copper sulphate) and white (zinc sulphate).

36. Gianluca Farusi, 'Monastic Ink: Linking Chemistry and History', *Science in School* 6 (September 2007), https://www.scienceinschool.org/article/2007/galls/; accessed 3 June 2023.

37. [Partridge], *The Widdowes Treasure*, B4r. 'Limme' derives from 'limn' which refers to the act of painting: *OED*, 'limn', v.3a. For ink recipes in general, see Daybell, *The Material Letter*, 30–52; Love, *Scribal Publication*, 90–137, esp. 101–7; and Wolfe, 'Women's Handwriting', 29–30.

38. For the thinning with vinegar, see Daybell, *The Material Letter*, 38 – Daybell refers to Jean de Beau-Chesne and John Baildon's writing manual, *A booke containing divers sortes of hands, as well the English as French secretarie with the Italian, Roman, chancelry & court hands* (London: Thomas Vautrouillier, 1571), opening gambit (unpaginated).

39. 'To make Inck', BL, Add. MS 45198, fo. 153r.

40. BL, Sloane MS 3505, fo. 80r (p. 154).

41. See, for instance, the recipe for red ink found in Folger, V.a.159, fo. 61v.

42. Ruscelli, writing under the pseudonym Alessio Piemontese, *Secrets*, 94v–95r; see also Wecker, *Eighteen Books*, 272, 329.

43. [Partridge], *The Widdowes Treasure*, B4v.

44. Bales's declaration, 31 July 1600, TNA, SP 12/281, fo. 73r (no. 34).

45. It is unclear whether Daniel added potentially damaging passages to the letters, amplified exisiting passages or simply made accurate facsimiles to increase the level of threat they presented.

46. Gordon, 'Material Fictions', 108, quoting Attorney General v. Daniel, Star Chamber Decree, with Daniel's annotations, TNA, SP 12/279, fo. 231.

47. Bales's declaration, 31 July 1600, TNA, SP 12/281, fo. 73r (no. 34).

48. Penny Bidgood, '1601–1610, Jane and John Daniell Pester the Authorities with Many Petitions', *The Power of Petitioning in Seventeenth-Century England*, n.d., https://petitioning.history.ac.uk/investigating-petitioners/1601-1610-jane-and-john-daniell-pester-the-authorities-with-many-petitions/; accessed 3 October 2023.

49. Bales seems to have been involved in the dismantling of Mary, Queen of Scots: see Chapter 2, pp. 99–100.
50. Bales to Viscount Cranborne, [1604], Hatfield, CP 108/36.
51. The original is in Latin: 'Mea guidem sententia Princeps Henricus vix est mediocri laude dignus scriptor, adeo puerilem scriptionem habet': TCL, R.7.23x, vol. 1, fo. 005r (translation TCL).
52. Elizabeth I needed to send scores of letters requesting that the recipients furnish her with horsemen, and, worried that there were too many for her hand to cope with, proposed that William Cecil be allowed to put her signature to these letters by way of a stamp. See the draft warrant 'for stamping of certain letters', Elizabeth to William Cecil, 18 March 1569, Hampton Court, Hatfield, CP 156/17. This was a practice that began under Henry VIII and was known as 'the dry-stamp'.
53. See Brayshay, 'Messengers', 288–92. The name 'recusant' is derived from the Latin for refuse, and refers to those individuals, typically Catholic, who refused to attend Church of England services as prescribed by law.
54. Warrant to Porter, 6 June 1600, no place given, TNA, PC 2/25, p. 21.
55. Basil Morgan, 'Smythe, Sir Thomas', *ODNB*.
56. Gary M. Bell, 'Waad, Sir William', *ODNB*.
57. Lewes's examination, 31 July 1600, Middlesex, Hatfield, CP 80/95.
58. Porter's examination, 31 July 1600, no place given, Hatfield, CP 80/95.
59. Ruscelli, *Secrets*, 94v–96v, explains how to make the 'blacking' used by printers in their ink by burning peach and/or apricot kernels with pine tree resin and capturing the smoke in a bag or on sticks (in both ways it coagulates); to make this into printer's ink it was mixed with varnish or oil (he suggests linseed or walnut oil) until it reached the appropriate consistency.
60. Porter's examination, 31 July 1600, no place given, Hatfield, CP 80/95.
61. Porter's examination, 13 August 1600, Middlesex, Hatfield, CP 81/26.
62. See Brayshay, 'Messengers', 311–12.
63. See ibid., 294; Porter's examination, 13 August 1600, Middlesex, Hatfield, CP 81/26.
64. Porter's examination, 13 August 1600, Middlesex, Hatfield, CP 81/26.
65. Lewes's examination, 31 July 1600, Middlesex, Hatfield, CP 80/95.
66. Porter's petition, [before 24 March 1603], Hatfield, CP, vol 800–899.
67. See Brayshay, 'Messengers', 295; A warrant to the keeper of the Gatehouse, 21 July 1615, no place given, TNA, PC 2/28, p. 58.
68. Warrant to Porter, 1 September 1617, no place given, TNA, PC 2/29, p. 123; warrant to Porter, 3 September 1618, Whitehall, TNA, PC 2/29, p. 505.
69. Shaw, 'Thinker', 10. Walsingham had introduced the practice of entrapment, the placing of both men and women into prisons specifically to gain the trust of prisoners with the aim of immediately betraying it: Marshall, *Intelligence* (2023), 57.
70. In what is a rather complex field, and in order to reduce confusion, we will use composite nouns to indicate which particular 'seal' we mean (seal-stamp; seal-design; seal-impression; papered-seal; exposed-seal aka bare-seal). We distinguish these from the adhesive, e.g. wax or wafer, that is, the substance 'applied to prevent or inhibit the opening of a letter or other document, or to bear an authentication device'. Furthermore, all of these types of 'seal' are related to the act of sealing, though a 'seal' per se is not needed 'to seal' a letter – this action is also encompassed by the term 'locking', which is discussed on pp. 56–66.

In doing so, we are following the protocols of DoLL in our descriptions and our use of specific technical terms.

71. For an example, see Roe to Elizabeth, 30 June 1620, TNA, SP 81/17, fos 93–4; 'Antique Wax Seal of a Boar Inscribed *Mediocria Firma*, Motto of Sir Nicholas Bacon', Eastbourne Auctions, Sussex, UK, 6 July 2023.

72. Donne, 'To Mr George Herbert with One of My Seals', l. 18.

73. The creator of the passport in Fig. 12 gave two explanations for the seal: the first was that he stole it, the second that it was counterfeit: see Chapter 3, p. 151.

74. 'Statement that all seals and stamps for Her Majesty's service should be graven by the graver of the Mint', [*c.* 1595], TNA, SP 12/255, fo. 89.

75. Girolamo Cardano suggests using the hair from a horse's tail for this purpose: see Wecker, *Eighteen Books*, in which some of Cardano's recipes are collected and translated into English, specifically 271.

76. Lucian, *Alexander the False Prophet*, 203–4 (paragraphs 20–2). See also Santi Russell, *Information Gathering*, 186.

77. Hippolytus, *Refutation of All Heresies*, 153. This method was still in use in the late seventeenth and early eighteenth centuries, as the commonplace book of the Hungarian composer Johann Sigismund Cousser shows: 'How a letter is to be opened secretly. Anoint the place of the seal, and then pour upon it very fine gyp with water, and a little fish glue, or gum arabic; Let it harden, and so you shall have a false seal': BRBL, Osborn Music MS 16, p. 147. For fish glue, see Petukhova, 'A History of Fish Glue'.

78. Hippolytus, *Refutation of All Heresies*, 153. It might be that a cast made from a seal with bristles would show the imprints of them without any actual bristles being present.

79. BRBL, Osborn MS b234, p. 8.

80. For the dragon's blood sealing-wax recipe, see Anon., *Valuable Secrets*, 62. Other colours were also created by adding different pigments to the mixture (shellac varied in colour depending on when it was harvested).

81. Calcagnini, 'Oraculorum Liber', 646, as translated by Ossa-Richardson, *The Devil's Tabernacle*, 142–3. Kollurion is a type of plaster: see Santi Russell, *Information Gathering*, 186. Substances of this hardness may have been suitable for creating a usable matrix for the creation of lead seals.

82. For a gypsum-based method of counterfeiting, see Lesson 1.1. Black and green waxes are relatively common, and would have been made by substituting lamp black or verdigris for red lead. There is some suggestion that scent was also added to some mixtures: in 1662 Cornelis van Aerssen had a red Spanish wax made in Paris that perfumed an entire room when melted onto the paper: [Huygens], *De Briefwisseling*, no. 5766.

83. Gregory to Walsingham, [n.d.] February 1586, 'from my poor house; half blind', BL, Harley MS 286, fo. 78r: see Fig. 38. For evidence that 'the usual metal' refers to the substance he used to create usable counterfeit seal-stamps see, for instance, Gregory to Robert Cecil, 1 August 1596, no place given, Hatfield, CP 43/36.

84. Gregory to Walsingham, 22 March 1586, 'From the office', TNA, SP 12/187, fo. 93r.

85. Gregory to Robert Cecil, [before 28 February 1594[/5]], no place given, TNA, SP 12/260, fo. 67r. The letter is undated and the *CSP Domestic* estimates that the letter is written in September 1596, but the contents suggest that it must have been written before his other letter to Cecil of 28 February 1594[/5].

86. Gregory to Robert Cecil, 28 February 1594[/5], 'From my poore house', Hatfield, CP 25/52.
87. For instance, della Porta does not include a gypsum-based method of casting counterfeit seals, though he does present one using isinglass, but this was not designed for the finer quality of seals that Gregory wanted to counterfeit. Della Porta admits his recipe is for a low-quality seal: 'If it should happen that we want a lesser [i.e., low-quality] seal, we must do thus. Take isinglass, and dissolve it in water. Anoint the figure with oil, that it may not stick to the glue. Compass the seal about with wax, that the matter run not about. Put the isinglass to the fire, and melt it, pour it upon the seal. After three hours, when it is cold, take it away, and let it dry. For the seal when it is dry, will be drawn less equally': della Porta, *Natural Magick*, 352.
88. Ibid., 351–2; for these recipes, see Lesson 1.2.
89. Gregory to Robert Cecil, [before 28 February 1594[/5], no place given, TNA, SP 12/260, fo. 67r.
90. Tremor is one of the indicative symptoms of the neurological onset of Wilson's Disease, a disease caused by a build-up of copper in the central nervous system.
91. Gregory to Robert Cecil, 1 August 1596, no place given, Hatfield, CP 43/36. Our emphasis.
92. Charles I writing (in cipher) of Jane Whorwood's letters to Henry Firebrace, I [Charles I] to D [Firebrace], 27 April 1648, BL, Egerton MS 1788, fo. 21r; also quoted in Akkerman, *Invisible Agents*, 21.
93. The field of letterlocking is extremely new, and was pioneered by Jana Dambrogio; she and Daniel Starza Smith remain the field's leading practitioners and theorists. For a far fuller explanation than we can possibly encompass in *Spycraft*, see their forthcoming *Letterlocking*.
94. For a detailed description of the various letterlocking categories and formats, and their relative security, see Dambrogio, Ghassaei, Starza Smith et al., 'Unlocking History', 7.
95. Lake to Robert Cecil, 28 January 1595[/6], 'from the court', Hatfield, CP 30/29. Some take 'plight' to mean 'pleat'. For an example of a pleated letter, see 'Amalia von Solms's Holograph Letter to Eleonore de Volvire: A Letter of Condolence (1670)', Vimeo video, 29 October 2016, https://vimeo.com/189438940; accessed 3 October 2023.
96. Roger Lockyer, 'Lake, Sir Thomas', *ODNB*.
97. Boswell to the English Privy Council, [April] 1629[/30], no place given, TNA, SP 63/250, fos 204r (p. 175), 205r (p. 177).
98. Akkerman, 'Postmistress', 175.
99. Della Porta, *Natural Magick*, 352. A more technical explanation of how folding and wax could be combined to increase security – and a statement demonstrating that this is the reason it is done – can be found in Wecker, *Eighteen Books*, 271 (again, Wecker derived much of his information from Cardano).
100. For an example of an address being partially written over the lock, see Nicholas Throckmorton to Elizabeth I, 24 September 1559, Rheims, TNA, SP 70/7, fos 80–1. We thank Emily Montford for bringing this letter to our attention.
101. Dambrogio, Starza Smith, Pellechia et al., 'The Spiral-Locked Letters', specifically 27.
102. For contemporary belief that Mary, Queen of Scots communicated ciphered messages through embroidery see Akkerman, *Invisible Agents*, 18–19.

103. See Dambrogio, Starza Smith, Pellechia et al., 'The Spiral-Locked Letters', 42–4.

104. James Stewart to Robert Cecil, 1603[/4], Hatfield, CP 103/61.

105. For the last actions of this James Stewart, and the treasonous nature of counterfeiting the king's sign manual, see Chapter 3, pp. 146, 151.

106. Dambrogio, Starza Smith, Pellechia et al., 'The Spiral-Locked Letters', 15.

107. W.A. Speck, 'Harley, Robert', *ODNB*.

108. With some spiral locks, this number would increase to anywhere up to thirty-two layers: see Dambrogio, Starza Smith, Pellechia et al., 'The Spiral-Locked Letters', 8.

109. Castelnau to Burghley, 23 October 1575, London, TNA, SP 70/135, fo. 263r.

110. Gregory to Robert Cecil, 12 October 1594, 'from my poor lodging', Hatfield, CP 28/91.

111. Silas Taylor to Williamson, 9 April 1672, Harwich, TNA, SP 29/305, fo. 125r.

112. Boswell to the English Privy Council, [April] 1629[/30], no place given, TNA, SP 63/250, fo. 205r–v (pp. 177–8).

2. CIPHERS & CODES

1. A hankering after female agency has turned Mary Phelippes into a codebreaker when the evidence sadly disagrees. William Richardson, 'Phelippes, Thomas', *ODNB* states that 'throughout their married life Mary supported and assisted her husband in his work'; Bezio, *The Eye of the Crown*, takes this one step further, claiming that Mary Phelippes was 'specifically employed in cryptography, making her, in essence, the first-known "professional" female spy'. Unfortunately, the sources Bezio cites do not provide the evidence.

2. Phelippes to Sir Robert Cecil, 6 March 1596[/7], Hatfield, CP 38/97; William Richardson, 'Phelippes, Thomas', *ODNB*.

3. See Ellison and Kim, 'Introduction', 4; Láng, *Real Life Cryptology*, 36.

4. The first recorded use of a homophonic cipher was in 1401, in a letter from Francesco I Gonzago to Simeone de Crema in Mantua: see Kahn, *The Codebreakers*, 108; and Lesson 2.1.

5. Cryptography was, however, also used for social purposes: see Akkerman, 'Enigmatic Cultures'. It was also used to protect scientific discoveries: writing the details of a discovery in cipher prevented it from being stolen by jealous rivals yet allowed for precedence to be established in cases where claims to originality clashed; see Biagioli, 'From Ciphers'.

6. Iordanou, *Venice's Secret Service*.

7. Kahn, *The Codebreakers*, 109–10, 112–13. To see how Argenti's mnemonic system worked, and a later system used by the she-intelligencer Isabella Rich built on the same principles, see Lessons 2.2 and 2.3.

8. A 'Great Cipher' owed its efficacy to the movement away from hierarchical, alphabetical or otherwise parallel and thus easily deducible relationships between plaintext and code found in many cipher keys: see Lesson 2.4.

9. Arthurson, 'Espionage', 149.

10. C.S.L. Davies and John Edwards, 'Katherine [Catalina, Catherine, Katherine of Aragon]', *ODNB*, is perhaps misleading on this point, and emphasises her struggles with deciphering and enciphering messages over her success in doing so. Katherine seems to have taught herself cryptography to enhance her own credibility and the security of her ambassadorial mission.

11. Ferdinand to Katherine, 15 March 1507, n.p., *CSP Spain*, supplement to vols i and ii, no. 13. See also Ferdinand to Katherine, 15 March 1507, n.p., *CSP Spain* i, no. 502.
12. Katherine to Almazán, 15 April 1507, Richmond, *CSP Spain* i, no. 516.
13. Katherine to Ferdinand, 17 July 1507, Greenwich, *CSP Spain* i, no. 526. Arthurson, 'Espionage', 149, has taken this to mean that Katherine passed on cipher keys to Henry VII; it seems equally, if not more likely, that the 'trustworthy person' who deciphered it was Katherine herself.
14. By September 1507, she was writing in cipher, but joked that her correspondents would laugh at her endeavours: see Katherine to Ferdinand, and Almazán, 7 September 1507, Woodstock, *CSP Spain* i, nos 541 and 542.
15. See also Dubois-Nayt and Nachef, 'Developing the Art'.
16. Cooper, *The Queen's Agent*, 202.
17. See Andrew, *The Secret World*, 162–4; Somer, book of cipher keys, TNA, SP 53/23.
18. Cooper, *The Queen's Agent*, 203.
19. Andrew, *The Secret World*, 169. For more on this event, see Chapter 5, pp. 195–7.
20. Walsingham to Somer, 22 April 1584, 'the court', including Somer's answer on the verso side with a copy of a deciphered letter, BL, Add. MS 33594, fos 38–40. For Somer's official ambassadorial instructions to France in 1581, see TNA, SP 78/5, fo. 91a; and the Low Countries in 1583, BL, Cotton MS Galba C/VII, fo. 180.
21. Thomas Wilson to Walsingham, 30 June 1578, from the court, TNA, SP 83/7, fo. 39r (no. 52).
22. William Richardson, 'Phelippes, Thomas', *ODNB*.
23. For example, the five most frequently used letters in English are 'e', 't', 'a', 'o' and 'i'; in Spanish they are 'e', 'a', 'o', 's' and 'r'; in French 'e', 's', 'a', 'i' and 't'; and in Polish 'i', 'a', 'e', 'o' and 'z'.
24. Saiber, *Measured Words*, 22, suggests that the original fifteenth-century manuscript was soon disseminated amongst the major courts of Europe, while also stating that the thirteen manuscript copies that survive post-date the original by a century or two.
25. F[alconer], *Rules*, 8–12. Falconer's work was one of many explaining these relationships, and explicitly named its influences by calling itself 'an account of the secret ways of conveying written messages, discovered by Trithemius, Schottus, Lord Fran. Bacon, Bishop Wilkins etc.'. Other expositions occur in, for example, Davys, *An Essay*.
26. See Saiber, *Measured Words*, 21–5. Lennon, *Passwords*, 26, suggests that it was first proposed by al-Qalqashandī in the fifteenth century, or possibly even by al-Khalīl in the eighth century, but Alberti appears to be the first European to discuss the matter.
27. See Lesson 2.5 for a link to various versions of these wheels which may be printed, cut out and put to use. For an example in brass, see the cipher wheel held in the Österreichisches Staatsarchiv in Vienna, which dates from *c.* 1750–1800: AT-OeStA/HHStA HausA Handarchiv Kaiser Franz 22-3.
28. These letters are 'h', 'k', 'w' and 'y' – the 'i' and 'j' are, like the 'u' and 'v', elided together. Superencryption is when a cipher is encrypted twice: see Lesson 2.6 to see how this can be achieved with Alberti's wheel (see also Saiber, *Measured Words*, 27).

29. The zigzag configuration (the letter order being 'a', 'c', 'e', etc. clockwise and 'b', 'd', 'f', etc. anticlockwise) may seem to add another layer of difficulty to the cryptanalyst's job, but in terms of frequency analysis the relationship between the cipher alphabet and the plaintext language does not change.

30. See also Kahn, *The Codebreakers*, xvi.

31. Bacon, *The Advancement of Learning*, 121–2.

32. Saiber, *Measured Words*, 22.

33. See Alberti, *Opuscoli Morali*; Saiber, *Measured Words*, 22.

34. Kahn, *The Codebreakers*, 132. It was not until the 1990s that scholars discovered that the angels concealed other messages: see Ernst, 'The Numerical-Astrological Ciphers'.

35. Roberts and Watson, *John Dee's Library Catalogue*, 6 (Dee to William Cecil, 15 February 1563/4). Dee made a second copy in 1591, which now resides in the National Library of Wales (Peniarth MS 423).

36. Roberts and Watson, *John Dee's Library Catalogue*, 359, point to *Polygraphie* (Paris: Jacques Kerver, 1561), Royal College of Physicians of London, D1/48-e-16, noting it 'has no mark of ownership and may not be Dee's, but the title across and down the fore-edge is in a hand like his'.

37. Note that this does not tally with the version of Alberti's cipher wheel as presented above, as they use different alphabets. For a cipher wheel using this same alphabet, see Lesson 2.5.

38. Trithemius's cipher wheel comprised a series of fixed spokes, each of which carried a single substitution alphabet (starting from each letter in turn, as in the Trithemius table). The single moveable spoke bore the plaintext alphabet from 'A' through 'Z'. By aligning this spoke with one of the static spokes, one could transform the plaintext into ciphertext. See Trithemius, *Polygraphiae*, 352–61, where there are several working cipher wheels embedded into the text.

39. Another way to indicate the procession of alphabets was a numerical key: see Lesson 2.7.

40. Elizabethan tables based on this one can be found in the archives: see, for example, a document entitled 'The Alphabet sent by Master Ashley with the cozening letters', TNA, SP 106/1, fo. 13r (no. 2).

41. For the workings of the keyword cipher, see Lesson 2.8.

42. For the workings of the autokey cipher, see Lesson 2.9.

43. The index wheels are supplied in an insert placed between pages 88 and 89 of della Porta's *De Furtivis*, Book 2.

44. Bod., MS Cherry 30, specifically fo. 3r.

45. Cooper, *The Queen's Agent*, 205–6.

46. Bright's cipher wheels still need to be checked against Walsingham's correspondence to ascertain if they were actually used – the pristine condition of the manuscript suggests that the answer to this question may well be no.

47. See Mary to the duchess of Nemours, 6 November [1581], Sheffield, Labanoff, ed., *Lettres*, v.273; and to Mauvissière, 8 October 1582, Sheffield, ibid., v.314. We thank Alison Wiggins for drawing these letters to our attention.

48. See Lasry, Biermann and Tomokiyo, 'Deciphering', 88.

49. Bossy, *Under the Molehill*, 14–28, 38, 43, 45–9; Lasry, Biermann and Tomokiyo, 'Deciphering', 28, identify seven letters that were 'probably leaked from Castelnau's embassy'.

50. Somer to Walsingham, 6 April 1585, Tutbury, TNA, SP 53/15, fo. 70r.

51. For Morgan, see Cooper, *The Queen's Agent*, 199–200.
52. See Guy, *My Heart*, 473–7. When Gifford was away, Phelippes wrote to Mary's secretaries under cover of the name of Gifford's alleged cousin, Thomas Barnes, aka Barnaby, to assure them that the deliveries would continue to run smoothly.
53. The beer barrel account derives from 'Mémoire de Monsieur de Chateauneuf sur la conspiration de Babington', no date, London, as given in Labanoff, ed., *Lettres*, vi.284–5. Châteauneuf mentions a wooden box in which sealed letters could be placed, which is presumably the genesis of Guy's account in *My Heart*, 480. The hollow bung is suggested in Alison Plowden, 'Gifford, Gilbert', *ODNB*, for instance.
54. For a more comprehensive survey of the various methods Mary and others used to sneak letters through enemy lines undetected, see Chapter 3, pp. 124–32.
55. Our interpretation of this episode is indebted to Alford, *The Watchers*, 193–240; Cunningham, *Imaginary Betrayals*, 110–32; Guy, *My Heart*, 477–97; and Pollen's notes in Pollen, ed., *Mary*.
56. See Guy, *My Heart*, 481.
57. Shrank, 'Manuscript', 212–13.
58. Compare, for instance, the draft and signed versions of Elizabeth to Nicholas Throckmorton, 17 July 1559, Greenwich, TNA, SP 70/5, fos 132 and 134; and Elizabeth to Throckmorton and Thomas Smith, 11 October 1562, Hampton Court, TNA, SP 70/42, fos 170 and 172. We thank Emily Montford for drawing our attention to this process.
59. In the hand of Phelippes, 'Arguments of Nau and Curles privitye to the whole conspiracye as well of invasion as rebellion and murder of the Q. person', endorsed '4 September 1586', TNA, SP 53/19, no. 85.
60. Beale, 'A Treatise', 428.
61. Faunt, 'Discourse', 501. Robyn Jade Adams has pointed out the spiralling levels of familiarity evoked by the latter phrase: 'the secretary occupying an exclusive locus figured in terms of spatial, personal and sensual intimacy; "his mouth, his eye, his eare"': see Adams, '"Both Diligent and Secret"', 58.
62. Cecil, *The State*, 3.
63. Beale, 'A Treatise', 427.
64. Somer to Burghley, 2 March 1584[/5], Tutbury, TNA, SP 53/15, fo. 48v.
65. For a Pasquier acting as Castelnau's secretary, see Paulet to Burghley, 25 August 1578, Paris, TNA, SP 78/2, fo. 145r (no. 65). For Jerome Pasquier acting as cipher secretary, see his 'answers', 30 September 1586, TNA, SP 53/19, fos 117–19; and his later confession, 5 October 1586, TNA, SP 53/20, fo. 11 (the latter document also has him down as master of the wardrobe).
66. For Pasquier answering to Nau, see his 'answers', 30 September 1586, TNA, SP 53/19, fos 118v–119r (pp. 54–5).
67. Copy, Babington to Nau, [before 12 July] 1586, BL, Cotton MS Caligula C/VIII, fo. 328r. We know the enclosure in cipher is Babington's letter to Mary because of 'Arguments of Nau and Curle', TNA, SP 53/9, fo. 85r.
68. Mary to Babington, 25 June 1586, Chartley, TNA, SP 53/19, fo. 10r; Pollen, ed., *Mary*, 15–16 (no. 7).
69. Phelippes to Walsingham, 8 July 1586, Stilton, TNA, SP 53/18, no. 38.
70. Somer may actually have died by this point: see Somer's will, November 1585, TNA, PROB 11/68/621.
71. Davison to Phelippes, 10 January 1586[/7], Ely, TNA, SP 12/197, fo. 17r (no. 11).

72. See Paulet to Walsingham, 26 July 1586, Chartley, TNA, SP 53/18, p. 154. He writes that Phelippes is coming to London; this means that it took up to four days to deliver a letter from London to Chartley, as Walsingham had ordered Phelippes to come on 22 July: see Walsingham to Phelippes, 22 July 1586, 'at the court', TNA, SP 53/18, fo. 141r.

73. Nau to Babington [copy in Phelippes's hand], 13 July 1586, TNA, SP 53/18, fo. 87r (no. 43). Also in Pollen, ed., *Mary*, 24 (no. 12).

74. This was the story told by Mary and her secretaries under interrogation. Many historians argue that the letter had to be translated into English because the cipher key shared with Babington was an English one, but the substitution alphabet with nulls and dowbleths would have been perfectly serviceable in French, and the nomenclator would merely have created a bilingual text: 'I pray you write *a* me *Samedi matin*.' Mary's secretaries could simply have created a French nomenclator had they wished to. Translating Mary's response into English or perhaps Scots served to remove it a step further away from her own voice, however, allowing her to recycle the argument of authenticity used successfully during the tribunal of 1568–9; see also Shrank, 'Manuscript', 203. Furthermore, a cryptanalyst expecting French would have worked some hours in vain using incorrect frequency tables before realising that the chosen language was, in fact, English.

75. For the deciphered text, see Lesson 2.10.

76. See Mary to Babington, 17 July 1586, TNA, SP 53/18, no. 53.

77. 'Ciphers, including those for papers seized at Chartley Castle on the discovery of the conspiracy in 1586', TNA, SP 53/22. For the variations, of which the key sent to Babington was one, see fos 6r–v (anon), 8r–v (anon), 9r–v (anon), 16r–v (between Curle and Barnes), 17r–v (between Her Majesty and Blunt), 18r–v (anon), 21r (anon), 27r–v (for Emilio), 28r–v (between Curle and Emilio), 34r–v (for the elder earl of Huntley), 35r–v (for the younger earl of Huntley), 44r–v (three keys, for Morgan), 48r–v (Pietro), 49r–v (Pierre Soigne and Emilio Russo) and 54r–v (with Thomas Throckmorton).

78. Janet Scott, Lady Ferniehirst, was the contact between Mary and the Scottish court. Dr Lewes was vicar-general to Cardinal Borromeo and English 'referendaire' of the pope: as identified in the archbishop of Glasgow to Mary, [n.d.] June 1584, deciphered by Phelippes, TNA, SP 53/13, p. 243 (no. 33). Lady Ferniehirst's coded letters to Mary, which only survive in deciphered form, date from October to November 1583, so the key given to her may date from around this time: see her letters dated 22 October and 4 November 1583, BL, Cotton MS Caligula C/VI, fo. 338; 4 November 1583, BL, Cotton MS Caligula C/VIII, fo. 63; and 25 November 1583, BL, Cotton MS Caligula C/VI, fo. 341.

79. This is exactly what happened to the researchers who decoded a sheaf of unidentified letters between Mary and Castelnau (amongst others) in 2023. Their first attempts at decoding the letters failed – it was not until they changed the assumed plaintext language from Italian to French that they met with success. See Lasry, Biermann and Tomokiyo, 'Deciphering', 12–15.

80. One of Mary's cipher keys seized at Chartley, for use with an unidentified correspondent, TNA, SP 53/22, fo. 1r; Láng, *Real Life Cryptology*, 33, 73.

81. Babington to Mary, 3 August 1586, London, TNA, SP 53/19, p. 350 (no. 9); Pollen, ed., *Mary*, 46–7 (no. 15).

82. 'Arguments of Nau', 4 September 1586, TNA, SP 53/19, no. 85.

83. Imprisonment was far more laissez-faire than it is now. Allowing Mary to ride on horseback or in her carriage was perfectly normal.
84. Phelippes to Walsingham, 14 July 1586, Chartley, TNA, SP 53/18, fo. 99r (no. 48). The *CSP* mistakenly summarises the letter as if Mary smiled at Phelippes; the original leaves no doubt that it was Phelippes smiling.
85. See Barbé, *In Byways of Scottish History*, 291, on the long-tailed myth.
86. Shakespeare, *Henry VI, Part III*, act 3, scene 2, l. 183.
87. Mary to Monsieur de l'Aubespine [Châteauneuf], 24 March 1585[/6], Chartley, TNA, SP 53/17, fo. 36r. The translation is taken from the *CSP Domestic*, as the original is in French (as shown in Fig. 24). Phelippes had presumably contacted Châteauneuf in March offering his help to Mary through the French ambassador.
88. Mary to Morgan, 27 July 1586, TNA, SP 53/18, fo. 158v. In this letter, Mary also tells Morgan that, when he was in Chartley at Christmas, she had tried 'at that time I made be sought about to try if he had been your [Morgan's] man or not'.
89. 'Phelippes's apology touching his medling in the Queen of Scots's cause', undated, TNA, SP 14/1, fo. 265v.
90. Mary to Morgan, 27 July 1586, TNA, SP 53/18, fo. 156v (fos 156–7, no. 74, is a draft; fos 158–9, no. 75, of the same manuscript volume, is a fair copy in Phelippes's hand, presumably the one sent to Walsingham).
91. Mary to Babington, 17 July 1586, Chartley, TNA, SP 53/18, no. 53.
92. Walsingham refers directly to 'the gallows upon the packet': see Walsingham to Phelippes, 22 July 1586, 'at the court', TNA, SP 53/18, fo. 141r, secured with a triangle lock cut from the substrate.
93. Phelippes to Walsingham, 19 July 1586, Chartley, TNA, SP 53/18, no. 61.
94. 'Arguments of Nau and Curle', 4 September 1586, TNA, SP 53/19, fo. 85r.
95. Phelippes to Walsingham, 19 July 1586, Chartley, TNA, SP 53/18, no. 61.
96. Walsingham to Phelippes, 22 July 1586, 'at the court', TNA, SP 53/18, fo. 141r.
97. 'Arguments of Nau and Curle', 4 September 1586, TNA, SP 53/19, fo. 85r.
98. The quote is from the biographical entry of Bales – 'Bales, Peter' – in *Biographia Britannica*, 537.
99. Walsingham to Phelippes, 30 July 1586, 'at the court', TNA, SP 53/18, fo. 189r.
100. Walsingham to Phelippes, 3 August 1586, 'at the court', BL, Cotton MS Appendix L, fo. 143v.
101. See Pollen, ed., *Mary*, 65–6. This Babington apparently achieved by a personal message, as it does not feature in his reply.
102. Andrew, *The Secret World*, 177.
103. Phelippes to Walsingham, 19 July 1586, Chartley, TNA, SP 53/18, no. 61.
104. See Hunt, '"Burn This Letter"'.
105. Wiggins and Scott, 'The Afterlives'.
106. See Pollen, ed., *Mary*, 'Introduction', cxci.
107. Guy, *My Heart*, 485.
108. See, for example, ibid., 490–1.
109. Unfortunately for Mary, Curle had kept the 'Englished' version of this particular letter locked in her cabinet – the same cabinet Walsingham had taken possession of in August: see Pollen, ed., *Mary*, 147.

110. Examination of Curle, 23 September 1586, and Nau, 21 September 1686, in ibid., 143, 145 (nos 43, 44).
111. That Nau and Curle appear to have been presented copies of the letter lacking the postscript and Babington with one bearing the postscript during their interrogations is largely irrelevant, if indeed it is true.
112. Anonymous to Phelippes, 22 February 1587, Mansfield in Sherwood, TNA, SP 53/21, fo. 37r.
113. William Richardson, 'Phelippes, Thomas', ODNB. For Owen's network of intelligencers, see Orofino, 'Coelum'; and Edwards, 'The First Earl of Salisbury', 2.
114. Some added code names to an alpha-numeric-symbolic substitution alphabet with nulls, such as 'Cipher for Master Bowes in Scotland', 8 September 1592, TNA, SP 106/1, fo. 32r (no. 9b), which figured the queen of England as 'Arabia Felix' or 'America', England as 'Mesopotamia' or 'Damascus', and Robert Bowes (Elizabeth's ambassador in Scotland) as 'Antonius Conradus'.
115. See Berloquin, Hidden Codes, 182, and Dubois-Nayt and Nachef, 'Developing the Art', par. 31.
116. Guy, My Heart, 82, referring to an undated letter of Mary to her mother, as printed in Labanoff, ed., Lettres, i.5–7 (specifically 7). Guy's endnotes at 524 point out that the most likely date of this letter is 1556.
117. Guy, My Heart, 82, also suggests that Mary did not encipher letters herself: 'She had learnt to mark the most confidential passages of her letters for encoding in cipher', a task which would then be undertaken by her secretary. The source for this particular part of her education, if it ever occurred, is not clear.
118. Penelope herself had already been enciphered, if only poetically: she was the female half of the sonnet sequence Astrophil and Stella (composed 1580s; published 1591) by Sir Philip Sidney.
119. Laoutaris, '"Toucht with Bolt of Treason"', 206, referring to Thomas Fowler to Burghley, 7 October 1589, Edinburgh, Hatfield, CP 18/50.
120. Lord Henry Howard to Edward Bruce, 27 August [1602], in Dalrymple, ed., Secret Correspondence, 209–10.
121. Akkerman, Queen of Hearts, 35–7.
122. Strasser, 'The Noblest Cryptologist'; Strasser, 'Die kryptographische Sammlung Herzog Augusts'. Elizabeth Stuart also corresponded with Sir Francis Bacon: see CES, i.356–8, 363, 557–8 (nos 260, 263 and 387). As such, she might also have been familiar with Bacon's so-called 'bi-literal cipher', as discussed in Chapter 3, 'Disguise & Distraction'.
123. See Akkerman, 'Women's Letters', 550; 'Key Frederick V' (CES, i.869–72).
124. Akkerman, Queen of Hearts, 221.
125. Bachrach, Sir Constantine Huygens, 9–10; De Leeuw and Bergstra, The History, 336.
126. Huygens, Mijn Leven, i.136–7; our translation.
127. Adriaan Ploos van Amstel to Huygens, 29 August 1637, Oudegein; Huygens to Amalia, 6 February 1647, no place given ([Huygens], De Briefwisseling, nos 1665 and 4538).
128. Huygens to Elizabeth Stuart, 12 July 1634, Nijmegen, translation from the French (CES, ii.300–1 (no. 170)).
129. See CES, i.873–5.

130. Roe to Elizabeth Stuart, 1 August 1636, no place given (*CES*, ii.501 (no. 273)).

131. Carleton to Lady Sedley, [n.d.] February 1621[/2], The Hague, TNA, SP 84/105, fos 196v–197r, as quoted in Akkerman, *Queen of Hearts*, 166. Elizabeth Stuart employed the famed French engineer Salomon de Caus to work on her mechanical devices in masques and automata for her gardens while she was in Heidelberg.

132. Elizabeth Stuart, for instance, mistransposes 'electorat' as '4bobz5yswey', when it ought to read '4hohf5yswey' (*CES*, ii.522 (no. 284)). It is an odd mistake to make from a Trithemian table, or indeed from simple counting, but is a perfectly reasonable mistake to make on a cipher wheel if reading the plaintext on the inner wheel and the ciphertext on the outer, that is, the 'wrong' way around. Because this is a counterintuitive way to use the wheel, it is extremely easy to place the plaintext on the outer wheel (as would be expected) by mistake – this is why she transposes 'e' as 'b' and 'c' as 'z'.

133. Replacing letters with numbers was also the principle of the Gronsveld cipher as described in 1665 in Gaspar Schott's *Schola Steganographica*. Rather than using a keyword as an encoding and decoding device, Gronsveld's cipher used numbers to represent which of the twenty-four shift ciphers was to be used (see Lesson 2.7). The table included by Selenus also ran in a different direction from the one favoured by Trithemius.

134. See *CES*, ii.522. 'I have had newes from K. [Arundell] 50. [Emperor] 6nfzn. [hath] 4kmyhq4. [giuen-] 4lmp. [him] 5mnw [hir] last 4dkwzhu [agswer].' In '5mnw' and '4dkwzhu', Elizabeth Stuart makes coding errors (using 'w' instead of 'x' and 'k' instead of 'q').

135. Roe to Elizabeth Stuart [in The Hague], 20[/30] October 1636, no place given (*CES*, ii.542 (no. 292)). See also *CES*, ii.588–91 (no. 321): Elizabeth continues to use the alphabet despite Roe's protestations.

136. I [aka Charles I] to D [aka Firebrace], Tuesday 22 August 1648, BL, Egerton MS 1788, fo. 45r. See Akkerman, *Invisible Agents*, 46.

137. F[alconer], *Rules*, 30, D4v.

138. Landesarchiv Oranienbaum, Abteilung Dessau, A 7b Nr. 124, a collection identified by Groenveld, '"Chijffre"', contains, amongst others, such cipher keys as used by Queen Henrietta Maria's advisor Henry, Lord Jermyn (item 6), her daughter Mary (item 7) and her secretary Robert Long (item 30).

139. For more on this, see Láng, *Real Life Cryptology*, 43–4.

3. DISGUISE & DISTRACTION

1. See, for instance, Paulet to Phelippes, 25 January 1585/6, Chartley, TNA, SP 53/17, no. 13, in which Paulet closes with his 'most hearty commendations and the like from my wife to yourself and our good friend Master Francis Bacon'. See also Stewart, 'Francis Bacon', 129: it was Bacon who recommended Phelippes to Essex in *c*. 1591.

2. For the deliberate introduction of boring subject matter to fool an interceptor, see Akkerman, *Invisible Agents*, 104.

3. Akkerman, 'Enigmatic Cultures', 79.

4. Bacon's proposed system is effectively the same as the modern 5-bit binary representation of the numbers 0 to 23, where 0 = 00000, 1 = 00001, etc.

5. Bacon, *De Augmentis*, 444–6. It has been suggested that Bacon's cipher owes much to the systems of Trithemius, della Porta and Vigenère. The latter

published his work just seven years after Bacon's sojourn in Paris and certainly had contact with various members of the embassy in the interim (see Spedding, Ellis and Heath, *Works*, i.841–4; Kahn, *The Codebreakers*, 137–48; Stewart, 'Francis Bacon', 133). While it is true that no cipher exists in a vacuum, Bacon's system is far enough removed from these various systems to warrant its own place in the pantheon.

6. This misapprehension of Bacon's cipher as a print rather than handwriting technology is behind much of the fuss over Bacon's alleged responsibility for the works of Shakespeare: see Stewart, 'Francis Bacon', 133–4. Kahn, *The Codebreakers*, 881–2, also erroneously identifies Bacon's cipher as a print technology.

7. Walsingham to Sadler, 17 October 1584, London, BL, Add. MS 33594, fos 83–6 (fo. 85r is the decoded copy of this letter, while fo. 86r bears the explanation of Curle's code). See also Daybell, *The Material Letter*, 158.

8. See Schiltz, *Music*, 346–8.

9. For an image of this cipher key, Archivo General de Simancas, EST, LEG, 1, 1, 1, 204, see Rivas, *Espias*, 138–9 (catalogue entry 16.3).

10. For an image of this cipher key, BL, Add. MS 45850, fo. 68, see Akkerman, *Invisible Agents*, 219.

11. See Underdown, *Royalist Conspiracy*, 345–6. It was not only Royalists who used this kind of steganography: in 1640 intercepted letters from Covenanters were sprinkled with mercantile discourse: Marshall, *Intelligence* (2023), 96 n. 195.

12. See Akkerman, *Invisible Agents*, 98.

13. 'Cipher with 9.30.40.44.14.49', Bod., Clarendon MS 94 (no. 13).

14. Untitled, Bod., Clarendon MS 94 (no. 28).

15. *OED*, 'jargon', n.1, 3–4.

16. Bacon, 'A True Report', 284.

17. Marshall, *Intelligence* (2023), 156.

18. See cipher for Francis Bolton, TNA, SP 106/1, fo. 27r (no. 6a); cipher for John Conyers, TNA, SP 106/1, fo. 71r (no. 26; endorsed 'Phoenix', most likely Conyers's code name). The first was unaccompanied by a substitution alphabet, so is more properly considered a list of codes. The nomenclator names appear to be made up, without any great significance other than they were intended to sound plausibly Dutch.

19. Master Briskett's cipher, [before 1587, probably Ireland], TNA, SP 106/1, fos 35r–38v (no. 11).

20. Cipher for Roger Aston, 1599, TNA, SP 106/1, fo. 14r–v (no. 2a). The archivist's pencilled index lists this as 'used in Scotland', so presumably refers here to King James, Queen Anna, Prince Henry and Princess Elizabeth.

21. Amorella to Fidelia, 8 January 1643/4, TNA, SP 16/506, fo. 8; see Akkerman, *Invisible Agents*, 169.

22. See Akkerman, 'Women's Letters', 557; Akkerman, *Queen of Hearts*, 254.

23. Akkerman, *Invisible Agents*, 47.

24. For the three cipher keys, see BL, Egerton MS 2550, fos 8r–v (for Lycanthropus and Labyrinthus, 1649), 49r (for Profligantes, n.d.); Akkerman, 'Women's Letters'; see also Lesson 2.3.

25. Akkerman, *Invisible Agents*, 170.

26. See ibid., 242–4.

27. Waad to Salisbury, 26 November 1605, no place given, Hatfield, CP 113/44.

28. For cipher jewels, see Akkerman, *Courtly Rivals*, 61, 67; Braganza, 'Many Ciphers'.
29. Bulwer, *Chironomania*, 64.
30. Squier's second examination, 23 October 1598, TNA, SP 12/268, fos 144v, 145r.
31. For more on Brilliana, the siege of Brampton Bryan and the beginnings of the wars in England, see Eales, *Puritans*, 149–77.
32. Ibid., 25–6.
33. Della Porta, *De Furtivis*, 107–11; *De Occultis*, 134–5.
34. Bod., MS Cherry 30, fo. 9r–v.
35. Private collection, Lady Harley to Edward Harley, 3 March 1642/3, Brampton Bryan, no. 189, fo. 3. The grille letters were edited by Lewis in the mid-nineteenth century, but his edition includes several errors. We cite the original manuscripts, however, to demonstrate the materiality of the grilles at work (nevertheless, the manuscript numbers match the letter numbering of the edition).
36. Private collection, Lady Harley to Edward Harley, 1 March 1642/3, Brampton Bryan, no. 188.
37. Private collection, Lady Harley to Edward Harley, 9 March 1642/3, Brampton Bryan, no. 195.
38. In her letter of 1 March, Lady Harley also instructs Ned to 'give the other [grille] to your sister', suggesting that Brilliana had sent her son two grilles. This also explains why it is that, when the letterbook contains four letters written with the grille, it also contains two grilles. These grilles are either Brilliana's and Ned's, Brilliana's and her daughter Brill's, or Ned's and Brill's.
39. Private collection, Lady Harley to Edward Harley, 1 and 9 March 1642/3, Brampton Bryan, nos 188 and 195.
40. Tacticus, *How to Survive under Siege*, 86 (31.10–31.13).
41. See Hexham, *A Journall*, 22–3 (10 and 13 August 1632), quoted in Scannell, *Conflict*, 136.
42. Tacticus, *How to Survive under Siege*, 85 (31.7).
43. Della Porta, *Natural Magick*, 346.
44. Britland, '"In the Hollow of His Wooden Leg"', 90, referring to *The Diary of Samuel Pepys*, vi.30 (diary entry dated 4 February 1665).
45. Marshall, *Intelligence* (2023), 114.
46. Britland, '"In the Hollow of His Wooden Leg"', 90–1 n. 12 referring to Stanley, *Private Devotions*, i.cviii n. 17. Note 17, in turn, refers to another source, Halsall, *The Journal of the Siege of Lathom House* (1823), 67–9, a source which does not print the passage in question. This rather unpleasant story may instead be derived directly from Tacticus, *How to Survive under Siege*, 85 (31.6).
47. Della Porta, *Natural Magick*, 343.
48. Lupton, *A Thousand Notable Things*, Book 9, 232. For a demonstration of this technique, see Lesson 4.4.
49. 'Sir Roger Twysden's Journal', 148.
50. Miscellany, 1587, BL, Harley MS 530, fo. 14v.
51. Bales, *The Writing Schoolemaster*, Q3v.
52. Huygens's *Mémoires pour mes enfants*, 131–2, identified in Ineke Huysman's blog https://brievenconstantijnhuygens.net/2020/06/07/smokkelbriefjes/. The same blog states that twenty-nine such tiny letters survive.

53. Rivas, *Espias*, 71 (catalogue entry 8.3). We are thankful to Carlos Infantes Buil, head of the reference department, for measuring the document, Archivo General de Simancas, EST, LEG, 591.40.

54. Mary to Monsieur de l'Aubespine, 31 January 1586, Chartley, TNA, SP 53/17, p. 205. Guy, *My Heart*, 480, missapprehends the shoe technique, thinking the message was to be hidden in the heel.

55. Marshall, *Intelligence* (2023), 135 n. 120, referring to Stevenson, *The Scottish Revolution*, 188.

56. Britland, '"In the Hollow of His Wooden Leg"', 89.

57. Barwick, *Life*, 61–2. Tacticus also recommended the use of books as cover for smuggling messages: Tacticus, *How to Survive under Siege*, 84 (31.2).

58. Akkerman, *Invisible Agents*, 4, 29.

59. [Rous], *A Brief Narrative*, 4.

60. [Ludlow], *The Memoirs*, i.67–8.

61. Strangeways to Thurloe, 1 December 1656, Durham, Bod., Rawl. MS A 45, fos 5–6, also cited in Akkerman, *Invisible Agents*, 89.

62. Corbet, *A Letter*, A3r–v.

63. W.T., *The Triall of Mr Mordaunt*, 2.

64. Tacticus, *How to Survive under Siege*, 85 (31.4, 31.4a; sandals. 31.8; corslet); and 88 (31.23; tunic).

65. [Chaloner] to Essex, 8 January 1596/7, Pisæ, Hatfield, CP 37/56.

66. Iordanou, 'The Invisible Trade', 228. Report sent to the Heads of the Council of Ten, 2 October 1572, Archivio di Stato di Venezia, Capi del Consiglio di Dieci, Lettere dei Rettori e di altre Cariche, busta 281, c. 227. We are thankful to Ioanna Iordanou for chasing up this document.

67. The *CSP Domestic* speculates that the needle pricks still visible in Segur Pardeilhan to Burghley, 22 October 1585, Frankenthal, TNA, SP 81/3, fo. 214, are the result of its having been 'stiched into a garment', though it may also be the case that they simply resulted from its letterlocking.

68. Anonymous Royalist to Charles II, 13 March [1659/60], no place given, BL, Add. MS 35029B, fo. 7r.

69. Brilliana also informs Ned that 'I have sent you your linen. Doctor Wright and Mistress Wright present their service to you': 1 March 1642/3, Brampton Bryan, no. 188. This may be a hint that a message lies within the fabric's fibres.

70. Henry Garnett to [Thomas Garnett and Anne Vaux], 26 February 1606, Hatfield, CP 110/16, and Garnett to Vaux, 3 March 1606, TNA, SP 14/216 (part 2), fo. 203r (two handkerchiefs and a bible); notes taken on interrogation of Garnett, [31 March–24 April 1606], Hatfield, CP 110/66.

71. 'For correspondence with Master Williams', Bod., Clarendon MS 94 (no. 10). Wildman, 'A Brief Discourse', 532–4.

72. 'For correspondence with Master Williams', Bod., Clarendon MS 94 (no. 10).

73. Wildman, 'A Brief Discourse', 532.

74. Akkerman, *Invisible Agents*, 100–1, citing one of Cromwell's sons, Henry, to Thurloe, 31 March 1658.

75. See Andrew, *The Secret World*, 131–2, for the location of the letter boxes.

76. [Lilly], *The Last of the Astrologers*, 77, also cited in Akkerman, *Invisible Agents*, 54.

77. Thweyng to Owen, 23 November 1587, Calais, BL, Harley MS 286, fo. 120.

78. Hodgetts, 'Elizabethan Priest-Holes I', 279.

79. Ibid., 283, quoting Caraman, *Henry Garnett*, 168.
80. Hodgetts, 'Elizabethan Priest-Holes I', 284–6.
81. Ibid., 291; quoting *Records of the English Province of the Society of Jesus*, iv.73.
82. Hodgetts, 'Elizabethan Priest-Holes I', 285.
83. Hodgetts, 'Elizabethan Priest-Holes III', 171.
84. Waad to Salisbury, 26 November 1605, no place given, Hatfield, CP 113/44.
85. Johanesen, ' "That *Silken Priest*" ', 39.
86. For indisputable evidence that Lucy was Buckingham's mistress, see Akkerman, 'A Triptych', 135–7.
87. John Hope to 'some at Brussels', 20 April 1628, 'from the Exchange', TNA, SP 16/101, fo. 93r.
88. Camden, *Annales*, sig. T2r. Johanesen points out that this event is not substantiated in the interrogations: Johanesen, ' "That *Silken Priest*" ', 47.
89. See Akkerman, *Queen of Hearts*, 189–90.
90. See ibid., 155 n. 83: Nethersole to one of the secretaries of state [Naunton?], 24 February 1621, Berlin, TNA, SP 81/20, fo. 200v.
91. Smith, *Royalist Agents*, 171.
92. Farr, *John Lambert*, 211. The wearing of masks to hide one's identity had become so common in Venice that in 1608 it was prohibited for citizens travelling on foot or by boat to don such disguises other than at carnival time: Andrew, *The Secret World*, 131.
93. Woolrych, *Britain in Revolution*, 735.
94. [Halkett], 'The Autobiography', 70–1.
95. Anonymous to [Hyde?], 1/11 May 1648, Honselersdijk, Bod., Clarendon MS 31, fo. 66r. For more on this episode, see Akkerman, *Invisible Agents*, 189–91.
96. Charles Paget to Mary, Queen of Scots, [4/]14 January 1584[/5], Paris, Hatfield, CP 163/1 (fo. 2r).
97. 'A summary of the examinations and confessions of the conspirators, George Gifford, Savage, Ballard, Babington, Tichborne, Barnewell, and others, suspected and charged as implicated in Babington's conspiracy', TNA, SP 53/19, no. 91 (pp. 553, 556).
98. Ibid. (pp. 558, 569, 573).
99. See also Marshall, *Intelligence* (2023), 205.
100. Walter Frauncis, mayor of Dartmouth to Sir Thomas Ridgewaie, 23 June 1603, Saint-Malo, Hatfield, CP 187/82.
101. The master of Grey to Archibald Douglas, [n.d.] November 1586, no place given, Hatfield, CP 15/61.
102. See Johanesen, ' "That *Silken Priest*" '.
103. Viscount Howard of Bindon to Salisbury, 10 April 1608, no place given, Hatfield, CP 125/87.
104. Akkerman, *Queen of Hearts*, 238.
105. T[homas] D[ouglas] to Mr Thomas Honiman, 24 November 1601, Gravesend, Hatfield, CP 89/126. The letter has been endorsed by Cecil's secretary as 'Thomas Douglas to my master'.
106. Rob Macpherson, 'Douglas, Archibald', *ODNB*.
107. Much of our account stems from Bindoff, 'A Bogus Envoy'. Bindoff bases his interpretation on three of Douglas's confessions: Douglas's first confession, 3 February 1605, [Heidelberg], TNA, SP 81/9, fos 84–7, Latin; Douglas's second confession, 10 February 1605, [Heidelberg], TNA, SP 81/9, fos 88–92,

Latin; and his third confession, 21 June 1605, the Tower, TNA, SP 14/14, fos 112–13 (no. 50).

108. Robert Cecil to George Nicolson, [January 1601/2], Hatfield, CP 86/87_2, also quoted in Bindoff, 'A Bogus Envoy', 17. It is Bindoff who states that the unnamed spy derided by Cecil in the letter is Douglas. For Cecil's take on Douglas's intelligence, in this particular instance regarding Lady Arbella's assumed conversion to 'Papism', see [Robert Cecil] to [Thomas Douglas?], [c. February 1602/3], Hatfield, CP 82/104_2.

109. In July 1602, thus in Cecil's employ, Douglas confessed to counterfeiting 'heritable writs': see Newton, *The Making of the Jacobean Regime*, 114.

110. Bindoff, 'A Bogus Envoy', 19, notes that Douglas identifies the particular monopoly differently in two of his examinations.

111. The sign manual usually refers to either the signature of the monarch or a written monogram made up of their initials. Fundamentally, it was a hand-written equivalent of the royal seal (or signet).

112. Bindoff, 'A Bogus Envoy', 32–3.

113. Douglas's first confession, as trans. in ibid., 21.

114. Stewart writes to Cecil begging that he 'may travel to the Emperor's wars [vs the Ottoman Turks] . . . if it please God and His Majesty I would be for a better use hereafter than to die and be tormented'. The letter was sealed with his spiral lock, suggesting that Stewart wanted the letter to make an impression before it was even opened: see Chapter 1, pp. 60–4).

115. In 1598, for example, Garrett Swyfte was merely detained at Newgate for upwards of four months on account of his having counterfeited Cecil's hand on a petition: see Swyfte to Sir Robert Cecil, 27 November 1598, Newgate, Hatfield, CP 65/108. For Porter's stamps, see Chapter 1, pp. 41–6.

116. Lingelsheim to Lesieur, 1 February 1605, Heidelberg, TNA, SP 81/9, fo. 73r, translated in Bindoff, 'A Bogus Envoy', 24.

117. In *Resolutiën Staten-Generaal, 1576–1625*, xiii.94 (entry 76), given as genuine.

118. Besides the forgery located by the authors (Fig. 36), there are only two other forged documents of Robert Gray that survive: James to the Elector Palatine, 18 November 1604, TNA, SP 81/9, fo. 61, and the passport (Fig. 12), attached to TNA, SP 14/14, fos 112–13 (no. 50). The passport is generic, 'addressed to all political, military, and naval authorities requesting free passage for its bearer, "Robert Gray, Armiger"'. A contemporary copy of the forgery of James to the magistrates of Cologne also survives: [June 1605?], Hatfield, CP 97/49. Another, to the archbishop of Cologne, dated 7 November 1604, was printed in 1615: Bindoff, 'A Bogus Envoy', 20.

119. See Lake to Cranborne, 16 March 1604[/5], Royston, CP 104/96.

120. Bacon, *Novum Organum*, 87.

121. Bindoff, 'A Bogus Envoy', 27, translating the confessions.

122. Akkerman, *Queen of Hearts*, 59.

123. Bindoff, 'A Bogus Envoy', 20, quoting the third confession.

124. Ibid., 37, quoting annotations to the 1615 printed forgery. Elphinstone, by then 1st Lord Balmerino, would himself be accused of counterfeiting the king's signature in 1607, and had possibly been doing so since 1599.

125. Lake to Cranborne, 16 March 1604[/5], Royston, CP 104/96. It is worth noting that Douglas's execution was expedited with uncommon haste – perhaps to prevent too many questions being asked about the affair.

4. INKS & INVISIBILITY

1. Mary, Queen of Scots to Castelnau, 5 January 1584, Sheffield Castle, TNA, SP 53/13, p. 506 (see also Macrakis, *Prisoners*, 32). Guy, *My Heart*, 474, mangles the translation of Mary's letter somewhat, conflating the two possible reveals for alum, water and heat (there is no mention of a heat source in Mary's letter): he writes, 'in order to read it, the paper must be dipped in a basin of water, and then held to the fire, the secret writing then appears white, and may easily be read until the paper dries'. While the water would, indeed, reveal the writing, holding the wet letter to the fire would help the paper to dry quickly, thus allowing the message to disappear more speedily, but it brought with it the risk of scorching any message into a permanent presence.

2. See also *A Queens Delight, Or the Art of Preserving, Conserving and Candying*, appended to W.M., *The Queens Closet Opened*. Pages 270–1 describe using alum with a water reveal and orange or lemon juice with a heat reveal.

3. Mary to Monsieur de l'Aubespine, 31 January 1586, Chartley, TNA, SP 53/17, p. 205; see also Guy, *My Heart*, 480. For a piece of clothing sent to Charles II with a message in alum, see anonymous Royalist to Charles II, 13 March [1659/60], no place given, BL, Add. MS 35029B, fo. 7r.

4. Cooper, 'Surveillance', 218.

5. Gregory to Salisbury, undated, [1606?], no place given, TNA, SP 14/24, fo. 67r.

6. Gregory to Walsingham, [n.d.] February 1586, 'from my poor house; half blind', BL, Harley MS 286, fo. 78r: see Fig. 38.

7. *OED*, 'reagent', n.2.

8. Macrakis, *Prisoners*, 11–12, translates Thévenot, Boivin and de La Hire, eds, *Veterum Mathematicorum Opera*, 102.

9. It may be that the Puritan-minded secretary of state had not read the work in question, the *Ars Amatoria* or *Art of Love*, which was considered if not obscene, then certainly inappropriate.

10. Macrakis, *Prisoners*, 14.

11. See Chapter 1, pp. 33–8.

12. George Holles to the marquess of Ormond, 3 December 1657, Rotterdam, Bod., Clarendon MS 56, fo. 271r; for a demonstration, see Lesson 4.4.

13. Father Talbot to the marquess of Ormond, 3 December 1657, no place given, Bod., Clarendon MS 56, fo. 269r.

14. [Halkett], 'The Autobiography', 121–2, also quoted in Akkerman, *Invisible Agents*, 195–6.

15. One of his primary sources was Pliny the Elder's natural history (77 CE), which not only included Ovid's milk-writing, but noted the utility of another form of milk, the sap of the tithymalus, a type of succulent often called a spurge, for writing on the skin of a messenger. See also Macrakis, *Prisoners*, 3–4. Others were happy to follow della Porta's lead, such as the compiler of a manuscript including extracts from della Porta, Cardano, Trithemius and others ('Des ecritures non apparentes', BL, Cotton MS Vespasian F/VI, fo. 169r.)

16. See Jonson, *Epigrams*, 159: epigram 92, 'The New Cry', ll. 25–9. For della Porta's thoughts on seals, see Chapter 1, pp. 54–5.

17. See Cowley, 'Written in Juice of Lemmon', ii.28–9.

18. For the chemical process behind this and other heat reveals, see Lesson 4.4.

19. It is Macrakis, *Prisoners*, 16, who refers to the rise of the lemon juice heat reveal in sixteenth-century Italy, but the secondary source she refers to does not confirm it; Van der Meer, 'The History of *Citrus*', referring to Anon., *Dat batement van recepten*, 7.

20. If the Chinese were aware of the possibilities of alum in the twelfth century, the Arab world was not far behind, and between the thirteenth and fifteenth centuries they were making invisible inks with onion juice, alum and even with copper sulphate or blue vitriol (again using gall-water as the reveal, thus reversing Philo's prescription): Qalqashandī, *Subh Al A'sha*, 23, also suggested using a mixture of sal ammoniac and milk as a viable invisible ink.

21. Macrakis, *Prisoners*, 15. Qalqashandī, *Subh Al A'sha*, 23. 'Dried lemon' is a better translation than the literal 'black lemon', and while the translation mentions egg yolk, egg whites do appear more logical.

22. For these substances, see *Natural Magick*, 341–2; and Lesson 4.1, which gives modern names for these substances where appropriate.

23. Boyle, 'Experiments', 200 (experiment 3). For his experiments with ink, see Boyle, 'Experiments', 248.

24. Gregory to Walsingham, [n.d.] February 1586, 'from my poor house; half blind', BL, Harley MS 286, fo. 78r: see Fig. 38.

25. Wilkins, *Mercury*, 42. Wilkins here refers to della Porta, *De Furtivis*, 46–7.

26. Aldrovandi, *De Animalibus Insectis*, quoted in Harvey, *A History of Luminescence*, 76.

27. Ibid., 76, 80–2.

28. See Lesson 4.1.

29. Cotgrave beat the English translation of della Porta printed 'for Thomas Young' to market by three years, but it also included other recipes such as pomegranate juice which 'will not be seen till the paper comes to be pretty warm at the fire': Cotgrave, *Wits Interpreter*, 173.

30. Ibid.

31. Della Porta also suggests applying the liquor with a sponge: see his *Natural Magick*, 340.

32. For Africanus, see della Porta, *Natural Magick*, 343; for della Porta's experiments with glow-worms, see Harvey, *A History of Luminescence*, 80.

33. Bowes to Burghley, 1 January 1592/3, Edinburgh, TNA, SP 52/50, fo. 1r–v.

34. Della Porta, *Natural Magick*, 341.

35. Daybell, *The Material Letter*, 168, refers to one letter between these correspondents, dated 24 June 1599, for which the reference is TNA, SP 12/271, fo. 61, but there are twenty-three more, dated between 25 February and 23 December 1598, for which the reference is TNA, SP 89/2, fos 247–96. Not all of these letters show invisible ink writing between the plain ink lines, but they have been tested for it; sometimes the reveal has rendered the plain ink writing illegible (see e.g. Fig. 41).

36. John Laughton, aka Inchiquin, to Mrs Grey, 31 August 1659, Paris, TNA, SP 78/114, fo. 346r. See Akkerman, *Invisible Agents*, especially 148–54 (also good for forging hands and ink recipes passing down the female line).

37. Edmund Wyndham to [Sir Richard Browne], 6 September 1659, Dieppe, BL, Add. MS 78196, fo. 72v.

38. Mary to Monsieur de l'Aubespine, 31 January 1586, Chartley, TNA, SP 53/17, p. 205.

39. For Gregory to Walsingham, [n.d.] February 1586, 'from my poor house; half blind', BL, Harley MS 286, fo. 78r, see Fig. 38; Gregory to Cecil, 4 May 1594, 'from my house in Whitechapel', Hatfield, CP 26/57.
40. Captain William Ellesdon to Charles II, [September 1660], no place given, TNA, SP 29/17, fo. 134r. Ellesdon petitions the king for a pension of £400 and points out that the like was given to Gregory.
41. Henry Garnett to Anne Vaux, 21 April 1606, TNA, SP 14/20, fo. 91r: 'the apprehension of Richard, & Robert with a cipher I know not of whose laid to my charge: though that which was singular oversight, a letter written in cipher together with the cipher: which letter may bring many into question'. When Garnett was interrogated in April 1606 he was asked 'of whose hand is the cipher that was found in his chamber and between whom': interrogatories addressed to Garnett, [n.d.] April 1606, Hatfield, CP 116/28.
42. William Richardson, 'Phelippes, Thomas', *ODNB*.
43. For deciphering as reading illegible hands, see Chapter 1, p. 33.
44. Gregory to Salisbury, [1606?], no place given, TNA, SP 14/24, fo. 67r.
45. Childs, *God's Traitors*, 292.
46. Garnett and Richard Blount to the Privy Council, 30 November 1605, [Hindlip Hall?], in *Records of the English Province of the Society of Jesus*, iv.66–9.
47. For the birth of the lions, see Sir Gawen Hervey to Salisbury, 29 July 1605, the Tower, Hatfield, CP 114/62. In the next month Salisbury received many letters from other attendants, such as Anthony Bodely and Ralph Gill, as well as Waad, keeping him abreast of all movements in the den. Waad, who on one occasion complained that the stench of the beasts was so vile it was making him ill (Waad to Salisbury, 24 August 1605, the Tower, Hatfield, CP 112/28), even discussed the likely failure of Salisbury's desire to keep one of the male cubs as a pet: Waad had attempted to tame one of the cubs before, but it had repaid his kindness by eating his dog (Waad to Salisbury, 27 August 1605, 'From the Lion's Tower', Hatfield, CP 112/39).
48. For the earl's indifference to religion, see Thomas Wintour's confession, 25 November 1605, TNA, SP 14/216 (part 2), fo. 14r (no. 116).
49. Thompson Cooper, revised by G. Bradley, 'Garnett, Thomas', *ODNB*.
50. Henry Garnett to [Thomas Garnett?], [23 February? 1606], [from the Tower?], TNA, SP 14/216 (part 2), fo. 200Av. The 'fair copy' of this letter made by a modern archivist, from which the date is taken, is TNA, SP 14/216 (part 2), fos 199r–200Bv (the manuscript volume is incorrectly foliated and has two folios 200). The inscription 'Henry Garnett' is likely Coke's.
51. Gerard, 'The Life', lxxix.
52. Ibid.
53. While lemon juice reveals in water, orange juice does not, and neither will react to heat once the paper carrying them has been dipped in water.
54. Leading contenders for the recipe of 'bisket bread' include Lady Fettiplace, whose household book (annotated as 1604) presents what looks remarkably like a meringue (see Hilary Spurling, 'Fettiplace, Elinor', *ODNB*), and Digby, *The Closet*, 211–12, describes a thin paste slowly baked in an oven.
55. Gerard, 'Narrative', 166.
56. See Akkerman, *Invisible Agents*, 106, for artichoke juice; also Lesson 4.4.
57. Gerard, 'Narrative', 168.
58. See, for instance, Waad to Salisbury, 17 April 1606, no place given, Hatfield, CP 116/16; Gerard, 'Narrative', 168.

59. Gerard, 'The Life', lxxx.
60. Ibid., cviii–cix. It is of course possible that there was a transcription or printer's error that led to 'Lemon' being substituted for 'alum'.
61. See, for instance, Fraser, *The Gunpowder Plot*, 302.
62. Childs, *God's Traitors*, 3.
63. 'The Examination of Anne Vaux the maid', 11 March 1605[/6], TNA, SP 14/216 (part 2), fo. 139r (no. 200).
64. Sir Edward Coke to Salisbury, [December] 1605, no place given, Hatfield, CP 113/148–9.
65. Examination of Elizabeth, wife of Wm Shephard, coachman to 'Mrs Perkins', 11 November 1605, Enfield Chase, TNA, SP 14/216 (part 1), fo. 113r; Johnson's first examination, 11 November 1605, TNA, SP 14/216 (part 1), fo. 112r.
66. For her change of lodgings, see 'The Examination of Anne Vaux the maid', 11 March 1605[/6], TNA, SP 14/216 (part 2), fo. 139r (no. 200). Mark Nicholls, 'Vaux, Anne', *ODNB*. See Childs, *God's Traitors*, 329–46, 351, for more on these events.
67. Interlocution [a report by John Locherson], 23 February 1605[/6], TNA, SP 14/18, fo. 167r.
68. Johnson's second examination, 25 February 1605[/6], TNA, SP 14/216 (part 2), fo. 124r.
69. The letter also has an enigmatic endorsement in Garnett's hand: 'Thom. This is the letter which I sent by the woman. Thomas Sayer alias Rookwood. Henry Garnett.' There is a second endorsement in another hand which reads: 'Garnett's letter to Rookeshood.' Some suggest that Thomas Sayer was a pseudonym for Ambrose Rookwood (Daybell, *The Material Letter*, 167), but this is problematic, as while Garnett does write of bribing his jailer to take a letter to Rookwood (interlocution, 23 February 1605[/6], TNA, SP 14/18, fo. 167r), Rookwood had been executed on 31 January. Some sources suggest, however, that Rookwood was a pseudonym for Thomas Garnett: *Records of the English Province of the Society of Jesus*, ii.581. We argue that the letter was addressed to cover names used by Thomas Garnett to be forwarded to Anne Vaux.
70. For possible use of handkerchiefs as carriers for messages, see Chapter 3, p. 132.
71. Even black ink turns brown over time, partly because of the acid that the gall-water supplies.
72. Henry Garnett to [Thomas Garnett and Anne Vaux], 26 February 1606, Hatfield, CP 110/16. HMC, xviii.60, mistakenly reads 'Alice' for 'Adieu', and some have thus assumed that Alice is an alias for Anne Vaux. The Cradle Tower also contained the cell from which Father Gerard had escaped in 1597.
73. Garnett to [Anne Vaux], 3 March 1606, TNA, SP 14/216 (part 2), fo. 202r (no. 242).
74. Gerard, 'Narrative', 171–2.
75. Relation of Henry Garnett concerning the Gunpowder Plot, 13 April [1606], Hatfield, CP 115/ no. 13, fos 23–6 at fo. 25v.
76. Anne Vaux to Henry Garnett, [before 3 March] 1606, TNA, SP 14/216 (part 2), fo. 206r. Transcription is of the nineteenth-century copy at fo. 207r. On 3 March, Garnett replies to this with the words 'The Latin was for Mr. Blunt [i.e., Richard Blount] or any of the Society, shew it them if you have it still, or I will write again': Garnett to [Anne Vaux], 3 March 1606, TNA, SP 14/216 (part 2), fo. 203r.

77. Anstruther, *Vaux*, 347–8; Caraman, *Henry Garnet*, 370.
78. Henry Garnett to Anne Vaux, 3 March 1606, TNA, SP 14/216 (part 2), fo. 203r.
79. Ibid.
80. Anne Vaux to Henry Garnett, [21 March 1606?], TNA, SP 14/216 (part 2), fo. 208r. Our emphasis.
81. A manuscript in a private collection describes the search at Hindlip in detail: 'Forth of this secret and most cunning conveyance came Henry Garnett the Jesuit, sought for, and another with him, named Hall [i.e., Father Oldcorne]; marmalade and other sweetmeats were found lying by them': as cited in Butler, *Additions*, iii.447.
82. Henry Garnett to Anne Vaux, [2 April 1606?], TNA, SP 14/216 (part 2), fo. 210r–v.
83. Anne Vaux to Henry Garnett, [3 April 1606], TNA, SP 14/216 (part 2), fo. 213r.
84. Henry Garnett to Anne Vaux, [21 April 1606], TNA, SP 14/20, fo. 91r.
85. Relation of Henry Garnett concerning the Gunpowder Plot, 13 April [1606], Hatfield, CP 115, no. 13, fos 23–6 at fo. 25v. Garnett also notes at fo. 24v that 'I thought the gentlewomen past all examinations & having none to name so free from danger as Mistress Anne Vaux'.
86. [Thomas Wilson] to [Salisbury], [n.d.] 1606, no place given, Hatfield, CP 193/95.
87. Gregory to Salisbury, [1606?], no place given, TNA, SP 14/24, fo. 67r.
88. Gregory to Walsingham, [n.d.] February 1586, 'from my poor house; half blind', BL, Harley MS 286, fo. 78r: see Fig. 38.
89. See della Porta, *Natural Magick*, 352.
90. Gregory to Robert Cecil, 4 May 1594, 'from my house in Whitechapel', Hatfield, CP 26/57.
91. Gregory to Robert Cecil, 28 February 1594[/5], 'From my poore house', Hatfield, CP 25/52.
92. Gregory to Robert Cecil, 12 October 1594, 'from my poor Lodging', Hatfield, CP 28/91.
93. Gregory to Salisbury, [1606?], no place given, TNA, SP 14/24, fo. 67r.
94. Garnett to Vaux, 3 March 1606, TNA, SP 14/216 (part 2), fo. 203r.
95. Gregory to Salisbury, undated, [1606], no place given, TNA, SP 14/24, fo. 67v.
96. Frisius, *De Radio Astronomica*.
97. Cardano, *De Subtilitate*, vol. 1, book 5; della Porta, *Magiae Naturalis*.
98. Wotton to Bacon, 17 December 1620, Vienna, BL, Add. MS 39254, fos 60–61b.
99. Gregory to Walsingham, [n.d.] February 1586, 'from my poor house; half blind', BL, Harley MS 286, fo. 78r: see Fig. 38.
100. Flis, 'Drawing', 150–1.
101. Della Porta, *Natural Magick*, 364. See also Borrelli, 'Introduction'; Borrelli, 'Optical Diagrams'; Dijksterhuis, 'Magi from the North'; Smith, 'Giambattista'.
102. Della Porta, *Natural Magick*, 366–7.
103. Ibid., 364.

5. STILETTOS & STORYTELLING

1. This account is taken from Iordanou, *Venice's Secret Service*, 198–200. Iordanou made these fantastic discoveries in the Venetian archives.

2. Coryate, *Coryat's Crudites*, X3.
3. Walker, 'I Spy with My Little Eye', 212. London's playgoers were also more than used to seeing poison depicted on the stage: see Pollard, *Drugs*; Sadowski, '"Foul,"'; and the edited collection by Hopkins and Angus, *Poison*.
4. Raymond, *An Itinerary*, Introduction (iv); 209–10.
5. Demmin, *An Illustrated History*, 400–2. *OED*, 'stiletto', n.1a; Tarassuk, 'Some Notes', 47.
6. Marozzo, *The Duel*, 293–337 (126–48 in the original Italian). The poniard, however, often had a secondary function as a gunner's tool for clearing fuse holes in cannon and/or measuring powder to adjust range of shot.
7. Burton, *The Baiting of the Popes Bull*, 44.
8. See Marshall, *Intelligence* (1994), 282–6. Iordanou, *Venice's Secret Service*, 190–1, 198–202.
9. Colm Lennon, 'Creagh [Crevagh], Richard', *ODNB*. For Poley being in Cecil's or Walsingham's service, see 'List of certain intelligencers', TNA, SP 12/265, fo. 207r.
10. See Wiggins, *Journeymen*, 18–20.
11. *RPS*, A1567/12/22; accessed 13 June 2023. Schwoerer, *Gun Culture*, 60–1. A proclamation was delivered by the monarch, and did not enjoy the legal status of a statute, which expressed the current state of the law of the land. Subjects were expected to obey it nonetheless.
12. Fletcher, 'Firearms', 17–18; Jardine, *The Awful End*, 85–90.
13. Jardine, *The Awful End*, 57–8; see also Fletcher, 'Firearms', 2, 7–9. The name 'dag' possibly derives from a part of its mechanism known as the 'dog', the spring-loaded wheel that pressed the pyrite against the 'pan', the area that holds the gunpowder charge used to ignite the full charge held in the barrel. When the wheellock was ready to fire, the pan was covered, only opening when the wheel rotated against the pyrite, enabling the spark to do its job, while also holding the powder both safe and dry until the moment of ignition.
14. Fletcher, 'Firearms', 18.
15. Schwoerer, *Gun Culture*, 59.
16. Jardine, *The Awful End*, 93.
17. Schwoerer, *Gun Culture*, 60–1.
18. For tensions between the nobility and the authorities on gun ownership and the connection to hunting rights, see Fletcher, 'Firearms', 24, and Schwoerer, *Gun Culture*, 49, 65, 123.
19. Stipriaan, *De Zwijger*, 628–30.
20. Jardine, *The Awful End*, 51, 54–8.
21. Gérard's 'belt and braces' approach may have been influenced by the 2nd duke of Guise's assassin in 1563, whose dag also 'received three pellets and three charges in one chamber': see Smith to the queen, 26 February 1562[/3], Blois, TNA, SP 70/51, fo. 115r. The two bullets remain in the Prinsenhof wall. It is not entirely clear what dag he used in the assassination, nor where he had acquired it, but it sufficed for the job at hand.
22. Stipriaan, *De Zwijger*, 678–86.
23. Stafford to Walsingham, 17 July 1584, Paris, Hatfield, CP 163/32–3 (fo. 33v).
24. 'The Examination of diverse persons taken by Mr [John] Dol[e]y touching John Somerfield', 28 October 1583, TNA, SP 12/163, fo. 57r; also referred to in Jardine, *The Awful End*, 106.

25. 'Articles to be administered to John Somerfeld', TNA, SP 12/163, fo. 54r.
26. Somerville's examination, the Tower, TNA, SP 12/263, fo. 16r.
27. William Wizeman, 'Somerville, John', *ODNB*; William Wizeman, 'Arden, Edward', *ODNB*.
28. Jardine, *The Awful End*, 107–11.
29. Ibid., 153–4, citing 'A True and Plain Declaration of the Horrible Treasons Practised by William Parry against Her Majesty', 7.
30. Jardine, *The Awful End*, 112–13.
31. Ibid., 153–8, citing 'A Proclamation against the common use of Dags, Handguns, Arquebuses, Callibers and Cotes of Defence (26 July 1579)'.
32. Baker worked on Sheer Lane, which also housed the business of a cutler, John Willington, who manufactured 'these murthering Daggers': Waad to Salisbury, 29 May 1610, no place given, Hatfield, CP 128/125.
33. Schwoerer, *Gun Culture*, 63.
34. Raymond, *An Itinerary*, A1r.
35. Museo Correr, Venice, inventory no: Cl. XIV n. 1515.
36. Raymond, *An Itinerary*, A1r–v.
37. Pollard, *Drugs*, 8–9.
38. Guy, *My Heart*, 54; John Masone to the Privy Council, 29 April 1551, Amboise, TNA, SP 68/6, fo. 215r (no. 332). A Scot named Robert Stewart was arrested: see 'Advices sent by Jehan Scheyfve', June 1551, *CSP Spain*, x (Vienna, Imp. Arch. E. 19).
39. Guerau de Espés to Philip II, 5 December 1570, London, *CSP Spain (Simancas)*, ii, no. 227.
40. Mary to Verac, 20 April 1571, Sheffield, TNA, SP 53/6, fo. 74r (no. 43); Potter, *Edinburgh under Siege*, 45.
41. Verac to Mary, 20 July 1571, Leith, TNA, SP 53/7, fo. 3r; see also the account of Verac's mission to Scotland, July 1571, TNA, SP 52/20, fo. 208v.
42. Mary to the archbishop of Glasgow, 8 May 1574, Sheffield, in Labanoff, ed., *Lettres*, iv.470. Our translation from the French.
43. One writer suggested unicorn hoof as the most efficacious material, presumably because of the rarity of hooved narwhals: see W[illiams], *Occult Physick*, 1–2: 'the hoof of the unicorn is better than his horn, and being worn about a man in any place, no infection can have power on him'.
44. Cockyn lived in Fleet Street, 'at the signe of the Elephant, a little above the Conduit', according to the title page of Bishop, *Beautiful Blossomes*.
45. Cockyn's reply, 28 April 1575, TNA, SP 53/10, p. 517.
46. Gibbs, *Poison*, 12–13. Recipes for both substances can be found in Culpeper's 1649 English translation of the *Pharmacopoeia Londoniensis*, *A Physical Directory*, 180.
47. Wymmes's depositions, 15–16 May 1575, TNA, SP 53/10, fo. 57; Good's examination, 16 May 1575, TNA, SP 53/10, fo. 58. For more on theriac, see Gibbs, *Poison*, 77–87.
48. 'Henrie Cockyn touching a letter [to Mary] written by Dr Good concerning the Lady Cobham', 20 May 1575, TNA, SP 53/10, fo. 61.
49. Good's examination, 28 April 1575, BL, Cotton MS Caligula C/V, fo. 11.
50. Cockyn had begged Walsingham not to implicate Lady Cobham, or her husband: see Cockyn to Walsingham, 21 February 1575, no place given, TNA, SP 53/10, fo. 11.

51. Mary to Castelnau, 8 December 1585, Tutbury, TNA, SP 53/16, p. 413 (no. 214). Trans. of the original French from the *CSP Domestic*.

52. Budiansky, *Her Majesty's Spymaster*, 166.

53. 'A copy of a letter found in Bruges by one Alleyn a merchant', 1574, BL, Lansdowne MS 18, fo. 159r.

54. 'Mr Walsingham's Report from Franchiotto, the Italian', 20 August 1568, no place given, Hatfield, CP 202/59. Trans. of the Italian from HMC, i.361.

55. 'Certain Cautions for the Queen's Apparel and Diet', undated [*c.* 1568?], Hatfield, CP 153/58.

56. Paré, *Workes*, 780.

57. Guy, *My Heart*, 453.

58. Matthews, 'Nicolas Cabry', 4.

59. Cabry to Walsingham, 10/20 August 1582, Paris, TNA, SP 15/27 (part 1), fo. 159r (no. 105). Trans. of the French from the *CSP Domestic*.

60. Cabry to Walsingham, 19/29 September 1582, Paris, TNA, SP 15/27 (part 1), fo. 166r (no. 110). Trans. of the French and Latin from the *CSP Domestic*. It is this recipe that Culpeper includes in his *A Physical Directory*, 180.

61. Cabry to Walsingham, 16/26 June 1584, Paris, TNA, SP 15/28 (part 2), fo. 27r (no. 77). Trans. of the French from the *CSP Domestic*. Another source sends 'a box of terra sigillata and two little pots of Metridatum & triaca; the best to be found': Edward Barton to [Walsingham?], 27 June 1589, no place given, TNA, SP 97/1, fo. 172v.

62. In 1625, Lady Roe sent some of the finest bezoar stones she had seen, which derived from a 'stag of Corason in Persia' to Elizabeth Stuart: Roe to Elizabeth, 20 February 1624[/5], Old Style, Constantinople, *CES* i.515.

63. BL, Royal Appendix MS 68, fo. 32b.

64. Labanoff, ed., *Lettres*, vii.243, 246.

65. Inventory of items in the custody of the servants of the late queen, 20 February 1587, Labanoff, ed., *Lettres*, vii.248; Akkerman, *Queen of Hearts*, 69.

66. Paré, *Workes*, 808, 813.

67. Intelligence from Lancelot Browne to unknown addressee, 1602, Hatfield, CP 96/162.

68. Duffin, 'Danny Jewel', 7.

69. Rankin, 'On Anecdote', 274–93.

70. French, *The Art of Distillation*, 100.

71. Begley and Goldberg, eds, *The Medical World*, 86–7, 151, 309, 349. The editors identify Digby's own recipe at 349: BL, Sloane MS 2071, fo. 44r–v.

72. Thomas, *Religion*, 224–5, 260.

73. 'Evidence extracted', TNA, SP 12/265, fo. 212r.

74. French, *The Art of Distillation*, 100.

75. 'A report of divers physicians [i.e., Henry Atkins, George Turner, Ralph Wilkinson, Richard Palmer, John Argent and W. Poe], concerning the feigned poison delivered by Bind' to the lord treasurer, [between 22 and 31] July 1609, Hatfield, CP 127/99.

76. Sarpi to de Lisle Groslot, 11 December 1607, cited in Robertson, *Father Paolo Sarpi*, 124.

77. See http://web.prm.ox.ac.uk/weapons/index.php/tour-by-region/europe/europe/arms-and-armour-europe-157/index.html; accessed 3 October 2023.

78. Robertson, *Father Paolo Sarpi*, 114–17.

79. Coke, *The Third Part*, cap. 7, p. 52.
80. 'Certain Cautions for the Queen's Apparel and Diet', undated [*c.* 1568?], Hatfield, CP 153/58.
81. Daybell, Norrhem, Broomhall et al., 'Gender', 584.
82. McIlvenna, *Scandal*, specifically 114.
83. 'Evidence extracted', TNA, SP 12/265, fo. 212r.
84. Edward Talbot's case, [1595], Hatfield, CP Petitions 2363.
85. Practices of Archibald Douglas, etc., in William Davison's hand, 23 November 1584, BL, Cotton MS Caligula C/VII, fo. 206r.
86. John Clarke to Leicester, February 1587, from prison, TNA, SP 12/198, fo. 199v (no. 81).
87. Paré, *Workes*, 781.
88. Item 4 of Wayland's examination, 28 February 1599[/1600], TNA, SP 12/274, fo. 77r (no. 53).
89. Wayland's examination, 28 February 1599[/1600], TNA, SP 12/274, fos 77v (items 7 and 8, for hemlock, the books and ungodly practices), 79r (item 15, for the perfume) (no. 53). By *De Historia Plantarum*, the examination probably refers to *Herbarious Latinus*, a work often attributed to Villa Nova, but in actual fact an anonymous compilation drawing on classical, Arabic and medieval sources published in 1484.
90. Normand, 'Venomous Words', 123.
91. See Gibbs, *Poison*, 13, 131.
92. Shakespeare, *As You Like It*, act 2, scene 1, ll. 12–14.
93. Boaistuau, *Certaine Secrete Wonders of Nature*, 41.
94. Paré, *Workes*, 796.
95. Lupton, *A Thousand Notable Things*, the first book, 14 (item 52).
96. Ibid., the seventh book, 167 (item 18). Lupton claims Antonio Mizauld, a French astronomer and physician, as authority.
97. Topsell, *The History*, 727 (also the source for Fig. 57). Topsell claims Hieronymus Massarius, a physician, as authority for the scarlet cloth.
98. Rendall and Rosner, 'Plays', 1–3.
99. Paré, *Workes*, 797. Paré here describes the sticky end met by some diners who had added unwashed sage to their aperitif – the sage had been sullied with toad saliva or urine.
100. Wayland's examination, 28 February 1599[/1600], TNA, SP 12/274, fos 77r (item 3, for the cup), 78r (item 9, for the salt) (no. 53). Toads excrete bufotoxin – which attacks the heart in a similar manner to digitalis (a drug derived from the foxglove) – from glands in their skin, particularly when stressed, which suggests that this method would at least make the intended victim extremely ill. In 1646 the Montpellier physician Pierre Jean Fabre suggested that a 'toad salt', highly effective at nullifying poison, could be extracted from the ashes of an incinerated toad: see Baldwin, 'Toads', 231, 236, 238.
101. Toads were also suspected of being used to harm others: see Thomas, *Religion*, 530, 626, 653.
102. Jardine, *The Awful End*, 66–8. Dried toads were also used as amulets, as they were supposedly protective against plague and other inconveniences: Thomas, *Religion*, 11.
103. See Gibbs, *Poison*, 13, 18, 27, 131; Rankin, 'On Anecdote', 277–8, 287.

104. Paré, *Workes*, 778–9.

105. BRBL, Osborn Music MS 16, p. 127.

106. Coke, *The Third Part*, cap. 7, p. 52. For the substances and the actions of these poisons see Lessons 5.1 and 5.2.

107. Paré, *Workes*, 809.

108. Raymond, *An Itinerary*, A1v.

109. Monson, *The Black Widows*, 94, 96, 99.

110. Duramy, 'Women'.

111. Peter Holmes, 'Stafford, William', *ODNB*.

112. William Stafford to Walsingham, 10 June 1585, TNA, SP 15/29, fo. 24r.

113. 'The true foundation and manner of the horrible treason, or William Stafford's account of his dealings with Mons. Bellièvre, the French ambassador', 11 January 1587, TNA, SP 12/97, pp. 1–2.

114. Ibid., p. 7.

115. Paré, *Workes*, 781–2. Here Paré references the electric eel. It seems unlikely that he and his works did not cross Walsingham's path while both attended the French court in the 1570s.

116. 'Necessity of the Sentence of Death against Mary', March 1587, BL, Cotton MS Caligula D/I, fo. 80v; Peter Holmes, 'Stafford, William', *ODNB*.

117. Essex to Anthony Bacon, LPL, MS 653, fo. 312, vol. 7, no. 17.

118. Jews being poisoners of Christians played up to stereotypes: see Harris, *Foreign Bodies*; Shapiro, *Shakespeare and the Jews*, 73, 92–3, 96–8, 100, 250 n. 139, 254 n. 10.

119. See Edwards, 'Sir Robert Cecil', 389.

120. TNA, PC 2/24, p. 259.

121. Chamberlain to Carleton, 22 November 1598, London, TNA, SP 12/268, fo. 186r (no. 115).

122. Squier's first examination, 19 October 1598, at the Tower, TNA, SP 12/268, fos 133r, 134r. Not only signed by Squier, but also by the interrogators Sir John Peyton, Attorney General Coke, Solicitor General Thomas Fleming, Bacon and Waad. Making poison balls seems indeed to have been a specialised skill. In 1599, John Daniel wrote to the queen that he had discovered some 'horrible practices' against her person in the Low Countries. A poisoner, one Thomsin, had planned to use such balls, which had been made especially by William Randall at Dunkirk. He smuggled them first to Saint-Omer, then to Calais and finally to Dieppe before Daniel (see the forging of Essex's letters in Chapter 1, 'Fraud & Forgery') dobbed him in: Daniel to Elizabeth I, [February 1599], 'beyond the seas', Hatfield, CP 186/19.

123. Squier's second examination, 23 October 1598, TNA, SP 12/268, fo. 144r; Squier's first examination, 19 October 1598, at the Tower, TNA, SP 12/268, fo. 134r–v.

124. Squier's second examination, 23 October 1598, TNA, SP 12/268, fos 144v, 145r.

125. See Stewart, ' "Master Smokey Swyne's-Flesh" '.

126. Edwards, 'Sir Robert Cecil', 377–414.

127. 'Substance of Franklin's arraignment', 27 November 1615, at the king's bench, TNA, SP 14/83, fo. 129r.

128. 'Deposition of Jas. Franklin', 16 November 1615, TNA, SP 14/83, fo. 62r–v.

129. Paré, *Workes*, 780.

130. Wiggins, *Journeymen*, 4; John Considine, 'Overbury, Sir Thomas', *ODNB*.
131. Coke, *The Third Part*, cap. 7, p. 48.
132. 'Evidence extracted', TNA, SP 12/265, fo. 212v.
133. Bellany and Cogswell, *The Murder*, especially 137–58.

CODA: THE BLACK CHAMBER

1. A little bit of luck did not go amiss, either, as was painfully apparent on 4 November 1605, when Guy Fawkes was discovered alongside several barrels of gunpowder, waiting for his moment. The plot was uncovered at the last minute because one of the plotters warned the 4th Baron Mounteagle not to be at Whitehall on the 5th. Had this warning not been sent, England might have seen a very different seventeenth century.
2. See Akkerman, 'The Postmistress'. Midura, ' "They Hide from Me" ', confirms Akkerman's point that Alexandrine led one of the first chambers in Europe. The English (and Venetian) chambers discussed in *Spycraft* are precursors of the French Cabinet Noir, founded by the Rossignols in the 1670s – on which see Kahn, *The Codebreakers*, 157–88, specifically 162 – and the Habsburg Geheime Kabinets-Kanzlei in eighteenth-century Vienna, on which see Stix, 'Zur Geschichte und Organisation der Wiener Geheimen Ziffernkanzlei'. There is no comparative overview of European black chambers, but see Andrew, 'The Nature of Military Intelligence', Oakley, 'The Interception of Posts' and De Leeuw, 'The Black Chamber'.
3. Marshall, *Intelligence* (2023), 73.
4. Akkerman, 'The Postmistress'. Akkerman, *Invisible Agents*, 1.
5. Midura, ' "They Hide from Me" ', 1–2, citing 'The Swedish Manifesto, 1630', as published in Wilson, ed., *The Thirty Years War*, 123.
6. Akkerman, 'The Postmistress', 182.
7. Marshall, ' "Secret Wheeles" ', 193.
8. Dorset to Salisbury, 9 August 1642, York, Hatfield, CP 197/127.
9. Marshall, *Intelligence* (2023), 121–5, 144–5.
10. 'June 1657: An Act for settling the Postage of England, Scotland and Ireland', in *Acts and Ordinances*, 1, 110–13.
11. In 1660 and 1663, Charles II issued similar warrants, permitting his government officials to open letters; tellingly, the Post Office Act of 1711 underwrote those warrants, which in modern times would be seen as a violation of privacy: see Kahn, *The Codebreakers*, 172.
12. Marshall, *Intelligence* (2023), 173 n. 96, 203.
13. When William Phelippes recommended his younger son to William Davison, Walsingham's right-hand man, he noted that the boy had been 'brought up with Master Francis Bacon these two or three years': William Phelippes to Davison, 5 October 1586, London, TNA, SP 12/194, fo. 13r. Thomas added his tuppence-ha'penny-worth, praising his brother's 'staid and secret nature' before suggesting that the boy would 'in short time be as able to serve your honour's turn as any inexperienced man you can choose . . . Master Bacon can yield some testimony of his honest, discreet behaviour, for some time he hath remained with him': Thomas Phelippes to Davison, 8 October 1586, Chiswick, TNA, SP 12/194, fo. 42r (no. 21). The *ODNB* erroneously ascribes the 'staid and secret nature' to Thomas rather than to the brother, though skulking was apparently a family trait.

14. As quoted in Marshall, *Intelligence* (2023), 146.
15. Ibid., 155, 176, 206.
16. Ibid., 207, 211; but see also Akkerman, *Invisible Agents*, 24; Akkerman and Langman, 'Accidentally on Purpose', 327–8.
17. Marshall, *Intelligence* (1994), 86, quoting Morland, 'Proposals', 265.
18. Phelippes to Robert Cecil, 6 March 1596[/7], no place given, Hatfield House, CP 38/97.
19. LPL, MS 931, no. 13: 'An old writing pale & almost worn out copied in a Minute'.
20. Marshall, *Intelligence* (1994), 87; 'The said Proposall [see no. 11 of the same MS volume] copied in a Minute', LPL, MS 931, no. 12.
21. Evelyn, *The Diary*, i.326, 27 November 1655.
22. The comparison to Watt's machine is from Marshall, *Intelligence* (1994), 87; Muirhead, *The Origin*, iii.30–3.
23. Expenses for a circular cipher, [1667], TNA, SP 29/230, fo. 82r.
24. Morland, *A New Method*, 7–8.
25. Dickinson, *Sir Samuel Morland*, 34; Strasser, 'The Rise of Cryptology', 28; Buonafalce, 'Sir Samuel Morland', 258.
26. Morland, *A New Method*, 11.
27. So long as correspondents had pre-agreed the order of the alphabet they were employing, and used a single starting letter as a key (Morland also suggested using a series of nulls – between, for example, letters four and seven – to further frustrate attempts at breaking the code). The two lower discs comprised twenty-five letters and were set in standard manner, with the outer turning around the inner. On top of this pair lay a third disc with a twenty-four-letter alphabet and a small letter-sized window (Morland is incorrect in stating it is a twenty-five-letter alphabet on the top wheel). By combining the Albertiesque polyalphabetic encoding wheel with the superimposed wheel, Morland hoped to achieve a superencrypted autokey cipher. Unfortunately, his mistaken attribution of twenty-five letters instead of twenty-four to the superimposed wheel means that his written example does not accord with his illustrations. It may well be that Morland's machine worked better in situ than it does on the page. See also Strasser, 'The Rise of Cryptology', 28.
28. Expenses for a circular cipher, [1667], TNA, SP 29/230, fo. 82r; Akkerman, *Queen of Hearts*, 166.
29. Morland, *A New Method*, 11.
30. Dickinson, *Sir Samuel Morland*, 99; Morland, 'Proposals', 265–6. Roger Whitley, the deputy postmaster between 1672 and 1677, failed to forward some £30,000 to the royal accounts; in 1684, he was finally sued and fined £20,000: Paul D. Halliday, 'Whitley, Roger', *ODNB*.
31. For an example of mirror writing or 'left hand', see BRBL, Osborn MS b234, pp. 15, 29.
32. LPL, MS 931, no. 11 (fo. 12r–v). See Lesson 4.2 for information on its feasibility.
33. Morland, 'A Brief discourse concerning the Nature and Reason of Intelligence', BL, Add. MS 47133, fo. 13r.
34. 'The Proposall which Sir Samuel Morland gave to Major Wildman', Expenses, [1667], TNA, SP 29/230, fo. 82r; LPL, MS 931, no. 11.

35. Alan Marshall, 'Morland, Sir Samuel', *ODNB*. For Wildman's offices being at Lombard Street, see the warrant dated 12 April 1689, Whitehall, TNA, SP 44/338, fo. 284r.
36. Morland, 'Proposals', 266.
37. Morland to the archbishop of Canterbury, 23 May 1695, Hammersmith, LPL, MS 931, no. 2.
38. Gregory to Robert Cecil, 16 January 1596[/7], 'from my poor house', Hatfield, CP 37/74.

LESSONS: THE SCHOOL OF SPYCRAFT

1. This technique was investigated and replicated by Laura James at MIT.
2. See Akkerman, *Invisible Agents*, 44.
3. See *CES*, ii.1057–76, esp. 1068–71.
4. See Leon Battista Alberti, *De Compenendis Cifris*, Miscellanea Correr 47 2130, fo. 7r, assigned the no. or year '2016' in Saiber, *Measured Words*, 26, 29–31. See also Lesson 2.5.
5. See, for example, the cipher key still attached to an anonymous letter to Constantijn Huygens, 27 July 1644, no place given, G1-8.4, Koninklijke Verzamelingen, The Hague (*De Briefwisseling*, no. 3637). The basic combination of a substitution alphabet (cipher) and a nomenclator (code) would form the basis of practically every cryptographical system until the mid-nineteenth century: Kahn, *The Codebreakers*, xvii.
6. Enciphered messages were often presented in this manner, with each word separated from the next, either with spaces as in this example or by periods like this: 'mrmyfal.nmw.oanmwaf'.
7. The pre-encrypted text is taken from Mary's letter to Babington as recorded in Pollen, ed., *Mary*, 43–4, from xiii. This extract runs to approximately 5 per cent of the final letter.

BIBLIOGRAPHY

PRIMARY SOURCES, MANUSCRIPT

BL *British Library (London)*

Add. Additional
Add. MS 10037. Jane Seagar, *The Divine Prophecies of the Ten Sibills*, 1589
Add. MS 32658. John Willis, *The Art of Stenographie*
Add. MS 33594. Correspondence and Papers of Sir Ralph Sadler, vol. 4 (1580–85)
Add. MS 35029B. Holograph letters of Charles I and Charles II
Add. MS 36308. A Note-book of recipes in several hands, 1619–74
Add. MS 39254. Political Tracts, temp. James I
Add. MS 45198. Brockman Papers, cxxxi.fos 126–53, Cookery recipes; 1678–1719, n.d.
Add. MS 45850. Miscellaneous letters and papers
Add. MS 47133. Egmont Papers
Add. MS 78196. Evelyn Papers, 1643–1660
Cotton MS Appendix L. State Papers, 1513–1637
Cotton MS Caligula C/V. Records and papers concerning England and Scotland, 1575–79
Cotton MS Caligula C/VI–VII. Records and papers (originals and copies) concerning England and Scotland, 1580–81
Cotton MS Caligula C/VII. Records and papers (originals and copies) concerning England and Scotland, 1582–84, including correspondence of Mary, Queen of Scots
Cotton MS Caligula C/VIII. Records and papers concerning England and Scotland, 1584–86
Cotton MS Caligula D/I. Records and papers concerning England and Scotland, 1587–89
Cotton MS Galba C/VII. Records and papers concerning England and the Low Countries, 1580–84
Cotton MS Vespasian F/VI. Miscellaneous letters and papers
Egerton MS 1788. Original letters from Charles I, when prisoner in Carisbrooke Castle, Isle of Wight, to Henry Firebrace
Egerton MS 2550. Keys to ciphers used by Sir Edward Nicholas, 1646–1658
Harley MS 286. State papers and letters relating to England, 1559–1648
Harley MS 530. A miscellany of transcripts and original copies of historical works

Harley MS 675. *The Original Cause of Peter Bales his Challenge for a Pene of golde of twentie pounds*, 1595–96

Lansdowne MSS 1–122. Burghley Papers

Royal Appendix MS 68. A book of such jewels and other parcels as are delivered to the charge and custody of Mistress Mary Radcliffe, one of the gentlewomen of the Queen Maiesty's Privy Chamber, and were parcell of such jewels and were in charge of Mistress Blanche Parry, July 1587

Sloane MS 2071. Theodori Turquet de Mayerne Ephemerides

Sloane MS 3505. Medicinal treatises

Bod. *Bodleian Libraries (Oxford)*

MS Cherry 30. Timothy Bright, *De clandestino scripto methodica tractatio a Timothea Brighto Cantabrigiensi ex secondo & tertio libro Johannis Baptistæ Portæ Neapolitani, De furtivus literarum notis, ad honoratissimum virtum, & serenissimae reginae Elizabethae a secretis D. Guliel Davisonum*, 1587

Clarendon MSS 31; 56; 94. Papers of Edward Hyde, 1st earl of Clarendon

Rawl. MS A 45. Thurloe Papers

BRBL *Beinecke Rare Book and Manuscript Library (Yale University)*

Osborn MS b234. William Hill's commonplace book, early seventeenth century

Osborn Music MS 16. Johann Sigismund Cousser's commonplace book, *c.* 1690–1720 [written during his time in England and Ireland]

Folger *Folger Shakespeare Library*

V.a.159. Giles Lodge's lute book miscellany

Hatfield *Hatfield House*

CP. Cecil Papers. Papers of William Cecil, Lord Burghley, and his son Robert Cecil, 1st earl of Salisbury

Landesarchiv Oranienbaum.

Abteilung Dessau A 7b Nr. 124. Cipher keys

LPL. *Lambeth Palace Library (London)*

MSS 647–62. Bacon Papers

MS 931. Gibson Papers

Private Collection

Papers of Lady Brilliana Harley

TNA. *The National Archives (Kew), formerly PRO / Public Record Office*

E 122. Records of the Exchequer, and Its Related Bodies, Customs Accounts

PC 2. Privy Council Registers

PROB 11. Probate. Registered copics of wills proved in the Prerogative Court of Canterbury

SP. State Papers. Records Assembled by the State Paper Office:

SP 12   Domestic, Elizabeth I
SP 14   Domestic, James I
SP 15   Domestic, Addenda, Edward VI–James I
SP 16   Domestic, Charles I
SP 29   Domestic, Charles II
SP 44   State Papers Entry Books, 1660–1828
SP 46   Domestic, Supplementary, 1231–1829
SP 52   Scotland Series I, Elizabeth I
SP 53   Scotland Series I, Mary Queen of Scots
SP 63   Ireland, Elizabeth I to George III
SP 68   Foreign and Calais, Edward VI
SP 70   Foreign, Elizabeth I
SP 78   Foreign, France
SP 81   Foreign, German States
SP 83   Foreign, Holland
SP 84   Foreign, Holland
SP 89   Foreign, Portugal
SP 97   Foreign, Turkey
SP 106   Foreign, Ciphers, Elizabeth I

TCL. *Trinity College Library (Cambridge)*

R.7.23x. Prince Henry's copybooks, *c.* 1600–1610

West Sussex Record Office

Add. MS 18006. Letters patent

CATALOGUES AND CALENDARS OF MANUSCRIPT SOURCES

Acts and Ordinances of the Interregnum, 1642–1660, edited by C.H. Firth and R.S. Rait. London: HMSO, 1911.
CSP. Calendar of State Papers.
CSP Domestic, Elizabeth I, 1581–90. London: HMSO, 1865.
CSP Domestic, Elizabeth I, 1595–97. London: HMSO, 1869.
CSP Spain, vol. 10. London: HMSO, 1914.
CSP Spain, Simancas, vol. 2. London: HMSO, 1914.
CSP Spain, Supplement to vols 1 and 2. London: HMSO, 1868.
Dalrymple, David, ed. *Secret Correspondence of Sir Robert Cecil with James VI, King of Scotland.* Edinburgh: A. Millar, 1766.
HMC. The Historical Manuscripts Commission, *Calendar of the Manuscripts of the Most Honourable the Marquess of Salisbury . . .*, 24 vols. London: HMSO, 1883–1976.
Morison, J.H., ed. *Prerogative Court of Canterbury: Letters of Administration 1620–30.* London: J.H. Morrison, 1935.
Records of the English Province of the Society of Jesus: Historic Facts Illustrative of the Labours and Sufferings of Its Members in the Sixteenth and Seventeenth Centuries, edited by H. Foley, 7 vols. London: Burns and Oates, 1875.
Resolutiën Staten-Generaal, 1576–1609, vol. 1, edited by N. Japikse. The Hague: Nijhoff, 1915.

Roberts, Julian, and Andrew G. Watson, eds. *John Dee's Library Catalogue*. London: The Bibliographical Society, 1990.

RPS. *The Records of the Parliaments of Scotland to 1707*, edited by K.M. Brown et al. St Andrews, 2007–23.

The Statutes of the Realm, vol. 4. London: Dawson's of Pall Mall, 1819.

Wilson, Peter H., ed. *The Thirty Years War: A Sourcebook*. New York: Palgrave Macmillan, 2010.

PRIMARY SOURCES, PRINTED

Alberti, Leone Battista. *Opuscoli Morali*, edited by Cosimo Bartoli. Venice: Franceschi, 1568.

Aldrovandi, Ulisse. *De Animalibus Insectis Libri Septem*. Bologna: Ioan: Bapt: Bellagambam, 1602.

Anon. *Dat batement van recepten: Een secreetboek uit de zestiende eeuw* [1549], Leiden University Library S 7579 25, edited by W.L. Braekman. Brussels: Omirel UFSAL, 1990.

Anon. *Valuable Secrets Concerning Arts and Trades or Approved Directions, from the Best Artists for the Various Methods*. London: Will Hay, 1775. [*Secrets concernant les arts et metiers*. Paris: Claude Jombert, 1716.]

Bacon, Francis. *The Advancement of Learning* (1605). *The Oxford Francis Bacon*, vol. 4, edited by Michael Kiernan. Oxford: Oxford University Press, 2000.

—. *De Augmentis Scientiarum* (London: John Haviland, 1623). In *The Works of Francis Bacon*, edited by James Spedding, Robert Leslie Ellis and Douglas Denon Heath, iv.275–498. London: Longman, 1870.

—. *Novum Organum* (London: John Bill, 1620). In *The Oxford Francis Bacon*, edited by Graham Rees with Maria Wakely, xi.48–372. Oxford: Oxford University Press, 2007.

—. 'A True Report of the Detestable Treason, Intended by Dr. Roderigo Lopez' (composed 1594, first printed in 1657). In *The Letters and The Life*, edited by James Spedding, Robert Leslie Ellis and Douglas Denon Heath, i.274–87. London: Longman and Roberts, 1862.

Bales, Peter. *The Writing Schoolemaster*. London: Thomas Orwin, 1590.

Barwick, Peter. *Life of the Reverend Dr John Barwick, D.D.*, edited and translated by H. Bedford. London: I. Bettenham, 1724.

Beale, Robert. 'A Treatise of the Office of a Councellor and Principall Secretarie to her Ma[jes]tie'. In Conyers Read, *Mr Secretary Walsingham and the Policy of Queen Elizabeth*, i.423–43. Oxford: Clarendon Press, 1925.

Bishop, John. *Beautiful Blossomes*. London: H. Middleton, 1577.

Blackwood, Adam. *History of Mary, Queen of Scots* [abridged – full text composed in French and published 1587]. Edinburgh: Maitland Club, 1834.

Boaistuau, Pierre. *Certaine Secrete Wonders of Nature . . .*, translated by E. Fenton. London: Henry Bynneman, 1569. [Boaistuau, *Histoires prodigieuses extraictes de plusiers fameux auteurs grecs & latins*, 1561.]

Botero, Giovanni. *The Reason of State*, translated by P.J. Waley and D.P. Waley. London: Routledge & Kegan Paul, 1956. [Botero, *Della ragione di stato*, 1589.]

Boyle, Robert. 'Experiments'. In *The Works of the Honourable Robert Boyle*, edited by W. Birch, iv.200, 248. London: A. Millar, 1744.

Bright, Timothy. *Charac[terie.] An ar[te] of shorte, swift[e], and secrete writing by character*. London: I. Windet, 1588.

Bulwer, John. *Chironomania: Or, the Art of Manuall Rhetoricke* [published alongside *Chirologia: or the Naturall Language of the Hand*]. London: R. Whitaker, 1644.

Burton, Henry. *The Baiting of the Popes Bull*. London: W[illiam] I[ones, Augustine Mathewes, John Jaggard? et al.?], 1627.

Calcagnini, Celio. 'Oraculorum Liber'. In his *Opera Aliquot*, 640–6. Basel: H. Froben and N. Episcopius, 1544.

Camden, William. *Annales*. London: Beniamin Fisher, 1625.

—. *Annales Rerum Anglicarum*. Frankfurt: Ioannis Brineri, 1616.

Cardano, Girolamo. *De Subtilitate*. Nuremberg: Johann Petreius, 1550.

Cecil, Robert. *The State and Dignitie of a Secretarie of Estates Place With the Care and Perill thereof . . .* London: [s.n.], 1642.

CES. Correspondence of Elizabeth Stuart, edited by Nadine Akkerman, 2 vols. Oxford: Oxford University Press, 2011–15.

Coke, Edward. *The Third Part of the Institutes of the Laws of England concerning High Treason, and Other Pleas of the Crown, and Criminall Causes*. London: M. Flesher, 1644 [composed between *c.* 1628 and 1634].

Corbet, Roger. *A Letter from his Majetties [sic] Court at Holmbie*. London: B.A., 1647.

Coryate, Thomas. *Coryat's Crudites*. London: William Stansby, 1611.

Cotgrave, John. *Wits Interpreter, the English Parnassus . . .* London: N. Brooke, 1655.

Cowley, Abraham. 'Written in juice of Lemmon'. In *The Collected Works of Abraham Cowley, 1618–1667*, edited by Thomas O. Calhoun, Laurence Heyworth and J. Robert King, ii.28–9. Newark, NJ: University of Delaware Press, 1989–99.

Culpeper, Nicholas. *A Physical Directory: Translation of the London Dispensatory*. London: Peter Cole, 1649.

Davys, John. *An Essay on the art of Decyphering in which is inserted a discourse of Dr Wallis*. London: John Davis, 1737.

della Porta, Giambattista. *De Furtivis Literarum Notis*. Neapoli: Mariam Scotum, 1563.

—. *Magiae Naturalis*. Neapoli: Matthiam Cancer, 1558.

—. *Natural Magick*. London: Printed for T. Young & S. Speed, 1658.

—. *De Occultis Literarum Notis*. Montisbeligardi: Jacobum Foillet, 1593.

Digby, Sir Kenelm. *The Closet of the Eminently Learned Sir Knelme Digbie Kt. Opened . . .* London: E.C., 1669.

Donne, John. 'To Mr George Herbert with One of My Seals', translated by Catherine Freis and Greg Miller. In *The Variorum Edition of the Poetry of John Donne*, vol. V, *The Verse Letters*, general editor Jeffrey S. Johnson, 423–8. Bloomington and Indianapolis: Indiana University Press, 2019.

[Evelyn, John]. *Diary and Correspondence of John Evelyn, F.R.S.*, edited by William Bray, 4 vols. London: Bell and Daldy, 1870.

Evelyn, John. *Numismata, a Discourse of Metals, Ancient and Modern*. London: Printed for Benj. Tooke, 1697.

F[alconer], J[ohn]. *Rules for explaining and deciphering all manner of secret writing*. London: Printed for Dan. Brown and Sam. Manship, 1692.

Faunt, Nicholas. 'Discourse touchinge the Office of principall Secretarie of Estate'. In Charles Hughes, 'Nicholas Faunt's Discourse Touching the Office of Principal Secretary of Estate, &c. 1592'. *English Historical Review* 20, no. 79 (1905): 499–508.

French, John. *The Art of Distillation . . .* London: Richard Coates, 1651.

Frisius, Gemma. *De Radio Astronomica et Geometrica*. Antwerp: G[regorius de] Bonte & Louvain: P[ierre] Phalèse, 1545.

Fuller, Thomas. *History of the Worthies of England*. London: J.G.W.L. and W.G., 1662.

[Gerard, John]. 'Father Gerard's Narrative of the Gunpowder Plot' [composed 1606]. In *The Condition of Catholics under James I*, edited by John Morris, 1–331. London: Longman, 1872.

—. 'The Life of Father Gerard' [composed 1609]. In *The Condition of Catholics under James I*, edited by John Morris, ix–ccliii. London: Longman, 1872.

[Halkett, Lady]. 'The Autobiography of Anne, Lady Halkett, 1677–78'. In *Lady Anne Halkett: Selected Self-Writings*, edited by Suzanne Trill, 51–143. Aldershot: Ashgate, 2007.

Halsall, Edward. *A Journal of the Siege of Lathom House*. London: Harding, Mavor and Lepard, 1823.

Harley, Lady. *Letters of the Lady Brilliana Harley, Wife of Sir Robert Harley, of Brampton Bryan, Knight of the Bath*, edited by Thomas Taylor Lewis. London: Camden Society, 1854.

Hexham, Henry. *A Journall, of the taking in of Venlo, Roermont, Strale, the memorable seige of Mastricht, the towne & castle of Limburch vnder the able, and wise conduct of his Excie: the Prince of Orange, anno 1632*. Delft: Iohn Pietersz Walpote, 1633.

Hippolytus. *Refutation of All Heresies*, translated by M. David Litwa. Atlanta: SBL Press, 2016 [*Refutation Omnium Haeresium*, 3rd century CE].

[Huygens, Constantijn]. *De Briefwisseling van Constantijn Huygens (1608–1687)*, edited by J.A. Worp, 5 vols. The Hague: Nijhoff, 1911–17.

Huygens, Constantijn. *Mémoires pour mes enfants*, edited by Theod. Jorissen. The Hague: Nijhoff, 1873.

—. *Mijn leven verteld aan mijn kinderen in twee boeken*, translated by Frans R.E. Blom, 2 vols. Amsterdam: Prometheus / Bert Bakker, 2003 [*De Vita Propria: Sermonum Inter Liberos*, 1678].

Jonson, Ben. *Epigrams* nos 59 and 92 (1616), edited by Colin Burrow. In *The Cambridge Edition of the Works of Ben Jonson*, general editors David Bevington, Martin Butler and Ian Donaldson, v.141, 158–9. Cambridge: Cambridge University Press, 2012.

—. *Masque of Queens* (1609), edited by David Lindley. In *The Cambridge Edition of the Works of Ben Jonson*, general editors David Bevington, Martin Butler and Ian Donaldson, iii.281–349. Cambridge: Cambridge University Press, 2012.

Labanoff, Prince Alexandre, ed. *Lettres, instructions et mémoires de Marie Stuart, reine d'Écosse*, 7 vols. London: Charles Dolman, 1844.

[Lilly, William]. *The Last of the Astrologers: Mr William Lilly's History of his Life and Times from the year 1602 to 1681*, repr. from the 2nd edn of 1715, with notes and introduction by Katharine M. Briggs. London: Folklore Society, 1974.

Lucian. *Alexander the False Prophet*, translated by A.M. Harmon. Loeb Classical Library 162, vol. 4. Cambridge, MA: Harvard University Press, 1925.

[Ludlow, Edmund]. *The Memoirs of Edmund Ludlow*, edited by C.H. Firth, 2 vols. Oxford: Clarendon, 1894.

Lupton, Thomas. *A thousand notable things, of sundry sortes Wherof some are wonderfull, some straunge, some pleasant, diuers necessary, a great sort profitable and many very precious*. London: Iohn Charlewood, 1579.

Marozzo, Achille. *The Duel, or the Flower of Arms for Single Combat, both Offensive and Defensive*, edited and translated by W. Jherek Swanger. 4th edn. [N.p.]: privately published, 2021. [Marozzo. *Opera Nova de l'arte de l'Armi*. Venice, 1536.]

[Mary, Queen of Scots], *see* Labanoff, ed.; Pollen, ed.

Middleton, Thomas. *Father Hubbard's Tales: or the Ant and the Nightingale*. London: T.C., 1604.

Monardes, Nicolás. *Dos libros* (1565). Seville: Hernando Diaz, 1569.

Morland, Samuel. *A New Method of Cryptography, Humbly Presented to the Most Serene Majesty of Charles II*. London: s.n., 1666.

—. 'Proposals for Secret Service, [1689?]'. In HMC, *Report on the Manuscripts of Allan George Finch, Esq., of Burley-on-the-Hill, Rutland*, ii.264–6. London: HMSO, 1913.

Ovid. *Ars Amatoria; or The Art of Love*, translated by Henry T. Riley, 1885; Project Gutenberg, 2014.

Paré, Ambroise. *The Workes of that Famous Chirurgion Ambrose Parey translated out of Latine and compared with the French*, translated by Thomas Johnson. London: Th: Cotes and R. Young, 1634.

[Partridge, John]. *The Widdowes Treasure*. London: I. Roberts, 1595.

Pepys, Samuel. *The Diary of Samuel Pepys*, edited by Robert Latham and William G. Matthews, 11 vols. London: Bell & Hyman, 1970.

Pliny the Elder. *Naturalis Historia*. Venice: Johannes de Spira, before 1489.

Pollen, John Hungerford, ed. *Mary Queen of Scots and the Babington Plot*. Publications of the Scottish Historical Society Third Series, vol. 3. Edinburgh: Printed at the University Press by T. & A. Constable, 1922.

Qalqashandī, Ahmad ib 'Alī. *Subh Al A'sha*, translated by C.E. Bosworth. In C.E. Bosworth, 'The Section on Codes and Their Decipherment in Qalqashandī's *Subh Al A'sha*', *Journal of Semitic Studies* 8, no. 1 (1963): 17–33.

Raymond, John. *An Itinerary Contayning a Voyage Made through Italy, in the Yeare 1646, and 1647*. London: Humphrey Moseley, 1648.

Ripa, Cesare. *Iconologia*. Siena: Heredi di Matteo Florini, 1613.

—. *Iconologia or Moral Emblems*, edited by P. Tempest. London: Benjamin Motte, 1709.

[Rous, Francis]. *A Brief Narrative of the late Treacherous and Horrid Designe . . .* London: Printed for Edward Husbands, 1643.

Ruscelli, Girolamo. *Secrets of the Reuerand Maister Alexis*, translated by Richard Androse. London: P. Short, 1595. [Ruscelli, *I segreti del reverendo dono Alessio Piemontese*, 1555.]

Schott, Gaspar. *Schola Steganographica*. Nuremberg: J. Hertz, 1665.

Shakespeare, William, plays. In *The RSC Shakespeare: The Complete Works*, edited by Jonathan Bate and Eric Rasmussen. Basingstoke: Macmillan, 2008.

Shelton, Thomas. *Tachygraphy*. [Cambridge]: R. D[aniel], 1641.

—. *Tutor to Tachygraphy*. London: M.S., 1642.

Stanley, James. *Private Devotions and Miscellanies of James, Seventh Earl of Derby*, edited by Francis Robert Raines 3 vols. N.p.: Chetham Society, 1867.

Tacticus, Aineias. *How to Survive under Siege*, translated and edited by David Whitehead. 2nd edn. London: Bristol Classical Press, 2002.

Thévenot, M., J. Boivin, and P. de La Hire, eds. *Veterum Mathematicorum Opera*. Paris: Ex Typographia Regia, 1693.

Topsell, Edward. *The History of Four-Footed Beasts and Serpents describing at large their true and lively figure*. London: E. Cotes, 1658.

Trithemius, Johannes. *Polygraphiae Libri Sex*. Oppenheim: Haselberg de Aia, 1518.

—. *Steganographia: Ars per Occultam Scripturam*. Frankfurt: Becker, 1606.

Twysden, Sir Roger. 'Sir Roger Twysden's Journal', edited by L.B. Larking. *Archaeologia Cantiana* 3 (1860): 145–76.

Vigenère, Blaise de. *Traicté des chiffres, ou secrètes manières d'éscrire*. Paris: Abel l'Angelier, 1586.

Webster, John. *The Duchess of Malfi* (1612–13). London: Nicholas Okes, 1623.

Wecker, Johann Jacob. *Eighteen Books of the Secrets of Art and Nature*. London: Simon Miller, 1660. BL, 64.e.11a.

Wildman, John. 'A Brief Discourse concerning the Business of Intelligence and How It May Be Managed to the Best Advantage'. In C.H. Firth, 'Thurloe and the Post Office'. *English Historical Review* 13, no. 51 (1898): 527–33.

Wilkins, John. *Mercury: Or the Secret and Swift Messenger*. London: Richard Baldwin, 1694.

W[illiams], W. *Occult Physick, or, The Three Principles in Nature*. London: Tho: Leach, 1660.

W.M. *The Queens Closet Opened*. London: Nathaniel Brook, 1655.

W.T. *The Triall of Mr Mordaunt, Second Son to John Earl of Peterburgh, at the Pretended High Court of Justice in Westminster-Hall, the First and Second of June 1658*. London: James Flesher, 1661.

SECONDARY SOURCES

Adams, Robyn Jade. '"Both Diligent and Secret": The Intelligence Letters of William Herle'. Unpublished diss., Queen Mary, University of London, 2004.

Akkerman, Nadine. *Courtly Rivals in The Hague: Elizabeth Stuart (1596–1662) and Amalia von Solms (1602–1675)*. Venlo: VanSpijk / Rekafa Publishers in conjunction with Haags Historisch Museum, 2014.

—. *Elizabeth Stuart, Queen of Hearts*. Oxford: Oxford University Press, 2021.

—. 'Enigmatic Cultures of Cryptology'. In *Cultures of Correspondence in Early Modern Britain*, edited by James Daybell and Andrew Gordon, 69–84 (notes at 266–71). Philadelphia: University of Pennsylvania Press, 2016.

—. *Invisible Agents: Women and Espionage in Seventeenth-Century Britain*. Oxford: Oxford University Press, 2018.

—. 'The Postmistress, The Diplomat, and a Black Chamber? Alexandrine of Taxis, Sir Balthazar Gerbier and the Power of Postal Control'. In *Diplomacy and Early Modern Culture*, edited by Robyn Adams and Rosanna Cox, 172–88. Basingstoke: Palgrave Macmillan, 2011.

—. 'A Triptych of Dorothy Percy Sidney (1598–1659), Countess of Leicester, Lucy Percy Hay (1599–1660), Countess of Carlisle, and Dorothy Sidney Spencer (1617–1684), Countess of Sunderland'. In *The Ashgate Research Companion to The Sidneys, 1500–1700, Volume I: Lives*, edited by Margaret P. Hannay, Michael G. Brennan and Mary Ellen Lamb, 133–50. Farnham: Ashgate, 2015.

—. 'Women's Letters and Cryptological Coteries'. In *The Oxford Handbook of Early Modern Women's Writing in English, 1540–1700*, edited by Elizabeth Scott-Baumann, Danielle Clarke and Sarah C.E. Ross, 547–61. Oxford: Oxford University Press, 2022.

Akkerman, Nadine, and Pete Langman. 'Accidentally on Purpose: Denying Any Responsibility for the Accidental Archive'. In *Archives: Power, Truth, and Fiction*, edited by Alison Wiggins and Andrew Prescott, 323–36. Oxford: Oxford University Press, 2023.

Alford, Stephen. *The Watchers: A Secret History of the Reign of Elizabeth I*. London: Allen Lane, 2012.

Allmand, Christopher. 'Information et espionage pendant la guerre de Cent Ans'. In *La France et les Îles Britanniques: Un couple impossible?*, edited by Véronique Gazeau and Jean-Philippe Genet, 163–8. Paris: Publications de la Sorbonne, 2012.

Andrew, Christopher. 'The Nature of Military Intelligence'. In *Go Spy the Land: Military Intelligence in History*, edited by Keith Neilson and B.J.C. McKercher, 1–16. Westport, CT: Praeger, 1992.

—. *The Secret World: A History of Intelligence*. London: Allen Lane, 2018; Harlow: Penguin, 2019.

Anstruther, Godfrey. *Vaux of Harrowden: A Recusant Family*. Newport: R.H. Johns, 1953.

Arthurson, Ian. 'Espionage and Intelligence from the Wars of the Roses to the Reformation'. *Nottingham Medieval Studies* 35 (1991): 134–54.

Bachrach, A.G.H. *Sir Constantine Huygens and Britain, 1596–1687: A Pattern of Cultural Exchange*. Leiden: Sir Thomas Browne Institute, 1962.

Baldwin, Martha R. 'Toads and Plague: Amulet Therapy in Seventeenth-Century Medicine'. *Bulletin of the History of Medicine* 67, no. 2 (1993): 227–47.

'Bales, Peter'. In *Biographia Britannica: Or, the Lives of the Most Eminent Persons Who Have Flourished in Great Britain and Ireland*, edited by Andrew Kippis, i.536–48. 2nd edn. London: W. and A. Strahan, 1778.

Barbé, Louis A. *In Byways of Scottish History*. London and Glasgow: Blackie, 1912.

Begley, Justin, and Benjamin Goldberg, eds. *The Medical World of Margaret Cavendish: A Critical Edition*. Cham: Springer, 2023.

Bellany, Alastair, and Thomas Cogswell. *The Murder of King James I*. New Haven: Yale University Press, 2015.

Berloquin, Pierre. *Hidden Codes and Grand Designs: Secret Languages from Ancient Times to Modern Day*. New York: Sterling Publishing, 2010.

Bezio, Kristin M.S. *The Eye of the Crown: The Development and Evolution of the Elizabethan Secret Service*. Abingdon: Routledge, 2023.

Biagioli, Mario. 'From Ciphers to Confidentiality: Secrecy, Openness and Priority in Science'. *The British Journal for the History of Science* 45 (2012): 212–33.

Bindoff, S.T. 'A Bogus Envoy from James I'. *History* 27, no. 105 (1942): 15–37.

Blakeway, Anne. 'Spies and Intelligence in Scotland, *c*. 1530–1550'. In *Crossing Borders: Boundaries and Margins in Medieval and Early Modern Britain – Essays in Honour of Cynthia J. Neville*, edited by Sara M. Butler and Krista J. Kesselring, 83–106. Leiden: Brill, 2018.

Borrelli, Arianna. 'Introduction'. In *The Optics of Giambattista della Porta (c. 1535–1615): A Reassessment*, edited by Arianna Borrelli, Giora Hon and Yaakov Zik, 1–10. Cham: Springer, 2017.

—. 'Optical Diagrams as "Paper Tools": Della Porta's Analysis of Biconvex Lenses from *De Refractione* to *De Telescopio*'. In *The Optics of Giambattista della Porta (c. 1535–1615): A Reassessment*, edited by Arianna Borrelli, Giora Hon and Yaakov Zik, 57–96. Cham: Springer, 2017.

309

Bossy, John. *Under the Molehill: An Elizabethan Spy Story*. New Haven: Yale University Press, 2001.

Braganza, V.M. 'Many Ciphers, Although But One for Meaning: Lady Mary Wroth's Many-Sided Monogram'. *English Literary Renaissance* 52, no. 1 (2022): 124–52.

Brayshay, Mark. 'Messengers, Pursuivants and Couriers: Agents of the English State, *c.* 1512–*c.* 1640'. In *Storia postale. Sguardi multidisciplinari, sguardi diacronici [Postal History: Multidisciplinary and Diachronic Perspectives]*, edited by Bruno Crevato-Selvaggi and Raffaella Gerola, 279–317. Prato, Italy: Istituto di Studi Storici Postali, 2020.

Brewerton, Patricia. '"Several Keys to Ope' the Character": The Political and Cultural Significance of Timothy Bright's *Characterie*'. *The Sixteenth Century Journal* 33, no. 4 (2002): 945–61.

Britland, Karen. '"In the Hollow of His Wooden Leg": The Transmission of Civil War Materials, 1642–9'. In *Insolent Proceedings: Rethinking Public Politics in the English Revolution*, edited by Peter Lake and Jason Peacey, 88–106. Manchester: Manchester University Press, 2022.

Budiansky, Stephen. *Her Majesty's Spymaster: Elizabeth I, Sir Francis Walsingham, and the Birth of Modern Espionage*. New York: Viking, 2005.

Buonafalce, Augusto. 'Sir Samuel Morland's *Machina Cyclologica Cryptographica*'. *Cryptologia* 28, no. 3 (2004): 253–64.

Burke, Peter. 'Early Modern Venice as a Centre of Information and Communication'. In *Venice Reconsidered: The History and Civilization of an Italian City-State, 1297–1797*, edited by John Martin and Dennis Romano, 389–419. Baltimore: Johns Hopkins University Press, 2000.

Butler, Charles. *Additions to the Historical Memoirs Respecting the English, Irish and Scottish Catholics: From the Reformation to the Present Time*, 4 vols. London: John Murray, 1821.

Caraman, Philip. *Henry Garnet, 1555–1606, and the Gunpowder Plot*. London: Longmans, 1964.

Chesters, Geoffrey. 'John Daniel of Daresbury, 1544–1610'. *Transactions of the Historic Society of Lancashire and Cheshire* 118 (1967): 1–17.

Childs, Jessie. *God's Traitors: Terror & Faith in Elizabethan England*. London: Vintage, 2015 (first published 2014).

Coatalen, Guillaume, and Fred Schurink. 'A Tudor Translator at Work: John Osborne's Manuscript Translations of Demosthenes's *Againts Leptines* (1582) and Aeschines's *On the Embassy* (1583)'. *Huntington Library Quarterly* 80, no. 2 (2017): 257–75.

Cooper, John. *The Queen's Agent: Francis Walsingham at the Court of Elizabeth I.* London: Faber & Faber, 2011.

Cooper, J.P.D. 'Surveillance'. In *Elizabeth and Mary: Royal Cousins, Rival Queens*, edited by Susan Doran, 196–247. London: British Library, 2021.

Croft, Pauline. 'The Reputation of Robert Cecil: Libels, Political Opinion and Popular Awareness in the Early Seventeenth Century'. *Transactions of the Royal Historical Society* 1 (1991): 43–69.

Cunningham, Karen. *Imaginary Betrayals: Subjectivity and the Discourses of Treason in Early Modern England*. Philadelphia: University of Pennsylvania Press, 2002.

Dambrogio, Jana, Amanda Ghassaei, Daniel Starza Smith et al. 'Unlocking History through Automated Virtual Unfolding of Sealed Documents Imaged by X-Ray Microtomography'. *Nature Communications*, 12, no.1184 (2021).

Dambrogio, Jana, Daniel Starza Smith, and the Unlocking History Research Group. *Letterlocking*. Boston: MIT Press, forthcoming 2024.

Dambrogio, Jana, Daniel Starza Smith, Jennifer Pellechia et al. 'The Spiral-Locked Letters of Elizabeth I and Mary, Queen of Scots'. *Electronic British Library Journal* (2021): 10–50.

Das, Nandini, João Vicente Melo, Haig Z. Smith et al. *Keywords of Identity, Race, and Human Mobility in Early Modern England*. Amsterdam: Amsterdam University Press, 2021.

Daybell, James. *The Material Letter in Early Modern England: Manuscript Letters and the Culture and Practices of Letter-Writing, 1512–1635*. Basingstoke: Palgrave Macmillan, 2012.

Daybell, James, Svante Norrhem, Susan Broomhall et al. 'Gender and Materiality in Early Modern English Gloves'. *The Sixteenth Century Journal* 52, no. 3 (2021): 571–606.

de Leeuw, Karl. 'The Black Chamber in the Dutch Republic during the War of the Spanish Succession and Its Aftermath, 1707–1715'. *The Historical Journal* 42, no. 1 (1999): 133–56.

de Leeuw, Karl, and J.A. Bergstra. *The History of Information Security: A Comprehensive Handbook*. Amsterdam: Elsevier, 2007.

Demmin, Auguste. *An Illustrated History of Arms and Armour: The Dagger, Poniard, Stiletto, Kouttar, Crease, Etc.* London: George Bell, 1877.

de Vivo, Filippo. 'Archival Intelligence: Diplomatic Correspondence, Information Overload, and Information Management in Italy, 1450–1650'. In *Archives and Information in the Early Modern World (Proceedings of the British Academy)*, edited by Kate Peters, Alexandra Walsham and Liesbeth Corens, 53–85. Oxford: Oxford University Press, 2018.

—. *Information and Communication in Venice: Rethinking Early Modern Politics*. Oxford: Oxford University Press, 2007.

Dickinson, H.W. *Sir Samuel Morland: Diplomat and Inventor, 1625–1695*. Cambridge: Heffer, 1970.

DoLL. 'The Dictionary of Letterlocking', edited by Jana Dambrogio, Daniel Starza Smith and the Unlocking History Research Group; https://letterlocking.org/dictionary.

Doran, Susan. *Elizabeth I and Her Circle*. Oxford: Oxford University Press, 2015.

Dubois-Nayt, Armel, and Valérie Nachef. 'Developing the Art of Secret Writing across Borders: The Journey of Marie de Guise's Ciphers between France and Scotland'. *Études Epistémè* 37 (2020): https://doi.org/10.4000/episteme.6511

Duffin, Christopher J. 'The Danny Jewel'. *Jewellery History Today* 22 (2015): 6–7.

Dunnigan, Sarah M. 'Scottish Women Writers, c. 1560–c.1650'. In *A History of Scottish Women's Writing*, edited by Douglas Gifford and Dorothy McMillan, 15–43. Edinburgh: Edinburgh University Press, 1997.

Duramy, Benedetta Faedi. 'Women and Poisons in 17th Century France'. *Chicago-Kent Law Review* 87, no. 2 (2012): 347–70.

Dijksterhuis, Fokko Jan. 'Magi from the North: Instruments of Fire and Light in the Early Seventeenth Century'. In *The Optics of Giambattista della Porta (c. 1535–1615): A Reassessment*, edited by Arianna Borrelli, Giora Hon and Yaakov Zik, 125–43. Cham: Springer, 2017.

Eales, Jacqueline. *Puritans and Roundheads: The Harleys of Brampton Bryan and the Outbreak of the English Civil War*. 2nd edn. Cambridge: Cambridge University Press, 1990; Glasgow: Hardinge Simpole, 2002.

311

Eamon, William. *Science and the Secrets of Nature: Books of Secrets in Medieval and Early Modern Culture*. Princeton: Princeton University Press, 1996.

—. 'A Theater of Experiments: Giambattista della Porta and the Scientific Culture of Renaissance Naples'. In *The Optics of Giambattista della Porta (c. 1535–1615): A Reassessment*, edited by Arianna Borrelli, Giora Hon and Yaakov Zik, 11–38. Cham: Springer, 2017.

Edwards, Francis S.J. 'The First Earl of Salisbury's Pursuit of Hugh Owen'. *British Catholic History* 26, no. 1 (2002): 2–38.

—. 'Sir Robert Cecil, Edward Squier and the Poisoned Pommel'. *British Catholic History* 25, no. 3 (2001): 377–414.

Ellison, Katherine, and Susan Kim. 'Introduction: Ciphers and the Material History of Literacy'. In *A Material History of Medieval and Early Modern Ciphers: Cryptography and the History of Literacy*, edited by Katherine Ellison and Susan Kim, 1–29. New York: Routledge, 2018.

Ernst, Thomas. 'The Numerical-Astrological Ciphers in the Third Book of Trithemius's *Steganographia*'. *Cryptologia* 22, no. 4 (1998): 318–41.

Farr, David. *John Lambert: Parliamentary Soldier and Cromwellian Major-General, 1619–1684*. Woodbridge: Boydell, 2003.

Fischlin, Daniel. 'Political Allegory, Absolutist Ideology, and the "Rainbow Portrait" of Queen Elizabeth I'. *Renaissance Quarterly* 50, no. 1 (1997): 175–206.

Fletcher, Catherine. 'Firearms and the State in Sixteenth-Century Italy: Gun Proliferation and Gun Control'. *Past and Present* 260, no. 1 (2023): 3–37.

Flis, Nathan. 'Drawing, Etching, and Experiment in Christopher Wren's Figure of the Brain'. *Interdisciplinary Science Reviews* 37, no. 2 (2012): 145–60.

Fraser, Antonia. *The Gunpowder Plot: Terror and Faith in 1605*. London: Weidenfeld & Nicolson, 2002 (first published 1996).

Gibbs, Frederick W. *Poison, Medicine, and Disease in Late Medieval and Early Modern Europe*. London: Routledge, 2019.

Gordon, Andrew. 'Material Fictions: Counterfeit Correspondence and the Culture of Copying in Early Modern England'. In *Cultures of Correspondence in Early Modern Britain*, edited by James Daybell and Andrew Gordon, 85–109 (notes at 271–6). Philadelphia: University of Pennsylvania Press, 2016.

Groenveld, S. ' "Chijffre pour la communication avec Mr. Jermijn, de l'année 1647": Geheimschriftsleutels als bron voor netwerkreconstructies rond Prins Willem II'. In *Jaarboek Oranje-Nassau 2009–2010*, edited by C.R. van den Berg, S. Groenveld, P.L. Lekkerkerk et al., 55–78. Rotterdam: Barjesteh van Waalwijk van Doorn, 2010.

Guy, John. *My Heart Is My Own: The Life of Mary Queen of Scots*. London: Harper Perennial, 2004.

Harris, Jonathan Gil. *Foreign Bodies and the Body Politic: Discourses of Social Pathology in Early Modern England*. Cambridge: Cambridge University Press, 1998.

Harvey, E. Newton. *A History of Luminescence: From the Earliest Times until 1900*. Philadelphia: The American Philosophical Society, 1957.

Head, Randolph C. 'Knowing Like a State: The Transformation of Political Knowledge in Swiss Archives, 1450–1770'. *Journal of Modern History* 75 (2003): 745–82.

Hodgetts, Michael. 'Elizabethan Priest-Holes I: Dating and Chronology'. *British Catholic History* 11, no. 6 (1972): 279–98.

—. 'Elizabethan Priest-Holes III: East Anglia, Baddesley Clinton, Hindlip'. *British Catholic History* 12, no. 2 (1973): 171–97.

Hogge, Alice. *God's Secret Agents: Queen Elizabeth's Forbidden Priests and the Hatching of the Gunpowder Plot.* New York: HarperCollins, 2005.

Hopkins, Lisa, and Bill Angus, eds. *Poison on the Early Modern English Stage: Plants, Paints and Potions.* Manchester: Manchester University Press, 2023.

Hulse, Lynn. 'Musical Patronage of Robert Cecil, First Earl of Salisbury (1563–1612)'. *Journal of the Royal Musical Association* 116, no. 1 (1991): 24–40.

Hunt, Arnold. '"Burn This Letter": Preservation and Destruction in the Early Modern Archive'. In *Cultures of Correspondence in Early Modern Britain*, edited by James Daybell and Andrew Gordon, 189–209 (notes at 287–91). Philadelphia: University of Pennsylvania Press, 2016.

Iordanou, Ioanna. 'The Invisible Trade: Commoners and Convicts as Early Modern Venice's Spies'. In *Shadow Agents of Renaissance War: Suffering, Supporting, and Supplying Conflict in Italy and Beyond*, edited by Stephen Bowd, Sarah Cockram and John Gagné, 227–50. Amsterdam: Amsterdam University Press, 2023.

—. *Venice's Secret Service: Organising Intelligence in the Renaissance.* Oxford: Oxford University Press, 2019.

Jardine, Lisa. *The Awful End of William the Silent: The First Assassination of a Head of State with a Handgun.* London: Harper Perennial, 2006.

Johanesen, Sarah. '"That *Silken Priest*": Catholic Disguise and Anti-Popery on the English Mission (1569–1640)'. *Historical Research* 93, no. 259 (2020): 38–51.

Kahn, David. *The Codebreakers: The Comprehensive History of Secret Communication from Ancient Times to the Internet.* New York: Scribner, 1967; rev. edn. 1996.

Keblusek, Marika. 'Introduction: Profiling the Early Modern Agent'. In *Your Humble Servant: Agents in Early Modern Europe*, edited by Hans Cools, Marika Keblusek and Badeloch Noldus, 9–15. Hilversum: Verloren, 2006.

Keens-Soper, Maurice. 'Wicquefort'. In *Diplomatic Theory from Machiavelli to Kissinger*, edited by G.R. Berridge, Maurice Keens-Soper and T.G. Otto, 88–105. New York: Palgrave, 2001.

Láng, Benedek. *Real Life Cryptology: Ciphers and Secrets in Early Modern Hungary*, translated by Teodóra Király and Benedek Láng. Amsterdam: Amsterdam University Press / Atlantis Press, 2018.

Laoutaris, Chris. '"Toucht with Bolt of Treason": The Earl of Essex and Lady Penelope Rich'. In *Essex: The Cultural Impact of an Elizabethan Courtier*, edited by Annaliese Connolly and Lisa Hopkins, 201–36. Manchester: Manchester University Press, 2013.

Lasry, George, Norbert Biermann and Satoshi Tomokiyo. 'Deciphering Mary Stuart's Lost Letters from 1578–84'. *Cryptologia* 47, no. 2 (2023): 101–202.

Lennon, Brian. *Passwords: Philology, Security, Authentication.* Cambridge, MA: Harvard University Press, 2018.

Loomis, Catherine. '"Little Man, Little Man": Early Modern Representations of Robert Cecil'. *Explorations in Renaissance Culture* 37, no. 1 (2011): 137–56.

Love, Harold. *Scribal Publication in Seventeenth-Century England.* Oxford: Clarendon Press, 1993.

McIlvenna, Una. *Scandal and Reputation at the Court of Catherine de Medici.* Abingdon: Routledge, 2016.

McInally, Tom. 'Scholars and Spies: Three Humanists in the Service of James VI'. *Recusant History* 31, no. 2 (2012): 135–46.

Macrakis, Kristie. *Prisoners, Lovers, and Spies: The Story of Invisible Ink from Herodotus to Al-Qaeda.* New Haven: Yale University Press, 2014.

Malay, Jessica L. 'Jane Seagar's Sibylline Poems: Maidenly Negotiations through Elizabethan Gift Exchange'. *English Literary Renaissance* 36 (2006): 173–93.

Malcolm, Noel. *Agents of Empire: Knights, Corsairs, Jesuits and Spies in the Sixteenth-Century Mediterranean World*. Oxford: Oxford University Press, 2015.

Marshall, Alan. *Intelligence and Espionage in the English Republic, c. 1600–1660*. Manchester: Manchester University Press, 2023.

—. *Intelligence and Espionage in the Reign of Charles II, 1660–1685*. Cambridge: Cambridge University Press, 1994.

—. '"Secret Wheeles": Clandestine Information, Espionage, and European Intelligence'. In *Beyond Ambassadors: Consuls, Missionaries, and Spies in Premodern Diplomacy*, edited by Maurits A. Ebben and Louis Sicking, 185–216. Leiden: Brill, 2020.

Matthews, Leslie G. 'Nicolas Cabry Master-Apothecary of Paris'. *Pharmaceutical Historian* (1987): 4–6.

Mazzola, Elizabeth. *Learning and Literacy in Female Hands, 1520–1698*. Ashgate, 2013; New York: Routledge, 2016.

Midura, Rachel. '"They Hide from Me, Like the Devil from the Cross": Transalpine Postal Routes as Intelligence Work, 1555–1645'. *History* 108, no. 381 (2023): 1–25.

Monson, Craig A. *The Black Widows of the Eternal City: The True Story of Rome's Most Infamous Poisoners*. Ann Arbor: University of Michigan Press, 2020.

Muirhead, James Patrick. *The Origin and Progress of the Mechanical Inventions of James Watts*, 3 vols. London: John Murray, 1854.

Newton, Diana. *The Making of the Jacobean Regime: James VI and I and the Government of England, 1603–1605*. Woodbridge: Boydell & Brewer, 2005.

Normand, Silje. 'Venomous Words and Political Poisons: Language(s) of Exclusion in Early Modern France'. In *Exploring Cultural History: Essays in Honour of Peter Burke*, edited by Melissa Calaresu, Filippo de Vivo and Joan-Pau Rubiés, 113–31. Farnham: Ashgate, 2010.

Oakley, Stewart P. 'The Interception of Posts in Celle, 1694–1700'. In *William III and Louis XIV: Essays 1680–1720 by and for Mark A. Thomson*, edited by Ragnhild M. Hatton and J.S. Bromley, 95–116. Liverpool: Liverpool University Press, 1968.

ODNB. Oxford Dictionary of National Biography

OED. Oxford English Dictionary

Orofino, Anna Maria. '"Coelum non animum mutant qui trans mare currunt": David Stradling (1537–c. 1595) and His Circle of Welsh Catholic Exiles in Continental Europe'. *British Catholic History* 32, no. 2 (2014): 139–58.

Ossa-Richardson, Anthony. *The Devil's Tabernacle: The Pagan Oracles in Early Modern Thought*. Princeton: Princeton University Press, 2013.

Perez, Béatrice, ed. *Ambassadeurs, apprentis espions et maîtres comploteurs. Les systèmes de renseignement en Espagne à l'époque moderne*. Paris: Sorbonne, 2010.

Petukhova, Tatyana. 'A History of Fish Glue as an Artist's Material: Applications in Paper and Parchment Artifacts'. *The Book and Paper Group Annual* 19 (2000): 111–14.

Pollard, Tanya. *Drugs and Theatre in Early Modern England*. Oxford: Oxford University Press, 2005.

Potter, Harry. *Edinburgh under Siege 1571–1573*. Stroud: Tempus, 2003.

Powell, Jason. 'Secret Writing or a Technology of Discretion? Dry Point in Tudor Books and Manuscripts'. *The Review of English Studies* 70, no. 293 (2019): 37–53.

Rankin, Alisha. 'On Anecdote and Antidotes: Poison Trials in Sixteenth-Century Europe'. *Bulletin of the History of Medicine* 91, no. 2, 'Special Issue: Testing Drugs and Trying Cures' (2017): 274–302.

Rendall, Edward B.M., and Isabella Rosner. 'Plays, Plague, and Pouches: The Role of the Outside in Early Modern English Plague Remedies'. *Journal of Early Modern Studies*, 'Special Issue: Plagues in Early Modern Europe' (2021): 1–15.

Rivas, Javier Marcos. *Espias: Servicios secretos y escritura cifrada en la monarquía hispánia*. [*Spies: Secret Services and Enciphered Writing in the Spanish Monarchy*.] Castellano: Ministerio de Cultura y Deporte, 2018.

Robertson, Alexander. *Father Paolo Sarpi: The Greatest of the Venetians*. 2nd edn. London: Sampson, Low, Marston, 1894.

Sadowski, Piotr. '"Foul, Strange and Unnatural": Poison as a Murder Weapon in English Renaissance Drama'. *Mosaic* 53, no. 3 (2020): 139–54.

Saiber, Arielle. *Measured Words: Computation and Writing in Renaissance Italy*. Toronto: University of Toronto Press, 2017.

Santi Russell, Frank. *Information Gathering in Classical Greece*. Ann Arbor: University of Michigan Press, 1999.

Scannell, Paul. *Conflict and Soldiers' Literature in Early Modern Europe: The Reality of War*. London: Bloomsbury Academic, 2016.

Schiltz, Katelijne, with a catalogue by Bonnie J. Blackburn. *Music and Riddle Culture in the Renaissance*. Cambridge: Cambridge University Press, 2015.

Schwoerer, Lois G. *Gun Culture in Early Modern England*. Charlottesville: University of Virginia Press, 2016.

Shapin, Stevin. 'The Invisible Technician'. *American Scientist* 77, no. 6 (1989): 554–63.

Shapiro, James. *Shakespeare and the Jews*. New York: Columbia University Press, 1996.

Shaw, Dannielle. 'Thinker, Gaoler, Soldier, and Spy: Sir John Peynton (1544–1630) and Early Modern Intelligence-Brokering in the Tower of London'. *History*, 'Special Issue: New Explorations in Early Modern Intelligence-Gathering', edited by Dannielle Shaw (2023): 1–20.

Shrank, Cathy. 'Manuscript, Authenticity and "Evident Proofs" against the Scottish Queen'. In *English Manuscript Studies 1100–1700*, vol. 15, *Tudor Manuscripts 1485–1603*, edited by A.S.G. Edwards, 198–218. London: The British Library, 2009.

Smith, A. Mark. 'Giambattista della Porta's Theory of Vision in the *De Refractione* of 1593: Sources, Problems, Implications'. In *The Optics of Giambattista della Porta (c. 1535–1615): A Reassessment*, edited by Arianna Borrelli, Giora Hon and Yaakov Zik, 97–123. Cham: Springer, 2017.

Smith, Geoffrey. *Royalist Agents, Conspirators and Spies: Their Role in the British Civil Wars, 1640–1660*. Farnham: Ashgate, 2011.

Soll, Jacob. *The Information Master: Jean-Baptiste Colbert's Secret State Intelligence System*. Ann Arbor: University of Michigan Press, 2011.

Spedding, James, Robert Leslie Ellis and Douglas Denon Heath, eds. *The Works of Francis Bacon*, vol. i. London: Longman, 1857.

Stevenson, David. *The Scottish Revolution, 1637–44: The Triumph of the Covenanters*. Edinburgh: John Donald, 2003.

Stewart, Alan. 'Familiar Letters and State Papers: The Afterlives of Early Modern Correspondence'. In *Cultures of Correspondence in Early Modern Britain*, edited by

James Daybell and Andrew Gordon, 237–52. Philadelphia: University of Pennsylvania Press, 2016.

—. 'Francis Bacon's Bi-literal Cipher and the Materiality of Early Modern Diplomatic Writing'. In *Diplomacy and Early Modern Culture*, edited by Robyn Adams and Rosanna Cox, 120–37. Basingstoke: Palgrave Macmillan, 2011.

—. '"Master Smokey Swyne's-Flesh": Francis Bacon and the Responses to the Edward Squire Conspiracy'. *British Catholic History* 36, no. 2 (2022): 119–52.

Stix, F. 'Zur Geschichte und Organisation der Wiener Geheimen Ziffernkanzlei (von ihren Anfängen bis zum Jahren 1848)'. *Mitteilungen des Österreichischen Instituts für Geschichtsforschung* 51 (1937): 132–60.

Strasser, Gerhard. 'Die kryptographische Sammlung Herzog Augusts: Vom Quellenmaterial für seine "Cryptomenytices" zu einem Schwerpunkt in seiner Bibliothek'. *Wolfenbütteler Beiträge* 5 (1982): 83–121.

—. 'The Noblest Cryptologist: Duke August the Younger of Brunswick-Luneburg (Gustavus Selenus) and His Cryptological Activities'. *Cryptologia* 7, no. 3 (1983): 193–217.

—. 'The Rise of Cryptology in the European Renaissance'. In *The History of Information Security: A Comprehensive Handbook*, edited by Karl de Leeuw and Jan Bergstra, 1–57. Amsterdam: Elsevier, 2007.

Szechi, Daniel, ed. *The Dangerous Trade: Spies, Spymasters and the Making of Europe*. Dundee: Dundee University Press, 2010.

—. 'Introduction: The "Dangerous Trade" in Early Modern Europe'. In *Spies, Spymasters and the Making of Europe*, edited by Daniel Szechi, 1–21. Dundee: Dundee University Press, 2010.

Tarassuk, Leonid. 'Some Notes on Parrying Daggers and Poniards'. *Metropolitan Museum Journal* 12 (1978): 33–54.

Thomas, Keith. *Religion and the Decline of Magic: Studies in Popular Beliefs in Sixteenth and Seventeenth-Century England*. London: Weidenfeld & Nicolson, 1971; London: Penguin, 1991.

Tosh, Will. *Male Friendship and Testimonies of Love in Shakespeare's England*. London: Palgrave Macmillan, 2016.

Underdown, David. *Royalist Conspiracy in England 1649–1660*. New Haven: Yale University Press, 1960.

van der Meer, Wouter. 'The History of *Citrus* in the Low Countries during the Middle Ages and the Early Modern Age'. In *Agrumed: Archaeology and History of Citrus Fruit in the Mediterranean – Acclimatization, Diversifications, Uses*, edited by Véronique Zech-Matterne and Girolamo Fiorentino, online (n.p.). Naples: Publications du Centre Jean Bérard, 2017.

van Stipriaan, René. *De Zwijger: Het Leven van Willem van Oranje*. Amsterdam: Querido Facto, 2021.

Walker, Jonathan. 'I Spy with My Little Eye: Interpreting Seventeenth-Century Venetian Spy Reports'. *Urban History* 29, no. 2 (2002): 197–222.

Wiggins, Alison, and Jade Scott. 'The Afterlives of Mary's Letters'. In *'In the End is My Beginning': The Cultural Afterlife of Mary, Queen of Scots*, edited by Steven Reid. Edinburgh: Edinburgh University Press, forthcoming 2024.

Wiggins, Martin. *Journeymen in Murder: The Assassin in English Renaissance Drama*. Oxford: Clarendon Press, 1991.

Wolfe, Heather. 'Women's Handwriting'. In *The Cambridge Companion to Early Modern Women's Writing*, edited by Laura Knoppers, 21–39. Cambridge: Cambridge University Press, 2009.

Woolrych, Austin. *Britain in Revolution, 1625–1660.* Oxford: Oxford University Press, 2002.

Woudhuysen, H.R. *Sir Philip Sidney and the Circulation of Manuscripts 1558–1640.* Oxford: Oxford University Press, 1996.

Zielinski, Siegfried. *Deep Time of the Media: Toward an Archeology of Hearing and Seeing by Technical Means,* translated by Gloria Custance. Cambridge, MA: MIT Press, 2008 [*Archäologie der Medien: Zur Tiefenzeit des technischen Hörens und Sehens,* 2002].

Zik, Yaakov, and Giora Hon. 'Giambattista della Porta: A Magician or an Optician?' In *The Optics of Giambattista della Porta (c. 1535–1615): A Reassessment,* edited by Arianna Borrelli, Giora Hon and Yaakov Zik, 39–55. Cham: Springer, 2017.

INDEXES

The **index of names and places** lists the individuals in the book and the locations they visited. In the case of sovereigns, stadtholders and all (foreign) princes, we have adopted the convention of including them under first names and given birth and death dates as well as period of rule between brackets: Elizabeth I (1533–1603), queen of England and Ireland (1558–1603).

We have indexed under individual names, rather than under titles, and next to birth and death dates indicated in which year a person received a title: Cecil, Sir William (1520/21–98), 1st Baron Burghley (1571). To assist the reader who might not be familiar with a family name, or who wants to remind themselves of how to distinguish one Cecil from another, we have cross-referenced extensively: Burghley, Baron, *see* Cecil, Sir William. For informative purposes, and to further avoid confusion of individuals, we have given the *floruit* period if birth and/or death dates are unknown, where possible.

All too often women appear only under one of their married names in indexes, the name they held in the period discussed, a practice which obliterates family connections. To make women visible, then, women are indexed under their maiden name, and all of their date(s) of marriage are given within parentheses: Ford, Catherine (1636–82), first marriage (1648) to Alexander Culpeper (d. 1649); second marriage (after 1649) to Ralph Grey (1630–75), later (1674) 2nd Baron Grey of Werke. In *Spycraft*, women are more often practitioners than dark artificers, but they had their parts to play. Catherine Ford, for instance, was a she-intelligencer who long remained in the shadows, but concocted the best, possibly poisonous, invisible ink. By indexing her under Catherine Ford, Catherine Culpeper but also under Lady Grey, she is less likely to escape the historian in the future.

The **index occultus** is a shadow index, an index of obscurity. It catalogues and cross-references the code names and nicknames used by intelligencers and spies.

The **index rerum** is a list of things. In a book so concerned with materiality it seemed obtuse not to accord to items a status similar to that we accord people.

Entries in **bold** indicate illustrations.

INDEX OF NAMES AND PLACES

INDEX OCCULTUS

INDEX RERUM